AHEAD of the CURVE

Andy Maguire in Congress and Beyond

MICHAEL TAKIFF

Prospecta Press

Paperback ISBN 978-1-63226-135-9
eBook ISBN 978-1-63226-136-6

Published by PROSPECTA PRESS
An imprint of EASTON STUDIO PRESS
P.O. Box 3131
Westport, CT 06880
www.prospectapress.com

Book and cover design by Alexia Garaventa
Manufactured in the United States of America

In memory of Beatrice "Bea" O'Rourke (1938–2023),
who lived courageously and believed in a better world.

A.M.

CONTENTS

1 *Foreword* MR. MAGUIRE GOES TO (AND BEYOND) WASHINGTON (by Michael Levin)

5 *Chapter 1* AN ACTIVIST BORN AND BRED: Growing Up Maguire

25 *Chapter 2* GETTING READY: Oberlin, Harvard, Africa

51 *Chapter 3* REMARKABLE OPPORTUNITY, REMARKABLE TIMES: At the United Nations during the 1960s

82 *Chapter 4* THE IMPRIMATUR OF THE MAYOR: Andy Maguire, John Lindsay, and a Job in Jamaica

116 *Chapter 5* DEMOCRAT FOR CONGRESS: Finding a Political Home during the Age of Nixon

152 *Chapter 6* DREAM JOB: Joining the House of Representatives

195 *Chapter 7* UNEASY ALLIANCE: A Second Term, a Frustrating President

207 *Photographs*

234 *Chapter 8* POTENTIAL UNFULFILLED: Jimmy Carter, Andy Maguire, and the Will of the People

267 *Chapter 9* HIGH STAKES: Working to Avert Generations of Trouble during the Age of Reagan

304 *Chapter 10* MCKINSEY MEETS THE PEACE CORPS: A Businesslike Approach to International Development

343 *Chapter 11* FRUSTRATION: A Variety of Pursuits, 2003–2014

379 *Epilogue* A PRODUCTIVE LIFE: Looking Back

389 *Appendix* THE MAGUIRE TEAMS

409 *About the Author*

411 *Acknowledgments*

413 *Note to Readers*

417 *Index*

FOREWORD

MR. MAGUIRE GOES TO (AND BEYOND) WASHINGTON

MICHAEL LEVIN

The story this volume tells is an unusual one.

This book is a personal memoir. It tells of an idealistic innovator who set out to deliver better lives to those for whom "betterment" seldom is realized—tied to events like McCarthyism, the US civil rights movement, the Middle East Six Day War, the 1960s housing/community crises in New York City, the Vietnam conflict, and the 1974 "Watergate Baby" revolution in Congress. Maguire's father, a charismatic Presbyterian minister dismissed from an Ohio pulpit for progressive political views, rebounded to become a high-level community organizer, eventual head of the national YMCA college-student division that sought to counter 1950s complacency and create a more open society. That history helped cement young Andy Maguire's commitment to his family's liberal beliefs. Moved by opposition to apartheid, an allergic reaction to inequality of all kinds, and hope for what might come after, he wangled an undergraduate reporting assignment to cover the SNCC's 1960 organizing meetings in North Carolina, picketed (and was attacked at) a segregated Woolworth's, then completed a prescient PhD in African Studies at Harvard, learning Swahili in the process. He was off to the races from there.

This book is about team building. Andy soon realized that no one can affect public issues by acting alone. His first State Department job at the United States Mission to the United Nations in New York confirmed that belief. From his next position, organizing local community improvements in the Queens borough of Mayor Lindsay's New York City—an unconventional step "down" from a promising diplomatic career—he reached out to enlist allies and previously ignored residents of all races and creeds. He and his young wife, Meg, moved to a gritty neighborhood as part of his commitment.

After Andy was elected to the US House of Representatives in 1974, there was no hierarchy in his office. Despite nominal staff chiefs, there was only one level—each staff member was equally listened to, no matter how young. (It has often been remarked that the House "runs on child labor.") Some staffers occupied desks in his personal inner sanctum. That approach was intentionally liberating compared to the operations of most established members and committees, especially for new arrivals from those operations or from federal or state agencies. As at Andy's later positions, he attracted a crazy-quilt cadre of brilliant but seemingly-uncredentialed men and women—college dropouts, former homemakers, young mothers trailing toddlers, in addition to accomplished strivers—who were unafraid to press new ideas and went on to remarkable careers.

This book is an implementation handbook. It's as much about *how* Andy did what he did, as *what* he did.

His achievements stand on their own. During his time in the House, his accomplishments include: the pathbreaking "Maguire Report" elevating cancer prevention to equal cancer treatment; upending of the House's regressive seniority system; an enacted amendment to stop clean-air areas from getting dirty. After he left the House, he testified at the first Senate hearing on climate change; headed an organization (characterized as "the Peace Corps with a business plan") that worked with low-income families and communities in less-developed countries to implement useful technologies and business strategies that raised output along with product quality and doubled or tripled local incomes; helped expand an international health initiative that vaccinated some twenty million children in the world's poorest countries.

But the ways Andy got these things done, within a widening circle of resistant institutions, offer a textbook in constructive change-making: get a platform; attract (and let loose) exceptional staff teams; use all available networks; build coalitions; find champions to advance the ball; seek out fault lines for possible compromise; treat objectors as equals, not enemies; listen, always listen.

Andy was a change agent before the term existed. In an early Democratic campaign for election as a Bergen County, New Jersey, freeholder, he crashed the county Republicans' annual banquet seeking swing support. That act evoked bemused astonishment—plus headlines and a solidified voter base. Andy continued to crash parties, whether as the first House second-termer named to a House-Senate Conference Committee or, later, as an advocate for a bipartisan New Jersey blue-ribbon commission (despite a hostile Republican governor) to mitigate effects of another Superstorm Sandy. When he introduced a bill reforming the Guaranteed Student Loan Program from outside the turf-conscious House Education Committee, the sense of trespass could have been cut with a knife. Yet key parts of that bill—including income-based repayment to reduce burdens on less-affluent students or those who choose public service—eventually became law.

This book is a coming-of-age tale. Maguire had to learn to curb his enthusiasm, not act as the smartest person in the room, not instantly dismiss views he believed unsupportable, not ignore the concerns behind questions, not think professional relationships replaced mutual trust. This did not stop him from telling President Carter to his face that deregulating natural gas prices made no sense in an energy crisis, or from writing Carter that his comments favoring tobacco price supports were at fault from a public health perspective and ridiculous in stating that cigarettes could be made "even safer." Still, Andy's lifelong learning process continued. Intellectually restless, relentlessly curious, he kept moving.

Beyond inevitable life losses, there were personal costs to being out in front, often on a limb. For Andy these included the ire of colleagues at a perceived upstart who recognized neither his proper place nor accepted social status quo. They included two marriages that ended, partly from his commitment to speaking for the voiceless and the demands on time and energy that work involved. They included periods of unemployment when he declined to pursue lucrative lobbying opportunities, instead seeking positions where he could maintain his principles while supporting a family.

Nevertheless, values prevailed. Andy was the parent who took his four kids out to play in single, separate, or merged households. When one of his daughters developed third-grade reading problems, he read with her each night for a year till those issues resolved. For half a decade he cared, arranged and rearranged care for his beloved third wife, Adele, after her Alzheimer's diagnosis. While she could still travel, he orchestrated family trips to California, Arizona, Switzerland, Maui, and the Galapagos. He paid off all his children's college costs, then substituted his low-cost personal loans for their graduate- and medical-school debts. The love behind those actions enriches his life now.

Maguire was a fly on the walls of southern dorm rooms at the birth of the modern civil rights movement, and a participant in UN meetings during the international crisis caused by the Six Day War. He was "in the room" during a seminal community-organizing period in New York City; during the post-Watergate revolution that transformed congressional operations; in Johannesburg commemorating the life of assassinated South African activist Steve Biko; when important advances in American public health and global sustainable development were formulated.

His story is an insider's footnote to fifty years of American and world history.

It's a tribute to the dedicated, unsung men and women who continue to pursue the promise of a better, more just, more equal life for all.

It's a record of a committed life, fully and consistently lived.

As an American Political Science Association congressional fellow for Andy Maguire in 1978–79, Michael H. (Mike) Levin designed initiatives in health and education policy that became law. He has advised Andy as friend and counselor for over forty years.

CHAPTER 1

AN ACTIVIST BORN AND BRED: Growing Up Maguire

I say that our objectives are not for the timid. They are not for those who look backward, who are satisfied with things as they are, who think that this great nation can ever sleep or ever stand still.

—**ADLAI STEVENSON**, 1956, in his speech accepting the Democratic presidential nomination

A DRAGON SLAIN: Taking Inspiration from a Villain's Demise

"We talked about McCarthy for years at the dinner table," recalls Andy Maguire. Joseph McCarthy, the snarling junior senator from Wisconsin, enjoyed only a brief ascendancy in American politics, from his burst into prominence with a speech in Wheeling, West Virginia, in February 1950, until his discrediting in mid-1954 and censure by the Senate that December. But during that time, no American held greater sway over the nation and its fears, as he alleged Communist infiltration of the central institutions of the United States government.

"My parents said he was un-American," says Andy, "that he violated every principle of honesty and fairness. He was building a reputation through political vendettas and baseless accusations. He was attacking the fabric of American life."

More than any others, two men were responsible for McCarthy's downfall. In May 1954, when Andy was fifteen, the Wisconsinite made the mistake of taking on the United States Army in televised Senate hearings. By that time, McCarthy's demeanor—his belligerence, his sinister smugness—along with his inability to back up his wild claims had begun to grate on public sensibilities. In one session, the Army's counsel, a soft-spoken Boston lawyer named Joseph Welch, summed up the nation's exasperation with McCarthy when he asked the senator, "Have you no sense of decency, sir? At long last, have you left no sense of decency?"

Around the same time, Edward R. Murrow, the anchor of CBS news, used his weekly television program *See it Now* to expose the senator for the liar and menace he was. "We proclaim ourselves," Murrow told his viewers, "as indeed we are, the defenders of freedom, wherever it continues to exist in the world. But we cannot defend freedom abroad by deserting it at home."

Welch and Murrow had defeated McCarthy; all that remained was the coup de grâce. In June, a fellow senator introduced a resolution to censure him; in August a committee opened hearings on the question; in December the Senate registered its condemnation. McCarthy's influence was broken—neither the press nor his Senate colleagues paid him much attention until his death in May 1957 due to alcoholism—even though witch hunts and blacklists would continue to plague the nation through the 1950s.

"That awful McCarthy era—I remember it as if it were yesterday," says Andy. "We watched the Army-McCarthy hearings and we saw the Murrow programs. Seeing Murrow, I thought, 'Somebody has finally figured out how to talk about this awful guy. Here's a major institutional player who is willing and able to do it.'"

Murrow, already familiar to Andy—Andy's father tuned in to the newsman's regular broadcast every evening—inspired the teenager to plan a life taking on large challenges and slaying large dragons. But not as a journalist. "I didn't want to be describing what other people were doing," he remembers. "I wanted to be one of the people who was doing.

That was a fundamental principle for me from day one: I wanted to be in there, where I could do something about the things that were wrong."

A TEACHER AND A PASTOR:
Ruth and Bruce Maguire

Gene Andrew "Andy" Maguire's father raised his son to be a man who could—and would—do something about the things that were wrong.

Bruce Maguire was a man of the liberal cloth. "My father was a social-justice Presbyterian pastor," Andy recalls. "He dedicated his life to the ideals within that calling, and I carried that work on."

Born in 1911, Bruce grew up in a household filled with religion—old-time religion. Staunch members of a conservative Presbyterian church in Youngstown, Ohio, Bruce's parents did not countenance drinking or dancing, or playing games on Sunday. Bruce's father, Andrew George "Andy" Maguire, broke records as an automobile dealer, selling an estimated twenty thousand Plymouths and DeSotos over his twenty-five years in business. "My grandparents were conservative not just socially but politically, too," says today's Andy Maguire. The earlier Andy Maguire was a rock-ribbed Republican. His wife, Jeannie, served as a local and national leader of the Woman's Christian Temperance Union.

But Bruce would find his own way to God. When it came time for higher education, he at first stayed within the fold, attending Muskingum College, a small, conservative Presbyterian school in New Concord, Ohio. There he met and fell in love with Ruth Leitch, a fellow student from a home much like his. The two would marry after they received their undergraduate degrees, while Bruce was enrolled in Pittsburgh-Xenia Theological Seminary. It was the seminary that opened Bruce's mind to a new world of religious inquiry and thought. "He was exposed to a whole list of liberal Protestant thinkers," says Andy, "like Harry Emerson Fosdick, John Bennett, the Fellowship of Reconciliation."

Fosdick, the first pastor of New York's famed Riverside Church, was the nation's leading opponent of fundamentalism. John C. Bennett would be known for his activism. "Church-state relations in the United States," he said while president of the Union Theological Seminary, "have never meant that churchmen should separate their Christian ethics from political action." The Fellowship of Reconciliation was, and is, an international, interdenominational association of church leaders who preach pacifism and nonviolence.

"My father read and talked and interacted with internationalist, social-justice leaders in the church," says Andy. "That's what he organized his life from. Not from his father's business." Bruce moved beyond the cramped Calvinism of his upbringing to a faith that, as he noted in an early sermon, called upon its adherents to "be courageous, daring, and willing to achieve a better social order for mankind." Decades later, as a grad student, Andy wrote a note to himself: "Let me never lose my capacity for rage against injustice. And may I always do something to try to correct it."

In his early pastoral positions—at Murray State College, in Oklahoma, at a church in a Kentucky suburb of Cincinnati—Bruce earned renown for the depth and power of his prayers and sermons. That reputation earned him, at age twenty-eight, the pulpit at Mt. Auburn Presbyterian Church, the largest Presbyterian church in Cincinnati.

Mt. Auburn was a plum position for a pastor of any age—the church was awash in resources, counting Cincinnati royalty like the Wittnauer, Procter, and Gamble families as congregants. The job seemed an ideal foundation on which to raise Bruce and Ruth's children—Andy, born in 1939, and Marjorie, born in 1941. But after Pearl Harbor, Bruce's job collided with his beliefs.

When the United States entered World War II, Bruce registered as a conscientious objector, and he brought his antiwar convictions to his sermons. "You have a pacifist preaching at the beginning of the war," says Marjorie "Marj" Maguire Shultz, Andy's sister. "According to my mother—I was barely a year old at the time—he always prayed for the soldiers, but I'm sure he wasn't beating the patriotic drum." While the congregation as a whole voted to keep Bruce, its wealthiest members wanted him gone. "The dispute went to the presbytery, the next step up in the governing structure of the church, and they threw him out."

The presbytery's action meant that no church would hire Bruce, so this father with two toddlers to feed was out of a job. "My mother, brother, and I went to live with her sister for a while until he found work," says Marj. "But even though he never went back to the church, he remained a pastor in his outlook. We three absorbed the energies and religious commitments of a pastor who was no longer a pastor."

A native of Pittsburgh, Ruth Maguire also hailed from a conservative Presbyterian household—again, no drinking, no dancing, no games on Sunday. A superior student in high school, after college she became a schoolteacher, instructing students in Latin, English, and public speaking. When she gave up her career to tend to her new family, she transferred her skills to the education of her own children. "In addition to what we were doing in school," says Andy, "we were tutored by our mother. And that included everything from sketching landscapes to playing the piano to playing softball."

Marj recalls instruction in public speaking. "Anytime we had to do even a two-minute talk at school," she says, "we would plan and rehearse it with her. When Andy ran for office in high school, he would practice his talk and she would provide pointers. We two kids absorbed the energies of a highly skilled, knowledgeable teacher."

Ruth taught her children not only by instruction but also by example, displaying a commitment to social justice they would carry on in their own lives and careers. "My mother adopted generous and creative initiatives to help those in need—on the other side of the globe, within the church community, in our own neighborhood," says Andy. Ruth and Bruce decided together on their charitable donations, giving to organizations focused on poverty, racism, civil liberties, and the peaceful resolution of conflict, both in the United States and abroad. "She also volunteered her skills and time at every church the family joined—in Ohio, California, and New Jersey." Struggling local families relied on Ruth as a major source of support. "One family she helped had a child with Down syndrome; another household had troubled teenagers. There was also an older couple we knew—they needed emotional support and quick action in medical emergencies.

"My mother's interests went beyond our immediate family. She harbored a deep commitment to a life of service."

If Bruce Maguire was disappointed that his church career had been cut short, he nevertheless landed a job perfect for his abilities, outlook, and goals: He was named the western regional director for the college program of the American branch of the Young Men's Christian Association, or YMCA. To take the job, he moved with his family to Los Angeles.

The "Student Y" had little to do with the Y's more familiar offerings: swimming pools, basketball leagues, day camps, low-cost accommodations. Rather, the college program aimed to lift students' social and political consciousness. Bruce now had a vehicle for communicating his values to young people all over the western United States—indeed, to many times the number of impressionable individuals who could ever fit into the pews at Mt. Auburn Presbyterian Church.

"Instead of pontificating from the pulpit," says Andy, "he reinvented himself as a guy who worked behind the scenes to push promising college students forward into leadership roles and to give them experiences they otherwise would never have had.

"Eventually, the Student Y got phased out, but at the time it was common in American colleges and universities, especially as a major presence on campuses in the western half of the country. The college program offered all kinds of discussion groups. It held events and ran work camps. It was all about ideas: What do we believe and what are we prepared to do about it? What must happen to eliminate poverty? What must happen to produce a racially just society? What must happen to make sure the world doesn't blow itself up?"

Bruce brought those subjects to the family dinner table, where the Maguires conducted a nightly conversation about politics, race, justice, morality, war, peace. Participation was not limited to the four Maguires: Because of the Y's national and international footprint, Bruce knew and worked with people from across the country and around the world. When they visited Los Angeles, these individuals would dine at the Maguire household, further broadening the educations of young Andy and Marj. Bruce also took his family to events like the Y's annual gathering at the Asilomar Conference Grounds located at the tip of northern California's Monterey Peninsula. "At Asilomar," says Andy, "my father introduced me to Howard Thurman, a major African-American theologian and theorist of nonviolence—he was said to have had a major influence on Dr. King. Dad also introduced me to representatives of the American Friends Service Committee. I read the book they published, *Speak Truth to Power: A Quaker Search for an Alternative to Violence*. It had an enormous impact on me."

Ruth and Bruce Maguire used dinner itself, not just dinner conversation, as a teaching tool. Once a week, Ruth would replace the usual fare—meat, potatoes, vegetables—with soup. The money the family saved with this "sacrificial meal" was dropped into a jar and eventually donated to a worthy cause.

"For years and years we contributed to the Heifer Project," Marj recalls, "an organization that raises animals to give to poor people. We did service projects, too. For example, Andy and I collected old newspapers from our neighbors. Once we'd come up with maybe two tons of it, our dad would rent a trailer. We'd take the newspapers to a place that recycled it, sell it for a few dollars, then talk about which charity the money should go to."

"Tithing was important," says Andy. "Sacrificing to help others was important."

Amidst the burgeoning consumer culture of postwar America, the Maguires stressed altruism. Amidst the dull conformism of mainstream culture, the Maguires questioned the status quo. Amidst complacency, the Maguires treasured activism.

Several years into his tenure with the YMCA, Bruce was offered a raise from $3,000 per year to $3,500. "He turned it down," Andy recalls, "on the grounds that he didn't really need it, that it should go to other purposes.

"Isn't that amazing?"

A CIVIC RELIGION: Seeking Social Change in 1950s America

The particular environment of the Maguire household shaped Andy's worldview. So did the larger environment in which he came of age: the United States of America in the 1950s.

During the '50s, America was afraid: of sex, of change, of racial rebalancing, and, especially, of communism.

American culture had loosened during the Second World War: With millions of men in uniform, millions of women worked outside the home for the first time, many doing "men's work" in munitions factories and shipyards. As servicemen and their sweethearts were separated by hundreds or thousands of miles, sexual mores slackened. Jazz, an invention of Black musicians, went mainstream, as swinging (if mostly white) big bands inspired a never-before-seen energy on dance floors across the country and in USOs overseas. Franklin D. Roosevelt had turned from Dr. New Deal to Dr. Win the War; either way, he represented an activist vision for the role of government in the life of the nation. The Soviet Union, dreaded by American leaders and citizens alike since its founding in 1917, became our nation's ally in the fight against Hitler. Shortly after the war, Jim Crow suffered its first setbacks in decades, as Harry Truman desegregated the armed forces and Jackie Robinson desegregated Major League Baseball.

But in the 1950s, the nation pulled back. Sexual repression once again became the norm, as G.I. Joe became the man in the gray flannel suit and Rosie the Riveter returned to the kitchen to mind the boom of babies born in the war's aftermath. Mainstream music became blander and slower. And even though rock 'n' roll would appear by mid-decade, record producers would hide the original rhythms of Black America behind acceptable white artists like Elvis Presley and Pat Boone. With the economy growing as no economy had grown before, the country saw no need for dynamic leadership from its president; most Americans were satisfied with the hands-off approach of Dwight Eisenhower. In 1954, the civil rights movement scored a landmark breakthrough with the Supreme Court's *Brown v. Board of Education* unanimous decision that mandated an end to segregation in public schools. The following year, a twenty-six-year-old African-American preacher named Martin Luther King Jr. led the Black citizens of Montgomery, Alabama, in a boycott of their city's buses. But these hints of progress enraged white citizens of the South and elsewhere. Real school desegregation, as well as meaningful civil rights legislation, would take years to be realized. Our onetime alliance with the Soviet Union yielded to the cold war, with US foreign policy centered on countering communism across the globe and our domestic scene dominated by a red-hunting hysteria that smothered dissent and ruined countless lives.

In a society dominated by retrenchment and fear, young Andy Maguire, tutored in public speaking by his mother and in public affairs by his father, saw the need for action.

"My parents were teetotalers," Andy recalls, "but that was the only restriction that lasted from their religious upbringing. They did not believe in not playing games on Sunday, they did not believe in not dancing, they did not believe in going to church six times a week. They moved beyond all that. Their real orientation was: How can we be effective—in our community, in the country, in the world?"

The family's efforts to be effective were not limited to acts of charity. The Maguires valued another way of improving the world: politics. And while churchgoing was not a daily habit, politics was.

"My father was a politics addict," Marj recalls. "The world would be in crisis if he didn't read his *New York Times* every day—he read it religiously, shall I say. And he watched Walter Cronkite or Murrow or whoever was the main newscaster religiously, every night. We never did anything else during the news hour."

Bruce Maguire did not distinguish between religion and politics. "The two were woven together," says Marj. "I think his religion included social justice and racial equality and attentiveness to countries, including ours, where people were suffering."

"My father represented a combination of religious faith and social justice," Andy recalls. "He was not interested in a heaven hereafter. He was interested in: What are we going to do, today, to make things better? Our mother was also oriented toward the here and now. She was enormously generous, always interested in specific people and what they were all about. My father was more directly intent on changing people. He wanted to be a change agent."

"After World War II," says Marj, "we briefly took in a displaced person from Hungary. Dad was excited by reading and talking about liberation theology in South America. He was a strong follower of Gandhi. Social justice and religion were basically identical for him."

"My father felt strongly the inadequacies of mainstream politics and religion," says Andy, "but at the same time was committed to making them work as best they could. He believed that God was calling us to a social activism that would right wrongs and achieve progress for all, that would make the Gospel real on the ground."

"It's too strong to say Andy was a re-creation of my dad," says Marj. "But my dad was obsessed with politics, and his son became obsessed with politics. Politics was among the highest callings my dad could have wanted for Andy."

For Bruce Maguire, no wrong needed righting more than the wrong of racism. He insisted that his children understand the centrality of America's original sin to America's past and America's present.

Andy learned lessons on racism not only from his parents but also from the neighborhood surrounding the Maguires' modest house at 1215 West Gage Avenue. "When we lived there," Marj recalls, "the area was pretty much working-class white, with some Hispanic families. It was about to be swept by white flight—it's basically South Central L.A."

"The neighborhood was in transition at the time," says Andy. "It's an all-Black community now. It was at the eye of the hurricane during the 1992 riots."

African-Americans nearly tripled their share of the city's population between 1940 and 1960, raising their numbers from 2.7 percent to 7.6 percent. Not all white residents took kindly to their new neighbors.

"As I was growing up," says Andy, "race conflict was intensified in certain parts of the city, including ours. My parents told me—I didn't see it—that somebody had burned a cross on the front lawn of a nearby Black family.

"Living in that neighborhood at that time, added to what I had grown up learning in my family, I came to understand that race was the fundamental issue in American life: that it underlay every other difficulty and reality; that active, direct, and institutionalized racism had always been, and was still, the single most corrosive aspect of what needed to be overcome in American life.

"You can draw a line from that neighborhood and from the teachings of my parents to my decision to study African history in graduate school and to writing my dissertation about Africa. I wanted to learn: What was it like where Black Americans came from? What has happened? What needs to happen now?"

"A FIRM CONFIDENCE IN JUSTICE": Supporting Adlai Stevenson

In Mahatma Gandhi of India, the Maguires found a hero who countered humanity's predilection to oppression and violence. They also found a hero at home, a politician—like Bruce a Midwesterner and a liberal Christian—who countered America's prevailing lethargy and self-satisfaction.

Illinois governor Adlai Ewing Stevenson II, a grandson of Adlai Ewing Stevenson I, Grover Cleveland's second vice president, served as the Democratic Party's presidential nominee in both 1952 and 1956. In neither year did he stand a chance of winning.

Stevenson's coherent speeches, his eloquent phrasing, his wit, his call for "sacrifice, patience, understanding, and implacable purpose," offered voters nothing as catchy as his opponent's slogan: "I like Ike." In 1952, Ike—Dwight David Eisenhower—ran a campaign based less on ideology than on personal appeal. The retired general who had served as supreme commander of the Western allies in the recently concluded world war, Eisenhower flashed a million-megawatt smile that got voters to overlook his rambling speaking style. Eisenhower had another advantage that year: the public's widespread disapproval of the incumbent president, Democrat Harry Truman, and its discontent with the stalemate in the cold war's first hot war, the Korean conflict.

Whereas in that first campaign Stevenson shunned advertising on television, deriding "this idea that you can merchandise candidates for high office like breakfast cereal," Eisenhower's operation embraced the new medium. The campaign's most popular ad, a sixty-second animation created by Disney Studios, showed a parade headed by Uncle Sam, behind whom a bass-drum-beating Republican elephant and a line of ordinary Americans marched in time to a sunny jingle: "You like Ike, I like Ike, everybody likes Ike for president." Meanwhile, a newspaper columnist dubbed Stevenson an "egghead." Although inspired by the candidate's bald head, the term soon came to describe the Illinois governor, and people like him, as overeducated snobs disconnected from the concerns of average Americans. "Eggheads of the world, unite," Stevenson quipped. "You have nothing to lose but your yolks!" But the Democrat's joke did not undo the damage the word did to his campaign.

Stevenson sought to make Joseph McCarthy an issue in the campaign, taking Eisenhower to task for his refusal to criticize his fellow Republican directly. Eisenhower was content to give voters the impression that Stevenson's loyalty was suspect, although the general left the dirty work to his running mate, a young California senator named Richard Milhous Nixon. Nixon, who had made his name pursuing Alger Hiss, the former State Department official accused of espionage, awarded Stevenson "a PhD from the Dean Acheson School of Cowardly Communist Containment." Sixteen years later, Nixon, at the top of the ticket, would leave the dirty work (and the alliteration) to *his* running mate, Spiro Agnew. But as Ike's hatchet man in 1952, Nixon showed that if he was gifted at one thing, it was the art of the smear: His slander of Stevenson not only rendered the Democrat a pinko, just like Dean Acheson, Truman's secretary of state, whom Nixon had already defamed. It also conferred on the Illinois governor the graduate degree most associated with effete intellectual snobs. (No, "latte-sipping" was not yet an epithet.)

An adherent to one of America's most progressive religious denominations, Unitarianism, Stevenson extolled liberal values—and he did so in complete sentences. "You have written a platform that neither equivocates, contradicts, nor evades," he told the 1952 convention. "You have restated our party's record, its principles and its purposes, in language that none can mistake, and with a firm confidence in justice, freedom, and peace on earth that will raise the hearts and the hopes of mankind for that distant day when no one rattles a saber and no one drags a chain."

While Stevenson's outlook, and his way of expressing that outlook, made him ill-suited to win the White House against a popular, ideology-free war hero, those qualities endeared him to the Maguire family and people like them.

"My parents were both extremely supportive of Stevenson," says Marj. "They thought he was concerned about the same things we were. And that his campaign and his speeches and his presence projected a thoughtful person, in terms of both US politics and world affairs. Somebody whose goals aligned with theirs.

"Though my dad grew up in a socially and religiously conservative family, in seminary he became close with national religious leaders committed to social justice. In his YMCA work he offered what many students felt were life-changing experiences: work camps abroad, internships so young people could test career choices, summer projects that served needy Americans and built skills. In politics he was an activist, speaking out and going door-to-door in support of candidates he favored. Still, he had a kind of ethereal idealism. Stevenson had some of that, too."

Every other summer, the Maguire family would take a long car trip east to visit Bruce's family in Youngstown and Ruth's family in Pittsburgh. Two of the trips coincided with the presidential campaigns of 1952 and 1956. When the Maguires weren't playing word games or singing songs to pass the long hours on the road, they were listening to Stevenson's speeches.

"I thought Stevenson was amazing," says Andy. "His ability to articulate and focus in and explain, in the most engaging but profound way, what it was he believed in and what we should be doing as a nation—it was remarkable.

"I campaigned for him with my father in 1952, when I was thirteen years old, door-to-door."

Andy and Bruce knocked on those doors in vain: Stevenson was trounced in 1952, winning only 44 percent of the popular vote and 89 of 531 votes in the Electoral College. Eisenhower's reelection four years later was even more decisive—the Democrat drew just 42 percent of the popular vote and 73 electors.

"The results in 1952 and 1956 were shocking to me," says Andy. "That this great country of ours would elect Dwight Eisenhower, a smiling general—not once, but twice—a man who by 1956 appeared to my family to be sitting comfortably in the White House and not doing much about much of anything, other than being a (quote) 'Republican'; that Stevenson, a man who was unusually brilliant and on target with respect to what he hoped to do for the nation, would be rejected—I was shocked and dismayed. Really, what did Eisenhower accomplish as president aside from building the interstate highway system? These two elections gave me my first experience in understanding the difference between how a lot of Americans think about things and how I think about things."

From Stevenson's speech accepting the nomination in 1956:

> My friends, we must place our nation where it belongs in the eyes of the world—at the head of the struggle for peace. For in this nuclear age peace is no longer a visionary ideal. It has become an absolute, imperative, practical necessity. Humanity's long struggle against war has to be won and won now. Yes, and I say that it can be won!
>
> It is time to listen again to our hearts, to speak again our ideals, to be again our great selves.
>
> There is, as we all know, a spiritual hunger in the world today and it cannot be satisfied by material things alone—by better cars on longer credit terms. Our forebears came here to worship God. We must not let our aspirations so diminish that our worship becomes rather the material achievements of bigness.

After the deprivations of the Great Depression and World War II, with those hardships now ended by the greatest economic expansion the world had ever seen, a critique of materialism hardly amounted to a winning electoral message, no matter its resonance with a family that ate a weekly sacrificial meal.

Even before campaigning for Stevenson, even before watching McCarthy's checkmating at the hands of Murrow and Welch, Andy could see his future. "At ten, twelve, I would go to YMCA retreats in the Sierras with kids my age. We would be encouraged to think deeply about our lives. It was all about your 'vocation'—this was my father's language, also. What is your vocation? What is your purpose in life? I remember being alone on a hilltop, looking at the stars, thinking, 'Here's what you're going to do: Make a difference.'" A few years later, participating in mock legislatures at YMCA youth and government events, Andy wrote one bill eliminating loyalty oaths for public servants and another abolishing the death penalty.

The outcome of the 1952 and 1956 presidential contests sharpened not only Andy's resolve to take action but also his vision of the obstacles ahead. "Stevenson's two losses told me that it would be tough sledding," he says, "and that I'd better strap on my boots if I wanted to be effective in making changes."

GREAT EXPECTATIONS: The Price of Growing Up Maguire

In the Maguire household's ethos of liberalism and devotion to justice, there was a blind spot. "The strongest thing I remember," says Marj, "is how close the family was, and how oriented it was toward political issues—peace and justice, essentially. But I felt like I got a little lost in that shuffle. Nobody was planning a career for *me* in politics."

The modern American women's movement started late for women who came of age in the 1950s—Betty Friedan's landmark book, *The Feminine Mystique*, often credited with sparking America's still-continuing reappraisal of gender roles, did not appear until 1963. The ideal American woman in the '50s did not work outside the home; she devoted her life to raising children, keeping a tidy house, and preparing and serving the food paid for by her husband's salary. If she was active outside the home, it was as a volunteer for the PTA or at church or in the community.

For all his progressive views, Bruce Maguire didn't entertain the idea that his daughter could accomplish as much as his son could. "My dad tried to raise Andy and me with the same ideas," says Marj. "I was every bit as much a receiver of the ideas. But as we got older, my father increasingly thought about Andy's future in those areas, not so much mine. I don't know what my parents would have done if, in high school, I'd pointed toward any kind of career, which I didn't. Maybe I'd be a teacher, maybe a secretary—until I had kids.

"I think my dad hadn't thought enough about this. As for my mother, she was a timid person in many ways—frightened of the marketplace. The dissonance between her and the male side of the family was strong." As Marj did start to think of a more ambitious career, Ruth tried to talk her out of it. "Partly, her advice came from her timidity. She spent more than one conversation trying to persuade me to become a secretary."

Marj would become a professor at the University of California at Berkeley Law School. She began her employment there as one of only two women on a faculty of forty-five to fifty men; as the years went by, her male colleagues would come up with a variety of excuses to deny her tenure despite a wealth of accomplishments and accolades: Her work has been cited in opinions of the California Supreme Court. In 1983 she was honored with Berkeley's all-campus Distinguished Teaching Award. She was recognized as Teacher of the Year in 2000 by the Society of American Law Teachers. Three years later she co-authored *Whitewashing Race: The Myth of a Color-Blind Society* (University of California Press), hailed as "a powerful book" that "disposes of the claim . . . that America has solved its race problem." (The volume remains relevant; it was reissued in 2023.) In 2008, the year she retired, she received the law school's own teaching award.

Considering the rigidity of gender stereotypes in the America of the 1950s, it's not surprising that Marj's view of Bruce differs from that of Andy. "I did idolize my father," she says, "but I also had real difficulty with him that I don't think Andy did.

"A story about my dad: When my husband, Jim, and I were in grad school, we lived in Chicago. One time my dad was in Chicago on business and he stayed overnight with us. Our little apartment was not close to the University of Chicago, where Jim was in school. So, every morning, I'd get up at six and drive him to the freeway, where another student would pick him up. They would drive to school and I would drive back home and go back to bed. I'm a night owl.

"This day, when I got up again, my dad said, in what sounded like the voice of God, 'You know, your mother has made me breakfast every day of our married life.' Here I was in graduate school, preparing myself for adult life. And because I got up to drive my husband to the freeway but didn't make him breakfast, my father was telling me, 'You are doing a bad thing!'

"He didn't say it angrily—he never did. Nor did he give us orders: 'Do this.' Instead he'd say, 'Could you have done something better in this situation?' Our whole life was driven by expectations. In much of my life I have been driven—and Andy has, too, I think—by what Andy interpreted as expectations but I interpreted as guilt. We had this amazing, outward-looking family. We were so educated, so oriented toward social justice and world peace and intellectual strength. But there was an overload of expectations from day one, all the way through my parents' deaths. Again, very little in the way of angry explosions or direct criticism. But questions: Are you doing the right thing? Are you doing as well as you could have?

"Andy may not feel it as much as I did. I felt it a lot. I have never been able to unscramble what in our lives was the product of our parents' aspirations and expectations for us, as opposed to what were choices we made ourselves.

"Another example of a crisis of expectations: Sexually untutored and inexperienced, like so many young people in the 1950s, Andy was suddenly informed by his girlfriend that she was pregnant with his child. Andy later discovered that she had lied to him—that another young man was the father—and ended the relationship. But in the meantime, it was as if an atomic bomb had been dropped on our family. During those times a college pregnancy might have upended the career my parents desired and anticipated for Andy. At least, that's what they feared.

"The level of expectation he lived with was a heavy burden. In a way I was glad I was a girl. Because I think the thought of failing to meet our parents' expectations fell much more heavily on him. I always felt sorry for him on that score."

CALIFORNIA NERD, NEW JERSEY STAR: School Years

Before taking on the world, Andy had to take on middle school. Adolescence would not be easy for this smart but awkward boy.

Throughout his education, Andy proved an outstanding student—Bruce and Ruth would have it no other way. "I always had a high level of confidence," he says, "that if I worked hard—and I always worked hard—I'd succeed. I always wanted to produce the best possible paper or exam or project. I was into excellence. I got that from my parents. There was no excuse for non-excellent performance."

But academic prowess had its drawbacks, especially when the straight-A student wore glasses. "I got nicknamed Mr. Magoo," says Andy, "after the nearsighted cartoon character. I had my lunch money extorted from time to time. Once when I went to the aid of a small defenseless kid who was being pushed around by a bully—I said, 'Don't do that to him'—I got whacked on the nose, painfully, by the bully, who happened to be a foot shorter than I was. I did nothing further and walked away, although my intervention did allow the younger kid to escape.

"When I read James Joyce's *Portrait of the Artist as a Young Man* in college, I felt a shiver of recognition at glasses-wearing Stephen Dedalus and the teasing he suffered on the playground: '*Pull out his eyes / Apologize / Apologize / Pull out his eyes.*'"

When Andy entered high school, it was time for a change. "On the first day," he recalls, "another bully started pushing me around. I broke. I decided I couldn't be bullied in high school, too. I found myself saying, 'OK, let's go.' We went at it behind the nearest building, with an audience of onlookers. My best friend's father had taught me boxing—I decked this kid with my first punch. Bullying was never a problem for me again."

As bookish as Andy was, he was also an athlete. "My parents," he says, "introduced me to tennis—they introduced me to everything, right? They were not great tennis players, but they enjoyed it. I decided that I would play tennis."

On weekends, Andy would visit nearby public courts, where he found a man who took pleasure in helping youngsters learn the game. "Even though I never had a paid tennis lesson, I became a good player," Andy says. "I watched tennis players on television, especially the great Australians like Ken Rosewall and Lew Hoad."

Unfortunately, neither Andy's brainpower nor his hand-eye coordination did him much good when it came to solving his most vexing problem: girls. "I didn't know what to make of them," Andy recalls. "I would go to dances, and I wouldn't know what to do on the dance floor or how to do it. I wouldn't even know how to ask a girl to dance. I'd see other guys going off with girls—I was in agony. I didn't have the skills, the persona, the wherewithal, the anything."

The clumsy teenager needed a change of scenery.

He got one.

In 1955, the YMCA student division made Bruce its national director, requiring the Maguire family to move east. The summer before Andy's senior year the family settled in Ridgewood, New Jersey, not only an easy commute to the Y's national headquarters in Manhattan but also home to a high school with a state-championship tennis team.

The school year got off to a marvelous start when Andy was befriended by a fellow senior. "This boy was a big deal in the school," Andy recalls. "He knew everybody. He shepherded me into relationships and activities. I quickly discovered that I could develop an entirely different persona from the one I'd been categorized into before."

He became a star.

The New Jersey kids sensed a California mystique in this new arrival from the West Coast. His homeroom elected him to the class council. The varsity football coach saw him throw a pass and lamented that he hadn't arrived a couple of years earlier, when he could have been groomed for quarterback. When he made the tennis team, the coach expected him to join the squad's lower ranks. After matches with all the top players, the kid from L.A. found himself ranked first.

"I had a devastating flat forehand," he recalls, "that I could put on a dime in any part of the court—the back corners and what have you. I had a perfectly efficient backhand, but not the sort you would hit winners with—more like a Federer-style slice backhand. It was the sort of backhand that would keep you in a rally until you had your forehand shot. I killed opponents with my forehand shot."

The summer before starting school in Ridgewood, as the family was staying in motels while looking for a house, Marj taught Andy to dance. "She could rock 'n' roll and swing," he says, "and I was a klutz." Voilà, klutz no more: "All of a sudden in high school, I was the California phenom on the dance floor."

In the spring, Andy managed the successful campaign of the junior seeking to be the following year's student-body president. When the outgoing seniors were deciding upon their class gift, Andy, in a speech coached by Ruth, urged his classmates to donate not the traditional plaque at the football field but rather, via UNICEF, books and science equipment to schools in Nepal. The class agreed to the future congressman's proposal. At a school assembly, Andy played a piano solo—a piece by the Spanish composer Isaac Albéniz.

One fact above all represents Andy Maguire's transformation from Mr. Magoo to Big Man on Campus: he dated cheerleaders.

Andy turned down a tennis scholarship offered by the University of Southern California. "I didn't want to be a student athlete," he says. "I had larger purposes in mind." Harvard and Oberlin, too, had larger purposes in mind for Andy—both offered him academic scholarships.

Andy's guidance counselor was appalled when the star student decided to pass on Harvard and thus also pass on bolstering Ridgewood High's statistics in sending students to the Ivies. "I wanted a small liberal-arts college that was coeducational," he says. The presence of women was important: Andy had only recently found his mojo with the opposite sex. Now was no time to stop the momentum by attending all-male Harvard. (The school didn't admit women until 1977.) But the presence of women was only one factor. Despite his academic achievements, despite the intellectual and spiritual content of his upbringing, despite the guests from many lands who had sat at his family's dinner table, the kid from the lower-middle-class Los Angeles neighborhood wasn't ready to rub shoulders with the sons of the American ruling class. "I was intimidated by the whole notion of the wealthy East Coast Ivy League school," he says. "At that time the Ivies were still hierarchical, all about whose family had the most money, how big your house was, who had the most expensive cars, where you lived—the whole thing."

Insecurity over social class aside, Andy perceived a solid academic advantage in attending the smaller school, regardless of the step down in prestige. "I researched it carefully," he says. "I decided that, for an undergraduate, education at Oberlin would be equivalent to, if not better than, education at Harvard. Harvard had all the big faculty names, but they were off writing books and doing research. I figured that at Oberlin I'd work with the professors themselves, not with teaching assistants.

"I did, however, promise myself that I would go to Harvard for graduate school."

If Andy suffered from social uncertainty, he harbored no doubts about his academic ability. He would enter Oberlin with his intellectual guns blazing.

Ruth and Bruce Maguire had prepared their son well. It was time to leave the nest.

CHAPTER 2

GETTING READY: Oberlin, Harvard, Africa

The old era is ending. The old ways will not do.

—**JOHN F. KENNEDY,** July 1960, accepting the Democratic presidential nomination

THE ROAD TAKEN: Outside vs. Inside

The United States of the 1950s was upended by the mass movements of the 1960s. The African-American civil rights movement demanded, and got, an end to Jim Crow, the South's comprehensive system of legalized oppression, even if the ultimate goal—equality in law and in fact—still seems a distant mirage. The movement's high-water mark came in August 1963, when a quarter million people joined Dr. Martin Luther King Jr. at the March on Washington. The student antiwar movement demanded, and got, an end to America's war in Vietnam, even if the victor in the 1968 presidential election, Richard Nixon, punished that small country with years of American firepower before concluding a peace treaty, in January 1972, that formally ended the conflict. In November 1969, half a million people, most of them young, gathered in Washington to bear witness against the carnage their government was inflicting, on Americans and on Asians, on the other side of the world.

Other movements would follow suit, most notably the women's movement and the gay-rights movement, both effecting major change in our country, if still far from rendering sexism and homophobia extinct.

Andy Maguire participated in the movements both for civil rights, if only briefly, and against the war, if only sparingly, as circumstances of his study and work prevented him from playing a greater role in those efforts. Nonetheless, his involvement, and the salience of both movements in 1960s America, illuminated for him a choice. "There were two routes if you wanted to make a difference," he recalls. "One was the Paul Potter-Rennie Davis route. The other was working from the inside."

Paul Potter and Rennie Davis were early leaders of Students for a Democratic Society, a nationwide organization of young activists. After its founding in 1960, SDS at first focused its efforts on the struggle for African-American civil rights. But it was America's involvement in Vietnam that gave the group its animating cause, leading to the formation of chapters on university campuses across the country as college students mobilized to oppose the war. As the '60s progressed, however, the group's increasingly radical politics drained it of its mass appeal.

"Rather than holding my placard as I marched up and down the streets," Andy continued, "I intended to get myself qualified—as qualified as the very best people in the world—to work on the things I cared about. Then, occupying key positions inside key institutions, I would bring about change.

"I later developed a lot more respect for the activist route. I recognized its enormous impact, working from the outside, on the conduct of the Vietnam War.

"But that wasn't the choice for me. The choice I made was to say: I will prepare myself to enter the major institutions in our society, institutions that have leverage on important issues. That's where I want to be."

If in the first seventeen years of his life Andy's parents prepared him to do big things, he spent the next ten years—from the mid-1950s to the mid-1960s—preparing himself.

Bruce and Ruth Maguire had raised their son to be aware of other cultures and receptive to big ideas. College further expanded his perspective.

"Oberlin," Andy says, "was a fabulous cornucopia of opportunities for me to learn and immerse myself in history and philosophy and modern religious thought and the arts. All of which I did."

At first, the earnest freshman intended to major in history, but he changed his mind after he saw the department chairman in action. "As interesting as his lectures were," Andy remembers, "they were the same lectures he'd been giving for thirty years. He was a troglodyte; I didn't want to work with him."

Instead, Andy majored in religion, while also taking memorable courses in art, economics, political theory, and literature. Today, two courses stand out in his recollection: "In Modern Religious Thought we read Soren Kierkegaard, Reinhold Niebuhr, and Paul Tillich. That course provided the next level, above what I'd gotten from my parents, in understanding theology and religion. I wanted that next level to enable me to consider: Where am I going from here? Niebuhr was famous for the realpolitik orientation of his theology, linking religion to social action.

"I also took a whole semester seminar on James Joyce with an amazing professor. We did *Ulysses* in detail, which was amazing, then made it partway through *Finnegans Wake*, which I found bewildering. I loved *Portrait of the Artist* and *Dubliners*."

Andy sang in the Oberlin College Choir. He acted in plays.

Curiously, considering his later career choices, he did not study American history or government. "In college I took Japanese history, in graduate school Soviet history and European history—I felt as though I already understood the United States. I didn't take a single government course, either—I already knew about the three branches of the US system. Nor did I want to study the different models of European democracy—it was easy to get a grip on that topic, I didn't need a class. Those subjects struck me as boring."

The diligent student did take time off for a social life. "At Oberlin I did not get pegged as a this or a that, the way I had in California," he says. "By the time I got there, I'd developed a more relaxed persona, one more attractive to other people, including women." While his persona might have been relaxed, contemporary attitudes toward sex were not. The Oberlin administration reflected those mores, as expressed by its "six-inch rule." "That was how much your doorway needed to be open if you had someone of the opposite sex in your room," Andy explains. "Can you imagine? Sex tended to be furtive in the '50s. Of course, in the '60s that all got blown away.

"And that was good."

THE TORCH IS PASSED: The Election of John F. Kennedy

Nothing so demarcated the transition from the torpor of the '50s to the tumult of the '60s than the election in 1960 of John Fitzgerald Kennedy, the Democratic junior senator from Massachusetts, as president of the United States.

Dwight Eisenhower's eight-year presidency had featured an avoidance of major governmental initiatives at home and major new commitments overseas. While the nation as a whole enjoyed a respite from domestic strife and foreign wars, by the end of Eisenhower's second term Americans were open to a more dynamic candidate. Jack Kennedy promised to "get America moving again."

Like the outgoing president, JFK was a hero of World War II. But while General Eisenhower had commanded the Allied assault on Nazi-occupied Europe, Lieutenant (Junior Grade) Kennedy had commanded a small boat in the South Pacific, the PT-109. The young naval officer drew accolades for his valor in the saving of crewmembers' lives after the boat's sinking. Kennedy was a generation younger than Eisenhower—only forty-three years old on Election Day, weeks after Ike had turned seventy.

Kennedy's Republican opponent in November 1960 was Vice President Richard M. Nixon, a man whose relatively young age—only four years older than JFK—belied his dozen years of prominence in American politics, first as a red-baiting representative and senator from California, then as Ike's backup for both of the general's terms. But Nixon was stiff where Kennedy was smooth, awkward where Kennedy was graceful, stilted where Kennedy was witty, homely where Kennedy had the looks of a movie star. Nixon's dutiful wife, Pat, was more than good-looking, but Jacqueline Kennedy boasted the beauty, clothes, and bearing of a model for *Vogue* magazine. Nixon, the son of a grocer, had attended Whittier College in California. Kennedy, the son of a tycoon and former ambassador to the United Kingdom—his pro-Nazi sympathies had caused FDR to recall him—had gone to Harvard. Nixon would nurse a lifelong grievance against people like Kennedy—born to privilege, with the self-assurance only people who have never faced rejection or failure can have.

Much of the campaign centered on each candidate's credentials as a cold warrior. Kennedy charged that Eisenhower had allowed a "missile gap" to develop, leaving the United States woefully behind the USSR in military preparedness. (There was no such gap.) In their four televised debates—the first debates in presidential campaign history—the two candidates sparred repeatedly over the need to defend two Taiwanese islands, Quemoy and Matsu, from Communist Chinese aggression. But at its essence, the contest presented a choice between yesterday and today, between maintaining the status quo and marching bravely forward: "We stand today on the edge of a New Frontier," Kennedy declared in his speech accepting his party's nomination, "the frontier of the 1960s, the frontier of unknown opportunities and perils, the frontier of unfilled hopes and unfilled threats."

Nixon made two crucial mistakes. The first was his noble-sounding but politically suicidal promise at the Republican National Convention to campaign in all fifty states. Nixon found himself wasting time in underpopulated states like Kansas, Nebraska, and, just days before the balloting, Alaska, while Kennedy crisscrossed closely contested states like Pennsylvania and New Jersey, chock full of electoral votes. (He won New Jersey's sixteen electoral votes by just 22,000 ballots out of some 2.7 million cast.)

Nixon's second error was cosmetic. The vice president showed up for the first debate underweight, looking haggard after a hospital stay for a knee that had become infected after he'd banged it on a car door. He refused an offer of makeup, needed a shave, and sweated profusely under the TV lights. Kennedy, properly made up, looked tanned, rested, and healthy. These appearances were deceptive—Kennedy suffered from a variety of serious ailments, including colitis and the adrenal disorder Addison's disease, but he had long hidden those maladies from public knowledge. Nixon accepted makeup for debates two, three, and four, but the damage had been done. Prior to the first debate, polls showed Nixon with a slight lead. Following that encounter, the candidates changed places. They remained there through Election Day.

But to win the race, Kennedy had to neutralize another issue, which had hung over the campaign from the beginning. All previous presidents had been members of Protestant denominations, as was Nixon. Kennedy, not many generations removed from the Emerald Isle, was Roman Catholic. Prejudice had helped doom the candidacy of the only prior Catholic presidential nominee, Al Smith, the New York governor who lost to Herbert Hoover in 1928. Nixon professed to avoid the topic of his opponent's religion—indeed, at every campaign stop he'd tell his audience, "And one thing I will not bring up is the religion of my opponent." But he did encourage sub rosa efforts by prominent Protestant ministers, most notably Billy Graham and Norman Vincent Peale, to organize fellow pastors likewise appalled by the prospect of a "papist" in the White House.

Just as Barack Obama, forty-eight years later, would feel compelled to deliver a speech on race as he asked Americans to make him the nation's first Black president, so did John Kennedy feel the need to reassure voters that as America's chief executive he would act in accord with US laws and interests, rather than at the direction of the pope. The venue he chose was a gathering of Protestant clergy in Houston, Texas. "I believe in an America where the separation of church and state is absolute," he told the ministers,

> where no Catholic prelate would tell the president (should he be Catholic) how to act, and no Protestant minister would tell his parishioners for whom to vote. . . .
>
> I believe in an America that is officially neither Catholic, Protestant, nor Jewish; where no public official either requests or accepts instructions on public policy from the Pope, the National Council of Churches, or any other ecclesiastical source; where no religious body seeks to impose its will directly or indirectly upon the general populace or the public acts of its officials. . . .

Kennedy's insistence on removing religion from the public square seems ancient today, when one party claims the mantle of Jesus and the other party struggles to keep up.

In the end, the country voted to move forward, but the margin was narrow: Kennedy won the popular vote by just 120,000 votes out of nearly 70 million cast, an edge of 0.17 percent, although by a more comfortable edge in the Electoral College. Partisans charged fraud, especially in Illinois, where Mayor Richard J. Daley was said to have turned out the graveyard vote, and Texas, where JFK's running mate, Lyndon Baines Johnson, was said to have pulled his home state's political strings. But the allegations were never proven.

On January 20, 1961, John F. Kennedy delivered one of the most memorable inaugural addresses in American history, matched only by Lincoln's second and Franklin Roosevelt's first. "Ask not what your country can do for you," he declared, "ask what you can do for your country."

The new president also promised that the United States would "pay any price, bear any burden, meet any hardship, support any friend, oppose any foe to assure the survival and the success of liberty."

Americans would pay a heavy price, indeed, to bear a burden in a faraway country named Vietnam.

A MAILROOM AND A MEETING: Learn Outside the Classroom

For all that Andy learned in the classrooms at Oberlin, no less important were the lessons he learned far away from the campus, in Washington, DC, and Raleigh, North Carolina.

Deferring his graduation from 1960 to 1961, Andy took off the spring 1960 semester to work as an intern in the office of US Senator Henry "Scoop" Jackson, a Democrat from Washington State. Andy landed the job thanks to his economics professor, an adviser to the senator.

Andy's first government job did not tax his abilities. "I cut out newspaper clippings about Jackson and pasted them in scrapbooks," he recalls. "I didn't have a grand project of the sort I liked to give my own interns when I was in Congress. I would never have an intern just pasting stuff into a book."

Nonetheless, the ambitious youth did not let the opportunity go to waste. "I was in his office," he says, "that's what was important. I watched what everybody was doing." The chief of staff brought Andy into meetings. "I got to see what the legislative assistants were working on. I even got to say hello to the senator when he came in."

Jackson's candidate for the Democratic presidential nomination was Kennedy, and in March, Jackson's office secured a place for Andy in the Kennedy campaign—he worked for six months in the mailroom at national campaign headquarters in Washington. "I sent piles and piles and piles of stuff to West Virginia before the primary there," Andy remembers. "One day I went with other campaign workers to Charleston, West Virginia, where we heard JFK speak to a stadium full of fans."

Before 1972, presidential nominations were decided by party insiders—city, county, and state bosses who controlled large numbers of the delegates selecting the nominees at the national conventions. Starting in the early 20th century, candidates competed in primary elections, but not to acquire convention delegates directly, as candidates do today. Rather, they competed in order to demonstrate their electoral chops to party leaders.

By the time West Virginia was ready to vote on May 10, Kennedy had already won seven primaries, but only one had been significantly contested: Wisconsin, where he'd won 56 percent of the ballots to 44 percent for Senator Hubert H. Humphrey, even though Humphrey represented the neighboring state of Minnesota. A liberal hero, Humphrey had leapt to national fame with his speech on civil rights that electrified the 1948 Democratic convention and sparked a walkout by politicians and delegates from the Deep South, furious over the then-Minneapolis mayor's urging that the federal government overrule their states' sovereign right to discriminate. "The time has arrived in America," Humphrey said, "for the Democratic Party to get out of the shadow of states' rights and to walk forthrightly into the bright sunshine of human rights."

Kennedy again faced off against Humphrey in West Virginia, which party heavyweights and the national press saw as a test case: Would the heavily Protestant, religiously traditional farmers and coal miners of the state vote to send a Catholic to the White House? Indeed they would, handing Kennedy another victory over his Senate colleague, this time by 61 percent to 39 percent. At the convention in Los Angeles, Adlai Stevenson and Lyndon Johnson would make last-minute bids for the nomination, but in West Virginia Kennedy had proven his point. He won the nomination on the convention's first ballot.

"Like so many others," says Andy, "I was inspired by Kennedy. I wrote a piece for the *Oberlin Review*, where I said that while Stevenson was inspiring and Humphrey was fabulous, Kennedy was the realistic candidate. He was the one with the best chance to win. I thought a third run for Stevenson would be a mistake and that Humphrey was too aggressively liberal a voice for the public at large. Kennedy was attractive and articulate, and he hadn't taken too many positions on too many issues. Plus, he'd skippered a PT boat during World War II and had a glamorous wife—the whole package. And then, in the debates he was a cool customer, while Nixon looked stressed out. And he'd forgotten to shave.

"The things on which history turns."

The Eisenhower era was over. Democrats were looking forward to great things. "After the two hugely deflating elections of 1952 and 1956," says Andy, "seeing in 1960 that a national victory was possible gave me a positive view of the way history could develop—which is a huge contrast to how I feel today. Never did I imagine we would ever see a president like George W. Bush or Donald Trump, and all of the depredations they have wrought upon our nation and the world."

While working in the Kennedy mailroom, Andy came across a chance to add another facet to his education.

Through his contacts at the Y, Bruce Maguire heard about a meeting to take place Easter weekend on the campus of a Black college in Raleigh, North Carolina. He related the information to his son, who decided he wanted to attend. However, he couldn't just show up. "I needed some sort of an imprimatur," Andy recalls. "So I telephoned the Student Y chapter at Oberlin to ask if I could be its representative. They agreed, and so I represented the Oberlin chapter of the Student Y at the organizing meeting of SNCC, the Student Nonviolent Coordinating Committee."

Although Bruce and Ruth Maguire had tried to educate their son on the subject of American racism, Andy had grown up far from the daily matter-of-fact cruelty of the Jim Crow South. He was not prepared for what he found only a few hours after setting off for the meeting.

In Washington he boarded a bus to Richmond, where, after a short layover, he was to catch a bus to Raleigh. Getting off the bus at the Richmond terminal, he was, as young men tend to be, hungry. He walked into the terminal's well-stocked cafeteria, but the menu did not offer what he wanted: a sandwich. So he walked out of the cafeteria and into the terminal's snack bar, and in that room he came to a realization: all the patrons were Black. He checked back at the cafeteria: all white. "I had known the facts of segregation in the South long before I entered that Richmond bus station," he wrote in a two-article account of his trip for the *Oberlin Review*, "but now I sat down in the waiting room and for fifteen minutes watched people divide according to race and file into the 'WHITE CAFETERIA' and the 'COLORED RESTAURANT.'"

The restrooms were segregated, too, as well as the water fountains and the waiting rooms. Segregation was alive and well in 1960 in the onetime capital of the Confederacy.

Segregated eating establishments were the target of the first major initiative of the civil rights movement in the 1960s. On February 1, 1960, four young African-Americans, students at North Carolina Agricultural and Technical College, another Black institution, entered the Woolworth's in Greensboro and took a seat at the five-and-dime's whites-only lunch counter. The students were refused service and asked to leave; they politely remained in their seats.

The Greensboro Four were not acting on a whim; with the help of a local white businessman, they had carefully planned their protest. Once the students had taken their places, the businessman alerted the press. Soon the "sit-in" was the subject of extensive coverage on local television stations.

Over the next several days, more and more students from local institutions joined the Greensboro protest. The action spread rapidly from Greensboro until, by the end of March, sit-ins at lunch counters and other segregated facilities were taking place in fifty-five cities across thirteen states. As footage from the extensive television coverage shows, crowds of whites abused the protestors, taunting and assaulting them, pouring ketchup and cigarette ashes on their heads. But the protestors did not fight back. They had been trained in the techniques of nonviolent action advocated by the man who had emerged as the leader of the civil rights movement, Martin Luther King Jr., who in turn drew his inspiration from Gandhi's campaign of nonviolent action that had brought about the end of British colonial rule in India.

With the initial success of the sit-ins, Ella Baker, the executive secretary of the Southern Christian Leadership Conference, saw the need for an organization aimed at recruiting and organizing young people for the civil rights cause. With $800 of SCLC funds—approved by the group's leader, King—she set up a meeting to create a new organization to marshal the energies of Black students. King was interested in creating a student wing of the SCLC; Baker sought a more independent group, led and run by young people. The meeting would take place at Baker's alma mater, Shaw University, in Raleigh.

Attendees at the meeting included people who were, or would become, civil rights luminaries: Charles McDew, Marion Barry, John Lewis, Julian Bond, and Stokely Carmichael, among others. Barry, later the mayor of Washington, DC, was made SNCC's first chairman; McDew and Lewis would follow.

SNCC would go on to organize the Freedom Rides of 1961, when African-Americans rode segregated buses, refusing to sit in the back rows, and Freedom Summer of 1964, when hundreds of mostly white college students from all over the country came to Mississippi to assist local residents in their efforts to register long-disenfranchised Black voters.

As the civil rights movement began to fracture, many young activists grew impatient with King's strategy of nonviolent action in a society that regularly employed violence and the threat of violence to enforce the second-class status of the descendants of the Africans brought here in chains. In 1966, SNCC elected as its leader one of those activists, Carmichael, who had abandoned King's vision of a "beloved community" and instead preached "Black power." "Violence is as American as cherry pie," said SNCC's next leader, H. Rap Brown.

Under intense surveillance and infiltration by the FBI, SNCC disbanded in the early '70s.

About thirty people attended the founding of SNCC. All but two were Black.

"The Student Nonviolent Coordinating Committee was formed and named," Andy recalls, "and officers were selected. The meeting was basically about, All right—how are we going to organize this thing? How are we going to expand what we're doing? Get more people involved? Make sure that it stays nonviolent?"

As Andy described in the *Oberlin Review*, additional questions under discussion included: "Should students go to jail rather than pay bail or fines? How should police brutality be dealt with? Should discriminatory laws and practices be tested by a few students only, or should masses of students submit themselves for arrest on the same charges? Should sit-ins or demonstrations continue while negotiations with store managers and town officials are in progress?"

Folk singer Guy Carawan taught the gathering "We Shall Overcome." "That was the first time I sang that song," says Andy. In fact, it was the first time many of the attendees had sung the song; the occasion has been credited with introducing it to the civil rights movement, which adopted the song as its anthem.

Andy's presence at the meeting helped him fulfill his sense of self and mission. "Being there," he says, "was entirely consistent with everything I'd always believed in, everything I'd wanted to see happen and to be present for. The civil rights movement was something I wanted to participate in and make some small contribution toward."

Andy struck up a friendship with Charles McDew, a young veteran of the movement who told Andy of his recent experience facing fire hoses in Orangeburg, South Carolina. The two men were among those who put their plans into action with a visit to downtown Raleigh to picket stores with segregated lunch counters. "There was a revolving picket line," Andy recalls, "which drew a huge crowd."

The picketers passed out leaflets explaining their case. Some white onlookers accepted the leaflets, others told the demonstrators to "stick it down your toilet," as Andy wrote in the *Oberlin Review*. A white child asked Andy for a leaflet, perhaps because Andy's was the only white face among the protestors. After Andy handed it to him, the boy's mother "ripped the leaflet from his hand and tore it to pieces while screaming a tirade of profanity at the child, who was too young to comprehend the leaflet or his mother's rage." The white citizens of Raleigh had taught another lesson to the naive, idealistic northerner. "Never have I experienced such hate as was expressed in the hard lines of those peoples' faces, in their sneering contempt, and in their harsh words. I experienced this for a few hours; the Negro endures it for a lifetime."

A young white man yelled epithets at all the protestors, but he singled out Andy, the only white marcher. The man did more than yell at the apparent race traitor. "He roared out of the crowd and clocked me," wrote Andy.

Although dazed, Andy recalled the instructions McDew had given him in nonviolence, and thus didn't strike back. "I just stayed in line and kept walking," Andy remembers.

The incident made the national news—after all, here was something remarkable: A white person had been attacked.

The following day, Easter Sunday, afforded Andy and his colleagues a chance to stage a different kind of demonstration. Four students from the meeting—Andy, McDew, the other white student, and another African-American—put on their Sunday best and crossed the street from the Shaw campus to Raleigh's largest white Baptist church. They tried to enter to attend the service. "We were met at the top of the steps by the ushers," Andy wrote, "who told us that we would not be admitted to the church. Not a surprise. This was a demonstration. We expected that to happen."

The students tried to open a discussion. "We told the ushers that we were all sinners," Andy wrote, "and wished simply to participate in the service of worship. We were told that we obviously didn't know our way around town; that we could satisfy our desire to worship by going elsewhere." But all should be welcome at a Christian church, the youths said. The ushers responded by speaking directly to Andy and the other white student: "You are not the white men you ought to be. You're as Black as your friends there.'" To the Black students the ushers said, "Go back where you belong."

When one usher, nearly losing control of himself, went back inside, another man, possibly the assistant minister, appeared. He told the boys, as Andy wrote, "that the church was 'working on this thing' but that he could not admit us for the sake of the congregation, which had not yet made a decision."

The boys went to a Black church. All four were welcomed warmly by its congregation and pastor.

Andy regrets that after this introduction to civil rights activism he was not able to become more involved. "In 1964 I would have taken part in Freedom Summer," he says, "when so many students went to Mississippi. But I was in Africa."

BONA FIDES: A PhD from Harvard

Andy returned to Oberlin in the fall of 1960. "Because I had only a semester to make up," he says, "but was staying for two, I luxuriated in various optional classes: modern poetry, Renaissance art, and the like."

Nevertheless, the serious matter of graduation—and what to do afterward—loomed. Andy considered attending Yale Divinity School or the Union Theological Seminary for a master's degree in religion, with the thought of becoming not an ordained minister but a professor of religion. "But by the time I actually had to make my decisions," he remembers, "I said, 'Look, time is passing. You've had great religion courses—that's good enough.' I wanted to be in the midst of shaping things. I wanted to be directly involved in the important issues as the post–World War II world moved through the 1950s and into the 1960s. I wanted action."

Even though Andy was eager to dive into the world of policy-making, he saw the need for another preparatory step: earning a PhD in government. "It was an era when advanced degrees were highly thought of and prized," he says. "Everybody I knew who wanted to be a serious player got an advanced degree. Plus, I thought I had a whole lot more to learn, and this was the best way to learn it."

Five years earlier, Andy had accepted Oberlin's, not Harvard's, offer of admission, but he'd promised himself that he'd get his PhD at Harvard. He had the grades to get into Harvard's graduate program—his record at Oberlin was stellar—but he needed something more. "A professor who taught me political theory," says Andy, "and graded my papers A-plus was connected to the government department at Harvard. I'm sure that's why I got in."

Andy had had his fun at Oberlin. At Harvard, he was all business.

"I wanted to get through there as fast as I could," he recalls. "I designed my course load to be 100 percent efficient in terms of meeting the requirements. I wanted to get on with it." Andy applied for and received various fellowships. "I never paid a dollar for any of my five years of graduate work," he says.

As one of his areas of concentration, Andy chose African history, studying with Professor Robert Rotberg, a 1955 Oberlin grad on the way to becoming a leading authority on Africa and international conflict. Rotberg became Andy's dissertation adviser.

With Rotberg, Andy worked out a plan: He would first take part in a Harvard-Radcliffe program that sent students to teach schoolchildren in Tanganyika, a newly independent nation in East Africa. "Rotberg thought Tanganyika was a particularly interesting country," says Andy, "because Julius Nyerere was an atypical African leader." A sophisticated political thinker, the new country's prime minister—he would become president in 1963—advocated what he called "African socialism," which owed little to Marxist-Leninist ideas but instead was modeled on traditional African "tribal communalism."

Why did Andy choose to focus his studies on Africa? The decision goes back to those nightly conversations around the Maguire dinner table as well as to Andy's long-standing desire to be in the middle of things. "Race was very much on the mind of my family and myself," says Andy, "and of all the people I was regularly in touch with and friendly with. Plus, at this time there was a great deal of excitement about decolonization. What better than to immerse myself in this environment of so many new nations emerging from a century or more of European colonial control? At the same time, I would learn about the origins of the African-American population in the United States: What drove the slave trade? How did African societies function before and after the arrival of Europeans?"

For ten weeks during the summer of 1962, Andy taught English and basketball at a boys' middle school in the town of Mwanza. "The kids were, in general, good students," he recalls. "They wanted to learn. We did a lot of interesting things in the classroom, and in the afternoons we would play basketball. They loved learning the game—how to dribble, how to hoist the ball up at the basket.

"It was great."

GRASSROOTS AND GRASSTOPS: Conducting Research in Tanzania

Between 1870 and 1905, during the "Scramble for Africa," European powers colonized nearly every inch of the African continent. France and Britain controlled the largest chunks of territory, but Belgium, Italy, Germany, Portugal, and Spain all joined in the plunder. World War I cost Germany its possessions, but those lands were not decolonized—they were divided among France, Britain, and Belgium. After World War II, with economies weakened by the conflict's devastation, Europe found it harder and harder to maintain its dominion over Africa. Self-determination movements were sweeping through the continent. Europeans' days of sovereignty there, indeed throughout the developing world, were numbered.

Setting the stage for African decolonization was the independence of India in 1947, the jewel in the British imperial crown. The sun had begun to set on the most far-reaching empire in history.

African nations followed—slowly at first, then in a torrent; some peaceably, some with strife. Italy, on the losing side of World War II, gave up Eritrea and Libya in 1947 and 1951, respectively. British colonies on the continent started their move to independence with Sudan in 1956; others quickly followed, including Ghana (1957), Nigeria (1960), Uganda (1962), and Kenya (1963). Among the nations that emerged from French colonization were Tunisia (1956), Senegal (1960), Ivory Coast (1960), and, after a long, bloody war, Algeria (1962). Belgium, the cruelest of the colonial powers, gave up its largest, most lucrative holding, what is now the Democratic Republic of Congo, in 1960.

Tanganyika, where Andy would teach and study, was colonized by Germany in the late 1890s and handed over in 1919 to Britain, which pulled out in 1961. In 1964, Tanganyika merged with another former British colony, the small, nearby island nation of Zanzibar, to form the country Tanzania.

"There were two ways to get to Tanganyika," says Andy. "One was to go through Europe, and the other way was through South Africa, flying first to Rio de Janeiro and then across. To begin my summer in 1962 I went via Europe. I came back via South Africa."

In Tanganyika Andy met people who belonged to the African National Congress—Nyerere had welcomed exiled members of the South African political party banned by the apartheid regime. These individuals, as well as Professor Rotberg at Harvard, connected Andy to a variety of important people in South Africa. In Johannesburg, Andy met political leaders from all the different racial communities, as categorized by the white-supremacist government: White, African (Black), Coloured (of supposedly mixed racial descent), and Indian (with descent from the Indian subcontinent or most other parts of Asia).

He met Helen Suzman, for many years the only anti-apartheid member of the South African parliament; Shun Chetty, a leading Asian human rights lawyer; John Dugard, a human rights activist and a Cambridge-educated professor of law at Witwatersrand University; and Winnie Mandela, wife of Nelson Mandela, the imprisoned leader who would be the first president of post-apartheid South Africa. The ANC exiles had also connected Andy with Gerard Ludi, a university professor and ostensible communist. "Ludi introduced me to a whole raft of African leaders," Andy recalls, "while also asking me about all the meetings I was having. Ten or fifteen years later—still well before the end of apartheid—I read in the international press that he had been a spy and was testifying in court against all these people.

"Interesting that I should remember his name after all this time."

On his return to Harvard, Andy and his adviser settled upon a subject for his dissertation—the changing social, economic, and political organization in Sukumaland, an upcountry area of Tanganyika, in the two decades leading to the country's independence in 1961. During his summer in Mwanza he'd picked up a smattering of the local language, Swahili, but to conduct his research he'd need more. Another application, another grant, and he was able to attend the School of Oriental and African Studies in London for the fall semester in 1963. "I didn't do anything there other than study Swahili," he says. "And go to the National Theatre." When he returned to Africa in early 1964, he was fluent.

His new linguistic skill proved essential to both components of his research: He pored over documents, many in Swahili, in district and provisional governmental offices. And he conducted dozens of one-on-one interviews—mostly in Swahili with people at the rank-and-file or, as Andy says, "grassroots" level; mostly in English with leaders, people at the "grasstops."

This white American encountered no trouble in securing cooperation from his interviewees. "In general," he recalls, "they were pleased to be paid attention to; delighted that their stories were important somehow; glad that someone from the United States would be interested in them. I can't remember asking for an interview I did not get."

PhD dissertations are supposed to encompass original research. Andy's certainly did. "What made my work new and important," he says, "was that it focused on the grassroots, where there was an awful lot going on. When political scientists from American or British universities came to write about a country emerging from colonial rule, they camped in the capital. They talked to the elite national leaders, they documented when the British did this or the French did that. To my knowledge and my professor's knowledge, nobody before me had ever learned the language and dug deep down. And talked to people whose names never became well known.

"My dissertation was full of the names of people who played a role at the grassroots in the organization of small fraternal associations of like-minded people. These associations led to the formation of economic cooperatives, so that people got a better deal for what they produced.

From the cooperatives, political organizations evolved as the grassroots helped push the country toward *uhuru*—self-determination, independence, freedom. What made the research especially fascinating was that this part of Tanganyika, Sukumaland, was well ahead of the rest of the country in terms of these moves at the local level."

Andy's dissertation was published in 1969 by Cambridge University Press under the title *Toward "Uhuru" in Tanzania: The Politics of Participation* as the first entry in a new Cambridge Commonwealth Series. Because of Germany's onetime rule over Tanganyika, the book was published in Germany in German translation. A condensed version, in Swahili, was published in East Africa for use in schools.

In the book's introduction, Andy writes, "The present work is a study in micropolitics because it is my belief that thorough and detailed case studies of selected areas within various nations are among the next necessary steps toward a fuller understanding of African politics, in both its pre-independence and post-independence phases."

The boy who had grown up longing to contribute had made his first contribution.

Andy would later look back on his work in Africa as superb preparation for service in the House of Representatives: "In Congress, I felt I was one of a small number of people who really understood what it was like to be on the ground in the developing world—as a resident and as an expert visitor. That knowledge was applicable to many other situations Congress was dealing with.

"While I was in the House we paid an enormous amount of attention to Central America—El Salvador, Guatemala, Nicaragua, Panama, Honduras. I understood the complexity of issues from the ground up. And, against the background of our own struggle for civil rights in the United States, we paid lots of attention to South Africa and Southern Rhodesia, which later became Zimbabwe. Not everybody had that level of consciousness about what was happening elsewhere in the world."

A LOVE AFFAIR GONE BAD: Africa and the United States in the 1960s

In 1957, in a speech on the Senate floor, John F. Kennedy took France to task for its war in Algeria and took Eisenhower to task for his failure to condemn not only that war but European colonialism in general. By refusing to lend US support to the burgeoning drive for self-determination around the world, the senator said, the Eisenhower administration risked allowing emerging countries to be drawn into the Soviet orbit.

> The most powerful single force in the world today is neither communism nor capitalism, neither the H-bomb nor the guided missile. It is man's eternal desire to be free and independent. The great enemy of that tremendous force of freedom is called, for want of a more precise term, imperialism—and today that means Soviet imperialism and, whether we like it or not, and though they are not to be equated, Western imperialism.
>
> Thus the single most important test of American foreign policy today is how we meet the challenge of imperialism, what we do to further man's desire to be free.

Toward the end of the Second World War, Franklin Roosevelt had urged his British and French allies to give up their empires, but his successors Harry Truman and Dwight Eisenhower did not press the case. Kennedy, an ardent cold warrior, saw Africa, along with Latin America and Asia, as a battleground in the competition between East and West. Kennedy encouraged African independence. And, recognizing that Africans might see the Soviet Union as a friend after decades of Western European colonial rule, he refrained from insisting on capitalistic and democratic purity in each new country's form of governance. What mattered was keeping the country out of the Soviet camp.

Kennedy undertook two important initiatives intended to change perceptions of the United States in the developing world. The Alliance for Progress was aimed at Latin America. For decades, the United States had been notorious in that region for the large US corporations exploiting its people and natural resources. With this new program, Kennedy sought to make the United States a constructive partner in Latin American development. The Peace Corps sent (mostly young) Americans to teach and build in countries throughout the less developed world. Critics have charged—with some justification—that despite the idealism of these programs' stated rationales, their real purpose was less raising living standards in the Third World than extending US influence there. (In the 1980s, Andy and a colleague at World Resources Institute co-edited a volume of essays by US experts, *Bordering on Trouble: Resources and Politics in Latin America*, that cast a critical perspective on a century of US government and corporate involvement in the degradation of Latin America's natural resources and de facto support for antidemocratic political leadership in many nations there.) But for JFK, that distinction was irrelevant. We needed these countries on our side. The best way to bring them to our side was to help them.

Kennedy's policy toward underdeveloped countries ran aground in Cuba. In April 1961, only three months after taking office, Kennedy authorized the Bay of Pigs invasion, a half-baked attempt by a group of US-based Cuban exiles to overthrow the government of Fidel Castro. The attack, planned under the Eisenhower administration, ended in ignominious failure. That episode, joined with US efforts to assassinate Castro, as well as Soviet leader Nikita Khrushchev's bullying of the young American president at their Vienna summit in June 1961, led to the USSR's decision to place missiles in Cuba. In October 1962, American discovery of those missiles, on an island just ninety miles off the coast of Florida, brought the world to the brink of nuclear war. Officials on both sides urged preemptive military action, but the cooler heads of Khrushchev and Kennedy prevailed, arranging a compromise: The Soviets agreed to withdraw their missiles from Cuba in exchange for JFK's announced agreement to stage no more invasions of the island as well as his secret agreement to withdraw US missiles from Turkey.

What turned out to be a more costly miscalculation came in US policy toward Vietnam. After humiliation at the battle of Dien Bien Phu ended France's war to preserve its colonial rule over Vietnam, the United States took over as the effective guarantor of the West's interests there. According to a 1954 peace treaty signed in Geneva, Vietnam was partitioned into a Communist-aligned north, headed by Ho Chi Minh with its capital in Hanoi, and a Western-aligned south with its capital in Saigon. The agreement further called for a plebiscite to be held in 1956 on the question of the country's unification. The Eisenhower administration, knowing that the vote would produce a unified Vietnam under the leadership of Ho, a nationalist hero to most Vietnamese, canceled the election.

A low-grade insurgency developed in South Vietnam, but Ike resisted calls to stage a major US military intervention to support the Saigon government. By the end of his administration, the US presence numbered under a thousand troops, all considered not combatants but "advisers." But Kennedy, with the status of the Saigon regime deteriorating, was sold by members of his team on the value of "counterinsurgency" warfare conducted by special operations forces. And in late 1963, the United States gave its approval to plotters who, on November 1, staged a military coup that toppled South Vietnamese president Ngo Dinh Diem, who was murdered the next day. In Dallas, Texas, three weeks later, Lee Harvey Oswald murdered the American president. On November 22, 1963, the number of US troops in Vietnam numbered sixteen thousand. They were still considered "advisers."

Whether Kennedy would have carried out the massive escalation implemented by his successor, Lyndon Johnson, in the face of the certain collapse of the Saigon regime is a question historians and partisans have long debated. Expecting to face the fiercely anticommunist senator from Arizona, Barry Goldwater, as the GOP nominee in the 1964 election, Kennedy might have cut US losses and left Vietnam following his reelection. But would the president who had promised to "bear any burden" have stood by in 1965 as Saigon was ready to fall to a Soviet ally?

Johnson didn't stand by. He laid the groundwork for intervention in August 1964, when two supposed incidents—one minor, the other fictional—of Communist aggression against US assets in the Gulf of Tonkin enabled him to go to Congress with the Gulf of Tonkin Resolution. The bill, which permitted him "to take all necessary steps, including the use of armed force, to assist any member or protocol state of the Southeast Asia Collective Defense Treaty requesting assistance in defense of its freedom," passed the House without a dissenting vote and the Senate with only two. Johnson then staged what he called a "sharp but limited response"—an air raid against oil storage tanks and boats in the North Vietnamese port city of Vinh.

Barry Goldwater did win the Republican presidential nomination that year. In the fall campaign, while the Arizonan advocated US military action in Vietnam, Johnson promised that he would not "send American boys nine or ten thousand miles away from home to do what Asian boys ought to be doing for themselves." In November, Johnson defeated Goldwater in a historic landslide.

Johnson reneged on his pledge only four months later. On March 8, 1965, the 3,500 men of the Ninth Marine Expeditionary Force came ashore in the South Vietnamese port of Da Nang, representing the first

US ground combat troops stationed in Vietnam. Relying on the authorization he'd been granted in the Gulf of Tonkin Resolution, Johnson continued to pour US service members into the fight. The number of troops in-country peaked in 1969 at 540,000.

Andy's two stays in Africa presented a contrast in attitudes toward his home country.

In 1962, as Africans were just beginning to experience independence, the people of Tanganyika admired the United States of America and its youthful president. "It was a love affair between Africans and the United States," Andy remembers. "John Kennedy in particular. Every other store or home had a framed photograph of him on the wall. They wanted to become part of the world—the modern world. They saw America as a beacon of freedom and accomplishment. The romance of Kennedy's persona translated across the globe."

The United States was given credit as a powerful country that opposed colonialism. "The Tanganyikans hated the British, the French, and the Belgians," says Andy, "but they did not hate Americans. They had a progressive president, Julius Nyerere—he and Kennedy got on well. It was no problem at all being an American in the summer of 1962 in Tanganyika."

When Andy began his second visit to Africa in early 1964, arriving in what was now Tanzania, attitudes toward the United States were still positive. John F. Kennedy was gone, but Tanzanians appreciated the young people of the newly created Peace Corps who had come to lend their hands to the nation's development. However, the summer of 1964 brought the Gulf of Tonkin Resolution, and American involvement in the war in Vietnam seemed certain to deepen.

While US involvement in Vietnam in 1964 was still minimal compared to the escalation that followed, the Africans Andy encountered saw the beginnings of another invasion of a small, poor country by a large, rich Western power. "By mid-1964, we were becoming more and more mired in Vietnam," says Andy. "Our involvement became an issue for knowledgeable Tanzanians, as it did for people all over the world."

In later years, while working full-time for the State Department and then the City of New York, Andy would on several occasions join hundreds of thousands of other Americans marching to put a halt to

America's war in Vietnam. But even in Africa in 1964—and even before that—Andy sensed a disaster brewing for the United States. "I'd read the books of Bernard Fall, who had analyzed the situation with the French. He understood the dynamics of Vietnamese society. I was gaining experience on the ground in Third World countries. I could see from the get-go—from Kennedy's sixteen thousand 'advisers'—that the United States was making a huge mistake. If you looked at the history of the Vietnamese and the French, it was crystal clear to anybody with a pair of eyes that this would end badly for us and for the Vietnamese."

In November 1964, the United States committed what to the Africans was an unforgivable sin by supporting Belgium's show of residual power in its former colony, the Congo, which had gained its independence in 1960. By 1964, the Simba Rebellion, backed by China and the Soviet Union, had fought the Congo's Western-aligned government for three years. In August the rebels gained control of the city of Stanleyville. After executing thousands of Congolese believed to be sympathetic to the West, the rebels began to take white residents into hostage. In November, 350 Belgian paratroopers, jumping from American military aircraft, landed to rescue the captives, evacuating them and many other white residents of the town. The Belgians soon mounted another operation that expelled the rebels from the city of Isiro, effectively ending the Simba Rebellion.

In Africa, no colonial power was more hated than Belgium, which had treated the Belgian Congo as one massive rubber plantation and its inhabitants as slave laborers. Regardless of the merits in this case, for many in nearby Tanzania, America's actions showed its anticolonial boasts to be hollow.

"It was only after the Belgians went into Stanleyville with US support," says Andy, "at the same time that our involvement in Vietnam was deepening, that attitudes toward us deteriorated."

How much they deteriorated was made clear by Andy's encounter with a local official, John Malecela, the regional commissioner of Tanzania's Lake Province.

"After Zanzibar became part of the new Tanzania," Andy explains, "'radicals' like Malecela, as opposed to activists who had come out of chiefly traditions, began to move up in the hierarchy. Malecela was not Zanzabari. He came out of Dodoma, the most undeveloped part of what had been Tanganyika, which is saying a lot. Other areas had coffee production, and tea and fish and the like. Dodoma is in the middle of a wasteland."

Educated at a mission school, Malecela did well enough to be sent to study in India and Europe. He also traveled in the United States. "He personally experienced the prejudice that Black people here experience; he came away from his visit hating the United States," Andy says. "He was smart and well spoken.

"I first encountered him on a parade route in one of the outlying districts, Geita, which happened to be the most confrontational district against the British in the 1950s. He was visiting, accompanied by a variety of elite Zanzibari political figures. In Africa at that time, whenever anybody of some importance came to visit, everybody would turn out. People lined the road leading into the main town. I not only showed up, I showed up wearing a dashiki, the traditional garb for a man in East Africa. I considered it to be a sign of respect.

"So here comes Malecela in this procession, standing in the back of a truck with the Zanzibaris, and here's this white guy standing on the side of the road, the only white guy anywhere. And he's in a dashiki.

"He glared at me."

Soon Andy got a message that Malecela wanted to see him at his office in Mwanza. The commissioner let loose with a long diatribe about the sins of the United States—racism, imperialism, capitalism—and accused Andy of being a CIA agent. Andy—who was not a CIA agent—remembers Malecela as evidence of American racism's corrosive effect on US diplomacy and our image abroad.

After this dressing down, Andy began to make carbon copies of his research notes and mailed them out of the country on a regular basis. "I was worried that the Malecela hammer might fall at any point," he says.

Malecela went on to an illustrious career, holding office as Tanzania's foreign minister and its prime minister. En route to those positions, he served as his country's ambassador to the United Nations. Andy worked at the United States Mission to the United Nations at the same time. One day, in the delegates' lounge, the two men came face-to-face. "We looked at each other," recalls Andy, "and finally said hello. I could see him saying to himself: 'How could that nobody researcher suddenly be at the UN with the State Department? That bastard. I knew he was CIA.'"

In late 1964, Andy passed through Nairobi en route to India to visit a friend doing research there. He arrived in the Kenyan capital in time for a celebration: Although the nation had gained independence from the United Kingdom in 1963, it was declared a republic on December 12 of the following year. The occasion is now celebrated as Jamhuri Day (*jamhuri* is Swahili for 'republic') each year on the declaration's anniversary.

Andy entered Nyayo National Stadium, which was filled with euphoric Kenyans. "I was there with my camera," Andy recalls. "They allowed me to go down on the field and photograph the dancers. Jomo Kenyatta, the country's president, headed up the festivities. Here I was, this little white guy from America—nobody interfered with me at all. I got the most amazing photos of all these tribal dancers."

Andy was invited to visit the US Embassy to Kenya and met the American ambassador. He also played tennis at the home of the embassy's senior political officer. The officer questioned Andy closely about his work and what he'd observed. "It was clear to me," Andy recalls, "that this man was interested in learning all he could about what was going on in key provinces of Tanzania."

Andy was not CIA, but this political officer evidently was. "Of course, they never tell you," says Andy.

SO LONG, HARVARD: Rejecting the Academy

Andy returned to the United States in March 1965 to finish writing up his research. In June 1966 he received his degree. Now he had to decide what to do with it.

For starters, a PhD from Harvard attracted many opportunities for academic employment. Amherst invited him to interview for a position on its faculty. "I got claustrophobia the minute I stepped on the campus," he recalls. "I said, 'I can't do this.'

"I wanted to lean in and make a difference. I didn't want to be *writing* about government and structures and processes and institutions and voting. I wanted to be *doing*. I'd spent years reading syllabuses and taking notes and writing papers and studying A-B-C and X-Y-Z. I thought, 'If I'm a professor, I'll be doing the same thing for the rest of my life.'

"I had hurried through my doctorate as quickly as possible, without taking a single unneeded course. I wanted to get through there and now I wanted to get out of there."

Andy applied for a job at the State Department. He came to the attention of Richard Pedersen, also a Harvard PhD and the third-ranking officer at the United States Mission to the United Nations. "Normally, if you enter the State Department," says Andy, "you take all the exams, you go into the Foreign Service. They send you to an outpost like Ouagadougou, where you stamp passports for a couple of years. Pedersen hadn't come in that way. In fact, he was one of the youngest ambassadors in the history of the State Department, only about forty years old at this time. I think he saw me as a replica of himself. He hired me.

"I came in not through the Foreign Service but through a designation called 'excepted service,' which was available only to missions, like those in New York and Geneva, where multilateral institutions were involved. There was some argument to the effect that you needed people with different kinds of views of the world."

As he'd planned, Andy's supreme credential—his PhD in government with specialization in African history—opened this first, crucial door for him.

Harvard was not amused. "When I told the head of the government department at Harvard that I was taking a job with the State Department," Andy says, "he went nuts. 'We prepare people here to do research and scholarship, and teach,' he said. 'Not go to work for the State Department.'"

Harvard would remain disappointed. The new PhD became not a scholar but a diplomat.

CHAPTER 3

REMARKABLE OPPORTUNITY, REMARKABLE TIMES: At the United Nations during the 1960s

I want to suggest to you that optimism should not be a cowardly escape but a confident crusade.

—LORD CARADON

A SOCIETY IN MOTION: The '60s

By 1966, when Andy finished his PhD and ventured into the world, what we now think of as "the '60s" had emerged in full force.

Two landmark pieces of civil rights legislation had been enacted into law: the 1964 Civil Rights Act, which banned segregation in most public accommodations, and the 1965 Voting Rights Act, which aimed to guarantee Southern African-Americans the franchise. The sexual revolution had begun, set off by the Food and Drug Administration's approval in

1960 of the first oral contraceptive. Sex before marriage was no longer hidden, it was expected—indeed, celebrated. If colleges like Oberlin still listed a "six-inch rule" in their student guidebooks, students no longer bothered to observe it.

For the first time in modern American history, a widespread "counterculture" developed. Baby boomers, spared the trials of their parents' coming of age—the Great Depression, World War II—sought ways to distinguish their generation from the one preceding. Young men grew their hair long and left it unkempt. Young women wore jeans and shorter skirts. A new kind of popular music emerged—loud and transgressive. ("But I can't understand the words," clueless parents would tell their clued-in children.) Rock stars like Jim Morrison and Janis Joplin stood as far outside mainstream culture as the favorite pop stars of young people just twenty years earlier, like Frank Sinatra and Peggy Lee, had stood within.

In 1961, comedian Lenny Bruce was arrested at a San Francisco nightclub for saying the word "cocksucker." Only seven years later, Broadway's biggest smash hit was *Hair*, a counterculture musical that featured full-body nudity by the entire young male and female cast. Use of consciousness-raising drugs—marijuana, LSD, hashish—became common among young people, and even some of their parents. In 1967, *The Graduate*, a popular movie about a young man alienated from the materialism of his wealthy parents and their friends, depicted his sexual affair with a middle-aged woman. The sex scenes crossed boundaries that had ruled Hollywood for three decades, even though those depictions now look tame compared to scenes in films released just a few years later.

Underlying the cultural ferment was the Vietnam War and its attendant anxiety. Never before had television brought the hard realities of combat to American living rooms, making plain the terror our nation was inflicting on a tiny country halfway around the world. But the president and his aides never made plain the reason for the terror or for the lack of apparent progress in achieving the terror's stated end: an independent and democratic South Vietnam. The government's evasiveness and deceit fostered widespread public distrust—not only of the war aims, but of government and authority in general. Young men on college campuses, unwilling to die in a conflict they viewed as illegitimate, clung to their college deferments to protect themselves. Draft evasion—legal, illegal, and in between—became a cottage industry in doctors' offices across the country.

But there was another reality in America, that experienced by the sons of the poor and working classes. In the conflict fought by their fathers, World War II, men from all walks of life—the sons of janitors just as much as the sons of the executives whose trash the janitors emptied—stepped forward to serve in the armed forces. But now the members of Congress saw fit to permit their sons and the sons of their socioeconomic peers to shelter in college. Undergraduate deferments did not end until 1970, when America's role in the war had begun to diminish. The young men who fought the Vietnam War were poorer, Blacker, and browner than the population at large. Class resentment, over the inequities of military service and the evident lack of respect among affluent youth for American institutions, would set the stage for a broad counterreaction to the cultural ferment of the 1960s.

The liberal consensus that had held sway in the United States since Franklin Roosevelt's New Deal would not survive that backlash.

AT THE CENTER OF THINGS: Working at the United Nations

"It was a remarkable opportunity," says Andy.

Born in 1939, Andy Maguire was not a baby boomer. He recalls dancing to the music of Jefferson Airplane and the Rolling Stones, but he had more serious business to take care of. In 1966, twenty-seven years old, he moved to New York City and began work at the United States Mission to the United Nations. The job represented a logical professional beginning for the ambitious new PhD, both as a place to make a difference and a launching pad for a difference-making career. "It's so important that the most powerful nation on earth make decisions that are helpful to the world," he says. "My whole game with getting a PhD in government, and getting it from Harvard, and going into the State Department—all of that—was saying, 'Hey, here I am.' I've got these credentials. I'm somebody who should be able, at some point during my career, to exert a positive effect on the course of world events. And God knows the world needed improvement."

Andy was assigned to the political section of USUN, as the mission was known in the State Department—the word *political* denoting responsibility for government-to-government policy issues. With the title

Adviser, Political and Security Affairs, Andy covered relations with countries in the Middle East and southern Africa. Along with the advisers covering other regions, Andy reported to the head of the political section, John Baker, who in turn reported to Richard Pedersen, the man who'd hired Andy.

A native Arizonan who earned his undergraduate degree at Stanford, Richard Foote Pedersen entered the State Department in 1950, joining USUN three years later. In 1969, William P. Rogers, Richard Nixon's first secretary of state, hired Pedersen as counselor to the United States Department of State—a position established in 1909 as a kind of omnibus consultant on matters of foreign policy. The job description did not come with the proviso of one's phone being tapped, but that's what happened to Pedersen the following year, after Nixon ordered US and South Vietnamese troops to cross into Cambodia—the White House (wrongly) suspected that Pedersen had been responsible for leaks to the press regarding that invasion. From the start of his administration Nixon marginalized Rogers, conducting foreign policy primarily through the White House national security advisor, Henry Kissinger. Nixon formalized the arrangement in 1973 when he ousted Rogers and put Kissinger in charge at Foggy Bottom. Pedersen then had to be gotten rid of, so Nixon dispatched him to Budapest as ambassador to Hungary. Pedersen later served for thirteen years as president of the American University in Cairo. Upon his appointment as State's counselor, the *Washington Post* wrote that Pedersen "has come closer than anyone to personifying the US Mission to the United Nations."

"Andy was the kind of person Dick Pedersen would hang onto, would bring in and operate with," recalls Donald F. McHenry. McHenry, who would serve as US ambassador to the UN during the Carter administration, worked at the time in the Office of UN Political Affairs at the State Department. That office oversaw and assisted not only USUN but also American delegations to international organizations around the world.

"Pedersen was a PhD," McHenry continued, "Andy was a PhD. Andy was a go-getter activist—Dick Pederson certainly was. Pedersen probably outranked his rank—that is, people thought he was higher up in the place than he was." Eventually, Pedersen brought his official position in line with his de facto duties. "He got his office turned into the number-three position at USUN. This gives you an idea of the man Andy was working for."

"Pedersen," says Andy, "was the senior brains of the mission, the principal strategist, figuring out what we were and were not going to do vis-à-vis our allies and adversaries. He was thoughtful and accomplished, a positive thinker and actor committed to his role. An American patriot who wanted our country to lead the world. He was a great mentor to me."

A notch above Pedersen stood the deputy chief of the mission, William Buffum, concerned more with administration than policy. Leading the delegation as the ambassador—more formally, the Permanent Representative of the United States of America to the United Nations—was Arthur J. Goldberg, the Chicago labor lawyer whom John F. Kennedy had appointed first as labor secretary, then, in 1962, to the Supreme Court. Goldberg succeeded Felix Frankfurter in what used to be called the High Court's "Jewish seat."

At the urging of President Lyndon B. Johnson, however, Goldberg surrendered that lifetime appointment to succeed Adlai Stevenson at the UN, where the two-time presidential nominee had served as ambassador since 1961. LBJ, one of the most persuasive operators Washington has ever seen, was notorious for "the Johnson treatment," his way of cajoling and bullying otherwise self-assured people to do his bidding. When Stevenson died in July 1965, Johnson invited Goldberg to join him on Air Force One en route to the funeral in Illinois. Aboard the aircraft, Johnson put the squeeze on the justice. Johnson wanted a man of Goldberg's stature representing the United States at the world body. But the president had another motive for his request—he wanted to name his old Texas friend Abe Fortas, also Jewish, to the Court.

Pedersen wasn't Andy's only mentor at USUN. Another was Frederick Vreeland, son of the photographer Diana Vreeland. "A very high-society guy in New York," says Andy. "Yale, CIA—that whole scene. He spoke fluent French, covered all the Arab states, and eventually served as ambassador to Morocco. He shepherded me around."

Andy had joined a high-functioning team that achieved important objectives. "Everybody was collegial," he recalls. "I could talk to any of the major people at will if I had questions. It was a superbly qualified bunch. Just extraordinary. The mission hadn't become politicized, the way it has in recent years. These people had been trained to think about the national-security interests of the United States, and spent their careers doing so."

"USUN was a great place to be," says McHenry. "Dick Pedersen was great with young people. And you could turn this staff loose. They weren't deskbound as we were in Washington. They were active. They took initiatives. It was a really distinguished group that came through USUN at that time."

"It was an amazing experience to have as the first chapter of my career," says Andy. "Totally amazing."

"Andy didn't wait for things to come his way," says Donald McHenry. "He explored differences with other countries and what they could all do to work out differences. And there were plenty of differences, particularly in the area of colonialism."

In later years, other issues would dominate the UN's agenda. "Andy came and left before the north/south questions arose with regard to economics," says McHenry. "That was more in the '70s. He was there before the great emphasis on the environment. Before Law of the Sea. Before petrodollars.

"The two big issues when Andy was there—and they were perennial issues—were the Middle East, with the Israeli-Palestinian question, and the whole series of questions about decolonization and discrimination.

"Andy was the kind of person who was sensitive on social issues and concerned that the United States be on the right side of history."

More than anything else, Andy's job consisted of taking in, managing, and communicating information—even highly classified information. "They would show me eyes-only communications from the secretary of state, if it was in my bailiwick," he recalls. "I also processed all the incoming cable traffic in my areas of responsibility and would take initiatives based on what I was reading, making recommendations to Baker or Pedersen, such as, How should we handle this matter between Jordan and Israel?"

By virtue of his clerical skills, Andy found himself present in all sorts of meetings, whether or not they related to his regional responsibilities. "I had developed a peculiar set of abbreviations so that I could take almost verbatim notes in any diplomatic meeting," he says. "So when Secretary Rusk"—Dean Rusk, secretary of state from 1961 to 1969—"came to meet with the Russians or the Israelis or whomever, I was the guy who took the notes and then wrote the cable that reported on the meeting back to the entire State Department universe. Obviously, Baker or Pedersen would read it before it went out, but I don't remember ever being corrected on anything.

"I was engaged with people at the top, from Secretary Rusk to Yitzhak Rabin"—the future Israeli prime minister who served as his country's ambassador to the United States from 1968 to 1973—"to Britain's ambassador, Lord Caradon.

"I was right there."

Andy's role in less formal settings was as important as his recording of sit-down meetings. "There was a constant flow of information, back and forth, between our team and other diplomatic missions—every day, all week long," he says. "A lot of that interaction took place in the delegates' lounge. At lunch hour, people like me, from all the delegations, went over there to chitchat and eat." Afternoons, Andy and colleagues would attend receptions at one embassy or another. "Everyone on our team always had an ear cocked to pick up anything that might be important.

"I would memorize what I'd heard from this or that diplomat. If I thought it had implications for anything I or any other person on our team was doing, I would write it down and pass it along."

Serving at USUN was a heady experience for this Californian/New Jerseyan just out of grad school. "Here I was twenty-seven, twenty-eight years old," he recalls, "and my colleagues in parallel positions were in their forties and fifties: Vreeland, the Asia specialist Donald Toussaint, others. A lot of people trusted me to turn in accurate reporting. I knew that if I wrote a memo, it might or might not result in an action—I was a support person, after all. But I did know that the memo would be read and thought about."

Still, Andy's education at USUN didn't always go smoothly. The novice diplomat had a lot to learn.

One evening, at a reception held at the residence of the United Kingdom's deputy ambassador, Andy heard a piece of information he thought Pedersen needed to know—and right away. Andy stepped into an unoccupied room and picked up a phone. The call was still in progress when the evening's host entered the room. "He read me the riot act for using a social occasion at his home to report to my colleagues," Andy says. At social occasions no less than at meetings of the Security Council, diplomatic protocol had to be observed.

Another reprimand came with an American accent. John Baker represented the United States on a joint UK-US-France committee that oversaw the United Nations Relief and Works Agency. Created in 1949, UNRWA provides humanitarian aid to Palestinians displaced by the founding of Israel in 1948.

Andy acted as Baker's staff member at the committee's monthly meetings. One day, as the time for the meeting was approaching, Andy discovered that Baker was in conference with Goldberg in the ambassador's office. Afraid as a junior official to interrupt the mission's most senior official, Andy remained outside, too timid even to ask Goldberg's secretary to intervene.

Finally, out came Baker, who said he'd forgotten about the meeting. He and Andy were twenty minutes late to the appointment. "Baker's anger at me was visceral," Andy recalls. "I learned two lessons: one, don't ever be late for a meeting with international counterparts, and two, if you are the responsible staff person and something is wrong, do whatever needs to be done to get it right—even if you have to interrupt the Permanent Representative of the United States of America to the United Nations."

Another lesson was easier to learn—and left Andy with a blueprint for his future as a leader. "Wherever I went with Baker," he remembers, "he introduced me as 'my colleague' rather than what he might have said: 'one of our political staff.' He was according me respect, and in public. I was grateful for it. I adopted the practice in all my later leadership positions. And that change in nomenclature affected the way I forever after saw my own staff—as *colleagues*, from whom I could learn.

"I always wanted to learn from people who knew more than I did in their areas of expertise, I always wanted people who could do things that complemented what I did. That's why I had such great staff, and why people tended to stay with me. When I was in Congress, there were plenty of members who mistreated their staff; as a result they experienced high rates of turnover. They didn't treat their staffers as equals or as colleagues, in the way my superiors had treated me when I was a junior official at USUN.

"I allowed—invited, urged, insisted—that the fabulous people who worked with me were my colleagues, in name and in fact. And that they were to come up with the very best ideas they could. I had my own ideas, but their ideas were just as important."

SIX DAYS, FIVE DECADES: War and Its Aftermath in the Middle East

In 1956, Gamal Abdel Nasser, the autocratic president of Egypt, seized control of the Suez Canal from the United Kingdom. In response, military forces of Israel, Britain, and France combined in an effort to reestablish UK control of the waterway. The three parties backed down in the face of pressure from America's president, Dwight Eisenhower, but Israel did secure an important concession: free passage of ships to and from Israel through the Straits of Tiran. In addition, Nasser accepted placement of international peacekeepers, the United Nations Emergency Force (UNEF), in the Sinai Peninsula and the Gaza Strip, near Egypt's border with the Jewish state.

The peace held for a decade. But in May 1967, Nasser, responding to a false Soviet warning that Israel was days from attacking Syria, readied for war. He moved Egyptian ground troops into Sinai and expelled UNEF. Still, war might have been avoided had Nasser not taken his next step: He closed access to and from Israel via the Straits, through which Israel imported 90 percent of its oil. At a Sinai air base the Egyptian leader posed for a photograph with a group of smiling airmen. The picture made its way around the world, along with Nasser's boast: "If Israel wishes to threaten war, we tell her, you are welcome."

Israel took him up on his offer, mounting a preemptive attack on the morning of June 5, 1967. Israeli war planes attacked Egyptian airfields, destroying—on the ground—nearly every plane in the Egyptian air force. Israeli ground troops advanced west into Sinai. Israel also responded to attacks from Syria and Jordan, both formally allied with Egypt, and from Palestinian and Egyptian forces in Gaza. The Jewish state prevailed on all fronts—and quickly. The warring parties declared a cease-fire after only six days of fighting, with Israel having taken control of the Sinai and Gaza from Egypt, the Golan Heights from Syria, and the West Bank from Jordan. Israel also occupied East Jerusalem, the ancient part of the city that included the al-Aqsa Mosque and the Western Wall, the only structure remaining from the Hebrew temple destroyed by Rome in 70 C.E. Jordan had held the Old City since 1948, denying entry to all Jews.

Tiny Israel had triumphed; the Arab world had been humiliated. Israel—and its friends around the world—were giddy with joy and relief. The Jewish state had more than temporarily escaped annihilation; it had dramatically and definitively served notice that it was in the Middle East to stay.

Israel's leaders envisioned that before long it would trade the land it occupied—most of it, anyway—for peace treaties with the Arab states. United Nations Resolution 242 called for such an exchange, although it avoided the most intractable issues a peace treaty between Israel and Palestine would have to address: the status of Jerusalem and the right of return for Palestinians who left or were driven out of the new state of Israel in 1947–48 in what they call *al-naqba*, the catastrophe. Israel did conclude peace treaties with Egypt, to which it returned the Sinai, in 1979, and with Jordan, in 1994. A deal between Israel and the Palestinians, however, today seems a near impossibility.

In the years since the Six Day War, positions on both sides have hardened. The leadership of the Palestinians has resisted the compromises a deal would entail. Meanwhile, demographic shifts in Israel have displaced the older, more left-leaning, more secular generation of Jews who arrived before and just after World War II and dominated Israeli politics for the first three decades of the state's existence. After the 1967 war, Jews from elsewhere in the Middle East, expelled by Arab governments, streamed in, as did Jews from the Soviet Union and, later, from former Soviet nations. Both groups were less likely than the earlier immigrants to favor accommodation with the Palestinians, as was Israel's increasing population of ultra-Orthodox Jews. The Labor Party, which had governed Israel from its founding until 1977, gave way to Likud, a more conservative, nationalistic faction. Sentiment grew for retaining control of the West Bank, both because it made up part of the ancient Land of Israel and because successive governments permitted more and more Israelis to settle in the area. Benjamin Netanyahu, the longest-serving prime minister in Israel's history, paid grudging lip service to the so-called two-state solution but in practice did everything in his power to prevent its realization.

Today, Israel continues to occupy the West Bank and Gaza. Demography dictates that if Israel maintains its rule over nearly five million Palestinians, it must eventually confront a choice: Either grant Palestinians equal rights and cease to be a Jewish state, or continue to deny those rights and cease to be a democracy. With each passing year, the latter option seems increasingly probable.

And so, Israel's stunning victory in 1967, rejoiced over at the time, has turned out to have been cursed.

On June 4, 1967, Andy went to bed at the US mission's sleeping quarters—someone was always on duty overnight; this night it was his turn.

In the early morning hours, the secure communications team, working in the mission's basement, woke Andy with a message: ISRAEL AND EGYPT ARE AT WAR.

"The people in the basement got incoming cables from all over the world," Andy recalls. "Those relating to your area would be on your desk when you arrived in the morning. But if there was an emergency, they'd wake you up. That was the case on the night of June 4.

"Yeah, I was the guy."

Andy telephoned his superiors, starting with Pedersen. "I didn't have much more involvement that day," Andy says. "It was all the top-level people talking to each other. They didn't need a staff assistant right then."

But in the months that followed Andy had plenty to do—he didn't get a day off until November. "Every Saturday, every Sunday, every holiday, I was in the mission," he says. "One hundred forty-eight straight days.

"Again, a pretty amazing experience for a twenty-eight-year-old."

The UN Security Council took up the issue; Andy attended every meeting.

On June 6, the second day of the war, the Security Council heard from Israel's foreign minister, Abba Eban, called by some the most articulate person in the world. In his resonant baritone, with an accent that attested to his South African birth and Cambridge education, he described Israel's situation as Nasser mounted his threat.

> In short, there was peril for Israel wherever it looked. Its manpower had been hastily mobilized. Its economy and commerce were beating with feeble pulses. Its streets were dark and empty. There was an apocalyptic air of approaching peril. And Israel faced this danger alone. . . .
>
> Now there could be no doubt about what was intended for us. With my very ears I heard President Nasser's speech on 26 May. He said:
>
> "We intend to open a general assault against Israel. This will be total war. Our basic aim will be to destroy Israel."
>
> On 2 June, the Egyptian Commander in Sinai, General Mortagi, published his Order of the Day, calling on his troops to wage a war of destruction against Israel. Here, then, was a systematic, overt, proclaimed design at politicide, the murder of a State.

"I was in the Security Council the day Abba Eban gave one of the best speeches I've ever heard," recalls Donald McHenry. "It was stirring. It was passionate. It was sweeping. At the end of it, you would have thought Israel had been attacked; in truth, it had not. You could make the argument that had they waited they would have been overrun. But anybody who heard that speech would have thought that Israel had been attacked."

Andy was present for the speech, as well, and had other dealings with the Israeli statesman. "Eban was enormously impressive," he says. "He had such a dignified presence. His elocution and his verbal style were elite. Extraordinary man. Brilliant. At the same time, warm and interactive. A superb representative of Israel."

Once the war had ended, with the Arab world in shock and Israeli forces occupying territory previously held by Egypt, Syria, and Jordan, the Security Council conducted intensive negotiations aimed at finding a way forward. The result was Resolution 242.

Andy recalls the subject matter of the meetings: "How do we come up with a resolution that will provide a road map with respect to negotiations between Israel and its neighboring states regarding borders and security? How could all the pieces fit together?"

The United States delegation worked closely with the United Kingdom's, which was headed by Hugh Foot, a veteran diplomat who had received a life peerage as Baron Caradon. Throughout his career he'd served in a host of overseas postings, beginning with an administrative role in Mandatory Palestine—what is now Israel and the Occupied Territories, administered by the UK under international mandate between the end of World War I and 1948.

Officially, the Security Council operated in two working languages, English and French.

"From the get-go we worked closely with Lord Caradon on the English version," Andy recalls. "The French were working on their own."

As the resolution took shape in both tongues, a subtle discrepancy arose. "You could always depend on the French to have some sort of an angle," Andy says. "They felt closer to the Arabs than did the British. We Americans pretended we were close to both sides, even though we knew that our domestic politics meant we would never do anything unacceptable to Israel. At the same time, we had spent decades developing close relationships with many Arab states. And some critics would argue that the State Department was populated by people—Vreeland, for example—who were prepared to make a fuller case for the Arab point of view. Ultimately, we got a clear understanding from the White

House that everything had to be worked out with Israel. It was a high-wire act.

"The French and the Americans have always had a rivalry of sorts. Whether regarding tourists or culture or languages or politics or diplomacy, the French always want to be big players, with their own point of view. And they had continuing relationships in the Middle East and in Africa with French-speaking former territories. It's not at all surprising that they should come up with a formulation in French that gave the impression that every piece of occupied land should be returned."

As Andy notes, 242 "was basically a territory-for-security document." The dispute centered on the treatment of the word *territories* (*territoires* in French). In both English and French, the resolution called for the termination of belligerency and the right of every state in the area to live in peace within secure and recognized borders. The English version further called for "Withdrawal of Israeli armed forces from territories occupied in the recent conflict." In French the text read, "*Retrait des forces armées israéliennes des territoires occupés lors du récent conflit.*" The English version notes "territories," without the definite article *the*, permitting the understanding that withdrawal might not be mandated from *all* the territories. The French "*des territoires*," by contrast, means 'from the territories,' implying complete withdrawal. "In the English," notes Andy, "because the State Department and Israel and Goldberg wanted a bit of flexibility, the resolution suggests that the settlement might not necessarily have to hew exactly to the Green Armistice Line of 1948 but might include some adjustments here and there that would be acceptable to both sides. The French version came closer to saying that the borders had to return to exactly the way they used to be.

"We got the resolution passed. The notion was that all parties had an interest in getting the matter resolved in a reasonably short period of time. Obviously, it would take years—none of the issues were easy. We thought that the exchange of Arab territory for Israel's security was the central challenge. There was never going to be a comprehensive right of return. There would be something symbolic. And we knew Jerusalem would be a headache.

"The Arabs, for their part, suffered under their leadership, beginning with Palestinian leader Yasser Arafat, who seemed less interested in a settlement than in being a world figure and feathering his own nest. Meanwhile, Israel was riven internally between those who wanted to make a deal in line with 242 and those who believed Israel should encompass all the land from the Jordan River to the Mediterranean.

"Those were the two main thrusts within Israel. You had people like Rabin and Levi Eshkol"—prime minister from 1963 to 1969—"who believed that their country's future was best protected by permitting the establishment of a Palestinian state, although with clear guarantees of security for Israel. But then you had Likud, first as an opposition faction, then, starting with Menachem Begin as prime minister, in control of the government. They didn't want to implement 242. And as the years have gone by, the West Bank has been increasingly home to Israeli construction projects and settlements."

> Surely, after what has happened we must have better assurance than before, for Israel and for the Middle East, of peaceful coexistence. The question is whether there is any reason to believe that such a new era may yet come to pass. If I am a little sanguine on this point, it is because of a conviction that men and nations do behave wisely once they have exhausted all other alternatives. Surely the other alternatives of war and belligerency have now been exhausted.
>
> —*Abba Eban*

"In 1967," says Andy, "I believed that the UN and the Americans could solve problems. I thought, 'Okay, we've got a blueprint for peace in the Middle East. It might take some time, but the parties will conclude negotiations within a few years.' I said to Pedersen, 'How long do you think it'll be? Five years?' His answer was: 'Fifty years.' That shows you how intuitive he was.

"It turns out that fifty years was optimistic."

Andy notes that any public servant must maintain optimism. "You need to believe that you're going to be able to make a difference," he says. "In my twenties my notion was that history would always be progressive. After dealing with *these* problems, we would move on to *those* problems. And when we dealt with *those* problems, we would deal with the next set. That was naive. Look at the debates in Congress today—too many of them resemble the debates of forty years ago, except that the place is so much worse now.

"But I'm still optimistic. I'll give you an example. The dangers Trump poses, both internationally and domestically, are enormous. But so far we've survived years of this disaster, including all that has come at us since Trump left the White House. Everybody is saying, 'No way can we survive more of this, it'll change America forever.' I don't believe that, even though it is becoming increasingly difficult to envision how and when the positive changes I expect will reassert themselves.

"That's how optimistic I am about the resilience of this country."

GUNBOAT DIPLOMACY: The United States, South Africa, and an Aircraft Carrier

"You have to remember," says Donald McHenry, "that when the question of apartheid first arose in the UN, there was an issue as to whether it was a legitimate subject. If it was considered a matter of domestic jurisdiction, the charter eliminated it as something to address. Indeed, one of the great compromises in those early days was that apartheid got on the UN agenda because of South Africa's treatment not of its Black inhabitants but of its inhabitants of Indo-Pakistani descent. So the issue was an argument between South Africa and India, not one about the bulk of South Africa's population. It was only later that the fig leaf disappeared. People got brave enough to list apartheid as the real issue.

"Of course, the big thing, the thing that really got worldwide publicity and brought apartheid before the Security Council, was the massacre that took place in South Africa in 1960."

In March of that year, South African police officers fired into a large crowd assembled in the township of Sharpeville to protest the country's pass laws, which required Black citizens to carry a passbook at all times and severely restricted their freedom of movement in white areas. The police killed 69 people that day; they wounded another 180.

Before Sharpeville, US foreign policy treated South Africa as a cold war comrade-in-arms, with the two countries engaging in substantial trade and in military cooperation. But in the '60s, America's stance toward the racist regime hardened.

"Beginning about '63," says McHenry, "and certainly by '66, one of our principal concerns was trying to restrict sales of military equipment. We'd stopped selling arms to South Africa under Kennedy. After that, the big bureaucratic squabbles were about, What is military equipment? A real issue had to do with light aircraft. A Cessna is not generally thought of as military equipment. On the other hand, if your prime reason for buying the Cessna is to spot movements of guerillas, that's a different story. For purely military equipment, the export goes through the Department of Defense. These other pieces might go through Commerce. And that's where the big bureaucratic battles start.

"Of course, the South Africans wanted to identify themselves as anti-Communist. And there were enough conservatives and bigots and right-wing nuts in the United States who bought that. But you also had the suppliers. A town in Wichita wants to sell Cessna airplanes. When you deny the sale, you hear from the Cessna Aircraft Corporation and from workers and from members of Congress. We were constantly dealing with such issues."

In February 1967, the USS *Franklin Roosevelt*, a Navy aircraft carrier just finished with an eight-month combat tour off the Vietnamese coast, docked in Cape Town, South Africa. US civil rights leaders and prominent lawmakers had opposed the visit, but the four thousand officers and men aboard the ship were eager for shore liberty. However, that liberty was canceled, and the ship's visit cut short, when the Department of Defense ruled that sailors would be permitted ashore "in connection with organized integrated activities only"—a condition the segregated city could not meet. A group of sixty sailors, Black and white, did go ashore to donate blood in response to a South African appeal. Medical technicians extracted the blood in an integrated setting. However, each portion of blood was marked with the race of the donor so as to be sure that white South Africans did not receive nonwhite blood. After refueling, the ship sailed home to the United States.

The following year, the Navy arranged for another carrier to dock in Cape Town. Andy Maguire, raised not only to see racial injustice but to fight it, set out to change that plan.

"I worked closely on the issue with Donald McHenry," says Andy.

McHenry recalls, "We asked, What do we need to do—you in New York, I in DC—to make sure that our Defense Department doesn't send the wrong signal by having its aircraft carrier call at Cape Town? This was a time when there were UN sanctions against South Africa and when the United States was critical of apartheid yet under increasing criticism around the world for being too snuggly with the South African government. USUN and DC would sometimes make joint recommendations and try to get them implemented, and in this case we succeeded. The damned aircraft carrier did not go to Cape Town."

The issue was more complicated than it seems on first examination. McHenry recalls the attractiveness of the destination for the sailors. "Cape Town at that time was a great place to stop," he says. "You had this large 'colored' population in the city, and they had nightclubs.

"But every time a ship docked there, it was a political hot potato for the administration. And there was a thought that if you stop in Cape Town, some other country, in Africa or Southeast Asia, might say you can't stop at our place. Nobody ever made that threat, but it's the kind of thing you have to think of. It was bad publicity for the administration.

"The first thing Johnson did was to prohibit the shore leave. But the military was saying, 'We can't make it around that far without refueling. We want to be able to stop at Simon's Town, which is sixty, seventy miles north of Cape Town. Or get the fuel delivered from Simon's Town.' But again, that was an indication of cooperation between the US military and the dreaded South Africans.

"Here again you have all these forces. You have a group that says, 'This looks terrible and you don't really have to stop there for fuel. We all know you can carry enough fuel to get you to another place for refueling, so don't give us that crap.'

"And then you have military brass saying, 'You got all of these horny men on the ship, they need to get off, and Cape Town's a nice place to do it.' Also on that side, again, was the argument that the South Africans were anti-Communist.

"There was a lot of back-and-forth with the people at USUN. Washington was split, as you would expect. Defense Department saying this, State Department saying that. Input from Commerce, from various people on the Hill pushed by one of those factions in the government or one of those factions outside.

"Finally, the decision was made not to do it."

After the *Franklin Roosevelt*'s visit in 1967, no US naval vessel docked at a South African port until 2008, nearly a decade after Nelson Mandela ended his post-apartheid presidency, when a nuclear-powered US aircraft carrier dropped anchor at Cape Town. Fittingly, the ship's name was the USS *Theodore Roosevelt.*

McHenry recalls the time in which Andy served in the State Department as a kind of golden age. "This was a period of time," says McHenry, "when, objectively speaking, the two great parts of the State Department were USUN and UN Political Affairs. There was a close relationship between the two units, not simply because you're working on the same subjects but because you were on the telephone constantly, many times a day. We sent personnel back and forth—more, I think, people going from Washington to New York than vice versa. I think the New Yorkers probably would have benefited had they come to Washington a little more, because then they would have been able to better understand complex problems like dealing with dual-use equipment.

"USUN didn't have to reconcile its views with all these other places that we at UN Political Affairs had to deal with. Plus, New York always had one thing—they knew it and we knew it. They had direct access to the president of the United States through the ambassador. At that time the ambassador had cabinet status, with the ability to go straight to the top. Goldberg, in particular, was not shy about calling Johnson. By personality, Goldberg would have done so. But even more, because he'd given up his seat on the Supreme Court. Johnson owed him."

After leaving State, Andy kept up his involvement in issues relating to South Africa. Sentiment started to grow in the United States for companies to divest holdings in South Africa and for the government to implement economic sanctions against the apartheid regime. Andy spoke on college campuses in favor of those moves. He maintained his interest in the country once he entered the House of Representatives.

"My views were well known in the State Department," he recalls, "so Dick Moose, head of State's Bureau of African Affairs, called me to ask if I'd lead an effort in Congress to support the Sullivan principles. Leon Sullivan, a minister in Philadelphia, had come up with a set of rules for US companies that employed workers in South Africa—rules dictating an integrated workplace and the like.

"Andy Young"—Carter's first UN ambassador, succeeded by McHenry—"was always drawing analogies between South Africa and the civil rights movement in America. I said to Dick, 'South Africa is a regime based on terror, on the most systematic racism the world has ever seen. They will not be budged by any ideas about how to work together as nice guys. No, I won't do that. Because that's not what the situation requires.'

"I did, however, author and get passed in the House the first piece of legislation that imposed a US government sanction on South Africa. The bill severely narrowed the Export-Import Bank's role in supporting exports to South Africa."

After the bill passed in the Senate, Jimmy Carter signed it into law.

Among its provisions, the Export-Import Bank Amendments Act of 1978 barred the "support of any export which would contribute to . . . apartheid," whether to the South African government or a private business, although allowing for relaxation of that prohibition upon a president's formal declaration "that significant progress toward the elimination of apartheid has been made."

From the *New York Times*, February 9, 1978:

> Representative Andrew Maguire, Democrat of New Jersey and a leader of a new ad hoc Congressional caucus on South Africa, commented in an interview, "We're saying that at the very least we can demur from using public funds and agencies to further encourage additional private investment, which cannot be defended either in terms of human rights or the long-term security of the investment community."

The son of Bruce and Ruth Maguire had kept faith with his family's principles.

A BITCH OF A WAR:
Lyndon Johnson's Dream and His Downfall

John F. Kennedy had long supported the aims of the civil rights movement, but their cause was not his cause—not really. A son of privilege, educated at Choate and Harvard, JFK had little experience of African-Americans and Latinos aside from the people serving him dinner or parking his car. And, like any Democratic president since the end of the Civil War, he relied on the votes—and the legislators—of the Solid South, the states of the Confederacy where the Party of Lincoln was almost as powerless as the Black people who had been disenfranchised since the end of Reconstruction.

During his first two years as president, Kennedy gave measured support to the movement but considered it a nuisance that only complicated his life and his politics. But events—the brutal treatment of civil rights demonstrators at the hands of Southern law enforcement, the resistance to the Supreme Court's 1954 *Brown* decision mandating the integration of public schools—intervened to deepen his commitment to ending Jim Crow. On June 11, 1963, hours after George Wallace, the scrappy, racist governor of Alabama, had fulfilled his promise to "stand in the schoolhouse door" in a futile—and staged—effort to obstruct the integration of the University of Alabama, Kennedy delivered a nationally televised address that finally placed him squarely on the side of those demanding justice.

> We are confronted primarily with a moral issue. It is as old as the scriptures and is as clear as the American Constitution.
>
> The heart of the question is whether all Americans are to be afforded equal rights and equal opportunities, whether we are going to treat our fellow Americans as we want to be treated. . . .
>
> One hundred years of delay have passed since President Lincoln freed the slaves, yet their heirs, their grandsons, are not fully free. They are not yet freed from the bonds of injustice. They are not yet freed from social and economic oppression. And this nation, for all its hopes and all its boasts, will not be fully free until all its citizens are free.

The president promised to introduce legislation that would attack Jim Crow by knocking down its two most prominent pillars: discrimination in public accommodations and denial of the right to vote.

But on November 22, Lee Harvey Oswald gunned down President Kennedy in Dallas. Five days later, Lyndon Baines Johnson, Kennedy's vice president, who had taken the presidential oath of office on Air Force One less than an hour and a half after JFK's death, addressed Congress and the nation:

> On the twentieth day of January, in 1961, John F. Kennedy told his countrymen that our national work would not be finished "in the first thousand days, nor in the life of this administration, nor even perhaps in our lifetime on this planet. But," he said, "let us begin."
>
> Today, in this moment of new resolve, I would say to all my fellow Americans, let us continue.

Johnson did more than continue. The early years of Johnson's presidency—1964, 1965, 1966—mark the high point of American liberalism.

Johnson did not grow up poor in Johnson City, Texas, but his family wasn't rich, either. He attended not Harvard but Southwest Texas State Teachers College and, after earning his degree, spent nine months teaching Mexican-American children at a segregated school in the small Texas town of Cotulla. He spoke of those children often as president. Johnson felt the need for justice in a way that a rich kid like Jack Kennedy could not.

During his Senate career, especially as Senate majority leader in the 1950s, LBJ bided his time, not revealing his passion for civil rights, although he did work hard to secure passage of the Civil Rights Act of 1957. Although toothless, the bill did put the federal government on record as supporting African-American voting rights in the South.

As president, LBJ was liberated. He pushed through Congress the Civil Rights Act of 1964, which integrated public accommodations. "White" and "Colored" water fountains, segregated restaurants in bus terminals, were things of the past. In his speech the following year supporting passage of the Voting Rights Act, he spoke of "the effort of American Negroes to secure for themselves the full blessings of American life."

Continuing, he said, "Their cause must be our cause too. Because it is not just Negroes, but really it is all of us, who must overcome the crippling legacy of bigotry and injustice. And we shall overcome."

Civil rights leaders—indeed, all who supported the struggle for the rights of America's Black citizens—were amazed and energized that a president of the United States had spoken, emphatically, the refrain from the movement's anthem.

The Voting Rights Act passed in 1965.

With his political power at its peak following his November 1964 landslide defeat of Senator Barry Goldwater, the Arizona conservative who had opposed the public accommodations bill, Johnson set out to create what he called "the Great Society." An avid New Dealer from his first campaign for Congress in 1937, Johnson now aimed to emulate and build on FDR's panoply of programs aimed at improving the lives of less-than-affluent Americans. Head Start, Medicare, Medicaid, the National Endowment for the Arts, the National Endowment for the Humanities, the Corporation for Public Broadcasting; federal aid to education, protection of endangered species, federal attention to highway safety and consumer protection—all these features of our national life had their start thanks to LBJ's ideals, his mastery of the levers of power, and the lopsided Democratic majorities his electoral coattails had produced in Congress.

But the quagmire of Vietnam was drawing Johnson in deeper, and he could find no way out. After Dallas, Johnson asked each member of Kennedy's cabinet and White House staff to stay on, telling them, "I need you more than President Kennedy needed you." Kennedy's national security team—Secretary of Defense Robert McNamara, Secretary of State Dean Rusk, National Security Advisor McGeorge Bundy, Walt Rostow at State and Bundy's successor starting in 1966—remained in place. David Halberstam, in *The Best and the Brightest*, his classic study of the men who designed and implemented America's war in Vietnam, looks at these four men and others in the administration. All had attended the world's most prestigious schools—Harvard, Yale, Oxford. All had held important positions in academia and business: McNamara had served as president of the Ford Motor Company, Bundy as dean of Harvard's Faculty of Arts and Sciences, Rusk as president of the Rockefeller Foundation, Rostow as an economics professor at MIT.

Yet for all their education and credentials, these men led the nation into catastrophe, unaware that the theories they devised in Washington did not apply on the ground in a country about which they understood next to nothing. Lyndon Johnson, the alumnus of West Texas State Teachers College, felt overawed by the pedigree and apparent brilliance of these men. Johnson had had premonitions that Vietnam would turn into a nightmare. Had he trusted his instincts as a savvy Texas politician, rather than the lofty pronouncements of men whose ignorance was exceeded only by their arrogance, America and Vietnam might have been spared the long years of devastation inflicted by this foolish war.

At first, Lyndon Johnson believed that only by escalating the war could he maintain the goodwill of Congress and thus its support for his burgeoning quest to create the Great Society. But by 1967 he realized that his war to bring freedom to Vietnam was sapping his government's ability to bring justice to the United States. The war demanded more and more of the country's treasure. As the conflict wore on without noticeable progress toward victory, the nation's citizens, and their representatives on Capitol Hill, became less willing to bend under the president's legendary will and legislative wizardry. While elements of the Great Society have endured to this day, other programs—aimed at urban renewal, job training, economic empowerment, low-cost housing—did not long survive

Johnson's presidency. And even programs that have survived have not enjoyed the full funding Johnson envisioned.

In January 1964, Johnson declared "unconditional war on poverty in America." But that war fell victim to his other war. After leaving office, Johnson wrote, "I knew from the start that I was bound to be crucified either way I moved. If I left the woman I really love—the Great Society—to get involved in that bitch of a war on the other side of the world, then I would lose everything at home."

In 1968, Richard Nixon won election to succeed Johnson, commencing Republican occupancy of the Oval Office for sixteen of the next twenty years. The Democratic presidents elected since have been no more than moderately liberal, not proposing—or not able to pass—major government initiatives, with the notable exception of Obamacare.

American liberalism still has not recovered from America's war in Vietnam.

As an officer in the State Department, Andy could not ignore the war that was not only tearing his country apart but also damaging its standing around the world. "By the time I was at the UN," he recalls, "we were deeply involved in Vietnam, which the Africans thought was insane.

"It was, of course."

Andy's assessment of the war did not conflict with the duties of his position at USUN, but it would have had he been assigned to a job involving Vietnam. "If that had been offered to me, I would have said no," he says.

The earnest young staff member believed he had an obligation to present the truth to his elders, so he bought copies of books on Vietnam by the leftist historian Howard Zinn and the liberal historian Arthur Schlesinger and gave them to Goldberg, Pedersen, and Toussaint. More than once he boarded a bus to Washington to take part in antiwar demonstrations.

"There weren't any prohibitions one way or the other," he says. "You had complete freedom of speech and could have your own views. When you weren't in the office, you could do whatever you wanted. There were multitudes of people at the demonstrations. I never worried about my boss seeing me."

Andy wasn't the only State Department official supporting the antiwar protests. "If you came to my house on 16th Street in Washington on the weekends," says Donald McHenry, "you would probably have found twenty or thirty kids sleeping there, scattered in every room. They had come to the capital to demonstrate, and my name was on the list of people offering their houses. After they arrived I told them who I was, but they didn't know before."

Andy had analyzed the war; he's still angry about it: "First, the planners of the war started from the proposition that Communism was the world's greatest evil, that it would spread unless it was stopped, and that it fell to us to stop it. That idea got elaborated into the notion of falling dominoes. If you lose Vietnam, you lose the rest of Southeast Asia, then the Philippines, then India, then Japan, until finally the Communists are washing up on the shores of San Francisco. All of which was faulty—and should have been known to be faulty at the time.

"Second, they totally misunderstood the fact that in Vietnam, Communism, as it was understood by the vast majority of citizens, was far more a matter of nationalism than of Marxism-Leninism. People are motivated to fight for their national identity and their national well-being.

"Third, you can't prop up a government, like South Vietnam's, that's run by incompetent and corrupt individuals with no natural base within the polity.

"Fourth, successful counterinsurgency warfare was an illusion.

"Fifth, you can't win by bombing the other army to bits, because bombs are imprecise. All they do is cause the opposition to seek methods other than moving en masse across open territory.

"So from every point of view: the history of Vietnam; the threat, or lack thereof, of Communism; the ridiculous notion that you had to draw a line and decide that everybody on this side of the line had to have a particular type of government; the counterinsurgency strategy, the bombing—all deeply flawed.

"Johnson bombed the hell out of North Vietnam. Nixon and Kissinger bombed the hell out of not just the north but also Laos and even Cambodia. Which, of course, led to Pol Pot and the murder of millions of people.

"The people who brought us the war—Walt Rostow, McGeorge Bundy, Robert McNamara—were clear in their own minds about what they were doing. They were going to exert military force to stop the spread of Communism. But McNamara didn't know anything more about Vietnam than he knew about any other part of the world. What he knew about was how to build second-rate cars.

"These men didn't understand the world they were operating in, they didn't have any reasonable principles of military engagement that could possibly work, and politically the whole thing was wrong from top to bottom. Not to mention the devastating effects on America: 58,000 soldiers killed, countless more who came back with permanent physical and psychological wounds, the damage to our economy, the damage to our social fabric, the damage to our understanding of priorities, the damage to our ability to exert leadership in the world, the damage to America's sense of itself. The list is long.

"The best and the brightest were the worst and the stupidest."

AMERICA'S YEAR FROM HELL: 1968

No year after 1945 has been more traumatic for our country than 1968.

Consider:

On January 31, as South Vietnam was celebrating the start of Tet, the Lunar New Year, South Vietnamese Communist fighters, called Vietcong by Americans, along with troops of the People's Army of North Vietnam, mounted assaults in over one hundred locations throughout South Vietnam. Their aim was to incite a general rebellion of the South Vietnamese people that would topple the Saigon regime.

Tactically, the Tet Offensive proved a catastrophic failure. The general rebellion did not materialize as US forces and those of the Army of the Republic of Vietnam—the army of the South Vietnamese government—beat back the attackers, inflicting grievous losses. Strategically, however, the offensive struck pay dirt. The most effective of the one hundred-plus assaults was one of the most limited: an attack upon the United States embassy in Saigon. Although the attackers did not pierce the walls of the embassy building, they breached the compound's outer walls before being routed or killed. Via newspaper headlines and photographs, via televised film footage, Americans learned that Vietcong guerillas had made their way "inside the embassy." That simple fact seemed to belie recent pronouncements by the commander of US forces in Vietnam, William Westmoreland, that victory was near—there was "light at the end of the tunnel." In Tet's aftermath, Walter Cronkite, the anchor of CBS News and "the most trusted man in America"—at a time when it was possible to have a most trusted man in America—conducted a fact-finding visit to South Vietnam. At the end of his tour he pronounced the war unwinnable and called for a negotiated settlement. Lyndon Johnson lamented to an aide that if he'd lost Cronkite, he'd lost middle America.

On March 12, Eugene McCarthy, a little-known US senator from Minnesota running on an antiwar platform, finished a strong second in the New Hampshire Democratic primary. Not even on the ballot in this presidential election year, LBJ won the contest with write-in votes. But the incumbent president's near loss, four years after his historic landslide, shocked political professionals and rank-and-file citizens alike.

On March 16, a more formidable antiwar candidate entered the race: New York senator Robert F. Kennedy, a brother of the late president and a man who shared with Johnson a mutual hatred. Kennedy's announcement put the president's reelection in serious doubt.

On March 31, Lyndon Johnson delivered a televised address to the nation. Hoping to bring about peace negotiations, the president announced a near-cessation of US bombing of North Vietnam. Near the end of the speech he spoke of the challenges to the nation, in Vietnam and at home, and then said, "I do not believe that I should devote an hour or a day of my time to any personal partisan causes or to any duties other than the awesome duties of this office—the presidency of your country.

"Accordingly, I shall not seek, and I will not accept, the nomination of my party for another term as your president."

He had told his wife and the operator of the teleprompter, but almost no one else. The announcement surprised his White House staff and cabinet as much as it did the public at large.

On April 4, standing on the terrace of his room at the Lorraine Hotel in Memphis, Tennessee, where he was leading a strike of city sanitation workers, Martin Luther King Jr. was shot and killed by a racist drifter named James Earl Ray. Disturbances broke out in African-American neighborhoods around the country—among them Chicago, Baltimore, and, most visibly, Washington, DC The day of King's funeral in Atlanta, Georgia's segregationist governor, Lester Maddox, locked the state house and surrounded it with guards.

On June 4, Robert Kennedy won the year's final presidential primary, in California. After the campaign's victory party in the ballroom of the Ambassador Hotel in Los Angeles, the candidate exited through the hotel's kitchen. There Sirhan Sirhan, a Palestinian nationalist angry at the senator's support for Israel, fired his handgun. Three bullets hit Kennedy, one in his head. He died twenty-six hours later.

In August, Democrats convened in Chicago for their quadrennial national convention. With Kennedy gone, the presumptive nominee was Hubert H. Humphrey, Johnson's vice president. Humphrey had run in no primaries; he had secured his delegate lead through outreach to party bosses around the country. Eugene McCarthy had been joined as a candidate by South Dakota antiwar senator George McGovern, who framed his last-minute bid as a landing place for supporters of the slain Kennedy. The scene inside the convention hall was tumultuous, as supporters of McCarthy, Kennedy, and McGovern loudly refused to fall in line behind the party's nomination of a man so tainted by his association with the president and his war. The scene outside was even worse, as Chicago police officers wielded nightsticks and tear gas to control crowds of youthful antiwar protestors. From the convention podium Senator Abe Ribicoff, of Connecticut, denounced the "gestapo tactics" of the Chicago police force. "Fuck you, you Jew bastard," Chicago mayor Richard J. Daley was seen to have shouted back from the audience.

The GOP nominee, named at the Republican convention in Miami Beach three weeks earlier, was Richard Nixon. Two years after losing to Jack Kennedy in 1960, Nixon had run for governor of California. On the night of the election, after conceding defeat, Nixon told the press, "You won't have Nixon to kick around anymore because, gentlemen, this is my last press conference." But in 1964, when many establishment Republicans shied away from the ultra-conservative Barry Goldwater—"extremism in defense of liberty is no vice," Goldwater had proclaimed—Nixon delivered a nationally televised endorsement of the Arizonan and appeared on his behalf throughout the country. Four years later, Nixon's efforts within his party had paid off.

The Democratic convention couldn't have gone any better for Nixon. The chaos in Chicago, added to the turmoil that had roiled the nation's streets and college campuses for years, helped frame a campaign centered on Nixon's pledge to restore "law and order."

George Wallace mounted a third-party run for president, with a law-and-order platform like Nixon's but turbocharged by his personal brand of belligerent populism. Wallace ranted against "pointy-headed Washington bureaucrats" who controlled other people's lives, officials who carried briefcases that made them feel important but, said Wallace, in fact contained only a peanut butter and jelly sandwich.

Humphrey campaigned gallantly, but the traditional Democratic coalition—working people, Northern liberals, Blacks, Jews—was missing what had been an important component: Southern whites, who were beginning their migration to the GOP. Nor could Humphrey hold on to more culturally conservative Northern Democrats who responded to Nixon's promise to quell the anarchy. But above all, Humphrey was done in by his association with Lyndon Johnson's war—the Minnesotan went to his grave regretting that in 1968 he did not do more to separate himself from his boss on the issue. Nixon promised that he had a plan to end the war but refused to provide details on the grounds that he didn't want to tip his hand to the Communists. In fact, Nixon had no plan to end the war; he had a plan to prolong it. Unbeknownst to the public, Nixon sabotaged budding peace negotiations between the two coalitions fighting the war—the United States and South Vietnam vs. the Vietcong and North Vietnam—by convincing South Vietnamese president Nguyen Van Thieu to refuse participation in the talks in expectation of a better deal from a newly elected President Nixon. The peace talks were stymied, but polling showed a surge toward Humphrey after Johnson announced a complete halt to the bombing of North Vietnam days before Election Day.

Had the election taken place a week later, that surge might have carried Humphrey to victory. As it was, the election was close—Nixon won the popular vote by only half a million ballots. But he won the Electoral College 301 to 191. Wallace prevailed in five Southern states, gaining him 46 electoral votes.

"Would you buy a used car from this man?" some wag had captioned a picture of Nixon. Yes, said the voters in 1968, we would.

Although Andy thrived at USUN, after a couple of years he was restless to move on. He ruled out staying at the State Department. "I probably could have had a stellar career in the diplomatic service of the United States—I was off to a rip-roaring start," he says. "But I didn't want to stamp passports somewhere in the Foreign Service. And I knew full well that no matter how many promotions I got I would be locked into pursuing whatever it was that people in Washington were telling me I should be pursuing."

Donald McHenry suggests that Andy's personality ill-suited him to a career at State. "Andy struck me," he says, "as a crusader, a liberal, a can-do person. At the cutting edge. Working to correct injustice. He'd have found the regular Foreign Service difficult, because he would have had to work with people and on subjects he found distasteful."

Even worse would be working in the new Nixon administration, which took office on January 20, 1969. "I was special assistant to the secretary of state when Nixon came in," says McHenry. "I spent two years with the Nixon crowd. I don't think Andy would have spent two days."

Frederick Vreeland set up an interview for Andy with McGeorge Bundy, president of the Ford Foundation since leaving the White House in 1966 and now looking for an assistant. "I met with Bundy," says Andy. "I didn't take the opportunity to mention that I saw him among those responsible for the atrocity of our involvement in Vietnam."

Bundy didn't hire Andy but did pass on his name to the foundation's government and law division, which offered him a job. "I would have been the guy who handed out the money instead of always having to apply for it," Andy recalls. "I guess Bundy told these guys, 'Look. This is a fine young professional, but he's not right for me.' I turned down the offer. Thank goodness Bundy didn't ask me to be his assistant; I probably would have said yes, and it probably would not have turned out well. After all, he was head of the world-renowned Ford Foundation.

"It's surprising how those responsible for catastrophic policies work off their sins. Bundy did his penance at the Ford Foundation, McNamara did his as head of the World Bank. Henry Kissinger, implicated in a host of abuses, has continued for decades as a widely quoted foreign-policy guru. After leaving government, Paul Wolfowitz, like McNamara, led the World Bank; as a key adviser to President George W. Bush and Vice President Dick Cheney he helped take us, without vision, strategy, or common sense, into our disastrous involvement in Iraq—an intervention that, similar to our war in Vietnam, has hobbled both that country and America for decades.

"I find it astonishing that, perched in influential national leadership positions, people can do the most execrable things and afterward be rewarded with top positions and widespread renown. It's difficult to ponder how certain powerful 'public servants' have twisted history in ways that cost millions of people their lives, yet go on to be honored."

Andy also rejected the life of a staffer on Capitol Hill. "I remember being at Rehoboth Beach," he says, "with all these important people from Washington, the summer when I was an intern in Jackson's office. Somebody was somebody's press secretary, somebody was somebody's legislative assistant. I thought, I want to be the one who makes the decisions. I'm not going to Washington to hold somebody's briefcase."

Andy had a connection in New York City via his father: Don Elliott, chair of the City Planning Commission in the administration of Mayor John V. Lindsay. "I talked to Donald H. Elliott about all the things that were motivating me," says Andy, "and we came up with a job as director of the Mayor's Office of Planning and Development in Jamaica, Queens.

"With the assassinations and the chaos at the Democratic National Convention, and the rise of consciousness about what was going on in depressed parts of our major cities and all the riots, I decided that nuances like the meaning of '*des territoires*' were less important than trying to make the right things happen at home. People like me needed to zero in on that work. I said, 'Okay. I need to come home. That's where I need to be.'

"I also thought that if I dove into the precincts of New York City, I would expand my knowledge and my experience, and thus my career choices for the future, allowing me to work in both domestic and foreign policy. I imagined that at some point in the future I might return to the foreign policy arena as the ambassador to the United Nations or an assistant secretary of state.

"None of that ever materialized. It might have if we'd had Democratic presidents between 1980 and 1992. Of course, in Congress, even though I wasn't on the Foreign Affairs Committee, I was able to select certain foreign-policy issues to be involved in—Zimbabwe, South Africa, the Middle East, Central America."

Andy was taken with Mayor Lindsay, elected as a liberal Republican reformer in 1965—a departure from standard Tammany Hall pols. "Lindsay was doing imaginative and constructive things—on poverty, race, development—in a complicated city with all sorts of problems," says Andy. "I was impressed with the way the Regional Plan Association and Lindsay and his top aides, especially Donald Elliott, were thinking about the things that caused the urban riots in 1968.

"And so I dove into it. I decided I'd rather be on South Road in poverty-stricken South Jamaica, trying to make things happen, than working in one big tower on the East Side of Manhattan, the UN, then moving to another, the Ford Foundation.

"I don't suppose there would have been a single person I might have consulted, at that time or since, who would have recommended I make that decision. It was an unusual career choice.

"But all my career choices have been unusual."

CHAPTER 4

THE IMPRIMATUR OF THE MAYOR: Andy Maguire, John Lindsay, and a Job in Jamaica

Not only is New York City the nation's melting pot, it is also the casserole, the chafing dish, and the charcoal grill.

—JOHN V. LINDSAY

OUTER BOROUGH: A Failure and a Plan in Queens

It was insult enough for John Lindsay that ordinary citizens came out of their homes to jeer him on February 12, 1969. "Lindsay, you're a bum," shouted one resident at New York City's 103rd mayor, who was touring a borough still buried under the twenty inches of snow that had fallen three days earlier. The people of Queens were livid over the botched cleanup. "You should be ashamed of yourself," said another. "It's disgusting." One resident brought up the mayor's well-known aspirations to the presidency: "He can't even run a snowstorm and he wants to run the country."

Lindsay could not have been surprised that Queens politicians would join their constituents in kicking him while he was down. One member of the city council called upon Governor Nelson Rockefeller to deploy the National Guard to the borough and suspend Lindsay from the mayoralty "pending an investigation into the handling of this crisis." (The governor declined the suggestions.) Nor could the mayor have been shocked when the head of the Uniformed Sanitationmen's Association—the union representing the workers charged with the cleanup—blamed the disaster on Lindsay's "systematic destruction" of the Sanitation Department.

But the mayor could not have anticipated the scolding he received from one of the world's leading diplomats. "We have never experienced such neglect in snow removal as now," read an undiplomatic telegram to the mayor from Ralph Bunche, not only the under-secretary-general of the United Nations and a Nobel Peace Prize laureate but also a resident of the Queens neighborhood known as Kew Gardens. Bunche noted the empty shelves in his local stores and bemoaned his aching legs, sore from trudging through snowdrifts to reach the subway the day before. "As far as getting to the United Nations is concerned," he continued, "I may as well be in the Alps. This is a shameful performance by the great City of New York, which should certainly condone no second-class boroughs."

Evidently, Bunche, like most Queens residents, considered Lindsay a man of Manhattan, of Broadway and Wall Street, of Fifth Avenue and the Upper East Side—a mayor too enthralled by the central city's bright lights, showbiz celebrities, and moneyed grandees to care much about the working stiffs who populated the outer boroughs. Watching the news on television, Queens inhabitants could see that despite Lindsay's (accurate) explanation that the snowfall had caught city officials—and local weather forecasters—unaware, Manhattan streets had been promptly plowed.

A timely visit from a cleanup crew was enough to mollify Bunche. "I just got a call from my wife," he said the day after sending the telegram, "and the street is clean as a whistle." The rest of the borough's citizens, whose votes Lindsay would need if he wanted to win reelection in November, would not be so easily appeased.

Two days before the blizzard, Lindsay had appointed Andy Maguire director of the newly formed Office of Jamaica Planning and Development. "What idiot," Andy asks, "early in his career decides to go with a guy who might lose an election in nine months?"

Even before the blizzard, John Lindsay's prospects for reelection were doubtful, for his first three years in office had been tumultuous. But that uncertainty didn't deter Andy from joining Lindsay's team. "I said to myself," Andy recalls, "'This is important. I'm going to do it, whether he gets reelected or not.' I've always had a low concern for risk."

Andy knew that his work in the Jamaica area of southeastern Queens would serve a political purpose for a mayor hoping to shed his identification with Manhattan. "That was how people saw him at the beginning," Andy says, "because he first addressed the zoning and development issues in Midtown and lower Manhattan, getting the world's greatest architects involved in all the planning and design. Plus, it was cultural: He's from the Upper East Side—who is this guy? But a combination of pressures from the boroughs, and then the snowstorm, caused him to focus on the outer boroughs. He set up not just the Office of Jamaica Planning and Development but also an office in downtown Brooklyn with basically the same mandate. The idea that he focused on Manhattan is a fair criticism of his first two years but not a fair criticism of where he ended up."

While creation of the OJPD made political sense, the agency had its origins in the work of a nonpartisan quasi-governmental agency. Created as a public-private entity in the 1920s to coordinate planning for economic development throughout the New York City metropolitan area—the city plus suburban counties in New York, New Jersey, and Connecticut—the Regional Plan Association published the two volumes of its first comprehensive, region-wide plan in 1929 and 1931, respectively. The RPA's second plan, completed in 1968 after a decade's worth of information gathering, came in the form of a series of targeted reports, one of which laid out a multifaceted blueprint for Jamaica's revitalization. That report's main author was F. Carlisle Towery, a native Alabamian who had left his home state in disgust with its racism.

With a degree in architecture from Auburn, Towery, who was three years older than Andy, received a scholarship to study architecture and urban planning at Columbia—"They needed some rednecks to balance out the class," he jokes. His work at Columbia led to a job at the RPA; from there he was appointed director of the Greater Jamaica Development Corporation, a new public-private entity created under the RPA's aegis. Towery remained with the GJDC until his retirement in 2014.

"The RPA did some really forward thinking," he says. "It was a prototype of how you dealt with regional planning. When they decided to put out their second regional plan, I worked hard to get Jamaica included in it as one of a dozen subcenters outside Manhattan that warranted special attention from government and the private sector. There were big trends in the region—heavy-duty trends of economics and transportation and zoning and you name it. RPA wanted to address them all."

The idea behind subcenters was to group elements that would, according to Towery's report, "attract people from several miles away—universities, department stores, major health services, central libraries, government headquarters, specialized entertainment and cultural attractions. . . ." Jamaica had "tremendous potential to become a great subcenter in the Region and the major focal point for life in the Borough of Queens."

"Jamaica," recalls Towery, "was picked by the RPA because it had some real anchors in it. One thing was its three department stores, which were doing huge retail sales." Jamaica was also a transportation hub, served by subway and the Long Island Railroad, although that transportation needed upgrading.

The RPA's plan would accomplish nothing without a willing partner in City Hall. John Lindsay, elected in November 1965, was that partner. "Lindsay was the first mayor I knew of who really cared about planning," Towery says.

"Lindsay's Jamaica initiative," says Andy, "was not only a response to the Regional Plan Association. It was part of his desire to reenvision the city. He was already trying to figure out how to use zoning to improve public amenities whenever somebody built an office tower. He was already saying, 'Let's have great architects doing this work, not some clown who might be cheaper. Let's make intelligent investment decisions in our communities.' That was all pre-snowstorm."

In November 1966, Lindsay appointed a new chairman of the City Planning Commission: Donald H. Elliott, "a marvelous public servant," according to Towery. Elliott, who had met Lindsay years earlier when they were both young lawyers at a white shoe firm, had been a key member of Lindsay's campaign team.

Once Lindsay took office, he gave Elliott the title of counsel to the mayor. However, as the *Times* noted, the thirty-three-year-old adviser had a "finger in many pies," with primary responsibility for the capital budget and governmental reorganization, as well as policy-making on housing and poverty. "The major source of his influence," the paper said, "is that he has the confidence of the mayor." One city official told the *Times* that Elliott "knows more about the government than most of them, but when he does not know something he admits it. His humility is very refreshing—and extremely effective. He is interested in government, not politics. He is the best example of what Lindsay is trying to do."

"Elliott was just a superb guy," says Andy. "Lindsay and his team, with Don Elliott as the point of the spear, was tackling major, important stuff."

Elliott and Lindsay confronted what they deemed an outmoded model for urban planning. For decades prior to their arrival, the lord of development in the New York area had been Robert Moses. Celebrated for his grand contributions to the city's infrastructure—Lincoln Center; the Triborough, Whitestone, Throgs Neck, and Verrazano bridges—Moses was also notorious for his imperious ways and his willingness to sacrifice communities, particularly poor communities of color, on the altar of his vision: colossal projects, with an emphasis on automobile transportation. The construction of the Cross Bronx Expressway tore a wound through a swath of poor neighborhoods in the South Bronx. The result, as anyone who has driven the Cross Bronx knows, was perhaps the ugliest several miles of highway on earth.

At his swearing-in as planning chair, Elliott made clear his and Lindsay's determination to break with the Moses formula. Instead of massive set pieces, Elliott recommended a more balanced approach. "Planning for action," he said, "cannot be limited to physical development. The goal is the development of the potentialities of this city. Encouragement of the private sector and city programs that go to the causes of our problems as well as their symptoms are legitimate concerns of the planning process."

Elliott furthermore announced a change not only in planning's end products but also in its process. He called for "a recognition of the resources of citizen participation. . . . Listening to the people affected and working with them is the only successful way to proceed."

Robert Moses hadn't overly concerned himself with "the people affected."

"It was the end of the Moses era," says Andy. "Lindsay, along with the Regional Plan Association that partnered with him, was trying to reimagine the city in a whole different way. With emphasis on not just high-quality design and public space, but on retrieving communities that had fallen into the ditch."

Jamaica hadn't fallen into the ditch, but it was teetering above it.

FRESH, NOT TIRED: John Vliet Lindsay

John Vliet Lindsay did not fit the stereotype of New York City mayors. For one thing, as columnist Jimmy Breslin would point out, he was tall—six-foot-four—whereas nearly all his predecessors had been short. His immediate predecessor, Robert F. Wagner Jr., was five-foot-eight, Fiorello LaGuardia a mere five-foot-two. Even the Prohibition era's Gentleman Jimmy Walker, at five-foot-eight, was barely taller than the chorus girls on his arm as he hopped between speakeasies.

Lindsay was a WASP—the first mayor of New York City in over half a century not to claim heritage in either Ireland or Italy. He was a Republican—the first to be elected mayor since La Guardia, who left City Hall in 1945, and only the second since Seth Low, who left in 1903.

And he was so damned good looking.

Lindsay's privileged Manhattan upbringing and elite education—the Buckley School, St. Paul's School, Yale—along with his height, his erect bearing, his exotic middle name (Dutch, not French), his blue eyes, and his impossibly perfect hair, led New Yorkers to believe him the product of an old patrician family. He wasn't. His mother's family had been in the New York area for three centuries, but her father was a successful contractor in New Jersey, not a fixture of New York's social register. Lindsay's paternal grandfather had emigrated to America in the 1880s from the Isle of Wight; in New York he worked as a bank clerk. Lindsay's father did strike it rich as an investment banker but was self-made—he had put himself through law school at night while working days as a low-level functionary on Wall Street. Lindsay's wife, born Mary Anne Harrison, had a more impressive pedigree: She was distantly related to two past presidents, William Henry Harrison and his grandson Benjamin. John and Mary Lindsay met at the wedding of a relative of two future presidents—he was an usher and she a bridesmaid at the wedding of Senator Prescott Bush's daughter Nancy, sister of George H. W. and aunt of George W.

Born in 1921, Lindsay accelerated his graduation from Yale to enter the World War II Navy; as a gunnery officer on a destroyer he saw combat in both the European and Pacific theaters. After the war he attended Yale Law School, worked at a big corporate law firm—he made partner in only four years—then became active in politics. That interest set him apart from his social peers. As one family friend said of John and Mary Lindsay in 1966, they "could so easily have turned into bloodless Long Island types like everybody else they knew." Instead, Lindsay cofounded the Youth for Eisenhower club in 1951 and after Ike's election the following year became president of the New York Young Republican Club. In 1955, he went to Washington as executive assistant to Attorney General Herbert Brownell.

In 1958, Lindsay ran for Congress, winning election in what was called the Silk Stocking District because it included the swanky Upper East Side in addition to parts of bohemian Greenwich Village and gritty East Harlem. In Congress, he compiled a record strong on support for civil rights and other liberal causes—he voted for federal aid to education and the establishment of Medicare. In 1964, he refused to endorse his party's presidential nominee, Barry Goldwater. He was an early critic of the war in Vietnam.

In the third decade of the twenty-first century, liberal Republicans are an extinct species. But Lindsay entered politics before the partisan realignment that began with the campaign of Barry Goldwater in 1964, accelerated with Nixon's Southern Strategy in 1968, and achieved critical mass with the election of Ronald Reagan in 1980. Southern whites, blaming the Democratic Party for ending Jim Crow, forgave the GOP for ending slavery. Thus did the Solid Democratic South that had prevailed since the end of Reconstruction become the Solid Republican South of today. And as conservative Democrats became Republicans, liberal Republicans became Democrats. Southerners have now dominated the GOP for a generation, enforcing the ideological purity of officeholders from town council to the White House. There is no room in today's Republican Party for a politician like John Lindsay.

Some of the US Senate's biggest names in the 1950s were liberal Republicans: Leverett Saltonstall of Massachusetts, George Aiken of Vermont, Clifford Case of New Jersey, Jacob Javits of New York, and Prescott Bush of Connecticut; in the 1960s, Charles Mathias of Maryland, Charles Percy of Illinois, and Mark Hatfield of Oregon.

New York State politics, in particular, were dominated by liberal Republicans. When Lindsay first ran for Congress, four of New York's five statewide officeholders were Republicans: governor, attorney general, and two US senators. Only the comptroller was a Democrat. In 1964, when Robert F. Kennedy moved to New York to take on incumbent Republican senator Kenneth Keating, both candidates claimed to be the true liberal in the race.

In 1965, Congressman Lindsay ran for mayor of New York City, winning not only the Republican nomination but also that of the state's Liberal Party. Opposing the city comptroller Abraham Beame, who owed his Democratic nomination to a set of party bosses, and the conservative writer, editor, and flamboyant television personality William F. Buckley Jr., running on the Conservative Party line, Lindsay did not have much trouble positioning himself as the most liberal option.

In his first major speech after declaring his candidacy, Lindsay put his political courage on display by taking on the New York Police Department. Recognizing that "too many New Yorkers who have no wish to thwart the law have come to view the policeman as an enemy rather than a friend," he proposed adding civilians to the Civilian Complaint Review Board. (The word *civilian* in the panel's name was misleading—the board, made up entirely of NYPD appointees, was charged with addressing civilian complaints against the police.)

Mutual respect between citizens and police officers, Lindsay continued, "will not happen until all the people of our city feel and believe they are being treated fairly, equally, and courteously and, if they are not, that they have a fair opportunity to have their complaints heard."

Lindsay proposed a stack of additional initiatives: an overhaul of the city hospital system, a renewed commitment to public housing, and measures for economic development including a doubling of the city's economic growth and what the *Times* called "a massive attack against job discrimination."

Lindsay's progressive platform found resonance among Black and Latino New Yorkers, as well as among liberal Jews. But the debonair congressman was running less on specific issues than on his contrast with the status quo. Twenty years of one-party rule, he charged, had diminished the city and left its people "beset with hopelessness and despair." In 1960, John F. Kennedy had promised to "get America moving again." Five years later, Lindsay, seeing a stagnant city whose problems had long been neglected, adopted as his campaign slogan a newspaper columnist's appraisal of him: "He's fresh and everyone else is tired."

In its endorsement of his candidacy, the *Times* echoed the sentiment:

> Mr. Lindsay brings youth, energy and intelligence to this formidable job of overseeing the affairs of a great city gravely in danger of decline. In him the Republican and Liberal parties have chosen as their standard-bearer a proved and authentic progressive. . . .
>
> John Lindsay would not make this a new city overnight. No one could. But we believe that he would make an excellent mayor, that government with him in City Hall would be an exciting adventure in willingness to try the new and to accomplish great things through dedication, spirit and decisive action.

In November, Lindsay prevailed with 45 percent of the vote, over Beame's 41 percent and Buckley's 13 percent.

"Why don't you grow up and stop being a juvenile?" said Michael J. Quill to John V. Lindsay late in the evening on December 31, 1965. Quill, head of the New York City Transport Workers Union, made January 1, 1966—the first full day of John Lindsay's mayoralty—perhaps the worst first day of any elected official's tenure in the history of elected officials.

Lindsay was sworn in as mayor in a private ceremony just after 6:00 p.m. on New Year's Eve. With the TWU's contract set to run out at midnight, he met Quill for a final negotiating session at the Americana Hotel, but the talks, while memorable for Quill's insults, made no progress toward a deal. In order to see New Year's revelers home, Quill kept his members on the job until 5:00 a.m.; at that hour, they walked out. The subways and buses New York depended on to function: shut down. A freedom fighter in Ireland during his youth, Mike Quill, sixty years old, spoke with a brogue as thick as his confidence that he could get the better of the inexperienced new mayor. And so he did. Lindsay, aware that his predecessor had bequeathed him a city deep in debt, tried to hold to a hard line in negotiations. But while Lindsay marshaled public opinion and the law—a judge briefly jailed Quill after ruling the strike illegal—the labor leader's doggedness wore the city, and its new mayor, out. The strike lasted thirteen days. The generous increases in the transit workers' compensation set a standard for the city's negotiations with other unions, making labor costs a major factor in bringing the city to the verge of default in 1975.

Labor troubles would beset Lindsay throughout his first term. In February 1968, the city's sanitation workers struck, leaving garbage uncollected for nine days. The only consolation to New Yorkers disgusted by the mountains of trash covering city sidewalks was that the stench was not what it would have been had the walkout taken place in July.

The most painful labor trouble—for Lindsay's political fortunes and for the fabric of life in the nation's largest and most diverse city—involved the city's teachers. Over a decade after *Brown v. Board of Education*, New York public schools were still largely segregated by race, while only a minuscule percentage of teachers and administrators were Black and Latino. To give minority New Yorkers a greater stake in the school system, the Lindsay administration, acting upon a recommendation by the Ford Foundation, instituted a pilot program of decentralized control of public schools. Three districts, all predominantly populated by people of color, were chosen for the experiment; one was Ocean Hill-Brownsville, a largely Black neighborhood in Brooklyn. In April 1968, the mostly Black and Puerto Rican local governing board dismissed, without cause, thirteen teachers and six administrators, nearly all of which happened to be white and Jewish.

In protest, district teachers staged a brief strike, but the local school board would not rescind its decision. In the fall, New York's largely Jewish teacher corps, led by another incendiary labor leader, Albert Shanker—in the movie *Sleeper*, Woody Allen's visit to the future reveals Shanker to have ignited a civilization-ending nuclear war—conducted a series of strikes that kept city children out of school for weeks. Ultimately, the state government intervened, taking control away from the local school board and reinstating the fired educators.

The monthslong dispute inflamed relations between two of the city's largest ethnic groups, Blacks and Jews, who not only had been natural allies in the civil rights movement but who also accounted for the majority of Lindsay's political support. And even non-Jewish white ethnic New Yorkers believed Lindsay had given the city over to "Black militants."

The struggle to end Jim Crow had presented, to Blacks and whites, a clear moral choice—it was easy to tell who were the good guys and who were the bad guys. But who was good or bad in this case—the long-ignored minorities who wanted to run their schools as they saw fit or the underpaid teachers who had dedicated themselves to the education of the young? In early 1966, after his success in ending Southern segregation enshrined in law, Martin Luther King Jr. mounted a campaign in Chicago to oppose Northern segregation—in housing, schooling, and employment—due less to law than to entrenched attitudes and to discrimination that was no less systematic for its not being codified in statute. The initiative achieved little of benefit to Black Chicagoans, but it generated a fierce backlash among whites. "I have seen many demonstrations in the South," said King after leading a march through a white neighborhood, "but I have never seen anything so hostile and so hateful as I've seen here today." With legal segregation in the South a thing of the past, American liberalism was now forced to confront dilemmas with no easy solutions.

"In recognizing the demands of deprived neighborhoods for a sign of concern," Lindsay said years later, "we did not realize how much the vast bulk of city people—hardworking, white middle-class citizens—felt estranged, too, from the process of government."

Lindsay did achieve significant improvement in the life of the city during his first term. He hired a Black man as commissioner of the nearly all-white fire department. While Lindsay surely deserves some blame for New York's mid-1970s financial crunch, he did take the fiscally responsible steps of raising the city's corporate tax rate and instituting the city's first personal income tax. He was able to follow through on his promise to reform city hospitals, and he revived city parks. Determined to alleviate poverty, he encouraged people to apply for public assistance and opposed requiring recipients to work in exchange for their benefits. The welfare rolls swelled.

Lindsay failed in his quest to change the composition of the Civilian Complaint Review Board—his order to that effect was successfully challenged in court by the police officers' union; when his proposal appeared as a citywide ballot question, the citizens voted it down. Crime continued to rise. But, thanks in no small part to the mayor's personal courage, New York avoided the riots that plagued Los Angeles, Detroit, Newark, and other big cities during the 1960s. On the night of April 4, 1968, as Washington and other cities burned after the murder of Martin Luther King Jr., Lindsay ignored his aides' warnings of danger and went to Harlem. Walking the streets in his shirtsleeves, he listened to and mourned with the neighborhood's Black residents. "You're the greatest mayor there ever was in this city," one activist said to Lindsay that night. "You come here to see the people before the riot, not after the riot." There was no riot in Harlem that night—or any other night during Lindsay's eight years as mayor.

But his attention to New York's Black and brown citizens and his willingness to take on the police department, while helping keep the peace during troubled times, did not endear John Lindsay to the white ethnic residents of Queens. And so, when the snow was not removed, they were not inclined to give him the benefit of the doubt.

Whatever the snowbound citizens of Queens thought of their mayor, Andy Maguire and Carlisle Towery had only admiration for him.

"I thought he was a miraculous leader," recalls Towery. "A leader if there ever was one. In my view he never got the credit he deserved for doing what he did for New York City. I was well aware of what he did for Jamaica.

"I never sat down at a table with him and said, 'Let's work the next four hours on what we're going to do in Jamaica.' I'd sit with him and in fifteen minutes he'd say, 'When are we doing this? When are we doing that?' He was an incredible motivator and manager. His staff was superior and they were intellectuals, not politicians. He had a wonderful urban design department and really professional transit guys. His staff was obviously first rate, and everybody acknowledged that. He didn't reap the political benefits he could have gotten by hiring politicians to fill these roles. He had a few politicians, and Lindsay wasn't unpolitical. But the people of importance were professionals first."

"I thought Lindsay was fabulous," says Andy. "I thought he was brilliant. I thought he really understood issues on the ground. And was dedicated to making changes, and upgrading the city in every imaginable respect.

"Now ultimately it turned out that his budget guys played some games with the operating budget and the expense budget, and the city got itself into a hole financially. But his objectives were always superb.

"He was concerned with using his powers for productive purposes, and helping large numbers of people and businesses in the city, and upgrading the quality of life—as opposed to just occupying a position and figuring out what the emoluments might be. Which was all too true of all too many Democrats and Republicans in the city. And everywhere, for that matter.

"I felt I was someone who could be like Lindsay."

KNITTING IT ALL TOGETHER: Andy and a Neighborhood in Transition

Although still the premier shopping and business district in Queens, Jamaica by the late 1960s had begun to decline. Its three department stores, including the first Macy's to be built apart from its flagship on Manhattan's 34th Street, were still open. But these and smaller retail outlets faced increasing competition for middle-class shoppers from the malls sprouting in suburban, automobile-friendly Long Island just a few miles away. As in all of New York—indeed as in the Northeast as a whole—manufacturing was leaving for less expensive climes. Globalization was not yet a word in common usage; the drive to produce goods overseas was still years in the future. But Northern companies were drawn to the states of the American South, where a less unionized workforce earned a less unionized wage. And hanging over the problems of New York—and of cities throughout the country—was the issue of "white flight." As African-American and Latino residents, often poor, moved into the city, white residents, often middle-class, moved out, taking the city's tax base with them.

Midtown and downtown Manhattan boasted the world's best shopping and enough office space for the headquarters of thousands of companies, small and large. But the Regional Plan Association, the Greater Jamaica Development Corporation, city hall, and the Office of Jamaica Planning and Development—Carlisle Towery, John Lindsay, Don Elliott, and now Andy Maguire—argued that Manhattan did not suffice to meet the city's business needs. "The idea," says Andy, "was that New York was so big—eight million people—that it needed more than one central hub."

Creating that hub required cooperation with the private sector and among all levels of government. Towery notes a linguistic trick that enabled him to communicate effectively with all parties: "I learned how to talk out of both sides of my mouth. When you're talking to government, you're talking about all the problems. When you're talking to the private sector, you're talking about all the opportunities."

"There were big important folks in the Jamaica area," says Andy, "who partnered with the Regional Plan Association, and with Mayor Lindsay and with Don Elliott, and with whomever they could find at the state level, to do this incredible, complex, long-term bootstrap operation that affected the lives of literally millions of people."

John Lindsay's deputy mayor was thirty-three years old. His parks commissioner was thirty-four. Top city hall assistants were as young as twenty-four. Interviewing a candidate for press secretary, Lindsay asked the man his age.

"Thirty-five," the applicant replied.

"A little old for this administration," said the mayor, "but I think I can use you."

New York's tabloids called the mayor's cadre of youthful aides the Kiddie Corps.

So, putting twenty-nine-year-old Andy Maguire in charge of the new Office of Jamaica Planning and Development was in character for a mayor, himself only forty-four the day he took office, who valued imagination over experience.

Andy explains city hall's thinking in hiring him: "The Regional Plan Association had this plan, and Lindsay bought the whole package. Meanwhile, the business community had formed the Greater Jamaica Development Corporation. So the RPA, the GJDC, and John Lindsay all combined to say, 'We've all got to coordinate.' He said, 'I'm going to put my representative into Jamaica.' That was me, a director of the office of Jamaica Planning and Development, who would work with all of these communities: businesspeople; white residents; the impoverished, drug-infested Black community to the south, South Jamaica; and, just east of Jamaica Center, St. Albans, the community containing the largest number of African-American professionals anywhere in Queens.

"My job was to knit it all together. And make sure that all the relevant city agencies—which included planning, economic development, housing, transportation, social services—were in fact making decisions and investments that were consistent with the overall strategy that Lindsay and the RPA embraced and were positively received by the leaders of the different communities."

"Lindsay," says Towery, "directed all the relevant agencies to report to Andy. Andy had mayor power."

"I was young," says Andy, "and had never done anything like it before. Fortunately, I was able to learn on the job that the key was people, forming relationships, building consensus. It was all based on getting the major actors together, on getting city agencies to make the necessary decisions. And if the city agencies were dragging their feet, it was all about going and sitting with whatever mayoral assistant was in charge of those agencies and making sure the agencies got heat from the mayor's office in order to get stuff done.

"How did I know how to do all that? Towery was a great mentor. He understood everything and taught me about it. I was the go-to guy for making sure that the city was participating fully in the strategy that the Regional Plan Association articulated and that the Greater Jamaica Development Corporation was created to push forward."

Not only was Jamaica's economy in the midst of a transition when Andy arrived in 1969. The population was changing, too.

Central Jamaica, although adjacent to two African-American communities—poor South Jamaica and middle-class St. Albans—was populated largely by middle-class whites. But African-Americans were moving into white areas and white residents were starting to flee.

"The area was declining in a lot of ways," says Towery, "even though it had grown in the prosperity of the postwar years. Many attributed the decline to racial pressures, and I think that was partly correct. Jamaica was a place where Black folks were pioneering. These were not impoverished people moving there—there was some real poverty, but mostly the trend was Black families getting their piece of the Big Apple, owning a house. In many cases, these were people coming from the South." The Great Migration, the movement of millions of African-Americans from the countryside and farms of the South to the cities and factories of the North, continued to increase New York City's African-American population through the 1960s, lifting Blacks from 14 to 21 percent of the city's population over the course of the decade.

"Many people were buying their family's first home—it was an ambitious place," Towery continues. "But some whites found the influx of Black residents to be threatening. The area just south of the Long Island Rail Road tracks was rather prosperous, with attractive single-family homes that Blacks purchased, replacing whites moving to the suburbs.

So there was white flight in the area called southeast Queens. It was an unsettling time for a lot of white people who owned homes in southeast Queens and were seeing Black families starting to tip the balance."

Just as Lindsay had tried to do with school decentralization, so he wanted to do with the Jamaica initiative: empower local Black communities. "Before Lindsay," says Andy, "urban planning was business as usual: Get as many companies as you could to put their headquarters in New York. Be responsive to communities outside Manhattan and in Harlem when they had specific complaints, but without any grand strategy about how you redefine the way a city functions, about what sort of institutions are critical and how they need to be clustered together, about how Black and white communities need to be brought together around those institutions, about how quality of life needs to be upgraded.

"I guess because of my commitment to racial justice, stretching back over my life, Elliott and Lindsay felt I could relate to the Black community. They were right about that."

Early on, Andy made a number of strategic decisions to establish credibility among Jamaica's Black residents. He set up his office not in the central business district but in the heart of depressed South Jamaica. "We needed to affirm that community," he says.

He and his new bride—he'd married Meg Green in 1968—moved into a house in Laurelton, just the other side of St. Albans. "There wasn't anything in South Jamaica that we were willing to live in," he recalls, "so we bought a nice, attached brick house, maybe three miles from the office. Even so, our choice was seen by everyone as a commitment to the community." Meg continued working as an urban planner, traveling weekdays into Manhattan.

Taking charge of a new agency, Andy hired an entire staff—planners, architects, engineers; specialists in economic development, housing, transportation, and more. The majority were African-American. "I hired my senior people from the Black community," he recalls, "so that it was a partnership from day one. The community understood that I wasn't some white guy parachuting in to tell Black people what the mayor wanted. With a strong and open effort, and some good luck as well, I was able to establish my credentials."

The African-Americans on his staff were not tokens. "My deputy was an African-American—a senior guy who was highly respected in the community," Andy says. "My principal organizer was a younger

African-American. I interviewed a ton of people; I picked the very best." Working against stereotypes, as had Lindsay with his choice for fire commissioner, Andy hired a Black engineer.

Much of Andy's efforts went into working with Black business, political, and church leaders. "We would meet with local African-American members of the city council and the state legislature," he recalls. "We'd talk about what needed to be done, which city agencies needed to do it, and whether we could do it faster. For example, when you needed something from the people in charge of sewers or roads, it would normally be half a decade at least before the plans moved from drawing board to implementation. Just because of the bureaucracy. We would figure out how to bring pressure on those bureaucrats—pressure from the elected representatives, from the mayor, from the business community—to speed everything up, making sure that programs and projects aligned with the mayor's strategy for urban revitalization while ensuring important progress on the ground.

"Sometimes members of my staff and I would meet with the Greater Jamaica Development Corporation, which had Black members; sometimes we'd meet with a small group of key actors in the Black community. One who comes to mind was Reverend Robert Ross Johnson, who led a major church in St. Albans and was keenly concerned about South Jamaica. He and his congregation wanted to get involved in affordable housing. Like so many of our projects, this one didn't achieve full fruition until after I left. But I had hired a crackerjack housing expert. She kept on that project after I left and got it done."

Of course, Andy had to work with white Jamaicans, too. "I didn't spend a lot of time with neighborhood groups in the white community," he says, "because the interests of the white community were represented within the Greater Jamaica Development Corporation. Those were the leaders from the business community who, by definition, were the leaders from the white community. Those were the bankers, the department store owners, the lawyers, the business owners, the white politicians who represented white parts of Jamaica in the legislature and the city council. One Black executive from American Airlines was a major player in the GJDC. He was concerned mainly with two issues: opening up airport jobs for people in South Jamaica and getting a train to the airport built.

"The job was nonstop consultation—figuring out what the priorities were, figuring out how we could get all the pressure and support networks aligned to make sure all the necessary pieces were falling into place. And always we had the imprimatur of the mayor. Generally, I would talk to Lindsay about the big picture but discuss week-to-week specifics of strategy and tactics with Don Elliott.

"We got stuff done."

IN WITH THE NEW: Modernizing Jamaica

Attracting businesses to Jamaica and keeping businesses in Jamaica—and finding them suitable office and retail space—formed a substantial part of Andy's work. But during his tenure, his office and Carlisle Towery's worked toward the construction of major pieces of infrastructure.

One goal was to relocate a train.

"The subway was not a subway when it got to Jamaica," says Andy. "It was an elevated train—an 'El'—that went straight down the main street. It was noisy and disfiguring."

The mayor and the governor both wanted the train rerouted. "If you looked around the city at that time," says Towery, "Els were being torn down all over the place. The El became a symbol of blight; removing it was seen as a necessary redevelopment. It wasn't difficult to get support for the project—the question was what you replace it with. Ultimately it was replaced with an underground stretch of track that was not exactly the way it had been aboveground: Three new stations displaced four old ones.

"The new line cost $440 million—I'll never forget that number. It was a lengthy, lengthy process to get it done. But it was an obvious thing to do if you were in the business of trying to redo a downtown into a modern center. You'd want to modernize the subway."

The RPA, GJDC, and OJPD also set their sights on a rail link from Jamaica to John F. Kennedy International Airport, then accessible only by bus or car, both subject to long delays in rush-hour traffic. The planned link, which would connect the airport to the new subway terminus, "made all sorts of sense," says Andy. "And that's what we have today."

Although the plan proposed extending the Long Island Rail Road to JFK, the ultimate solution was a light-rail line that connects Jamaica and other points in Queens to all the airport's terminals.

The Archer Avenue subway line opened in 1986, the Air Train in 2003.

More important to planners even than the rerouted subway was the establishment in Jamaica of a new public school of higher learning, another star in the CUNY (City University of New York) college constellation. "York College," Towery recalls, "became the objective that could do all kinds of things to boost and unify Jamaica and the city. It was the key project."

While the idea of a new college in Queens drew support from a wide range of political and business leaders, those leaders were not unanimous on the particulars. As Towery recalls, "A lot of people immediately said, 'Well it's okay if you want to put a college there, but it should be a junior college.' There was a long fight about why it had to be a full four-year institution.

"Once that fight was won, the argument was over where to put it."

The matter of the new school's location became tangled in city politics. "The borough president wanted to put it on Fort Totten," Towery recalls, "which was out on the waterfront and up on Northshore. The federal government had offered the city 150 acres. We went to see the borough president, who had already made up his mind. 'The land's free,' he said, 'and I've already got it.'"

Fort Totten, at the northeast corner of Queens, is nowhere near a subway line. However, the setting suited the school as conceived by the college president who had already been hired—he envisioned a leafy suburban campus, accessible by automobile, with most students living in residential dormitories. "But," says Towery, "the RPA, thank God, the Greater Jamaica Development Corporation, Black leaders, and the Jamaica Chamber of Commerce—we all worked like crazy and got the decision turned around and the president replaced.

"It took the mayor to overcome the borough president's outright opposition and it took a lot of guts to designate for the college this tough area in Jamaica.

"It was a city urban renewal plan. It didn't have the heavy hand of the federal government, which, for example, got Lincoln Center built. The local community had to be included and convinced and involved, and then you had to convince city government and state government and then federal government. It was a huge, huge challenge to get it designated there."

Jamaica's accessibility by public transportation, planners believed, made it the ideal location for the new school. The RPA's Jamaica report noted that large percentages of New Yorkers did not own cars. Locating the college in Jamaica would be a service to those less affluent citizens, particularly citizens of color. From the report: "The current necessity to break the cycle of poverty and to bring Negroes and Puerto Ricans into the full life of the nation adds emphasis to this point of accessibility to all potential students."

"It took a two- or three-year battle to get the decision made to put York College, a brand-new four-year college of the City University of New York, in downtown Jamaica," says Towery.

In 1967, with the parties still arguing, York College began offering instruction in rooms rented in the Oakland Jewish Center in Bayside, Queens. The following May, the CUNY Board of Higher Education, yielding to community sentiment, agreed to locate the college in downtown Jamaica. The city's fiscal crisis in the '70s delayed construction; in the meantime, professors taught classes in a variety of Queens locations. Construction began in 1980; classes were held in York's Academic Core in 1986. A performing arts center opened in 1990, athletic fields in 1991.

Today enrollment numbers 8,300 students, 40 percent of them African-American and 13 percent Latino, reflecting the original intention of the Lindsay administration to offer New Yorkers of color a share in the life of the city. But the school also reflects the story of Queens in the intervening years, as the borough has become the most ethnically diverse place on earth. Students come from 120 countries of origin and speak more than eighty native languages.

"Jamaica needed a new courthouse," says Andy.

While the largest decisions about the rerouted subway line and the location of York College were made before Andy's arrival, he was instrumental in the siting and building of a new home for the Queens Civil Court.

"The Queens Civil Court," notes Towery, "was in the basement of Queens Borough Hall and in serious need of more and better space."

"The old court was a testament to the lack of investment in an outlying borough," Andy recalls. "A replacement courthouse had been on the agenda for years; funds had finally been budgeted. The remaining issue was: Where?"

By the time Andy got involved, the authorities had chosen a spot. "Originally," he says, "the new building was to go up on a parcel of land that was triangulated by Queens Boulevard, the Long Island Expressway, and the Grand Central Parkway. The site *was* centrally located in Queens. However, a building at that location would provide no beneficial secondary and tertiary effects on its surrounding community. The courthouse would just be sitting there, between the busy roads. The argument Elliott and I made with the mayor's support was that a significant public investment like a courthouse should be placed where it strengthens other nearby institutions and businesses, and becomes a centerpiece for the redevelopment of a declining area.

"My first major assignment at the Office of Jamaica Planning and Development was to make the rounds for this project—talk to all the relevant politicians on the city council, talk to all the presiding judges of the court. Get them to agree to a change in location. Don Elliott and Mayor Lindsay wanted consensus. They wanted everybody to feel good about it."

Andy identifies the judges as the reason for the original location. "They thought it would be easy to get to," he says. "And since they were the major constituency for courthouses, the government followed along. These judges had no interest in redeveloping fading downtown areas. In fact, they objected to being in a place like Jamaica, which was declining, where there were racial issues, and so on."

"The court's leadership was resistant to the idea of moving to Jamaica—most of the judges were white," says Towery.

"When I met these judges," says Andy, "I represented the mayor, who was trying to do something serious about Jamaica and about the outer boroughs in general. Lindsay felt deeply that public investments needed to play a significant role in improving city life. It was important in such cases for the mayor to be present and accounted for.

"Here the point was not just constructing a much-needed building but producing the secondary and tertiary effects of strengthening the community. It was hard for the judges to argue with those aims.

"I was able to assemble widespread agreement among the relevant parties. And so, the City Planning Commission changed the site to one we'd identified on Sutphin Boulevard.

"The courthouse was relocated to downtown Jamaica, with all the associated ancillary services—lawyers' offices, title insurance companies, food, other businesses—certain to be clustered around. Fortunately, in the end that's what happened."

"With a big push from the mayor, OJPD, and the Queens Bar Association," says Towery, "the court's leadership agreed to a site adjacent to the existing prominent, prestigious, and elegant State Supreme Court, Civil Term, long in Jamaica, where there were common operational modes and missions. A win-win, to be sure."

Andy didn't hire the architects, didn't see the construction to its 1997 completion. "I was only there a short time," he says, "but I bought into a strategy. I wanted to make sure the courthouse relocation achieved the maximum number of sensible, interlocking planning and multiple economic development and space use objectives. I wanted to be part of the courthouse relocation—indeed, of the entire Jamaica initiative.

"Nevertheless, Towery should get most of the credit for all the projects that were put in place over time—he spent most of his near half-century career there. As so many other key actors came and went at every level of government and in the private sector, he saw the whole thing through over all those years. I'm proud of the early work that made possible the fruition of the work we did."

Jamaica served as one more classroom in Andy's continuing education. "In Jamaica," he says, "I learned a lot about how local, state, and federal government could either be at odds or work together. All levels were involved in everything we did. This job was where I wanted to be, and I leaned into it. I left behind the rarified atmosphere of the State Department and the nuances of international diplomacy in favor of digging into where people were hurting.

"As Americans, we should have been doing much better in working directly with our people who were in distress. We still should."

LATE-INNING COMEBACK: The Election of 1969

John Lindsay needed a miracle to win reelection in November 1969.

In the aftermath of the snowstorm, Lindsay made it his business to show up in Queens when he could, but his standing with white working-class New Yorkers was slow to improve. That weakness created an opening for John Marchi, a right-wing state senator from Staten Island. Challenging Lindsay for the Republican mayoral nomination, Marchi offered a change from the perceived chaos of Lindsay's first term, pronouncing himself "very, very hawkish" on crime and pledging "to restore some kind of tranquility in the life of the people." The Conservative Party's leaders had already designated Marchi as their nominee, just as the Liberal Party had selected Lindsay. On primary day, Marchi added the Republican line to his candidacy, edging out the incumbent by 3 percentage points. Lindsay would have to run on the Liberal line alone.

That same day, however, the mayor got good news. On the Democratic side of the race, the top contender had appeared to be former mayor Wagner, who'd left his post as US ambassador to Spain after only nine months to make a bid for his old job. Positioned as the centrist, establishment candidate, Wagner faced effective opposition from both left and right. His chief liberal opponent was Herman Badillo, a native Puerto Rican then serving as borough president of the Bronx. On the right stood city comptroller Mario Procaccino, a native of Italy who had grown up in the Bronx. Badillo called Procaccino a racist; the comptroller responded, "I've got twenty-five years behind me to prove I'm no racist. I say I'm for you, whatever you are—but you've got to behave yourself, and I tell it to everybody, Black and white, straight out." Two minor candidates rounded out the roster: a liberal congressman, James Scheuer, and an obstreperous novelist, Norman Mailer. The large field meant a divided vote. Procaccino prevailed with only 33 percent of the vote. (Because of that result, lawmakers changed the state's primary rules to require a runoff election between the top two finishers if no candidate earned at least 40 percent of the vote.)

The voters, it seemed, had rejected liberalism in both primaries. But therein lay Lindsay's advantage: With two conservative candidates in the race, liberals had no choice but to support the incumbent. Marchi, the conservative Republican in a Democratic town, trailed throughout the campaign, leaving Procaccino to take the early lead. But the city comptroller proved to be a miserable campaigner. Some evenings he would visit a neighborhood, rattle after-hours storefront security gates, and shout to anyone listening that when he became mayor, stores wouldn't need such protection. He matched his odd behavior with odd words. He said that one of his running mates, a candidate for city council president, "grows on you like a cancer." In Harlem, he told an audience, "My heart is as Black as yours." Nonetheless, Procaccino coined a lasting contribution to the American political lexicon: "limousine liberal." His application of the term to Lindsay may have been unfair—while the mayor had come from a privileged background, he made good on his commitment to poor and underserved New Yorkers. But the term took hold and has persisted as a way of describing wealthy people whose compassion for the poor is matched by their unwillingness to spend time anywhere near them.

After Ocean Hill-Brownsville, Lindsay needed help in rebuilding Jewish support, so key in 1965. He got that help from the person with as much credibility among Jews as anyone in the world: the prime minister of Israel. With the main purpose of assisting her good friend John Lindsay in his campaign, Golda Meir visited New York for three days at the end of September. At a ceremony on the steps of city hall, Meir all but endorsed her host: "Mr. Mayor, you represent the great city of New York. There's no other city like it—you represent the people whose spirit has led the world for all that is good." At a dinner in Brooklyn, Lindsay, the ultra *goy*, joined Meir and the hundreds of guests in singing "Hava Nagila."

And then came the miracle.

From their maiden season in 1962 through 1968, the Mets had been lovable losers—a good year meant finishing in next-to-last place. But in the summer of 1969, led by one newly minted New York icon, star hurler Tom Seaver, and one longtime New York icon, manager and former Brooklyn Dodgers first baseman Gil Hodges, the Mets were in a race with the Chicago Cubs to win the Eastern Division of the National League. The Mets nipped at the heels of the first-place Cubs through July, but in mid-August fell nine and a half games off the pace. The Mets then went on an improbable run to win the division, take the league championship series from the Atlanta Braves, and wallop the heavily favored Baltimore Orioles in the World Series. The team captured the imagination of New Yorkers of every background. And what better analogue to John Lindsay, given up for dead, now surging back?

Lindsay, not previously known as a baseball fan—his tastes ran to tennis and yachting—leapt aboard the Mets comet, entering the clubhouse for each of the three victory celebrations: division, league, and World Series. On more than one occasion, live television and press photographers captured a smiling Lindsay being doused with champagne by joyful players—to the immense delight of campaign aides. The usually dignified mayor, now baptized as a regular baseball-loving guy, even returned the favor, turning over a bottle and soaking a player or two.

Lindsay staged a tickertape parade for the Miracle Mets—he rode in the procession and presided over the ceremony that followed.

All New Yorkers, not just the Blacks and Jews who made up Lindsay's base, could take pride in the city's new heroes—who happened to play their home games in Queens.

The mayor's attention to Queens also included touting the work of the Office of Jamaica Planning and Development. On October 24, he announced a $380 million set of improvements to Jamaica. The package included all the OJPD's major initiatives—the El, the train to JFK, York College, the courthouse—among other items.

Andy was present at the announcement. From the *Times*:

> City participation is necessary to stimulate private development, according to Dr. Andrew Maguire, director of the Mayor's office of Jamaica Planning and Development.
>
> Although the area is the city's third largest retail area (the first two are Herald Square in Manhattan and downtown Brooklyn) "it's an old place," Mr. Maguire said, "with image problems."

Of course, Lindsay had his own image problems in Queens; perhaps $380 million could repair them. As the *Times* noted:

> Asked at a City Hall news conference whether the timing of the announcement was designed to get him votes, Mr. Lindsay replied, to the guffaws of aides and newsmen:
>
> "The fact that it's made a couple of weeks before the elections is coincidental—conceivably helpful, but still coincidental."

As Election Day neared, Democratic leaders who couldn't stomach a candidate as conservative as Procaccino endorsed Lindsay. Even the president of the sanitation workers' union, who had been quick to hold Lindsay responsible for the snow snafu only months earlier, supported his reelection.

In his most effective campaign ad, Lindsay made a confession—not exactly apologizing, but admitting he'd erred: "I guessed wrong on the weather before the city's biggest snowfall last year, and that was a mistake. But I put six thousand more cops on the street, and that was no mistake.

The school strike went on too long, and we all made some mistakes. But I brought 225,000 new jobs to this town, and that was no mistake. . . . And we did not have a Detroit, a Watts, or a Newark in this city. And those were no mistakes. The things that go wrong are what make this the second-toughest job in America. But the things that go right are what make me want it."

Lindsay's contrition, his attention to Queens, his luck in opponents, his character witness from Israel, and the miracle of the Miracle Mets added up to a victory on November 5. He didn't get a majority—he didn't need one, taking 42 percent of the vote to Procaccino's 35 and Marchi's 23.

John Lindsay won only two of the city's five boroughs. One was Manhattan, where he prevailed by 47 percentage points. The other was Queens. He beat Procaccino there by half a point.

WHAT (NOT) TO DO: Learning the Levers of Power and Politics

"There would always be plans on the drawing board for how you're going to upgrade this park or repair this malfunctioning sewer line," Andy recalls. "We brought pressure.

"This is where I learned that you approach this stuff from the bottom and from the top. From the bottom you get the staff who actually do the work in the given agency. You sit down with them and talk about how important a matter it is and how it dovetails with what the mayor wants to happen out there, and how time is of the essence. You work from the bottom with all of the elected officials, who have their own calling cards with decision-makers and community leaders.

"At the same time, you go to the top. You start by approaching the department staff—at the Department of Public Works, for example, if it was a sewer issue. If that doesn't work, you work with the mayor's assistant for sewers. You write a memo to them saying, 'This is what we need you to do.' Talking points—bang, bang, bang. One page, a page and a half. You sit down with them, and you say, 'Look. These folks in the agency are ready to go, but they need to get the word from the mayor.' You get the relevant mayoral assistant to tell Public Works that the mayor wants something. Top-down: 'I'm calling from Mayor Lindsay's office.'

Everybody knew that you didn't mess with these mayoral assistants—and he had half a dozen of them—because they *were* the mayor. You work the citizen community boards in your part of the city. You get the city council member, the state assemblyman to talk to the sewer guy.

"So the decision-maker is getting it from all angles. From below and from above. I was the orchestrator of that whole process.

"Towery taught me how to do that, because he was always doing it himself. But sometimes he needed me. That's what I added to his mix. Something we wanted wasn't just a request from a constituency in Queens, the Greater Jamaica Development Corporation. It was a priority of the mayor of the City of New York."

"There were some questions of origination," Towery recalls. "Which project did the city originate or which did we. We didn't get in each other's way; there was plenty to do for everybody. Sometimes I would take the lead and sometimes Andy would. I don't ever remember a moment of competition because the job was so big and we were so ambitious about getting it done and so well aware of what it would take to get it done.

"I don't think we ever thought it would be as easy as it became. I don't want to overstate that—it was never easy. But we accomplished things. We took them on and Lindsay urged us to take them on and Don Elliott urged us to take them on."

"The Jamaica Center revitalization has been a huge success," says Andy. "There have been a lot of accomplishments. I played a role early on. I turned things over to my successors and to Towery."

Towery's example showed Andy what to do. However, Andy says, "sometimes you learn by figuring out what *not* to do."

In 1970, Andy took a brief leave of absence from his job at the OJPD to work in the campaign of Arthur Goldberg, running to defeat Nelson Rockefeller's bid for a fourth term as governor. Steve Smith, a Kennedy brother-in-law and political operative, was the chief strategist running the campaign, although he was not formally the campaign manager.

"I was there for Goldberg," says Andy. "I wanted to be his aide, and he wanted me around, because I'd worked with him at the UN for three years. Richard Reeves wrote a piece in *New York* magazine about my suddenly emerging as one of Goldberg's lieutenants in this campaign. Well, I wasn't being paid. Once I suggested to Steve Smith that maybe they should be paying me something. Smith grabbed me and pulled me into a closet and read me the riot act, basically saying, 'We don't care whether you're here or not.'

"As a candidate, Goldberg was a disaster. Every time there would be a press conference, it would be carefully orchestrated. The staff would tell him, You're going to get up there and talk about this issue in Syracuse—or Rochester or wherever. Then Goldberg would inevitably start the press conference by saying, 'As I have always said in the past . . .' He'd had the same habit while at the UN. You can imagine how appreciative newspeople would be to hear this time after time. They were looking for a new story which we could have given them but didn't.

"He also had an attitude of noblesse oblige: I'm a former Supreme Court justice. Now I'm making myself available to be your governor. The president asked me to do this. Democrats in New York have asked me to do this. It was saying, in effect, 'You should be grateful I'm here,' which doesn't translate well in a political campaign."

Another deficiency was that Goldberg had all the charisma of wet cardboard. Although he won the primary, in November he lost to Rockefeller by a dozen points.

"The Goldberg campaign taught me that lesson: What *not* to do," says Andy. "It would prove valuable when I ran for Congress."

"The more I think about Helmsley," says Andy, "the angrier I get. And it's fifty years later!"

Andy and Towery worked closely with Jamaica's business community, forging productive relationships, especially through the local Chamber of Commerce and its president, Vincent Albanese. But they were thrilled when they seemed to attract to Jamaica a world-class player. "Harry Helmsley," recalls Andy, "was a big deal in New York City—a major real-estate magnate, a so-called civic leader, reputed to have a social conscience. He was super wealthy—many New Yorkers thought he could do anything." Helmsley had built perhaps the most impressive real-estate portfolio in the history of New York, owning a variety of hotels and residential buildings and some of the city's best-known office towers, among them the Graybar Building and the Empire State Building.

While Andy was at the OJPD, Helmsley showed interest in expanding his holdings to Jamaica. "Among our projects," says Towery, "was the

Jamaica Center Urban Renewal area, ten acres of land designated by the city mainly for office space. The city was losing office jobs. We argued successfully for the city to use its powers to designate the area and then to create sites for development. It was a major undertaking of getting four sites ready for development by acquiring them, rezoning them, reshaping them. That started under Andy, and it lasted a long time.

"Helmsley's organization signed an intention to lease the land for development of an office building—the potential tenant was Chase Manhattan Bank, which was moving some of its back-office functions from Lower Manhattan. I saw the drawings for the building they were planning—it was a large one, maybe half a million square feet.

"We got all excited about that. I went and I met the guy from Chase who was in charge of the unit that would be coming. I believe his square footage was 250,000. But they ended up going to existing space in Rockefeller Center. That tells you something about the economy then, that it was a bargain for Chase to move its unit there.

"The Helmsley commitment was what we were salivating for: back-office jobs in Jamaica. But when Chase decided against it, Helmsley pulled out. I had a long talk with his project manager. He was very regretful about it."

Towery's nearly half century working in Jamaica enables him to look back on Helmsley's change of mind with equanimity. Not Andy. "Towery," he says, "is amazing in his ability to bounce back, continue on, make things happen in spite of reverses, of which this Helmsley item was one of the biggest. This was a crippling blow.

"Here are the mayor and his team working overtime to reenvision the city," Andy says, "and what it could become for all New Yorkers, including those in the outer boroughs always thought of as backwaters by the Manhattan crowd. And what does Harry Helmsley do? He signs up for the Jamaica Center Urban Renewal project, which could have been an early, powerful support to the new college and a business center to be served by a new underground line, he plays around with it, then he backs out. No doubt he found more attractive, prestigious, and more lucrative opportunities to be exploited in Manhattan. It could have been so huge if he had followed through on what he had committed to do.

"Helmsley bailed not only on helping significantly to better Jamaica's future but on the innovative mayor who was tackling the issues involved in redeveloping centers for the outer boroughs that would then anchor communities of millions of New Yorkers who live in those boroughs. And this would have been hugely beneficial to the city as a whole, including Manhattan, where there would be dynamic multiplication factors between what was going on in Manhattan and what was going on in the boroughs. It would have benefited everyone over time, even you, Harry Helmsley!

"I can still see him getting up from behind his huge desk, all six-foot-three inches of him, chatting up Elliott and Towery and me about what a wonderful idea this was.

"What a self-centered jerk he was to have pulled out later when, even without his initial prime tenant, he had plenty of wherewithal to have made it work."

FORGOTTEN MAN: John Lindsay and the Passing of 1960s Liberalism

In the summer of 1968, Lindsay was still glamorous enough, and his wing of the party strong enough, that he was on the short list to be named Richard Nixon's running mate at August's Republican convention in Miami Beach. But Southern conservatives, led by the segregationist Senator Strom Thurmond of South Carolina, threatened a revolt if Nixon chose the New York mayor—or any other progressive—so Nixon gave the nod to the relatively obscure governor of Maryland, Spiro Agnew. Agnew's main qualification seemed to be the hard line he took toward the African-American riots that had afflicted American cities—he'd earned a reputation, as one delegate to the convention put it, "as a shoot-the-looters boy." During the campaign and in the Nixon administration, Agnew would develop a vicious (and multisyllabic) brand of vitriol aimed at Nixon's opponents on campus, in the press, and in Congress.

Today, Richard Nixon's domestic governance would, in most GOP eyes, mark him as a RINO, Republican in name only. At the time, Nixon was considered a conservative. But he wasn't a "movement conservative" like Barry Goldwater, seeing in all but the most essential services of government a threat to "liberty." The many resentments that filled Nixon's complicated brain did not include the visceral detestation of taxation that marked the thinking of Ronald Reagan. Nixon believed in government. He didn't challenge the New Deal consensus on Social Security and banking regulation. He did not attempt to do away with the major elements of Lyndon Johnson's war on poverty.

Nixon did not announce any vast new social programs of his own. Nevertheless, he didn't go after Medicare or Head Start, and he oversaw a fivefold increase in the number of Americans on food stamps. By executive order he created the Environmental Protection Agency and appointed a first-class public servant, William Ruckelshaus, as its first administrator. When Congress created the Occupational Safety and Health Administration, Nixon signed the bill in the Oval Office with cameras clicking. Nixon's most startling departure from Republican orthodoxy came in 1971 when, to curb rising inflation, he instituted perhaps the most intrusive peacetime intervention in the US economy in American history: mandatory price and wage controls. And for all his tough talk about the supposed excesses of the liberal Warren Supreme Court, the three justices he appointed would, over their long tenure, cover the entire judicial spectrum: William Rehnquist, one of the most conservative justices in modern history; Lewis Powell, a classic swing vote; and Harry Blackmun, a moderate conservative at first who would go on to be a hero to America's liberals.

In purely policy terms, Richard Nixon was no more conservative than the nation's next two Democratic presidents, Jimmy Carter and Bill Clinton. But Nixon's most profound effect on American politics did not come in his domestic agenda or even in the criminal behavior that forced him to resign in 1974. Rather, he initiated the reactionary, exclusionary populism that has come to full flower in the demagoguery of Donald Trump. In 1968, Nixon weaponized white resentment. "Law and order" served as a racist code phrase, a way of letting whites, North and South, know that, like them, Nixon was fed up with the country's focus on the concerns of minorities, even if he needed to express his disgust in words that allowed the pretense of a race-neutral appeal. And when, as president, Nixon was confronted by massive student antiwar demonstrations, he called for support from "the great silent majority" of Americans, people who worked for a living, sent their sons to war, and felt no kinship with the protesting youngsters who had no idea how privileged they were.

What is the heart of Trumpism if not racial and class resentment?

All his life, Nixon had resented real and imagined elites—the wellborn, the Ivy Leaguers, supercilious newspaper columnists, the Kennedys, the Jews, holier-than-thou politicians who relied on Nixon to do their dirty work. The grocer's son from Whittier had much in common with the developer's son from Queens, who to this day privately craves the approval of the Manhattan elites he publicly scorns—the truly wealthy real-estate men, the respected philanthropists, the reporters and editors of the *New York Times*.

The distance from 1968's "law and order" to 2016's "Make America Great Again" is no more than a small leap of imagination.

In August 1971, John Lindsay bowed to reality and changed his party registration to Democrat. Not only did he see a Republican Party that had moved away from people like him; he also recognized that Nixon would be nominated for a second term in 1972. Lindsay still had national aspirations, and the Republican Party and its incumbent president stood in his way. In late December, he declared his candidacy for the White House.

Selling himself as a spokesman for America's cities, Lindsay competed in two primaries, Florida and Wisconsin. But after taking less than 7 percent of the vote in both contests, he dropped out of the race. The holder of the second toughest job in America would not be promoted to the toughest.

In his second term, Lindsay managed to govern more efficiently than he had in the first, dealing more skillfully with the municipal unions and with the city's political power brokers. Even so, he was unable to avoid another ugly situation that aggravated tensions between Black and white New Yorkers. Residents of the mostly white, mostly middle-class Queens neighborhood, Forest Hills, were furious over plans to build a large low-income housing complex there. The dispute lasted more than a year before Lindsay agreed to significant cutbacks in the plan.

When John Lindsay left office at the end of 1973, the city he'd sought to make more just and more humane still suffered from disorder. Crime continued to rise, the subways were covered with graffiti, and poverty still prevailed in too many neighborhoods. Two years into the administration of his successor, Abe Beame, the city nearly declared bankruptcy. It took a federal bailout to save the city from immediate default; it took damaging budget cuts imposed by an outside fiscal control board to avoid later default.

In 1977, New Yorkers elected as mayor another congressman from the Silk Stocking District, Ed Koch. Though known as a liberal member of

Congress, Koch pulled back from Lindsay's vision of justice and equality; by the time he left office after three terms, he and the city's Black community were barely on speaking terms. A Black mayor, David Dinkins, followed Koch; while he tried to bring liberal reforms to the city, he did not inspire the citizens' confidence that he was able to master the levers of government. Running for reelection, he was defeated by the former US attorney for the Southern District of New York, Rudolph Giuliani, who took a more conservative turn on most issues. Crime finally started to recede—at least as much a result of demographics as of any police strategy. Again, Giuliani gave Blacks and other minorities little reason to trust him, but the city did, for the majority, anyway, become more livable.

Lindsay's last political hurrah came in 1980, when he ran in the Democratic primary for the Senate seat held by an ailing Jacob Javits. The former mayor finished third in the primary; the victor in November was the Republican, Al D'Amato, a conservative from Long Island. Lindsay spent ten years as chairman of the board of the Lincoln Center Theater and was credited with the institution's revival. But he faced hard times toward the end of his life. He worked for two law firms; both went out of business, leaving the former mayor, afflicted by cardiac ailments and Parkinson's disease, without health insurance. What's more, his eight years as mayor had left him seven short of the fifteen needed to qualify for a city pension. Mayor Giuliani and Council Speaker Peter Vallone arranged for him to hold a largely ceremonial municipal job, providing him with health insurance and, after two years, a pension under revised city rules.

He retired to Hilton Head, South Carolina. The elegant mayor with movie star looks spent many of his last years living with his wife in a one-bedroom apartment. He died in December 2000 at age seventy-nine.

Lindsay represented the urban version of the heyday, then the last gasp, of a liberalism that had started with the New Deal—a belief in government's ability to make life better coupled with a commitment to expanding civic participation to marginalized people. New York City did not become more manageable or livable over his eight years in office. Could any mayor have reversed the rise of crime and disorder that plagued America's largest city from 1965 to 1973? No. But Lindsay was in charge and Lindsay is blamed. Subsequent mayors proved that the city could be governed—never mind that starting in the 1990s urban crime decreased across the country, never mind the profound impact, good and bad, of gentrification, never mind improvements that Lindsay set in motion. After all, his vision laid the foundation for the revival of Jamaica Center, which came to pass only many years after he left city hall.

The passing of John Lindsay from the political scene paralleled the passing of the liberal moment of the '60s. For a few years, as the frozen culture and politics of the '50s had thawed, it seemed that idealism would be enough to open hearts and change minds in the service of justice and progress. Now, those who sought to bring about significant change—the Andy Maguires of the world—would have to face the hard problems no merely moral stance could solve.

CHAPTER 5

DEMOCRAT FOR CONGRESS: Finding a Political Home during the Age of Nixon

Our citizens do not know whom to believe, and many of them have concluded that all the processes of government have become so compromised that honest governance has been rendered impossible.

—SAM ERVIN

"Midway through my time with Lindsay," says Andy, "I began to think, 'Look. What you really need to do is get yourself elected to Congress.'"

Meg Maguire, Andy's first wife, dates Andy's ambition earlier. "I don't remember the moment of decision," she says. "All I know is that he wanted to do that the whole time we were in Queens."

"Looking back," says Andy, "the 1968 assassinations of King and Kennedy, the gunning down of students that year in Orangeburg, South Carolina [twenty-eight injured, three killed when state police fired into a crowd of civil rights protesters], riots in cities across the country, including near where I grew up in Los Angeles in 1965 and close to my family home in New Jersey in 1967, the chaos and beating of protesters at the Democratic National Convention in Chicago—all this struck me with such urgency that I left the State Department for an inner-city post with Lindsay. Now I wanted the influence and, yes, the power, that elective office can bring."

Since his youth, Andy Maguire had set his sights on being an agent of progressive societal change. Essential to his ambition was becoming a person who made decisions rather than one who implemented decisions made by others. He had prepared himself, through academic, international, and urban experience that translated into sterling credentials. The House of Representatives formed the logical next step.

But where to run? Andy looked for places to which he could claim a connection.

One possibility was Ohio. "I'd gone to college there," he says, "and my grandfather, Andy Maguire, had been a leading citizen in Youngstown. My name (his name) would have had resonance. But near as I could tell, Democrats in all the potential districts were strongly ensconced. I would have had to become active in the Democratic Party, then wait in line for an opportunity to run, which might have taken years if it happened at all."

Another option was the area in which he was living and working at the time. However, he says, "Queens was just as hopeless as Ohio. Joe Addabbo had represented Jamaica since 1961 and was popular. There weren't any neighboring districts that made sense, either."

However, there was a third locale: New Jersey. "Ridgewood," he recalls, "where I'd attended my senior year of high school, was in a Republican area, with a longtime Republican congressman. But one Saturday I went to a Harvard-Princeton football game in Princeton with a high school buddy who was an alum. He said, 'You ought to take a look at how things are changing in Bergen County. It's not impossible to think about a Democrat winning.' The Democrat who ran for Congress in '70 got only 41 percent of the vote. It was a heavy lift from that number to winning.

"But I did take a look at it."

"There was an opening," says Meg, "and he seized it."

OUT OF GAS: A Nation Finds Its Limits

In the 1970s, the United States lost its swagger.

The country had emerged from World War II not only victorious but whole—among the world's major industrial powers, only the United States had, aside from the attack on Pearl Harbor, been spared war on its homeland. In the quarter century that followed the war, the country enjoyed not only unprecedented military power and international influence but also an economic expansion the likes of which the world had never seen. Dominant in global markets, American factories, negotiating contracts with strong labor unions, were able to pay workers a wage sufficient to bankroll a middle-class life.

More and more American families could afford automobiles; the cars would fuel the growth of suburbs. With the help of loans granted under the GI Bill, manual laborers who a generation earlier would have been confined to a lifetime in cramped quarters could now own a house—with a yard, a picket fence, and a refrigerator stocked with food to feed the children they were raising amidst a nationwide baby boom. Both custom—a lingering mindset from the ordeal of the Great Depression—and law meant that the social compact did not strain under the extreme inequality of wealth that afflicts our nation today. CEOs of large companies earned on average twenty times the salary of a line worker, not the roughly three hundred times they earn now. The marginal tax rate stood as high as 92 percent and didn't dip below 70. The Korean War had ended in stalemate, but at least America had protected South Korea from conquest by its evil twin to the north. Even the Vietnam War—for the first couple of years—seemed to be the action of a confident nation bringing altruistic power to bear on behalf of a worthwhile cause, the worldwide struggle against Communism.

It seemed America's prosperity and primacy would rise forever.

But America would become mired in Vietnam, leading us to see ourselves, in Richard Nixon's words, as "a helpless, pitiful giant," a Gulliver tied down by Lilliputians in a distant, poor land inhabited by people who wore odd clothes, spoke an odd language, and were of what most Americans, consciously or not, considered an inferior race. Spending on America's expensive enterprise in Southeast Asia, conducted without corresponding tax increases, caused prices to rise: the annual rate of inflation, which had not topped 2 percent since 1958, inched above 6.

America, the public believed, had never lost, and would never lose, a war. Yet, even after the peace agreement of 1973 that left South Vietnam an independent state, that prize hardly seemed worth the sacrifice of so much blood, treasure, and domestic tranquility. Veterans returning home from the war found themselves shunned and scorned, uncomfortable reminders of the nation's tragic collective folly.

The full scale of America's failure in Vietnam would not become clear until the fall of Saigon on April 30, 1975, but in the meantime the nation was dealt a blow almost as unsettling. In October 1973, on the eve of Yom Kippur, the holiest day on the Jewish calendar, Arab states mounted a ferocious attack on Israel. Caught by surprise, Israeli forces were pushed out of much of the Sinai and the Golan Heights, which they had occupied since the Six Day War of 1967. The United States poured arms to its ally Israel; the Soviet Union resupplied Israel's foes. After a few days, Israel mounted a counterattack that regained the lost territory and then some. The Yom Kippur War ended in cease-fire after nineteen days of fighting. The borders returned to those in place since 1967.

To punish the United States, as well as other Western nations that had supported the Israeli cause, Arab oil-producing states stopped selling them oil. The embargo caused worldwide oil prices to shoot upward, disrupting the entire American economy. Average Americans noticed the change most immediately in the cost and availability of gasoline. By early 1974, the price of a gallon of gas was rising at an annual rate of over 40 percent. Motorists from coast to coast were forced to do what had previously been unthinkable: wait in line to fill their gas tanks—*if* the stations' tanks had not already run dry. In New Jersey, car owners were allowed to buy gas only on alternate days, which day depending on whether the last digit of their license plate was odd or even.

The automobile, the symbol of American prosperity and freedom, had become a daily reminder that the United States of America no longer bestrode the world like a colossus, that our nation, like every other nation, was vulnerable to forces beyond its borders and beyond its control. Before long, consumers saw the increased price of oil affect everything they bought—by October 1974, the general rate of inflation topped 12 percent. Perhaps the bounty and the power of the United States were not limitless after all.

And then there was Watergate.

GETTING COMFORTABLE: Settling In Among the Democrats of Bergen County

If Andy was to establish a political career in Bergen County, his first task was to familiarize himself with its politics. "I went back to where I'd graduated from high school," he says, "where my parents lived, and I figured out who everybody was. It was like going to see all the presiding judges in Queens. You ask every important person, 'Can I come over and have coffee with you?' It didn't take long for me to identify Barbara Werber as a terrifically important person. And she took an interest in me."

After 1968, when the Democratic Party, torn by the Vietnam War, had seen its candidate lose the White House to Richard Nixon, a reform movement sought to wrest control of the party from the bosses who had given Humphrey the nomination and to orient the party toward a more liberal ideology. Rob Esposito, who joined Andy's campaign as a teenage volunteer and would go on to a long career in campaign management, recalls the state of the party in Bergen County. "The fissure in the national party reflected itself here, in terms of an old guard and a new guard," he says. "The new guard was represented by Barbara Werber, from Ridgewood."

Andy fell in quickly with Werber and her allies. "For decades, the county party had been run by organization Democrats," he says. "But Werber came along after 1968 and began to build a reform Democrat operation. This was opposed to the Vietnam War and very progressive on civil rights, on women's rights—the whole nine yards of stuff I identified with. She, and they, quickly concluded that I was part of them, which I was."

Historically, New Jersey's Seventh Congressional District had belonged to the GOP. "Going back to the 1950s and '60s," Esposito recalls, "Bergen was often referred to as the 'banner Republican county in New Jersey.'"

But now Werber had found someone with the ambition and credentials that could make him the first Democrat to represent the district in Congress in sixty years. "She knew I wanted to run for Congress," says Andy. "We talked about it from day one. She looked at my résumé—graduated from Ridgewood High School, PhD from Harvard, State Department, United Nations, working for a Republican mayor in New York—and thought it added up to a sellable package, with potential to get a Democrat elected in a Republican county. So she told me, 'Here are the twenty-five people who you need to go and sit down with.' Which I did—one by one by one by one."

After introducing himself to Bergen County, both on his own and under Werber's tutelage, Andy was ready to run for elective office—but not yet for Congress. The party's congressional candidate in 1972 would be Arthur Lesemann, an antiwar Democrat and lawyer active on the Fair Housing Council of New Jersey, who had run a respectable losing race in 1970 and was expected to do the same two years later. Andy would seek a lesser post: freeholder. At the time, Bergen County was governed by a nine-member board of freeholders. Three of those seats were up for normal reelection in 1972; there was also a contest to serve the final year of an unexpired term of a seat recently vacated when its holder resigned to take another job. The board had appointed Kenneth Sherwood, the Republican mayor of Upper Saddle River, as that freeholder's replacement. Now Sherwood was running to keep the position.

As Matty Feldman, the county Democratic chair, assembled that year's ticket, he took care to balance the competing wings of the party. "The progressive or liberal wing of the party was starting to rise to power," says Jerry Breslin, a senior Democratic operative who was aligned with the county party's regulars.

"Werber," says Andy, "had enough leverage in '72 with Feldman and Breslin that they wanted to give her something. What she took was me running for the one-year unexpired term."

Andy's running mates, the Democratic candidates for the three full-term seats, were all current officeholders: Gerald Calabrese, mayor of Cliffside Park; Frank Herbert, a council member from Waldwick; and Bill Meisner, a council member from Saddle Brook.

Breslin, who managed the ticket's campaign, remembers his first impression of Andy: "One, he was obviously bright. Number two, highly energetic. Number three, driven. Number four, very liberal. But even though we were at opposite ends of the split in the party, I don't recall any dispute between us."

Andy had found his political home. "I thought I might win the freeholder race," he says. "Still, in my mind, it was a prep for Congress. Werber and I discussed it. It was never her intention or mine that I would be ceilinged out on the freeholder board.

"I explicitly gave myself five years from the moment I left the Lindsay administration to get myself into Congress or I would do something else. I'd go back to the State Department, I'd teach at a university. Whatever. I didn't want to operate as a public official at a local or even state level. My goal was Washington, because I knew Washington was the place to be. There I would be involved with every level of government. I would draw on and leverage what I'd learned in grad school, at State, and in New York City.

"I targeted Congress. Five years. I made it in less than three."

"Obviously, I had to be living in Bergen County," says Andy. "So Meg and I bought a house in Ridgewood."

For a while, Andy commuted to his job in Queens, but that arrangement couldn't last. "I continued in my job," he says, "until I had to tell Dick Aurelio, the deputy mayor, what I was up to. It would have been fine had Lindsay not been lining himself up to run for president as a Democrat. Aurelio told me, basically, 'You're doing a great job, but we can't afford to have a mayoral appointee commuting from New Jersey. You're going to have to step down'—which I did. It makes perfect sense if you think about it.

"With her urban planning career, Meg earned enough money to support me. But I still felt obligated to contribute financially, so I went back to my contacts at the Ford Foundation and said, 'Do you have anything you'd like me to do?'

"They signed me up as a consultant. I did an investigation and a report on the theory and practice of workplace organization. I earned enough money to support myself while I set up to run for freeholder, and even for a while afterward—until I got organized for the congressional race."

SEWERS AND SPAGHETTI: Andy Sets Himself Apart

At times, the four freeholder candidates issued joint statements and made joint appearances. "Breslin was running the campaign and we did a lot of things together," Andy recalls. "It was a well-run campaign. Breslin was good."

Nonetheless, Andy found ways to distinguish himself. "I was the only freeholder candidate who was out there every single day, all day long," he says.

Almost by accident, Andy found a signature issue. "One of my supporters," he says, "was an engineer, Arthur Wrubel. He wanted to help—everybody who was oriented toward reform in the party wanted to help me. Nobody had ever paid any attention to the Bergen County Sewer Authority—it had been locked up by both political parties for decades as a patronage prize and had always used the same engineering consulting firm. Wrubel says to me, 'This is my field of expertise. I've taken a look and I can tell you that the engineering firm is ripping off the county and the taxpayers. This is a public interest issue you could really run with.'

"Wrubel provided me with analysis of the particulars relating to Sewer Authority contracts—this was one of the biggest pieces of county finance. He ran the numbers for me, prepped me on what was being done with the money, why there was what we came to call a scheme for pyramiding profits."

The engineering company, Clinton Bogert Associates of Fort Lee, would be paid not a flat fee for a project but a percentage of construction costs over time. And the process would take time—it might be years before construction would start. Meanwhile, the estimated cost would rise, causing the amount paid to the engineering firm to rise as well. The pyramiding occurred when the fees paid to Bogert were included in figuring the total cost, so that with the next payment, the company would receive not only a percentage of building costs but also a percentage of its own percentage.

"I started going to every freeholder meeting," Andy says, "armed with facts and figures—like the extra $300,000 the engineers were pocketing—and raise a ruckus about the Sewer Authority.

"And I would get press.

"There's another important piece here. The *Bergen Record*, a superb newspaper, had done an investigative reporting job on the Sewer Authority. So all of a sudden the Sewer Authority was a major public issue."

At the beginning of May, the week after the *Record* published its series of articles, Andy went to the monthly meeting of the board of freeholders loaded for bear. The *Record* reported the meeting in detail.

Andy charged the authority with a litany of sins, among them "at least the appearance of poor planning, inefficient and costly management . . . tolerance of a critical health hazard and of pollution of our rivers," and dishonesty: "Different versions of the facts seem to have been given by the authority to contracting communities, prospective bond purchasers, and the court." Such mismanagement could be costing county taxpayers millions, Andy told the board.

The upshot of Andy's troublemaking was that the freeholder director instructed the county counsel to conduct an in-depth study of the Sewer Authority's operations.

"The *Record* would report on what I was saying," says Andy, "because it was a different kind of politics being conducted at the normally boring monthly meetings of the freeholder board. It was a politics emphasizing substantive and important public-dollar issues. Also, my efforts followed on the articles—that was appealing to the paper: 'Hey, here's a guy who's taking our work seriously and doing something about it."

By knowing the right person, Arthur Wrubel, and taking his advice, Andy had not merely seized upon an issue, he had created one—and it was his alone.

Andy's focus on a previously unknown issue, the Sewer Authority, along with the dramatic confrontations he staged, revealed that he understood what it took to draw publicity. His most audacious bid for press came in September, when he crashed a party.

The idea for the stunt came from a woman who would be one of the most important players in launching Andy's career. As Andy recalls, "Werber said to me, 'You should talk to Gina Glantz. She's a savvy, smart person.' At the same time, Bob Welker, a colleague of Gina's who later designed the literature and logo that captivated voters, encouraged Gina to meet me. I went to see Gina and we hit it off, so she became a strategist for my freeholder campaign." Gina Glantz, who worked in New York promoting a tobacco company, had recently moved to Ridgewood from Brooklyn, where she had published a community newspaper. "She came up with a preposterous idea: Since I was looking to attract Republican and independent voters, as well as traditional Democrats—with my Harvard degree, my work at the State Department, and my work with a Republican mayor in New York, my profile was totally different from any candidate Bergen County had ever seen—she said, 'You know, the Republican Party is having its annual dinner. Why don't you go and shake every hand you can find?'"

The menu was spaghetti that night in Upper Saddle River, enjoyed by five hundred Republicans, including Governor William Cahill.

"I got all dressed up in my suit and tie," Andy says, "brought my handout campaign literature, and walked in. Of course, nobody expected to see me there—it was not the practice of Democrats or Republicans to be interlopers at the other party's annual dinner. I walked from table to table, greeting every person, shaking hands whenever I could, leaving a piece of campaign literature, saying, 'I'm looking for Republican support.' The people were flummoxed that I was there."

For the most part, the encounter was polite; when diners began to chant "Out! Out! Out!" the event's organizers quieted them down. Andy exchanged no angry words, but he did hand a letter to the Bergen County GOP chairman. Stating that Andy considered his opponent, Kenneth Sherwood, to be the chairman's puppet, the letter challenged the chairman to a debate to discuss "the record of your authoritarian patronage-oriented misadministration of this county's government."

"I was there fifteen to twenty minutes before eventually the powers that be came over and told me that I had to leave, which I did, of course." says Andy. "On my way out, a top Republican freeholder came up to me and said, 'Maguire, you've got a golden pair of balls.'

"Meanwhile Gina had alerted the press—they're all standing outside waiting to see what's going to happen. As I walk out, cameras flash. It was front-page news in the *Record*. And an important community paper, the *Ridgewood News*, featured multiple photos of my visit. Talk about a creative idea that blasted my name all over the county! This was the kind of thing Gina knew how to do and how to think about."

On Election Day 1972, Richard Nixon outpolled George McGovern in Bergen County by 138,000 votes. Although all the Democratic candidates for freeholder also lost, they came closer. Andy's losing margin was the smallest of the four—under 10,000 votes among some 364,000 cast.

"Andy ran an excellent race," recalls Rob Esposito. "He was an unusually energetic and high-profile candidate for that level of office. He wasn't part of the old guard, he was something different. And, of course, he had those credentials. You put those credentials on the table, you're going to get noticed.

"Andy got noticed."

Andy had been defeated in his first run at elective office. But only months after beginning in Bergen County politics, he'd established himself as a force to be reckoned with.

THE BIG STAGE: Richard Nixon and Global Affairs

The Nixon administration carried out its domestic policy with competence, responsibility, and even, with the creation of the Environmental Protection Agency, some foresight.

But the truth is, Richard Nixon cared little about domestic affairs. When he looked in the mirror before shaving his infamous round-the-clock five o'clock shadow, he didn't see a man who would bring justice to the underprivileged or even prosperity to the middle class. He saw a historic actor on the world stage—Metternich, de Gaulle, Churchill. Nixon aspired to reorder great-power geopolitics—and before he was done, he would.

In 1968, American voters elected as president a man who claimed to have a plan to end the Vietnam War. That man was lying. But, in office, he did draw down America's participation in the war through a policy he called Vietnamization—a gradual transfer of the responsibility for fighting Vietnam's Communists from the Americans to the South Vietnamese. In mid-1969, American troops reached their peak number in Vietnam, 540,000; from that point the number rapidly decreased. Only about 24,000 US service members remained in January 1973 when the warring parties signed the Paris Peace Accords to end the conflict. Nixon had, indeed, ended America's war in Vietnam, if years later—and at a cost of incalculable additional carnage—than might have been the case had he not sabotaged Lyndon Johnson's peace talks in the fall of 1968.

The peace would not be durable; the North Vietnamese felt no obligation to keep their word to the "colonialist" power that had brought so much destruction to their country. In early 1975 the north and its southern allies launched an offensive against the Saigon regime; on April 30, Communist troops captured the south's capital city. As would have been the case twenty years earlier if not for US meddling, the country was unified under the government created by Vietnam's national hero, Ho Chi Minh, who had died in 1969. With all of Vietnam now in Communist hands, it was time for the dominoes to fall—except they didn't. Indonesia, the Philippines, South Korea, Japan, and Australia did not succumb to Marxist domination. Soviet-backed guerillas did not land on the shores of San Francisco. Fifty-eight thousand Americans and perhaps two million Vietnamese had lost their lives in the Vietnam War, and for what? "I will not be the first American president to lose a war," Nixon had pledged over and over again. But he *was* the first—along with six other presidents: Harry Truman, Dwight Eisenhower, John Kennedy, Lyndon Johnson, Richard Nixon, and even Gerald Ford all owned shares in America's humiliating defeat.

The road from 540,000 troops to the Paris Accords was not a straight one; while drawing down the US presence in Vietnam, Nixon also expanded the war's scope. In March 1969, not two months after his inauguration, he initiated a secret, savage bombing campaign aimed at disrupting Vietnamese Communist supply lines in the adjacent country of Cambodia. On April 30, 1970, with that bombing still underway, Nixon ordered US and South Vietnamese ground troops into Cambodia. This escalation—of a war that was supposed to be ending—inflamed American public opinion, causing cities and campuses to explode in protest. Ohio governor James Rhodes called in the National Guard to deal with demonstrations at Kent State University; on May 4, panicked guardsmen fired on the crowd, killing four students. Eleven days later, two students were killed under similar circumstances at Jackson State College in Mississippi.

If Nixon's treatment of Cambodia produced unfortunate consequences within the United States, his actions proved catastrophic for the people of Cambodia. The bombing and the invasion, added to US support for forcing out the country's longtime ruler, Prince Norodom Sihanouk, in favor of a client autocrat, Lon Nol, created instability that allowed the radical insurgents known as the Khmer Rouge to seize control of the country in 1975. During its four years in power, the Khmer Rouge would perpetrate a warped ideological genocide against its own people, slaughtering as many as two million Cambodians—out of a population of 7.8 million—before Vietnamese troops invaded to topple the regime in 1979.

Deaths of civilians seemed not to trouble Nixon or his chief foreign policy aide, Henry Kissinger, initially Nixon's national security advisor and de facto secretary of state, then secretary of state in name as well. Neither Nixon nor Kissinger ever expressed any regret for their role in bringing to power the murderous Khmer Rouge regime. Nor did the pair suffer pangs of conscience when, in 1973, they supported the military coup that deposed and killed Chile's duly elected socialist president,

Salvador Allende, and installed as leader Augusto Pinochet, a general whose iron hand would rule the country for seventeen years. "I don't see why we need to stand by and watch a country go communist due to the irresponsibility of its people," Kissinger said at the time. "The issues are much too important for the Chilean voters to be left to decide for themselves."

These interventions notwithstanding, to Nixon and Kissinger Chile, Cambodia, and even Vietnam were sideshows, important only insofar as they related to the balance of power among the major nations of the world. During his initial months in office, Nixon encouraged the leaders of the USSR to believe he was crazy—nuts enough to launch a nuclear attack for no good reason—and thus realize they had to negotiate with him. And soon, they did just that.

But Nixon's masterstroke came when he introduced a new factor into US-Soviet relations: the People's Republic of China. Since the success of Mao Zedong's Communist revolution in 1949, the United States had refused to establish diplomatic relations with mainland China, instead continuing to recognize as the country's legitimate government the regime Mao had displaced. In exile, General Chiang Kai-shek ruled only the island of Taiwan, which he persisted in calling the Republic of China. In July 1971, Nixon astonished the world by announcing that he would visit China within the following ten months. Nixon flew to Beijing in February 1972. American television networks covered the weeklong visit with breathless wonder: Not only was an American president touring the Great Wall and shaking hands with Mao, but it was *this* American president, the famous red-baiter of the 1950s.

US policy-makers had always considered "Red China" and the Soviet Union two giant components within an indivisible global Communist monolith. But Nixon and Kissinger perceived the tensions that lay beneath Moscow and Beijing's avowed solidarity. Nixon, with his personal history of tough talk about world communism, had the leeway to open relations with Mao's China that a Democratic president would not have enjoyed. Playing the "China card," Nixon reset the balance of power between the United States and the USSR. And he set in motion America's eventual recognition of the Beijing government, acceptance that made China's entry into the world community possible once Deng Xiaoping took the reins after Mao's death in 1976 and injected capitalism into the state-owned Chinese economy.

In May 1972, Nixon followed his triumphant visit to China with a trip to Moscow. There, he and Soviet leader Leonid Brezhnev signed a pair of arms control treaties that, for the first time, put limits on each superpower's nuclear arsenal. The treaties had been under negotiation for two and a half years.

The spectacular trip to China followed closely by the signings in Moscow presented to the American electorate the persona of Richard Nixon he had long coveted: World Statesman.

Up for reelection in November, Nixon could have trusted that identity to earn him an easy victory. But he didn't.

LANDSLIDE: Richard Nixon, George McGovern, and a Setback for American Liberalism

Americans in 1972 did not see a likable man in the White House—no one actually *liked* Richard Nixon—but they did see a competent leader, a "professional" president, as Henry Kissinger noted in one of that year's campaign ads.

But Nixon, whose incisive intelligence was matched by his gnawing insecurity, was not content to leave his reelection to the vagaries of public opinion—to paraphrase Kissinger, the issues were much too important for the American voters to be left to decide for themselves. The president decided to stack the deck.

The Democratic candidate Nixon most feared was Edmund Muskie, early in the year considered the front-runner for the nomination. A moderately liberal senator from Maine, Muskie had impressed the nation as Hubert Humphrey's running mate in 1968 by his intelligence and his dignified demeanor. Nixon preferred to face another leading candidate that year, George McGovern, a decidedly liberal senator from South Dakota.

The first nominating primary would take place in New Hampshire on March 7. A few weeks before, two Nixon aides, hired to carry out dirty tricks, sent a letter to the arch-conservative *Manchester Union-Leader*, the state's most influential newspaper. Muskie, the letter alleged, had laughed at an aide's use of the word *Canucks*, a derogatory epithet often used to describe Americans of French Canadian background—not an insignificant share of New Hampshire's population. The incident never happened, but the paper treated it as fact, publishing the letter along with an editorial stating, "We have always known Senator Muskie was a hypocrite, but we never expected to have it so clearly revealed."

Amidst falling snow, Muskie took to the steps of the newspaper's headquarters to angrily deny the charge and condemn the paper's right-wing publisher, William Loeb, as a "gutless coward" for publishing not only the letter but also a separate article containing baseless slander of Muskie's wife. Reporters from the *Washington Post* and *New York Times* reported that Muskie was in tears as he made his speech; Muskie denied crying, noting that melting snowflakes had been running down his face, and one of those reporters later confessed uncertainty as to whether the senator had shed tears. But the tears became the accepted truth: Bad enough that the normally contained politician had lost his temper, but crying in public? Muskie had committed an offense unforgivable within the era's standards of masculinity.

The questionable tears and the unquestionable flash of temper broke Muskie's candidacy. He did win the New Hampshire primary, but the margin did not meet pundits' expectations for a front-runner from a neighboring state, and he never recovered. He withdrew from the race in late April.

The beneficiary of Muskie's precipitous withdrawal was George McGovern, a senator from South Dakota known for liberal views and for his early and vocal opposition to the Vietnam War. After their loss in 1968, the Democratic Party created a commission, chaired by McGovern, to reform the process that had allowed Humphrey to win the nomination without contesting a single primary. The panel shifted control of delegate selection away from party bosses; the result was an increase in the number of state primaries. In 1972, McGovern and his campaign brilliantly worked the system he had created. After Muskie withdrew, McGovern's chief foe for the nomination was Humphrey, but the South Dakotan sealed the nomination with a victory in the California primary, the nation's last.

The liberal senator, who advocated amnesty for draft resisters exiled in Canada and was associated in the public mind with spoiled hippies and vacuous left-wing Hollywood celebrities, would in the best of circumstances be an underdog against an incumbent just off the plane from Beijing and Moscow. But errors at the Democratic convention in Miami Beach ended McGovern's general election campaign before it started.

First, because of embarrassing wrangling over the vice presidential slot, it was 3:00 a.m. eastern time when McGovern delivered his speech accepting the nomination. His most important opportunity to reach American voters came when those voters were in bed.

Even more calamitous was his choice of a running mate. McGovern offered the position to at least half a dozen of the nation's best-known Democratic senators; all of them, sensing sure electoral defeat, turned him down. McGovern and his team settled on a young senator from Missouri, Thomas Eagleton. Upon making the choice, the campaign staff asked Eagleton if there was anything in his past that might embarrass McGovern. Eagleton said there was not.

There was.

Two weeks after the convention adjourned, reports surfaced revealing that some years earlier the Missourian had undergone electroconvulsive therapy for depression. Amidst the furor, McGovern announced that he was "one thousand percent" behind his chosen nominee. But, bowing to the reality that voters would not place a man with Eagleton's history a heartbeat away from the presidency, McGovern soon asked his running mate to withdraw.

Again, McGovern asked virtually every prominent Democrat to join the ticket; no one wanted to go down with a sinking ship. He settled on Sargent Shriver, a brother-in-law to the Kennedys who had served as the first head of the Peace Corps but had never run for elective office. It didn't matter; the ticket was doomed.

McGovern's liberal critique of the nation didn't resonate with the electorate. The South Dakotan had made his name opposing America's war in Vietnam. But by Election Day 1972, not only were few Americans still engaged in that war but the draft was also scheduled to end within months. McGovern's most widely discussed domestic policy proposal was reform of the income tax to include a guaranteed income, starting with a grant of a thousand dollars to every American. Although similar to plans long proposed by conservative thinkers, the idea was easily distorted as a form of universal welfare only a far-left liberal would favor.

"Come home, America," McGovern said in speeches and commercials. But America felt at home with Nixon, the competent leader at home and master of the spectacular gesture abroad. Unable to connect with working- and middle-class voters, the South Dakotan lost even his home state. He won only Massachusetts and the District of Columbia, suffering the worst Electoral College defeat in US history to that point. The loss has been matched only once since, in 1984, when Walter Mondale captured just one state and the District in his defeat by Ronald Reagan.

McGovern's defeat left American liberals demoralized. To leaders of the Democratic Party in the years that followed—in fact, to the present day—the landslide loss in 1972 imparted a lesson for presidential politics: Don't nominate a liberal. Mondale's loss, as well as that of Michael Dukakis in 1988, reinforced that warning. The next two successful Democratic nominees, Jimmy Carter and Bill Clinton, came to the race with reputations as Southern moderates. Even Barack Obama appeared more pragmatist than progressive. McGovern's loss might have been inevitable, but the wipeout wasn't. McGovern's missteps, especially his botched selection of a running mate, torpedoed not only his candidacy but years of American liberalism itself.

And Richard Nixon? He'd been elected to a second term. He would serve less than half of it.

A FORMIDABLE FIELD, AN OUTSTANDING CAMPAIGN: The Democratic Primary for Congress, 1974

"When the freeholder race was over," says Andy, "I was primed to target the congressional race. And so, with the help of Werber and Breslin and the county Democratic Party generally, I lined up support." Werber, by this time the Bergen County Democratic chair, would remain officially neutral in the primary, but no one doubted where her sympathies lay. "I went around to every single Democratic town in every part of the district—thirty-four towns. I don't remember not getting the support of a single local potentate. I convinced people that I was something special and would make a real charge at the seat.

"It was the same with fundraising. I went around to all the reform-oriented Democrats in Bergen County and urged them to support my race. I ended up spending more than every candidate for Congress in the state that year, except for one Republican."

By January 31, 1974, when Andy announced his candidacy in a booster's living room, "surrounded by 75 people and a table of liquor and three platters of hors d'oeuvres," according to the *Record*, he'd lined up as many as two hundred endorsements from political and other leaders around the county.

One leader Andy approached was Arthur Lesemann. "Andy asked Art if he would run again," says Gina Glantz, "because Art deserved first dibs on the 1974 race. Fatefully, Art said no."

Glantz recalls the nation's mood in 1974. "The president was threatened with impeachment," she says. "Gas was scarce due to the Arab oil embargo, and the price was high. Russia asked for and got subsidies for its wheat, increasing the cost of bread at home." In 1972, the Soviet Union, facing back-to-back poor harvests, negotiated a deal to buy hundreds of millions of dollars' worth of American wheat. US negotiators, unaware of the Soviet shortfalls, wound up selling the wheat below market price. A worldwide grain shortage ensued, causing global food prices to rise by at least 30 percent. "Democratic candidates across the country lined up to take advantage. Expectations ran high most everywhere."

The seventh district of New Jersey, however, was not among those thought to be ripe for Democratic picking. In GOP hands since 1914, the seat was now occupied by William Widnall, born in 1906, the longest-serving member among House Republicans—and, if he won reelection, soon to be the longest-serving Republican in House history. Widnall was not unpopular. "Bill Widnall was a Rockefeller Republican," says Rob Esposito. "He was a gentleman, and actually was progressive on housing issues and other sorts of things. He was not a bad guy."

However, the redistricting that followed the 1970 census had changed the composition of the district, adding likely Democratic voters. Reapportionment plus the scandal afflicting Richard Nixon drew Democratic candidates to the race. "In years prior," says Esposito, "the party had to recruit somebody to run, because nobody wanted to do it. As we're moving into '74, people are thinking, 'Maybe I can pick off this old guy.'"

As Glantz notes, four candidates opposed Andy in the race to win the Democratic nomination, to be decided by a primary on June 4: "Ned Parsekian, a former state senator and the commissioner of motor vehicles, was best known and the favorite; Eddie Hynes was a popular state assemblyman from the most Democratic part of the district; Gill Job, the Bergen County surrogate and a newly minted Democrat hailed from a famous Republican family (his brother was the longtime elected sheriff); and Marge Wyngaarden was an activist and feminist pioneer. Andy was a failed candidate for Bergen County freeholder, a foreign policy expert, and a member of Mayor Lindsay's staff. His first mention in the press regarding the race was when the *New York Times* did a round-up of candidates and misspelled his name as 'McGuire.'"

Andy faced a formidable field. To win, he'd have to wage a superior campaign.

Andy's most beneficial decision was the hiring of his campaign manager. "My selection of Gina Glantz," he says, "who had never run a campaign before, was a brilliant choice. We were a terrific pair."

"Andy picked me as his campaign manager, a complete novice in the world of organized politics," says Glantz, who would go on to a long career in local, state, and national campaign management. "A graduate of Berkeley, I had gone door-to-door in support of the repeal of an (un-) fair housing ballot measure in California. In New York, while working in advertising, I had railed against injustice but done little to affect it. After being fired when my boss discovered I was pregnant—this was before antidiscrimination laws—I started a community newspaper, a monthly that did some good, in Brooklyn where I lived with my family. Ultimately, we moved to Ridgewood, New Jersey, a decent commute to Wall Street, where my husband worked. It was time for me to go back to work and I found a good, if not particularly fulfilling, job: promotions manager at the New York office of Alfred Dunhill of London.

"Andy took a chance on me, in part because of our friendship, in part because I understood communications and seemed to have a knack for organizing, and in part because, since I was new to the area, he could avoid the political pitfalls in picking one local activist over another. For me, it was easy to leave hawking cigars to try my hand at campaign management—after all Andy said I wouldn't have to do it full time.

"Not long after, my ever-tolerant husband began answering the phone, 'Hello, I don't know where she is' and told folks that a warm presence in bed was most likely our cat."

Despite Andy's assurances, Gina and other key operatives soon found they were engaged way more than full time. What became known as "Political Parents Without Partners" was organized as Gina's husband, Ron, Andy's wife, Meg—who contributed enormous amounts of work behind the scenes—and Kathy Rae, director of research and the mother of three youngsters, took turns arranging play groups that managed child care within the exigencies of a fiercely contested political campaign.

All generations were involved in Andy's campaign. Two senior Republicans, one a white shoe Wall Street lawyer, Howard O. Colgan Jr., the other the managing director of a local accounting firm, served as chair of the campaign and finance director, respectively. Bea O'Rourke, a radical Catholic with strong ties to religious communities and progressive organizations in Bergen County and statewide, enlisted her networks and was a major factor in establishing Andy's credibility in the primary campaign. Esposito mobilized and brilliantly managed scores of young volunteers. High schoolers Thom Kleiner and Art Feltman started with Andy's campaign and went on to elected office themselves, Kleiner in New York, Feltman in Connecticut. Amy Chapman joined the campaign while in middle school, embarking on a career that eventually led her to become political director for a national labor union. Some college graduates were volunteers before launching their own careers. Lionel Johnson became vice president and director of international government affairs for Citigroup, then served as Clinton's deputy assistant secretary at Treasury. Ted Hoff became a sought-after management consultant, was on the faculty at the Harvard Business School, then became vice president of IBM. A volunteer driver, David Nemtzow, obtained a Harvard MA in public policy, was president of the National Alliance to Save Energy, then a director in the Energy Department's Office of Energy Efficiency and Renewable Energy.

The antiwar movement and the 1972 McGovern campaign had created a supply of activists in Bergen County. "Even though McGovern lost by a landslide," says Esposito, "Andy had diehard people—like me. He had the peaceniks, he had the new guard. All of these people wanted change. We had momentum: We were new, we were bright, we were fresh. We had a picture-perfect candidate for the moment. Timing is everything in politics. The campaign was a sponge to get people involved."

One of those who got involved was a computer expert named Don Henry. "Don Henry walked into the headquarters and announced he could guarantee we would win," says Glantz. "It sounded like a good idea to me, so I listened with fascination as he described what computers could do. Computers at the time were gigantic machines sealed off in large, vacuum-packed warehouses. Immediately I put together an organizing strategy based on what computerized data and computer-generated materials could provide, which by today's standards will seem almost laughable. We produced voter lists and accompanying punch cards that came with addresses and precinct numbers along with information on whether the individual had voted in the D or R primary in the last election. We bundled the punch cards into sets of fifty and placed them in envelopes printed with the words, 'Have you turned in your cards today?' on the flap. Undoubtedly we became the first campaign to have a budget line for rubber bands to hold such cards together."

"Unlike everyone else," says Andy, "we were the only campaign who knew who our voters were. And on Election Day we knew whom to get to the polls and whom not to get to the polls."

"Maguire put together a campaign the likes of which Bergen County had never seen before," says Esposito, "in terms of emerging computer technologies and emerging direct-mail marketing and grassroots fundraising. And Andy being a full-time candidate. And fundraising and massive volunteer recruitment."

Glantz recalled two other invaluable individuals: "What computers did not do—or at least we didn't know how to use them to do it—was create targeting. In the Maguire campaign that was left to two remarkable men: Fred Waring, a college administrator, who could see things in numbers unlike anyone I have ever known, and Mike Rappoport, a college professor who became our pollster."

"This incredible set of people," Esposito says, "developed what, at the time, was a very sophisticated, computer-driven, analysis-driven, poll-driven primary race. Waring says, 'Looking at past primaries—and not just for Congress—I'm projecting the turnout in this primary will be twenty thousand, with 10 percent of the vote from Teaneck, 7 percent from Hackensack,' and so on. In other words, we analyzed the territory in terms of where the votes would be.

"And Maguire's burning up the phone, raising money in the morning every day. This started in March. He is out knocking on doors. He does what we call the 'neighborhood tour.' We target election districts where the homes are close together and where we think turnout will be high."

"We produced walk lists and devised a personal voter contact system that required a lot of energetic volunteers," says Glantz.

"The day before Andy goes on a neighborhood tour," says Esposito, "we have a flying squad of kids who lit-drop the homes with a flyer that says: 'Meet Andy Maguire, Democrat for Congress. He'll be at your door tomorrow.'

"The next day, there he is. And to make it go faster, we did this: We'd have five people with him. A tour director would stand in the middle of the road, directing Andy and the four others, two on each side of the street. The tour director tells a volunteer, 'Go to house 33.' The person knocks on house 33 and says, 'Hi, I'm a volunteer for Andy Maguire. Did you see the flyer yesterday? He's right over there. He wants to come say hello to you.' We'd hold the person at the door so that Andy was not constantly waiting."

"If someone was home Andy would stride up to introduce himself," says Glantz. "One of his major personal expenses was sneakers—he must have gone through dozens over the course of his campaigning. The volunteer would mark up the punch card to show the results of the conversation. If no one was home, the volunteer left a giant door hanger saying, 'Sorry I missed you' and personally signed by the candidate."

The volunteer would use the punch cards to record information about each voter. So, after a visit by the campaign, with or without Andy, the voter would receive a personalized letter, referring not only to the voter's name but also the issue he or she had cited as most important. "We created volunteer 'Chris,'" says Glantz, "as in 'My volunteer, Chris, told me that you care about education . . . ,' figuring that 'Chris' could be the man or the woman who was at the voter's door." The envelope would also contain a policy paper on the issue.

"We generated almost ten thousand letters in the primary," says Glantz, "and signed each one under the supervision of Andy's mom, who overcame her discomfort with the forgeries by making sure the signatures came close to his."

"Andy called for impeachment," says Glantz. "He talked about the lines at the gas station across from our headquarters, stressing the economic pressures folks were feeling."

"People felt there was too much inflation," Andy recalls, "too much dominance by banks and oil companies. Ordinary folks weren't getting a fair shake, the political system was tired, and wasn't delivering either in the county or in Congress."

"He never wavered on controversial social issues," says Glantz, "always stating clearly his opposition to the death penalty and his support of legalized abortion." *Roe v. Wade*, the Supreme Court case legalizing abortion, had been decided in January 1973. A year later, evangelical Protestants had not yet made the issue the rallying cry of their political movement, but the Catholic Church was vocal in its disapproval.

"No one worked harder," says Glantz, "cared more about the people he would serve, or knew more about the issues the new Congress would face."

Andy also used specific issues to attack specific opponents, and he didn't mince words. "Politics was kinder back in 1974," says Glantz, "so when we ran print ads against our primary opponents, the reaction from Bergen political leaders was cringeworthy, especially when we went after the best known of our opponents, Ned Parsekian, for refusing to release his tax returns."

"It doesn't really matter why Ned Parsekian is keeping his finances secret," read one Maguire print ad. "After two years of Watergate, isn't it about time that politicians played straight with the people?"

Andy also went after Gill Job, the recently converted Republican. A print ad noted that in 1960 Andy had worked for Kennedy, who was pictured in the ad, while Job had worked for Nixon. "Down through the years," the ad read, "Gill Job has supported Nixon high price, high profit policies and Nixon special interest candidates."

"As for the other two opponents," says Glantz, "state legislator Eddie Hynes was too nice to attack and Marge Wyngaarden too insignificant to pay attention to." Wyngaarden, who before entering the race had supported Andy, dropped out well before primary day and endorsed Parsekian.

Aware that Bergen County's Jewish population could be important in the primary, Andy emphasized his support of the Jackson-Vanik Amendment then before Congress. Eventually approved within a 1974 trade bill, the amendment, whose chief Senate sponsor was Andy's former employer, Henry "Scoop" Jackson, conditioned trade with the Soviet Union on the Kremlin's allowing Soviet Jews to emigrate. Andy recognized the issue's value to his campaign. "But," he says, "I also thought Jackson-Vanik made sense. I thought what the Soviet Union was doing to dissidents, including Jewish dissidents, was outrageous. Not allowing them to leave the country was outrageous. This was a matter of principle."

And there was the Bergen County Sewer Authority. Andy continued to agitate, attending public meetings and raising hell. "Who advised you to adopt these outrageous practices?" he asked the commissioners at one of the authority's monthly public sessions. At a freeholders meeting, Andy criticized a commissioner's reappointment to the Authority: "He has no expertise. These appalling errors in judgment may cost the county's taxpayers hundreds of thousands of dollars." Two weeks later, the Sewer Authority defended itself in a six-page letter addressed to Andy. The candidate had not only gotten under the skin of the commissioners but was also still drawing attention via an issue he owned.

While some of Ned Parsekian's positions lacked the clarity of Andy's—Parsekian qualified his endorsement of abortion choice and of Jackson-Vanik—the race did not turn on issues. "Maguire concedes that he and Parsekian, both liberals, probably differ little on issues," noted the *Record*. Indeed, while Andy put forth a host of detailed policy proposals, his appeal transcended them.

In 1960, John Kennedy had promised to "get the country moving again." Five years later John Lindsay's slogan had been "He is fresh and everyone else is tired." Andy's campaign looked to create around its candidate a similar aura. Andy exhorted voters to join him in a rejuvenation of good government: "Let's make the system work again," read his literature. Time after time, ordinary voters and elected officials referred to Andy as "tall," "energetic," "young," "attractive," someone who "campaigns with intensity." People cited his unique résumé—bare of service as a local elected official but rich with education and with experience in international affairs and urban administration. Andy turned his age and background from potential liabilities into decided assets: "Although I'm younger than Mr. Parsekian"—he was, by seventeen years—"I think I can offer the kind of expertise needed to tangle with issues on a national level."

"Andy Maguire is a native of Bergen County," his ads announced, "but he represents something new and exciting in Bergen County leadership."

The energy of the volunteers and the candidate, the savvy of the campaign manager, the expertise and creativity of all involved in the computerized operations seemed to be paying off.

"As election night approached," Glantz recalls, "there was a palpable sense of momentum and some confidence given that we had reached the ten thousand-plus 'Andy-identified' vote total that Fred Waring thought we needed to win. In fact, the final vote total for Andy was 11,274.

"Ultimately, Andy took an astounding 51.7 percent, more than double Senator Parsekian's total. Surrogate Job came in at 11 percent;

Assemblyman Hynes at 9 and Marge Wyngaarden at 2. Clearly, talking to, identifying, and getting out our voters was a winning formula."

"We put a great team together," says Andy, "and blew the others out. Everybody was astonished. And then people began to think, 'Maybe this guy could actually run a race against this venerable Republican, William Widnall. Which we then did. It was a miracle. Objectively speaking, it was a miracle."

"I woke up the next day exhilarated and fretting over a $17,000 campaign deficit," says Glantz. "Andy called early in the day to say that he had been transformed overnight. Folks he ran into, including the owner of the small store where he bought his daily newspaper, looked up and with deference said, 'Congressman . . .'

"We celebrated, took a week off, and then gathered to plan the general election."

DAILY DRUMBEAT: The Two Years of Watergate

The sabotage of Edmund Muskie was but one incident among an abundance of illegal and unethical actions undertaken by the thirty-seventh president of the United States and people working for him. Collectively, the effort had two major aims: to punish Nixon's perceived enemies and to ensure his reelection in 1972.

The act that gave the scandal its name—and bestowed on every subsequent American scandal, in or out of government, the suffix *-gate*—took place early in the morning on Saturday June 17, 1972, when five men broke into the headquarters of the Democratic National Committee, located in a Washington building complex named the Watergate. The burglars intended to photograph documents and add to the wiretaps installed in a previous, undetected break-in. But a night watchman noticed something amiss and called the police. Five burglars were arrested. One of them, James McCord, was identified as a security coordinator for Nixon's campaign, formally titled the Committee to Re-elect the President, known as CREEP to friend and foe alike.

The next day, the White House press secretary, Ron Ziegler, dismissed the incident as a "third-rate burglary" that meant nothing to the White House. But within a week, in the Oval Office, Richard Nixon and H. R. Haldeman, the White House chief of staff, discussed the payment of hush money to the defendants and the use of the CIA to keep the FBI off the case.

Between the break-in and Election Day, the press steadily unearthed more about the burglary and the burglars. Two diligent reporters at the *Washington Post*, Bob Woodward and Carl Bernstein, began producing a series of scoops that slowly exposed connections between CREEP and the burglars and hinted at a program of sabotage and subterfuge much larger than one overnight break-in. McGovern tried to make an issue of Nixon's corruption. However, since the reports had not yet implicated the White House, the Democrat could not convince voters to care about them.

But only months after Nixon's triumph at the polls, the scheme began to unravel. In a Washington courtroom, Judge John Sirica pressed the burglars for more information on the origins of the break-in. By April, White House counsel John Dean began cooperating with the Justice Department. The information he relayed to prosecutors implicated two of Nixon's top aides, Haldeman and domestic policy adviser John Ehrlichman. Hoping to protect his presidency, Nixon, at the end of April, reluctantly asked the two men to resign. They did, the same day Nixon fired Dean.

The shake-up did not protect Nixon; his troubles were just beginning. In May, the Justice Department appointed a special prosecutor to handle all Watergate-related matters: Archibald Cox, a law professor at Harvard.

Even worse for Nixon, from mid-May to mid-August a select Senate committee on Watergate conducted daily hearings, nationally televised live with a replay in the evenings. Chairing the committee was Sam Ervin. The North Carolina Democrat would prove an unlikely hero to liberals—he'd previously been known for his opposition to the civil rights movement. Ervin's repeated protestations that he was just a "country lawyer" masked his legal and political sophistication and his unwillingness to be lied to. The committee's vice chair, Senator Howard Baker, Republican of Tennessee, had been asked by Nixon to be his defender on the panel. Baker stood instead for the rule of law, asking over and over the most memorable question of the era: "What did the president know and when did he know it?"

The Ervin committee saw a parade of witnesses that included large and small players in the scandal. Among the senior government officials who appeared—and they all appeared—only John Dean told the truth, laying out in detail the cover-up and Nixon's role within it. In addition,

Dean revealed the existence of a White House "enemies list," which included politicians, reporters, a labor leader, and even actor Paul Newman. The idea, said Dean, was to "use the available federal machinery to screw our political enemies."

Amidst the committee's riveting daily television drama, the press exposed yet another nefarious activity of the Nixon administration. In 1971, Nixon had hired a group of men to use whatever means needed to combat leaks of classified information. The unit, self-labeled the White House Plumbers and supervised by some of the same people involved in the June burglary, broke into the office of a Beverly Hills psychiatrist to seek information on one of his patients, Daniel Ellsberg. A longtime national security hand, Ellsberg had copied the Pentagon Papers, an exhaustive study of US involvement in Vietnam commissioned by Robert McNamara, and leaked it to the *New York Times*.

Nixon might have been able to weather the scandal—the hearings pitted the testimony of John Dean against that of just about everyone else. But in July, White House aide Alexander Butterfield told the Ervin committee that the Oval Office was equipped with a taping system that recorded all the president's conversations there. Before the committee, Dean had quoted Nixon extensively; now there could be irrefutable corroboration.

Cox sought the tapes; Nixon refused to turn them over. One Saturday in October, Nixon ordered Attorney General Elliot Richardson to fire Cox; when Richardson refused, Nixon fired him. Nixon ordered Richardson's deputy, William Ruckelshaus, to fire Cox; when Ruckelshaus refused, Nixon fired *him*. Finally, the Justice Department's number-three, Solicitor General Robert Bork, gave Cox his pink slip. But the public outcry to the "Saturday Night Massacre" was so loud that Nixon had no choice but to appoint another special counsel. Leon Jaworski picked up where Cox had left off, giving Nixon no respite.

Of course, Nixon knew what was on the tapes. A superior lawyer, he also knew that the courts would most likely order the tapes turned over to Jaworski. His last best hope of remaining in office lay in his vice president, who would become president if Nixon were removed. Few in Washington believed Spiro Agnew qualified to be president—certainly no Democrat wanted this intemperate attack dog to occupy the Oval Office. But in early October Agnew resigned to avoid imprisonment over corruption charges unrelated to Watergate. Nixon's "impeachment insurance" had run out.

Agnew was replaced by Gerald Ford, nominated by Nixon under the Twenty-Fifth Amendment and confirmed by the Senate. A conservative from Grand Rapids, Michigan, Ford, the House minority leader, was no one's idea of a dynamic leader, but neither was he controversial. Democrats would have no compunction replacing Nixon with Ford.

In March 1974, as Andy was mounting his campaign in the congressional primary, Leon Jaworski sent to Judge Sirica's court an indictment charging seven close Nixon associates—including Haldeman, Ehrlichman, and John Mitchell, Nixon's former attorney general and 1972 campaign manager—with conspiracy to cover up the scandal.

In May, the House Judiciary Committee, chaired by Peter Rodino, a New Jersey Democrat, initiated an impeachment inquiry. At the end of June, Richard Nixon traveled to Moscow to sign another arms agreement. For a few days, he could once more be Nixon the statesman, not Nixon the apparent crime boss. But the visit did nothing to slow the scandal's inexorable progress toward his demise.

In July, the legal wrangling over the tapes ended with the Supreme Court's unanimous decision ordering Nixon to give the tapes to Jaworski. Days later, the House Judiciary Committee, on a bipartisan vote, approved three articles of impeachment.

On August 5, Nixon made public what would be known as the "smoking gun tape," which proved Nixon's involvement in the cover-up just days after the break-in. Three distinguished Republican legislators—Barry Goldwater of Arizona, plus the Republican leaders in the House and Senate—visited the White House to tell the president that he faced not only impeachment but also certain conviction in the Senate.

The president had only one option. On August 8, he announced his resignation, effective noon the next day. "The long national nightmare is over," now-President Ford told the American people after Nixon's departure. A month later, Ford, intent on not extending the nightmare via a lengthy trial of his disgraced predecessor, granted Nixon a full pardon for any federal crimes he might have committed.

The resignation of Richard Nixon did not cap public fury at the party of the president who had put the nation through the long, sickening ordeal, and the pardon only further inflamed that feeling. In November 1974, the electorate rendered its verdict, repudiating the Republicans by giving Democrats a net gain of forty-nine seats in the House and four in the Senate.

The consequences of Watergate did not end with Nixon's resignation or with the wave election that followed. By 1974, Americans knew they had been lied to—for years, by a series of presidents—about Vietnam. Now a president had lied, flagrantly and almost daily, about his own corruption and abuse of power. The daily drumbeat of disturbing revelations, laid bare by the press, the courts, and Congress, conditioned Americans to distrust their government and their presidents. Skepticism is healthy in a democracy, but cynicism, an inevitable consequence of Vietnam and Watergate, is corrosive. Nearly five decades after Richard Nixon's resignation, our body politic has still not recovered.

ENERGY, AGGRESSIVENESS, TENACITY: Winning Election to Congress

"The strategy for the general election mirrored that of the primary," says Gina Glantz. "Organize, organize, organize and let voters know that the incumbent had flaws. We met with volunteers every week to train them on canvassing. We worked hard to keep volunteers engaged. We had a Halloween party where Andy and I came as a donkey. I was in the rear, fearing the amusement of some if Andy were designated the 'ass.' I wrote *The Maguire Wire*, a regular newsletter regaling tales from the field, citing press, and updating canvassing progress. The force of volunteers created a genuine sense of how he valued and was valued by the community."

Andy started his general election campaign by breaking tradition. "Before me," he recalls, "people nominated in the June primary would take the summer off, doing nothing for the remaining three and a half weeks of June, all of July and August, and early September. The argument was: Voters take vacations. My response was that voters take vacations but for two-week periods and at different times, so you'd find an awful lot of voters around at every part of the summertime. It was excellent campaign time. We just did it, day after day. And we combined it with the top-grade computerized targeting and the excellent campaign literature."

"The general election was the primary writ large," says Esposito. "Same techniques. Andy was a door-to-door machine."

"I loved doing that," says Andy. "I went to ten thousand doors in every campaign I ran. I loved talking to people, particularly those who had a different view about X, Y, or Z. We'd stand on their porch, or sometimes they would invite me in, and we'd have a conversation.

"I remember talking to a guy on his porch who was very much against gun control. We talked through the whole thing—about sportsmen and hunting and assault rifles and registration and the legitimate uses of guns. We ended up on very good terms, because we came to a rough understanding on the issue. I regarded leadership as being both an advocate and an explainer. You had to connect with the individual person. And you had to listen.

"It was amazing how many people, after a short conversation, agreed that I could put a Maguire bumper sticker on their car. By the time the election came, there were bumper stickers all over the district."

"He was very, very good at door-to-door campaigning," says Marj Shultz, Andy's sister, who took off six weeks from law school to work on the campaign. "He would zip around, wearing running shoes with his suit. He emphasized moving fast.

"He had a great many strengths. He was articulate and knowledgeable about substance. Outgoing, not at all shy. Partly because of our background and upbringing, he was comfortable with people from the bottom rung to the top, of all races and religions. He was always a sort of tense individual, striving to achieve. That probably put some people off, but I think most voters were responsive to his having strong goals, strong morals, and strong views about what makes good government and about how to talk to people about their needs and concerns."

Marj worked primarily on small-dollar fundraising, teaming with her father, an experienced fundraiser from his work at the YMCA. "Andy's dad had all these shoeboxes of alphabetized records," says Rob Esposito. "He was always prospecting for donors. He did all the back work and the organizing of the fundraising and the finance committee." Plus, Andy's wife, Meg, a city planner in New York City and later Newark, provided the paycheck that made it possible for her husband to fundraise and campaign full-time.

Gina Glantz calls Andy's parents, Ruth and Bruce, jointly "the conscience of the campaign," but Bruce exerted the greater influence. "Bruce was a moral force in the campaign," says Esposito. "He played a significant role just in terms of his presence. Not because he was overbearing—he was not. And not because he tried to make you afraid because he was the candidate's father. It was just the nature of his character. Bruce Maguire was a big piece of the campaign's success."

"My dad attended most of the staff meetings," says Marj. "My mother played a more functional role I think at that point. Both she and my father were meticulous record keepers and would have had every donor's name and address and contact point and phone number in readily accessible files. My dad more than my mom was involved in discussing campaign strategy. Andy spent a lot of time talking things over with him."

Bruce and Ruth Maguire knew that Andy had been pointing toward this run for most of his life. "My dad very much wanted him to run," says Marj. "They were very proud of him and excited that he was running, but also worried: Would there be enough money? Would he be able to do it? Would he strike the right notes?"

Andy's positioning as a fresh alternative, effective during the primary, made even more sense in the general election as he tried to unseat William Widnall. Sixty-eight years old, a congressman since 1950, Widnall was an uninspiring speaker with visible health problems—his diabetes affected his gait.

"He'd been a fixture for decades," says Andy. "He had little presence in the district—he certainly wasn't out campaigning the way I was. He was not a dynamic figure by any means."

"I wouldn't say Widnall was not sharp," says Esposito, "but he had always looked at his seat as safe. Everyone had. He was a fine congressman, but he was a sleepy congressman. He wasn't active and out there, he wasn't engaging the public."

"Widnall, a nice enough guy, had no expectation whatsoever that he was in danger," says Andy. "He thought his reelection would be automatic, as it always had been. Nobody had ever gotten more than 43 percent of the vote against him."

Widnall was unprepared for a candidate like Andy. "I really don't see such a bleak prospect ahead," the incumbent told the *Record* in July. "Just because this guy comes in with a lot of energy and a lot of money, I'm not going to lie down and die." The newspaper did find some evidence that Widnall was taking the race seriously, among them his larger-than-usual campaign budget of $30–35,000 and his plan to spend the August congressional recess in the district instead of at his Connecticut vacation home.

"I think I know how to handle someone like him," Widnall quipped, "and I'm not going to tell you how."

But he didn't know how to handle someone like Andy. As the *Record* reported in October, Widnall tried to counter "the Maguire image of energy, aggressiveness and tenacity" with "an image of quiet dignity, of statesmanlike competence, of respected seniority."

But Widnall lacked the skill and the presence to make that image work. "Widnall was an embarrassment at the debates," says Esposito. "And he shuffled. You felt sorry for him."

At a debate in October, Widnall lost his composure under attacks by Andy and by independent candidate Milton Gralla, a businessman from Teaneck.

"Widnall," reported the *Record*, "threatened by a serious campaign battle after 25 virtually unchallenged years, reacted with uncharacteristic anger and defensiveness to accusations he hasn't revealed his financial assets and has accepted contributions from financiers."

The congressman could only sputter under the assault: "I resent the smears and innuendos directed at me," he said, before giving a disjointed account of his financial history—the value of his house, shares of IBM stock he'd inherited from his mother. Raising his voice, he added, "And I resent the insinuations being made continually that because I received contributions from bankers I, therefore, am a tool of their industry. Nobody ever bought me. No one buys my integrity."

The "quiet dignity" of the incumbent was tested away from the debates, as well. "We produced a number of what we euphemistically called 'comparison' pieces," says Glantz, "citing how the incumbent voted vs. how Andy would have voted. The congressman was so unnerved by the tactic that one day he called me directly to complain. I was polite—and delighted. I figured a call from him meant a lot of nervousness on his part."

Widnall could not match the star power Andy brought into the district. Two hopefuls for the 1976 presidential race, Scoop Jackson and Minnesota senator Walter Mondale, visited on Andy's behalf. A thirty-one-year-old senator from Delaware, Joe Biden, headlined a fundraiser and talked about the "malarkey" spoken by some of Andy's critics. Bill Bradley, a star forward for the New York Knickerbockers, winners of two recent NBA championships, and a man with political aspirations of his own, appeared. In September, he and Governor Brendan Byrne, a landslide victor the previous year, teamed up to face Andy and a local assemblyman, Albert Burstein, in a doubles tennis match at the Maywood Tennis Club. Burstein and Andy, whose campaign biography noted he'd been a tennis star at Ridgewood High, walloped their opponents in the half-hour match, after which the thirty-five-year-old candidate, forgetting he was no longer eighteen, tried to jump over the net. He "landed in an inelegant heap on the other side," the *Record* reported. Widnall saw the mishap as a symbol. "In an effort to show his exuberance and youth," the incumbent said, "he tried to jump over the tennis net and fell flat on his derriere. And that's what's going to happen in this campaign."

But Andy was more deft at campaigning than he was at jumping.

"Widnall was a great hedger," says Andy.

Andy defined his proposals in detail: "We must reduce the federal budget, reform the tax structure, enforce antitrust laws. The president should convene key labor and industrial leaders and put pressure on them to downturn costs voluntarily. If that does not work, I would favor a reinstitution of wage-price controls, across the board, including rents and interest rates."

Widnall made statements like "I recognize very deeply the opportunity and the obligation I have to make an input of some kind to make a change in these conditions affecting so many people adversely."

Andy hammered Widnall on the economy and charged that he had voted to let millionaires avoid paying income tax. Andy emphasized the issues of inflation and jobs. He talked about the price and supply of gasoline, arguing that the United States should put pressure on the oil-producing states of the Middle East: "We have things they want, like machinery, medicine. The Arabs should not be allowed to get away with extortion."

Andy supported full abortion rights; Widnall, although he would not commit to supporting a constitutional amendment outlawing abortion, received the endorsement of the county right-to-life organization.

Continuing to talk about Jackson-Vanik, Andy added criticism of the sale of subsidized wheat to the Soviet Union. Widnall had supported the deal. "The wheat issue was connected to what the Soviets were doing with dissidents and the people who wanted to leave," says Andy. "We needed to get tougher with these guys."

While Andy did see the wheat deal in the context of human rights and superpower geopolitics, he and his campaign made it an issue for the kitchen table. "The Russian Wheat deal," read a Maguire print ad. "It cut bread prices in Moscow. By raising bread prices here. . . . Andy Maguire says that the American family shouldn't be forced to subsidize Russian food shoppers."

Before Nixon resigned on August 8, Andy highlighted his and his opponent's stances on impeachment: Andy supported impeachment, unequivocally; Widnall said he'd support it if the vote from the Judiciary Committee was bipartisan. Curiously, after Nixon resigned, Watergate became less a topic of conversation than a backdrop. "You didn't need to talk about it," says Andy, "because there wasn't anything much to add to what had already happened. Of course, it worked in our favor." And in September, Ford's pardon of Nixon delivered the coup de grâce—to Widnall and to Republicans across the country. Americans were in no mood to see Richard Nixon walk away from his crimes.

The issues and the energy were all working in Andy's favor. So was the money: Andy raised $101,000 to Widnall's $38,000. Gralla, financing his own campaign, spent $25,000.

Widnall was outspent, out-organized, and out-hustled. His only remaining play was to paint Andy as a wild-eyed liberal. Fourteen years later, George H. W. Bush would turn *liberal,* a proud descriptor for millions of Americans, into an epithet so damning it could hardly be spoken—the "L-word," it would be called. The gambit didn't work in 1974 in Bergen County, however, because Andy didn't play along.

Widnall, the *Record* reported in July, "tells friends that he believes he can turn his opponent's zealous, kinetic, intense reformer image against him by telling the moderately conservative district that Maguire is a well-meaning but politically immature liberal."

"I am not a liberal," said Andy later in the campaign. "Unlike the classical liberals, I do not believe in the government having to be involved in regulating every activity across the board. In some cases, the government should get out of the regulatory business." At the October debate, challenged on union contributions to his campaign, Andy protested that he had received "more contributions from business executives than from labor." And it didn't hurt that a columnist for the *Ridgewood News* headlined his piece "The Democrat who Speaks Like a Republican."

While a less skillful candidate and campaign might have found an elite background a detriment in appealing to working-class voters, Andy & Co. made his résumé an advantage. "There wasn't a backlash about good credentials," Andy says. "They were respected. In addition to getting traditional Democratic votes—from blue-collar areas, from progressives—I was able to attract votes from the northern part of the county where people were better off and tended to be more independent and Republican." Andy did set out forthright positions on what have come to be called culture-war issues—abortion, capital punishment—but the focus of his campaign was bread and butter. People cared about taxes and inflation. And, in the wake of Watergate, they cared about honesty. In 1969 Mario Procaccino lost a campaign in which he'd labeled Lindsay a "limousine liberal." Widnall was no more successful against Andy.

"There were still plenty of thoughtful moderate Republicans," Andy says, "many of whom were my neighbors in Ridgewood. Howard O. Colgan, Jr., a white-shoe Wall Street lawyer and life-long Republican chaired my campaigns and hosted a fundraiser at his home with Senator Hubert Humphrey as the special guest. Moderate Republicans like these thought that despite Widnall's statements about me, I was just fine. They saw in me somebody they could work with."

"In the end," says Glantz, "Andy's message was compelling and his forthrightness appealing. But it was his boundless energy and personal contact that contributed most to his win. I imagined conservative voters thinking, 'Gee, he is so energetic and personable he couldn't possibly be as liberal as some claim.' There was no question: Andy Maguire wanted the job and would work incredibly hard to represent the people of the district.

"And so he did."

Andy prevailed with 49.9 percent of the vote to Widnall's 44 and Gralla's 6.

The Maguire campaign held its election-night celebration at the Hackensack Women's Club ballroom. The *Bergen Record* described the scene when victory had been assured:

> As Maguire appeared at the entrance, half the hall, crowded with more than 400 persons, started a deafening, primitive foot stomping and hand clapping rhythm.
>
> Teen-age girls gave some fair imitations of swoons. One clutched her friend and gasped, "Oh, I can't stand it. I just can't. I'm going to … Oh, my God!" Maguire, brushing past the girl, had patted her.

> For a while, Maguire was the Messiah, Mick Jagger, Don Quixote, and Socrates rolled into one for Bergen Country Democrats. And he loved it. "Oh, but it's good to win!" he shouted, grinning broadly. Within the next 10 minutes he would repeat the same joyous cry four times. "It's so good to win!"

"It was great," says Rob Esposito. "Great. Never anything like it since. Never. Maguire '74 campaign. Never anything like it since."

CHAPTER 6

DREAM JOB: Joining the House of Representatives

There are men of character in the U.S. Congress, both House and Senate. There are women of character, too. But the evidence for "character" needs to be something other than the iteration of the word itself.

—MARJORIE GARBER

"I was in constant motion," says Andy Maguire, describing his six years representing the Seventh Congressional District of New Jersey in the United States House of Representatives. "When I left the office to go to a committee meeting, I'd have a whole briefing pack. Plus, I always carried four-by-six cards around in my pocket with lists of all the things I was supposed to be working on and the calls I would make when I had a free thirty seconds.

"I wanted to get as much good stuff done as I could, in as many places as I could, as often as I could. I loved being there, working on multiple issues simultaneously, on and off my committees.

"I would spend hours in the office during evenings, writing personal notes, making phone calls. I remember walking home at ten or eleven p.m. to my place on Capitol Hill—walking across the front of the Capitol, all lit up, and thinking, 'This is amazing.'"

"I feel more alive than I ever have in my life," Andy told the *New York Times* late in his first term. "This place offers you everything that you would ever be willing to do times ten by way of challenge."

"That's how I felt," Andy says now. "It couldn't have been more galvanizing. It was such an exciting opportunity. For somebody coming from where I was coming from, who wanted to do what I wanted to do—to improve American lives and build a better world—it was miraculous."

WHO THE HELL ARE YOU?
The Freshmen Take On the Old Guard

The net change of forty-nine seats produced by the 1974 elections for the House understated the infusion of new blood into the body: In addition to the forty-nine Democrats, Andy among them, who had won their seats by defeating Republicans, another twenty-six replaced members of their own party. These seventy-five freshman Democrats were, on average, younger and more liberal than the colleagues they were joining, albeit no more diverse: Only four were women and only one was Black.

Recognizing the strength in their numbers, the class of 1974—the "Watergate babies," as they would come to be known—began to organize. Two fellow newcomers had begun to set up a class office, a place, as Andy says, to "obtain information and serve as kind of a nerve center." Andy and another two colleagues joined in. "We five classmates introduced the new members to the whole of Congress. Communications went out to everybody, we had a whole series of meetings, including a lot of time with leaders of reform efforts already there. Over the previous one or two Congresses, these members had put together a series of reforms they hoped to institute within the Democratic caucus."

The reformers in the previous Congress had not added up to a majority of Democrats; the new class changed the math. Those already-serving reformers "saw us as the conquering army they had been waiting for," says Tom Downey, a '74 class member from Long Island, New York. "We felt the whole world was watching."

Watergate, inflation, and lines at the gas pump had accounted for the election of so many Democrats in 1974; virtually none of the new members had made reform of congressional procedures an issue in their campaigns. But under the tutelage of the incumbent reformers, the freshmen identified a hierarchical system that, if not dismantled, would stifle them. Leadership allotted committee chairmanships by seniority, meaning that most of the important committees were led by Southern Democrats who had been in office for decades, remnants of the Democratic Party's now-fading domination of Dixie. These powerful, mostly conservative men expected first-term legislators to follow orders, speak when spoken to, and, above all, refrain from introducing legislation of any consequence.

"Even before they were sworn into office," says John Lawrence, a former House aide and onetime chief of staff to Speaker Nancy Pelosi, as well as the author of *The Class of '74: Congress after Watergate and the Roots of Partisanship*, "the freshmen started supporting changes that checked the power of more senior members and increased the power of newer members. The freshmen were full participants, making and remaking major policy from the day they arrived. Of course, senior members looked and said, 'Who the hell are you?'

"Freshmen weren't supposed to speak out in committees. There were even committees where they didn't get to ask a question until all the other members had asked all the questions they wanted. Not that the members asked their questions in order of seniority; no, when the guys in front of you had run out of every conceivable question they wanted to ask, only then would the freshmen be recognized.

"The new members said, 'Nope, we're changing the rules. We want to offer amendments. We want to manage our amendments on the floor.' This stuff was unheard of, but once this group arrived, they had the ability to enforce these changes within the caucus. I think they came in here with an inflated sense of how much they'd be able to accomplish, because they didn't necessarily understand the nuances of the political process. They came in feeling like, 'Hey, we've got the numbers, we've got the public behind us, we've got the rule changes to empower us—we're going to change the world.'"

After the reformers voted down the seniority system, the new class brought the current chairmen before them for interviews. The wet-behind-the-ears upstarts would sit in judgment as to whether the graybeards were worthy of keeping their jobs.

Four aged potentates lost their chairmanships in the new Congress. The most powerful to go fell first, but not to the reformers' axe. Wilbur Mills, the sixty-five-year-old Arkansan who chaired the Ways and Means Committee, where tax laws were written and committee assignments for all members were decided on, had served in the House since 1939. In October 1974 he was caught driving while intoxicated near the Washington Mall; one of his passengers, Annabel Battistella, a South American stripper known professionally as Fanne Foxe and the Argentine Firecracker, bolted from the car and into the nearby Tidal Basin. In November, the veteran legislator, drunk again, joined Ms. Foxe and her husband onstage at a Boston burlesque house. Mills resigned his chairmanship and entered detox.

The others who became former chairmen did nothing so colorful; the caucus simply decided they deserved the boot: Edward Hébert of Louisiana, seventy-three, a member of the House since 1941, who chaired the Armed Services Committee; William Poage of Texas, seventy-five, a member since 1937, chair of Agriculture; and Wright Patman, another Texan, eighty-one, in the House since 1929, who chaired Banking.

"The committee chairs had to be voted on," Andy recalls, "not just plugged in by seniority. That caused quite a bit of consternation among the old guard in Congress and among the media and the public. It was really our debut as a group that could deliver a lot of votes.

"The three chairmen we voted out were older Southerners, extremely conservative across the board on key issues—they had been holding up progress on civil rights or the environment or whatever people really cared about. Also, they were extremely autocratic in how they ran their committees. In the case of Patman, who was progressive on banking issues, he was getting to be senile. Poage was tied up with a variety of special interests.

"We had to make choices considering what was realistic and what wasn't. One factor was: Is there somebody we really like who is prepared to step up and be the new chair? In the case of Patman, it was a superb congressman from Wisconsin, Henry Reuss. For Agriculture there was Tom Foley, of Washington State, who later became Speaker.

"One of the chairs we didn't get rid of was the head of the Appropriations Committee, George Mahon, another long-serving Texan. When he spoke before the group, he brought in Louis Stokes, an African-American representative from Ohio. Mahon stands up there in front of the group, and he drapes his arm around Stokes, good ol' boy style.

"Poor Stokes, he was trapped. He had to say a few words about the chairman. It was a little cameo that was very revealing."

CLOSURE: Congress and the Fall of Saigon

"What I found," says John Lawrence of the Watergate class, "was that not a lot of them decided to run because of Watergate. Overwhelmingly they told me they ran because of Vietnam."

In December 1974, the People's Army of Vietnam—the fighting force of Communist North Vietnam—mounted an offensive that ended in early January with the capture of a South Vietnamese provincial capital. The operation's swift success, made possible by the crumbling of the south's defenses and the lack of an American response to that collapse, convinced North Vietnamese military planners to stage another offensive, this one aimed at unifying the country once and for all.

Beginning in March, the offensive encountered feeble opposition; before long, northern forces were taking one southern city after another. By the end of the month, the North Vietnamese occupied Da Nang, where, ten years earlier to the month, 3,500 fighters of the Ninth Marine Expeditionary Force had landed, marking the first insertion of US ground combat troops into the conflict.

South Vietnamese president Nguyen Van Thieu begged Washington for aid. On April 10, President Gerald Ford urged Congress to authorize an immediate infusion to the South Vietnamese. "I have received a full report from General Weyand," the president said, "whom I sent to Vietnam to assess the situation." Frederick Weyand was the last commander of US forces in Vietnam before the January 1973 peace treaty. "He advises that the current military situation is critical, but that South Vietnam is continuing to defend itself with the resources available. However, he feels that if there is to be any chance of success for their defense plan, South Vietnam needs urgently an additional $722 million in very specific military supplies from the United States."

Even though the Ford administration pitched the aid as a final appropriation—one last gesture, not to be repeated, to honor America's commitment to the people of a beleaguered democratic republic—Congress was having none of it. Even Arkansas Senator John McClellan, long one of the war's most consistent supporters, had given up on preserving an independent South Vietnam. "Further military aid," said the aging Democrat, "could merely prolong the conflict, and perhaps postpone, briefly, the inevitable—a Communist victory, a complete takeover."

The new members of the House of Representatives were equally unwilling to aid the sinking Saigon regime. To Andy, Ford's request showed that he had not learned the lessons of America's long, painful involvement in the struggle over Vietnam. "It's the same illusions, the same arguments, that were used ten years ago," Andy told the press. "It's very sad, because the president is not facing the facts, or acting in the real interests of the United States, or responding to the wishes of the American people that there be no further military aid in Southeast Asia."

Tom Downey, a member of the House Armed Services Committee, recalls a hearing on the aid package. "I got a chance to question General Weyand," says Downey. "I had a quote from an American general, Jack Graham, in 1950 and then one by the French commander at Dien Bien Phu, both saying that with additional money they could handle the Viet Minh." Led by Ho Chi Minh, the Viet Minh was the political and military organization that resisted French occupation, which effectively ended with the defeat of the French at Dien Bien Phu in 1954. "I read both quotes and I said, 'Do you know where these are from?' He said, 'That sounds like me.' I said, 'No, that was an American general in 1950 and the French commander at Dien Bien Phu.' Andy and Toby Moffett"—a freshman from Connecticut—"and I were strongly opposed to that aid. We worked collaboratively trying to make sure Congress didn't approve it."

In March 1965, US television viewers saw young women placing leis around the necks of the American Marines wading ashore in Da Nang. On April 30, 1975, as North Vietnamese troops captured Saigon, television cameras captured an exit that was not cordial but desperate. "We witnessed helicopters being pushed off the decks of aircraft carriers full of evacuees," says Downey. "We saw American soldiers punching people who were attempting to ascend a stairway to get into one of our helicopters atop the US embassy. These were not pretty sights. They were bitter vindication that the policy all along was wrong, but they were still an embarrassment to the country. And consider all the men and women on both sides who died.

"I was glad it was over."

When Saigon fell, the two halves of Vietnam were joined to create a single nation-state. The United States had invested 58,000 lives in its mission to keep Vietnam divided.

That mission had failed.

LUCKY BREAK: Onto the Commerce Committee

The new reforms made it easier for freshmen to land seats on the committees of their choice. Andy's choice was Commerce (formally the House Committee on Interstate and Foreign Commerce). "I had been involved deeply in foreign policy with the State Department and with my academic studies," he says, "but I felt that Congress had little to do with running American foreign policy. The main thing was, I wanted to dive into domestic issues. The Commerce Committee was the best place to do that."

Seeking the seat, Andy set about politicking. "Everybody in the world is out there brokering," he said to the *New York Times*, "and I'm brokering like mad, too. I've consulted with members of the New Jersey delegation, and I've talked with the Speaker and the majority leader. You talk to people, and you hope you leave them with a good impression."

A seat was open on Commerce. However, the chairman of the New Jersey delegation, Democrat Peter Rodino of Newark, gave the slot to another New Jersey freshman. Andy, much to his displeasure, was assigned to Banking.

"I was immediately deluged by every banker in New Jersey," he recalls. "There was something they were all in a twitch about—something called Regulation Q. I can't remember whether they had to have it or they wanted to get rid of it." Regulation Q, among its other restrictions, forbade banks from paying interest on checking accounts. "The banking industry wasn't where I wanted to spend a lot of time. True, the committee dealt not only with financial institutions but with housing, too. Nevertheless, Banking had little to do with the real guts of major domestic issues at that time."

Before January was up, however, a deus ex machina rescued Andy from the hated assignment. A conservative Oklahoma Democrat who sat on Commerce, aggrieved by the overthrow of the three conservative Democratic chairmen, became a Republican. As all the GOP seats on the committee were already filled, the apostate was assigned elsewhere. Andy was chosen by Democratic whip John Brademas to fill the vacant Democratic seat.

From this base, Andy would pursue the central theme of his time in Congress: protecting ordinary Americans from the cruelties of an unfettered marketplace.

AMERICA REASSURED: President Gerald Ford

Gerald Ford may not have been the most learned man ever to inhabit the White House, he may not have sparkled with the most charisma, he may not have engendered the most confidence in him among the nation's citizens. He may not have been the most inspiring orator, visionary thinker, or masterly operator in bending Washington to his will. But he was as well-suited to the role history conferred upon him as any president to hold the office. Hungover after the Nixon flameout, the country needed calming. The sight of Ford—respectable, uncomplicated, anything-but-dazzling good ol' Jerry Ford from Grand Rapids, Michigan—working at his desk, puffing on his pipe, scratching the ears of his golden retriever, reassured a nation hoping to recover from the trauma of the previous two years.

Not that the nation loved everything Ford did. Just a month after he took office his approval ratings tumbled in response to his pardon of his predecessor. But Ford had the humility to explain his reasoning under questioning at a hearing of the House Judiciary Committee. And as unpopular as the pardon was at the time, it spared the nation the spectacle of a former president in the dock for months if not years—an ordeal that would have prolonged the "long national nightmare" Ford aimed to end. Nevertheless, the pardon did reinforce the perception that a president could not be held accountable for his crimes, confirming Nixon's belief, as expressed to interviewer David Frost in 1977, that "when a president does it, that means it's not illegal." Ronald Reagan and George H. W. Bush paid no price for the Iran-Contra scandal, which revealed that they sanctioned a secret foreign policy carried out in violation of the express will of Congress. George W. Bush suffered no penalty for his approval of torture, in violation of international law and the rules of common humanity. And Donald Trump got away with a whole range of crimes—obstruction of justice, solicitation of a bribe, emoluments, interference in elections—before he led an attempted coup against the nation's constitutional order, a crime for which the Senate refused to hold him accountable. At this writing, two and a half years after Trump grudgingly vacated the White House, Merrick Garland's Department of Justice has finally brought charges against the former president. Perhaps a president will at last be brought to justice for grievous crimes committed against the nation's body politic.

Unfortunately for Ford, his image as an unpretentious Midwesterner came to be paired with the perception that he was an amiable bumbler. Ford was one of the most athletic men ever to occupy the White House—he declined offers to play in the National Football League after starring as a center and linebacker on the University of Michigan's football team that won consecutive national championships. But he earned a reputation as a world-class klutz after slipping down the last few steps of a rain-slicked metal staircase as he was exiting Air Force One in June 1975. A new television show, *Saturday Night Live*, premiered that autumn. One of its cast members, Chevy Chase, skilled in the art of the pratfall, regularly depicted the president falling down, spilling water on his suit, or talking into the wrong end of a telephone handset. Ford laughed at the jokes—he even posed with Chase as they pretended to trip—but he knew the damage it caused to his reputation. Ford's tendency toward malapropism—"I always watch the Detroit Tigers on the radio," "If Lincoln were alive today, he'd roll over in his grave"—didn't help, either.

Ford contributed to this image in matters of policy, too. Perhaps his most awkward misstep came in his campaign to fight inflation. Richard Nixon's price controls had not been able to tame inflation, which stood at 10.9 percent when Ford took office in August 1974 and ticked above 12 percent in that year's fourth quarter.

Speaking to a joint session of Congress on October 8, 1974, Ford called inflation "public enemy number one" and pointed to a button he was wearing on his lapel: WIN, it said. Somehow he didn't explain in the speech that the word was serving as an acronym for "Whip Inflation Now," a slogan coined the week before by a New York ad agency. He announced that he was enlisting Sylvia Porter, a well-known personal finance columnist, to help mobilize Americans to be "volunteer inflation fighters." In Kansas City a week later, addressing the annual convention of the Future Farmers of America—a speech the major television networks, at his request, broadcast live—he announced a series of steps that Americans could take to curb the scourge of rising prices. Some of the recommendations came from the Citizens Action Committee to Fight Inflation, headed by Porter, some had been sent in by ordinary citizens. Among Ford's advice to Americans:

- "Save as much as you can and watch your money grow."

- "Shop wisely, look for bargains, go for the lowest-cost item, and most importantly, brag about the fact that you are a bargain hunter."
- "Do it yourself. Plant WIN gardens."

Don't waste electricity, the president urged the public. Drive a bit more slowly. Wear warmer clothes so that you can turn down the heat in your home. Don't waste food—follow the stricture preached by Ford's father: "Clean up your plate before you get up from the table."

The president also requested that businesses and labor resist the temptation to raise prices and demand higher salaries.

The program quickly devolved into farce. The Citizens Action Committee asked for groups to be set up around the country, but the committee's chief business representative, the president of the Chamber of Commerce of the United States, declined to recommend that businesses cooperate. The White House commissioned Meredith Wilson, author of the beloved musical comedy *The Music Man*, to come up with an anti-inflation song. Titled "WIN!" the marchlike song had these lyrics:

Win! Win! Win!
We'll win together,
Win together, That's, the true American way, today.
Who needs inflation?
Not this nation.
Who's going to pass it by?
You are, and so am I.
Win together.
Lose? Never!
If you can win, so can I.

The song, the White House said after its submission, would be released "at the appropriate time."

The White House did convince the Penn State Nittany Lions to wear WIN buttons on their parkas on the sidelines at the Cotton Bowl on New Year's Day 1975. But while Ford wanted Americans to moderate their spending habits, businesses, as the *Times* reported, turned WIN into a sales pitch:

> In Bridgeport, Conn., "FriendFrost backs the President's program to Whip Inflation Now by going all out to help you save money on TV and appliances."

> Hans Home Furnishings, in Lincoln, Neb., displays Uncle Sam pointing his finger and admonishing customers to Whip Inflation Now by buying a new bedroom suite.
>
> "We're behind you Mr. President," says the Frontier Carpet Center in Phoenix, Ariz., in a newspaper ad. "President Ford says to seek out and buy bargains—here are the best carpet bargains in town."

"Thus," the *Times* said, "the message with most inflation advertising is quite clear: Buy now, buy more. And that is just the opposite of what government economists say is needed."

While inflation did slowly moderate in 1975, the WIN campaign became a subject of derision. In November 1974, White House Press Secretary Ron Nessen wore his WIN button upside down to read NIM—for "no immediate miracles," he quipped. By March 1976, Porter and her Citizens Advisory Board had had enough, abandoning the WIN buttons.

"As an acronym," she said, "it is dead and God bless it."

SEIZING THE MOMENT: A Focus on Energy

In 1975, in Congress and around the country, one topic was on everybody's mind: energy. With this issue, Andy would make his presence known in Washington.

"If you were an activist entering Congress," says John Lawrence, "and your support in your district had come about because of long lines at gas stations, energy was going to be at the top of your list. Many of the best and brightest in the class of '74 tried to get onto the Commerce Committee and onto the Energy Subcommittee or the Consumer Protection Subcommittee as quickly as they could." Andy sat on those two subcommittees, as well as on Oversight and Investigations. "Members saw energy as an area likely to be the subject of legislation. And they were correct."

As the international price of oil shot up in response to the 1973 Arab embargo—from $24 per barrel that November to $56 only two months later—US companies, operating under limits imposed by the Nixon price controls in 1971 and by an act of Congress in 1973, were forced to maintain lower prices. In January 1975, President Ford, influenced by oil lobbyists, members of Congress from oil-producing states, and an inclination to trust free markets, included in his State of the Union address a request that Congress lift those restraints.

With so many members of Congress representing the oil patch, Ford figured his proposal would meet little opposition. A handful of freshmen, however, were not compliant. Of that handful, none was more visible or effective than Andy.

"First of all," says Andy, explaining his thinking at the time, "the energy companies had gotten exactly what they wanted from Congress for decades. If the oil companies were allowed to triple the price today, they would triple it again tomorrow.

"Second, if you talked about the merits of the proposals that were then being made, there were Milton Friedman Chicago economist types saying, 'Yeah, let the price float. Never mind that OPEC just tripled the price gratuitously. It should be a free market.' But there was also a group of people, and I was one of them, who said, 'The energy sector is tantamount to a public utility. We need to treat it as such and continue to regulate it.'

"We worked on a proposal for gradual decontrol. Why? Because the third main point was that every price in the country on every item of goods was related to the price of oil. If you suddenly decontrolled the price of oil, which is what Ford and the Republicans wanted, and what Dingell wanted"—John Dingell, the veteran Michigan Democrat who chaired the Energy Subcommittee—"because he was a new chairman and he wanted to make an impression on the president of the United States, you would have had an economic catastrophe, particularly for people who could least afford an economic catastrophe.

"And fourth, you would be allowing OPEC, on the other side of the world, to dictate your price of oil.

"Those were the four reasons. It was outrageous."

Dead set against Ford's proposal, Andy was no happier with the product of a joint Senate-House energy task force formed by Speaker Carl Albert and headed by Representative Jim Wright, from Oklahoma and Texas, respectively. As far as Andy was concerned, the proposals of Ford and Wright were "Tweedledum and Tweedledee." Andy and Toby Moffett, his closest ally on the issue—and, throughout Andy's six years in Congress, on many issues—decided that to prevent immediate full decontrol of oil prices, they needed to create their own bill. Andy, Moffett, and three other freshmen opposing decontrol, all only a few months into their tenure, staged their own press conference and then began to assemble a majority for their side.

The freshmen had the fire, but they needed a veteran experienced in writing legislation. They found that veteran in Bob Eckhardt, a Democrat from Houston, Texas. Although previously allied with big oil, Eckhardt now parted with the industry, calling for decontrol of prices—but implemented gradually, to ease the shock to the economy. He composed an amendment to be added to the session's main energy bill.

Andy and Co. faced opposition from Dingell. The subcommittee chair wanted a bill, any bill, but only as long as it was one Ford would sign. "There's no way the president is going to sign what you guys are for," Dingell told the freshmen.

After a tie vote on the Eckhardt amendment in subcommittee, the measure went to the full committee, chaired by Harley Staggers of West Virginia. Andy and his allies lobbied their colleagues hard, winning the vote of Staggers, albeit no other support from him. When the vote was held, the outcome came down to a single member, Williamson Stuckey. The Georgia Democrat had promised his vote to Andy, but only if Andy needed it. "Bill," said Andy, kneeling by Stuckey's chair, "we need you. Now. This is the time. Now!" Stuckey, serving his fifth term, kept his promise to the representative who had barely begun his first.

Andy Maguire, freshman legislator, had managed to bring to the floor a bill opposed by his subcommittee chairman, the oil industry, the Speaker, and the president.

"I thought Ford was a really decent guy," says Andy. "He had been a perfectly respectable leader on the Republican side of the aisle. Nothing flashy, nothing particularly inspiring. Nothing with a longer view. There were certainly Republicans in the House who were far superior to him in ways that measure people. But a decent guy.

"In the case of oil policy, he became a tool for the oil companies, which is classic Republican stuff and classic Southern Democratic stuff. I don't think Ford had any particular thoughts about the economy or what was needed to advance American interests domestically."

Ford offered various compromises on oil pricing, but the House, including those New Jersey colleagues who had been publicly critical of Andy's activism, stood firm.

On October 30, 1975, Andy published an op-ed on the subject in the *Bergen Record*. Noting Ford's announced intention to veto the energy bill on its way to his desk, Andy wrote that Ford's plan "for a national oil policy consists of a single priority—doubling oil prices once again." Andy conceded that the assumption behind the administration's plan—that higher prices would encourage conservation and production—was "elegantly simple."

"Unfortunately," he went on, "things aren't that simple. Any conservation achieved would be at devastating cost." Small businesses would go under, unemployment would rise. "We would find ourselves back in the same kind of inflationary recession we are just barely beginning to escape in the aftermath of the price rises which followed the Arab boycott."

The stalemate ended when the major oil companies, rather than continue to agitate, opted for a quick resolution that would set pricing they could plan around. The bill, said the head of the Petroleum Industry Research Foundation, "is not a very good law, but the nation and the industry can live with it."

And so Congress passed the legislation, and so President Ford signed it.

"It's inconceivable," Andy said fifteen months later, "that the Energy Policy and Conservation Act of 1975 could have been passed into law but for the work that I and several others did—and I as a smacking new freshman."

There was more to the bill than pricing. The Energy Policy and Conservation Act of 1975 created the strategic oil reserve, implemented the first CAFE (corporate average fuel efficiency) standards regulating the miles vehicles traveled per gallon of gasoline, and set standards for energy efficiency of large appliances.

"They were huge, high-stakes battles," says Elgie Holstein, the staffer who served as Andy's in-office expert on energy. Holstein later served on Clinton's National Economic Council, as chief of staff to the secretary of energy, then as a director with the White House's Office of Management and Budget, where he oversaw US natural resources, energy, and nuclear energy programs. "Andy felt passionately that the OPEC nations were an economic and commodity cartel that was controlling the price and supply of the world's oil and, because of market linkages, affecting natural gas prices as well. He believed that America needed to develop energy independence.

"The widely held view was that America needed to reduce its dependence on imports, which had grown quite high." In 1970, the United States imported about forty million barrels of oil per month, or around one fifth of all oil consumed; in 1977, imported barrels per month averaged over 200 million, nearly half the total used. "The view also was that we needed to move quickly to develop alternative sources of energy because until we did, our economy would continue to be held hostage by the so-called Arab or OPEC cartel. Our international affairs would be distorted as well, because of the enormous transfer of wealth to the OPEC nations and the ways that transfer was changing the dynamics of our relationships in the Middle East.

"Within Congress and within the Commerce Committee, the fundamental debate took several forms, one of which was the huge and continuing battle over whether to maintain price controls on oil and gas and for how long and how they should be set. Another aspect was what we at that time called energy conservation and has come to be called energy efficiency. The Republicans and oil-state Democrats argued that we needed to produce more fuels. We needed to open more areas for oil and gas production, we needed to get rid of price controls so that companies would have more incentive to drill. And so, in many of the congressional debates Andy was involved in, that tension between conservation and production played out as a fundamental theme.

"There's no question that the major pieces of legislation Andy worked on at that time became the bedrock for many of the things that have become our nation's energy policy and, more recently, our climate policy. An example would be the CAFE standards. Andy Maguire was in the center of that difficult debate to put those standards into law. Also appliance efficiency standards—when you go to buy a new refrigerator or water heater, you see a range of choices, but those choices over the years have gradually moved to the more-and-more efficient end of the spectrum. You'll see a label on those appliances that tells you how much it's going to cost every year.

"Those changes, those rules, those programs were all put in place by Andy and his colleagues, starting on that committee, and they have saved enormous amounts of energy over the years, starting our economy down the path of developing energy-efficient products. There were failures, too. Andy tried to require a home energy audit prior to the sale of any house;

such audits did not become law in part because the real estate industry, as it always does, opposed anything they thought might impede sales.

"I remember writing some of the letters we would routinely send to constituents over Andy's signature. He would talk about the need for controlling energy prices to prevent these steep runups in gasoline and home heating costs. He would talk about the need for new conservation programs nationally, so that we would start to reduce our use of imported oil, and oil generally, and build on those conservation goals over time. That's exactly what has happened. And also, he talked about investing in new technologies that were non-polluting and did not rely on petroleum.

"This was the dawn of renewable energy, which was not widely economical at that point. But Andy understood that we needed to devote research and development efforts to develop those technologies. He was on the committee that created the US Department of Energy during the Carter administration in order to perform that energy R&D, as well as to give the US government something it had not had in a serious way, and that was lots of energy data so that decision-makers could better understand the energy sector.

"Those debates evolved over time, but the bases for today's energy debates were shaped in the big energy debates of the 1970s and in the big policy initiatives, many of which were enacted, some of which were not, with Andy's active participation."

RULE OF LAW: Gerald Ford's Department of Justice

Perhaps Gerald Ford's most beneficial contribution to the nation came via his attorney general.

The reputation of the United States Department of Justice had been battered during Watergate. Nixon's first attorney general, John Mitchell, spent time in prison after conviction on charges of conspiracy, perjury, and obstruction of justice for his role in the scandal. Mitchell was succeeded by his deputy, Richard Kleindienst. As deputy, Kleindienst was pressured by the Nixon White House to drop litigation against the conglomerate ITT; he not only didn't report the conduct but he also lied about it to Congress. As attorney general, he was told that the Watergate break-in had originated within the Nixon campaign; he ordered the investigation to proceed normally but did not otherwise act on the information he'd received. Nixon's third attorney general, Elliot Richardson, resigned rather than obeying the president's order to fire special Watergate prosecutor Archibald Cox. Nixon's fourth and final attorney general was William Saxbe, an Ohioan who left his Senate seat to take over the job in January 1974.

The Department of Justice had been further compromised by the efforts of Nixon and his aides to use the CIA to prevent the FBI—an agency of the department—from looking into the burglary. And the damage done to the FBI's reputation by Watergate was followed by revelations that poured out of a wide-ranging Senate investigation headed by Frank Church, Democrat of Idaho, that revealed massive and long-standing violations of Americans' constitutional rights by the FBI, as well as the National Security Agency and the CIA. The Church Committee added to what the press had begun to discover about the Bureau's decades of illegal investigation and harassment under J. Edgar Hoover, whose forty-eight-year tenure as director had ended only with his death in 1972.

When Saxbe retired as attorney general in early 1975, Ford looked for someone beyond reproach to scrub the department and restore it to public confidence. He found that Mr. Clean in Edward Levi, the president of the University of Chicago. Scrupulously nonpartisan, Levi had earned respect as one of the nation's premier legal scholars. During his nearly two years as the head of Justice, Levi instituted a series of consequential reforms: He ended the FBI's practice of targeting Americans for their political views and confined the CIA's intelligence gathering to foreign operations, as the law specified. He instituted two watchdog offices in the Department of Justice: the Office of Professional Responsibility, to investigate wrongdoing within the department, and the Office of Public Integrity, to address ethical violations across the federal government. "He brought two qualities to the job," Supreme Court Justice Antonin Scalia said years later, "a rare intellectuality and a level of integrity such as there could never be any doubt about his honesty, forthrightness, or truthfulness."

By the end of the Ford administration, Levi had repositioned the Department of Justice once more as the impartial defender of Americans' rights. "Mr. Levi," said Ted Kennedy at the time, "entered office under the most difficult and trying circumstances, yet he leaves a department once again characterized by integrity, intellectual honesty, and commitment to equal justice."

His successor under Jimmy Carter, Griffin Bell, followed up on Levi's actions with a set of rules designed to insulate the department from interference by the White House.

The rules held up until they met Donald Trump and William Barr.

RIGHTEOUS INDIGNATION: Fighting Market Manipulation to Keep New Jersey Warm

Closely related to Andy's work on oil were his efforts concerning natural gas.

During the winter of 1974–75, southern New Jersey faced a potential 35 percent shortage in its supply of gas, causing large employers to contemplate shutting down. South Jersey Gas, the local utility company, worked with utilities in the northern part of the state and elsewhere to procure sufficient supplies to keep the businesses open. But the company operating the pipeline that serviced the area warned of more severe shortages the following winter.

Two Democrats from the area called for hearings by the Commerce Committee's Oversight and Investigations Subcommittee, on which Andy sat. Subcommittee chair John Moss, of California, agreed to the request, convening the sessions in June 1975. At those and subsequent hearings, the committee found that large producers were withholding gas in order to influence pricing.

The companies were unhappy with what they could charge for their product—the federal government regulated the price of natural gas under legislation passed during the 1930s. Arguing that price restraints depressed production, the producers found a sympathetic ear in the Ford administration, which proposed lifting the curbs. Andy, to no one's surprise, became a leading congressional critic of Ford's intentions. Indeed, when public television's *Robert MacNeil Report*, precursor of today's *PBS NewsHour* and the unofficial arbiter of official Washington's pecking order, needed an opponent of deregulation to discuss the issue, it turned to the freshman representative from the Seventh District of New Jersey.

Gas producers had an incentive to withhold their product. "There were two markets for natural gas," explains Elgie Holstein, "one with a low price and one with a high price." Federal price controls applied only to gas sold across state lines; companies were free to determine the price of gas sold within the state where it had been extracted.

"The widespread belief by Andy and me and many other people," says Holstein, "was that gas producers, let's say in Oklahoma, were purposely not selling their gas into interstate commerce, not putting it in those big pipelines that go thousands of miles, because they didn't want the lower price. And so the assertion was that natural gas was being withheld from consumers in New Jersey and other places and diverted to intrastate markets to take advantage of the *higher* price. The oil industry didn't necessarily deny this. They said this was the market at work, that producers were going to sell their gas wherever they could get the best price, and so we needed to decontrol it."

In November, with another winter on its way, Andy chaired a field hearing of the subcommittee in Newark. Interrogating an attorney representing the Transcontinental Pipeline Corporation, the largest purveyor of gas to the Northeast, Andy said, "Is Transco delivering less to New Jersey than they are contractually supposed to?"

"Yes, and to other states as well," answered the lawyer. "We are not obligated except to the extent that the gas is available from the producer."

"What if I told you that there is gas not being produced that can be, and not being delivered that could be, and that, in part, the crisis is manufactured?"

"If these are producers on our line, I'm not aware of this."

Soon afterward, the subcommittee issued a report finding that Mobil Oil Corporation had delayed extraction of gas promised to New Jersey and Ohio in an attempt to wait for a better pricing scheme. "This is just the latest flagrant example of deliberate withholding," said Andy. "I am taking under consideration the possibility of taking Mobil to court on this. I want them to perform, to deliver." Andy accused not just Mobil but the entire industry of dishonesty. "When we subpoenaed the big companies' records, we found they were consistently underreporting their reserves by 35 to 40 percent. They had two sets of books. It seems to be an orchestrated campaign by producers to withhold gas from the public so price controls will be lifted."

Together with his Commerce comrade-in-arms Toby Moffett, Andy requested that the Congressional Research Service conduct a study of the effect of lifting price curbs. The study concluded that such a move would prove catastrophic to the US economy, boosting inflation, lowering the gross national product, and costing as many as 700,000 jobs.

In February 1976, the House narrowly defeated a bill that would lift all controls on natural gas. Once again, Andy's efforts had paid off for American consumers: He estimated that his victory would save US families some $220 per year.

That victory didn't cause Andy to drop the fight; he continued to take aim at gas producers for withholding supplies. At a field hearing he chaired in Hackensack in August, Andy excoriated Gulf Oil for not delivering all the gas called for in a contract with Public Service Electric & Gas, the utility serving much of northern New Jersey. "This is a specific, glaring failure to deliver large amounts of gas in this state," Andy said. "It is a first-class outrage against any notion of law or good faith or public interest."

In early 1978, it was Texaco's turn to face Andy's ire. As a result of a petition he filed, the Department of Energy forced the company to send gas to New Jersey and other northeastern states to compensate those states for gas Texaco had been withholding to power boilers at a Texas refinery. "I thought that was completely unacceptable," Andy said. "This is a great victory for us in the Northeast who have been victimized."

OPTIONS: Ford, Kissinger, and the Politics of the Cold War

Just as Lyndon Johnson, to his detriment, retained the national security team of the president he unexpectedly replaced, so too did Gerald Ford keep as his secretary of state Nixon's foreign policy guru, Henry Kissinger.

Once Saigon fell on April 30, 1975, Gerald Ford was the first president since the end of World War II to be unburdened by the struggle to fight communism in Vietnam. But the end of the war created other consequences. Looking to retain influence in the region after Vietnam's unification, Ford and Kissinger visited Indonesia on December 6, 1975. The country's anti-communist dictator, President Suharto, informed his visitors that he was about to send troops to occupy East Timor, a new nation whose left-leaning government had recently declared independence from Portuguese colonial rule. East Timor shared the island of Timor with West Timor, a province of Indonesia.

The Indonesian army depended heavily on arms supplied by the United States, but Congress had forbidden those weapons to be used except in defensive operations. Ford nonetheless told Suharto, "We will understand and will not press you on the issue." Kissinger's concern was that the operation end quickly so that he could more easily manage any controversy that arose in the United States over the invasion's obvious violation of the will of Congress.

The following day, after Ford and Kissinger had left Indonesia, Suharto launched what would turn out to be a savage war and occupation. Within two years, the Indonesian army would force nearly half of East Timor's population into relocation camps. Military action, disease, and starvation would take the lives of at least 100,000 East Timorese—perhaps more than twice that number.

In their memoirs, neither Ford nor Kissinger say anything of their assent to this crime against humanity.

For two years before Ford took office, diplomats from the Western democracies and from the Soviet Union and its allied nations had been holding negotiations in Helsinki, Finland, on a set of statements putting in writing principles of territorial integrity and human rights in Europe. Among the provisions of the Helsinki Accords, finalized in the summer of 1975, were those recognizing the boundaries among European nations as set at the end of the Second World War, promising non-intervention in any country's internal affairs, and calling for the honoring of human rights such as freedom of emigration and of the press. The Soviet bloc had been eager for the West's formal assent to its hegemony over Eastern Europe, but had only grudgingly agreed to endorse the human rights it regularly denied its citizens.

All of America's NATO allies planned to sign the accords at a summit meeting in August. When Ford announced his intention to do the same, he was met at home with a wave of opposition. Americans of Eastern European descent protested that the accords amounted to US acquiescence to Soviet domination of its nominally independent neighbors, such as Poland and Hungary, and of formerly independent nations, such as Latvia, Lithuania, and Estonia, that had been subsumed into the USSR. Critics also pointed out the obvious: The Soviet Union had no intention of abiding by the accords' declarations on human rights.

Acknowledging the validity of the opponents' positions, Ford said that the "Helsinki summit is linked with our overall policy of working to reduce East-West tensions and pursuing peace," and was only a "modest undertaking" compared to the US-USSR arms-control efforts he'd inherited from Nixon and continued to support. "If even a part of it succeeds, the lot of people in Eastern Europe will be that much better and the cause of freedom will advance at least that far.

"I saw an editorial the other day entitled, 'Jerry, Don't Go.' But I would rather read that than headlines all over Europe saying, 'United States Boycotts Peace Hopes.'

"So I am going, and I hope your support goes with me."

Seeing unanimous support for the Helsinki Accords within NATO, Ford had little option other than to sign them. But that same summer he faced a related problem for which he did have options but mismanaged them.

Aleksandr Solzhenitsyn, the dissident Russian novelist who had been expelled from the USSR the previous year, had recently taken up residence in the United States. In June, George Meany, the anti-Communist president of the AFL-CIO, invited the writer to speak at a dinner in Washington. At the dinner, Solzhenitsyn denounced détente. Helsinki, he said, amounted to Western nations' approving of "the slavery of their brother countries of the East, all the while believing they are strengthening the prospects for peace."

Solzhenitsyn wanted to take his argument directly to the president of the United States. Influential lawmakers, including Republican senator Jesse Helms, of North Carolina, and the cold war Democrat Scoop Jackson, urged Ford to host the writer at the White House, but Ford, unwilling to jeopardize détente, refused. Publicly, Ford claimed he was too busy to meet the writer. Privately, he saw Solzhenitsyn as a "goddamn horse's ass" interested in visiting the White House for publicity that would sell his books. Ford did not appreciate the significance and moral authority of the author of *The Gulag Archipelago*, the acclaimed masterpiece detailing the horrors endured by those sent to rot in any one of countless Soviet prison camps and labor colonies. Neither, evidently, did Henry Kissinger, who, at least one White House assistant implied, was behind Ford's decision. "With all due deference to Dr. Kissinger," the aide wrote in a memo to the president, "I believe that if détente is so fragile that it cannot stand a meeting with Solzhenitsyn, it will fall on some other account."

The US press slammed Ford, a president who, suggested the *New York Times*, didn't "know the difference between détente and appeasement." The editorial continued, "Perhaps not since he pardoned Richard Nixon has President Ford looked so badly in public as he has since his recent unplanned confrontation with Mr. Solzhenitsyn. It all began with a white lie that the President had no time for the most eloquent living Russian spokesman for freedom."

Recognizing the public relations debacle, Ford attempted to arrange an informal meeting at the White House with Solzhenitsyn. But the writer, replying through his biggest Washington booster, Jesse Helms, demanded a formal written invitation, which Ford would not extend.

Helsinki and Solzhenitsyn and détente would come back to bite Gerald Ford the following year, as voters were preparing to decide whether he merited another term as president.

IMPRESSING, ANNOYING, INSPIRING: Andy and the People of Congress

"The Three Musketeers," the *New York Times* called Long Island's Tom Downey, Connecticut's Toby Moffett, and New Jersey's Andy Maguire. The three freshmen quickly became best friends and trusted colleagues. At thirty-five upon entering the House, Andy was the eldest of the trio—Moffett was twenty-nine and Downey twenty-five, the constitutional minimum for House service. "These three liberal Democratic Representatives from districts within a 100-mile radius of the Empire State Building," said the *Times*, "revel in taking on formidable opponents, often in the name of protecting both country and consumer."

"We played basketball together in the House gym," says Downey. "There was a picture of us in one of the Sunday supplements of the *Times* showing the three of us running together. It worked for the paper that one of us was from Connecticut, the other from New York, and the third from New Jersey—a metropolitan-area thing. In fact, because we were all from the area, there was a certain kinship to begin with."

"We would constantly get calls in the office from his buddy Toby Moffett or his buddy Tom Downey," says David Dreyer, who worked in Andy's office answering constituent mail. "You'd hear basketballs being dribbled in the background. They'd say, 'This is Toby'—or 'This is Tom'—'Where is he?' They wanted to play ball and were waiting for him to get there."

"Andy had a good jump shot," says Downey, "he ran up and down the court. He was a very good athlete and he was a very, very good tennis player—much better than I was."

Even in the gym, Andy was known for being driven by his work. "When we would be playing basketball or paddleball in the late afternoon," he says, "I'd be called to the phone by my staff working on this, that, or something else. The joke about me in the gym was that I had a shoe phone." (*Get Smart*, a popular TV sitcom of the 1960s, centered on the exploits of a bumbling spy with a rotary-dial phone in his shoe.)

"Yes," says Downey, "I remember him leaving the game."

No less than his intellect and unusual background, Andy's industry distinguished him in Congress—no member worked harder. "After a reception or dinner, Andy would come back to the office at ten at night," says Michael Levin, a lawyer who joined Andy's staff in 1977. "I normally was not there at that hour. He would call me and say, 'Listen, I've got a problem with something. Can you help me?' Sometimes we would take care of it on the phone, sometimes I'd come back down to the office, and we would sit there until one or two in the morning, trading drafts until it was done."

Andy's devotion to duty set an example for his staff. "It was impossible" says Elgie Holstein, "to listen to Andy talk about the issues of the day without comprehending that his commitment to trying to improve the country was bone deep. We saw his passion for changing the political system—not just for bringing about change in policy but also for things like ethics in government and bringing vibrancy to the job of representative.

"No doubt, Andy could be an intimidating boss, especially for a guy like me just starting out. But I quickly learned that he respected anybody who did their homework and worked hard, which I and the other members of the staff certainly did. Andy could become frustrated and abrupt if you let him down, but you learned quickly to not let him down. I don't remember Andy ever yelling at me. I do remember him yelling in frustration sometimes, but never singling people out or dressing them down. He let you know if he was unhappy with your performance, but in so doing he raised everyone's level of performance. He once said to me, 'Look, I'm the kind of guy who's going to run with the ball you hand me.' What he meant by that, and what a young person like me and many of the staff treasured about working for him, was that if we did our work and made the case, Andy would run with that case. There were plenty of congressional staff people then—as there are now—whose bosses will wander off to a committee hearing or to the floor of the House and cast a vote, and the staff people aren't sure how these bosses are going to vote when they walk out the door. Or the representative will be in a hearing and pay no attention to the briefing memo that a staffer stayed up all night to prepare. That's the worst kind of experience for a staffer to have.

"On the other hand, if you're in your early twenties and you work for a member of Congress who tells you, 'I'm the kind of guy who runs with the ball you hand me,' it gives you an incredible sense of responsibility. Which I took to heart and was deeply grateful for."

"A congressman makes waves," read the headline over the *Bergen Record*'s long profile of Andy just two months after he'd entered Congress. "Maguire," the article noted, "is regarded in Washington as one of the dozen potential standouts of this year's highly acclaimed freshman Democratic House class of 75 members. He's regarded among the brightest of the freshmen, certainly one of the most ambitious, and also as an awesomely hard worker."

Several times during Andy's tenure in Congress, the *Record* and even the *New York Times* reported on his dedication to the job and to the causes he chose. "I've never seen him waffle on an issue," said a senior House staffer to the *Record* in 1976. "He's completely consistent. You may not agree with him, but you can never accuse him of talking out of both sides of his mouth. He adheres to that solid liberal-consumer position. I wish to hell we had a hundred like him around here."

Each of these appraisals, however, noted that Andy was not universally popular among his colleagues—he was thought by some to be brash, arrogant, abrasive, disrespectful of his elders and of House traditions. Longer-serving members of the New Jersey delegation provided the most critical reviews. Andy, said the *Record*'s March 1975 profile, has been "marked as a man in a hurry, who has little instinct for the feelings of others as he works feverishly to win a point or pass a bill. Overall, veteran members from his own state regard him with suspicion. They grumble that he's too abrasive, too pushy for his own good.

"'He's like the kid in school trying to get all As, who doesn't care what he does to get them,' said one New Jersey Democrat."

A veteran Republican seemed to suggest that Andy needed to smile more: "I'm not sure he has yet developed that political flair, that knack to make others like him that is so necessary to get ahead."

Speaking today, Andy is familiar with all the complaints. "Sometimes," he says, "the judgments of 'many veterans of the House' boiled down to comments made by a single member of the New Jersey delegation. For example, Joe Minish." Joseph Minish, a former labor leader, represented parts of Essex County, including a section of Newark, from 1963 to 1985. "'Arrogant and abrasive' came from him. Stuff like that spreads like wildfire. Minish was on my case from day one. He didn't like any of this new member stuff. He didn't like any of the activism on issues. He was an old-timey Democrat, totally lacking in imagination or initiative or creativity. He and a pair of like-minded colleagues would sit in the first or second row of the House chamber, and when something interesting was developing in debate, they would call out, 'Vote! Vote!'—interrupting regular procedure. As best I can recall, this was Minish's only discernible contribution to the work of the House.

"I think the dislike for me very much originated among the troglodytes in the New Jersey delegation. Another one was Henry Helstoski, in the district neighboring mine. Also, Bob Roe on the other side of my district. They were all cronies. I'm sure they were nonplussed to the max that this whippersnapper suddenly emerged in North Jersey, in a district where a Democrat was never supposed to be electable, and was causing all this uproar.

"Mind you, that dynamic was not the general rule in my relationships with my colleagues in Congress and the New Jersey delegation as a whole. I had considerable regard for and positive interactions on policy with Peter Rodino (as New Jersey dean, a bellwether for the delegation), Frank Thompson, Jim Howard, Republican Matt Rinaldo, and my incoming classmates Helen Meyner, Bill Hughes, Jim Florio, and Republican Millicent Fenwick. I worked closely with Senators Pete Williams and Clifford Case (a Republican), and later with Bill Bradley when he joined the Senate. I felt I had good reason to think the respect among all of this group was mutual.

"I built coalitions—newer members, older members, Democrats, Republicans—to get done what I, and often they, thought was important. Often, we succeeded."

At the time, Andy freely admitted he was not going to be voted prom king. "I'm not the best-liked guy in the Jersey delegation in any vote of my colleagues," he told the *Times* in 1977. "But I've been a very effective member of the delegation." Andy pointed to his accomplishments on energy and other issues, while confessing that he eschewed the "old boy, slap-on-the-back syndrome." The author noted Andy's "disdain for what he feels is an unwarranted attachment of Congressmen for cronyism, swapping favors, protecting each other's flanks and respecting seniority."

"I don't play the old game," Andy said, "I have a different set of attitudes about what's important."

A Republican colleague, a friend and frequent ally of Andy's, weighed in: "Rep. Millicent Fenwick, the Somerset County Republican who at times speaks as the delegation's unofficial den mother, says that aside from a few longtime feuds, most of the New Jersey congressmen are friends. But not Maguire.

"'He's too busy to be cozy,' she says."

Andy started impressing/annoying his colleagues as soon as he entered Congress. During his brief stint on the Banking Committee—in his first three weeks in office—he managed to irritate the panel's veteran members by proposing that Congress require, not merely recommend, that the supposedly apolitical Federal Reserve Board lower interest rates. Despite the veterans' scorn, Andy's proposal did stir enough interest to make it past an initial vote before the committee killed it. And at a committee hearing, he brought distress to the hyper-dignified chairman of the Fed, Arthur Burns, by challenging his oft-stated contention that any move by Congress to improve the economy was "political":

> The suspicion occurs to me that [your] distinction [between political and nonpolitical] may be somewhat artificial, and may, in fact, go this way: That what you and the Fed do, and want to do, and want to continue to do, determines what, in your mind, is not political; and what you do not want to do determines in your mind what you then label as political.

Certainly, the chairman of the Fed must have realized that part of his job involved dealing with aggressive questioning from members of Congress. But so accusatory? From a freshman? In Congress for less than a month? Hadn't legendary Speaker Sam Rayburn advised new members, "If you want to get along, go along?"

Today Andy suggests that he might have tried harder to develop friendships with more of his New Jersey colleagues. In the March 1975 profile, the *Record* tells the story of one New Jersey congressman who was "infuriated" by his new colleague. The unnamed representative "carried around in his wallet a newspaper clipping in which Maguire was reported as saying that freshmen members before this year were expected to sit around quietly for a decade before they could attain influence.

"'He thinks I just sat around here for ten years,' the congressman said angrily, shaking the clip in his right hand. 'Wait till I see him; I'll confront him with this right between the eyes.'"

"Minish," says Andy, identifying the unidentified congressman who never did confront Andy with the clip, right between the eyes or anywhere else.

"Did I need to say that about sitting around for ten years?" says Andy today. "No, I didn't. If I were to do it again, I wouldn't say it. That sort of thing is unnecessary. What you do is, you buckle down and you work. You find your allies and you get the job done.

"I was part of the Watergate class, which was active in a way that was unprecedented. We did have—and certainly the press understood it—a lot of troglodytes in the Congress, some heading important committees. Sometimes you just had to say it."

If one word among the many applied to Andy annoyed him and his staff during his congressional tenure—and does to this day—it was "abrasive." Reporters included the word in a number of profiles throughout Andy's time in the House.

"What 'abrasive' translates into," says Andy, "is this: 'Andy has an advanced position on X, which he would really like other people to join him in. And then off Andy goes, with or without me.'

"I would be described that way no matter how big a coalition of votes I put together to make sure we got something passed. The people who don't like activists, who don't like Harvard PhDs, who don't like anyone who thinks he or she has a good idea about a direction we need to take as opposed to just following along—such people will describe the ones they dislike as abrasive, even if personally someone is not abrasive."

"What some people called abrasive," says Elgie Holstein, "a term that bugged me then and now, had a lot to do with the fact that Andy was *relentless*, which is a far better word to describe his behavior.

"Relentlessness. Enormous focus on the things he was passionate about.

"The fact of the matter is that, then and now, if you look at the collection of people who manage to get elected to the United States Congress, there's a dizzying array of personality types. Yes, there's this caricature of the baby-kissing backslapper. But the fact is that there are shy ones, there are ambitious ones, there are aggressive ones. There are dumb ones and brilliant ones, funny ones and serious ones. There are hyper-partisans and there are bridgebuilders. Andy was a young guy with a strong intellect and a super-strong commitment on the issues who was finding his way through an institution that puts a premium on getting along, because a certain amount of that is required. But I never saw Andy pick a fight with anybody. He never said a word in my presence about somebody being out to get somebody else or about any vendetta against anybody. Never. He disagreed with members, sometimes passionately, and there were some members he liked better than others.

"'Abrasive,' a term that used to crop up back then and infuriate all of us, tends to be used by people whose image of what a congressman should be has to do with a comic-book backslapping version of what a congressman should actually be like."

"Part of that image," says David Dreyer, "is because he was in the class of '74 that overthrew the patriarchy. The patriarchy doesn't like that. No, he didn't have a good bedside manner in dealing with people. He was the young man in a hurry who felt a sense of urgency, which I found admirable. He's one of the most intense people I've ever met. He sure got a lot done in the three terms that he served, and if he didn't win popularity contests among the go-along-to-get-along crowd, so be it."

Andy was well aware of his reputation. Michael Levin, recalling his job interview with the congressman and his chief of staff, Bob Kerr, says, "The first thing Andy said to me was, 'I hear you're too arrogant to be effective.' And I said, 'That's what I hear about you.' Everybody burst into laughter, and I was hired."

"By the way," says Andy, "all of my friends and all of my critics in the New Jersey delegation voted with me on the big issue that first year, energy policy and oil pricing, despite the fact that some of them considered me pushy. Every single one of them, including the one who complained about me the most, Joe Minish. The same was true on many other issues I championed. What's wrong with that?

"Joe Minish never said five words to me on any subject. I was never abrasive to Joe Minish. He chose to be abraded."

"Peers of Andy," says Holstein, "Toby Moffett or Tom Downey, might joke that Andy was not the coolest guy to take to a bar. But I don't think they would have changed the relationship they had with him."

"When someone doesn't agree with you," says Downey, "and holds strong convictions, 'abrasive' is usually a substitute for your not liking that the person disagrees with you.

"There *were* times when Andy could be difficult to deal with. I'll give you an example. We started a caucus of members—it was Andy's idea—called the Bipartisan Monitoring Group on South Africa."

"I created this caucus," says Andy, "with people like Tom Downey and other Democrats and some Republicans, to highlight what was going on under apartheid in South Africa. The South African authorities were torturing and killing people. We wanted to call attention to that, in Congress and for the public. This group was very much modeled on the monitoring that was going on of Refuseniks in the Soviet Union, highlighting the treatment of dissidents and of Jews who wanted to emigrate. The immediate occasion for creating this group was the murder in 1977 of Steven Biko, the Black consciousness leader who was hauled around by the police for countless miles naked and beaten to a pulp before he died in custody."

The following year, Andy went to South Africa. "The South African government couldn't prevent me from coming," he recalls, "because I'd been invited by the South African Institute of International Relations, which was linked with the World Peace Foundation in Boston, which was in turn headed by Robert Rotberg, my thesis adviser at Harvard."

During his two-week tour of the apartheid nation, Andy met with activists who confirmed reports of murder, torture, and unjust imprisonment. On behalf of the NAACP, he presented a humanitarian award in memory of Biko; Biko's family did not accept the award, instead asking that it be presented to another Black activist, then in prison.

"While I was there," Andy says, "I worked with a South African lawyer on all of the political detentions. We went to a prison, where I asked to be admitted to talk to a political prisoner and was refused. I gave a scathing press conference at the airport before I left the country, which made headlines in both Black and white media."

Speaking to the American press upon his return, Andy advocated for the gradual withdrawal from South Africa by US corporations operating there "so the government can see the consequences." Continuing, Andy said, "This government is not a democracy. It is in fact a police state with respect to nonwhite people. I left South Africa enormously discouraged about the future of the country. It is on a suicidal course."

Even before his trip to South Africa, Andy and his colleagues in Congress caught the attention of the apartheid regime. "Downey and I really drove the thing," says Andy. "We organized a bipartisan group to call on the South African ambassador to the United States. We took out a special order on the House floor where a dozen members spoke or entered prepared remarks about the killing of Steve Biko and the brutalization of black African citizens. Eventually a delegation of very senior South African officials asked to meet with the monitoring group and of course we said yes." The country's foreign minister, Pik Botha, had arrived in the United States; he, accompanied by other officials from the embassy and from Pretoria, met with Andy & Co. "I think they thought that we didn't know as much as we did about what was actually going on in South Africa and that they would kind of bring us to a better understanding of why things were the way they were. But the meeting broke up when they walked out because we weren't prepared to talk to them about anything other than the oppression under apartheid."

"In the meeting," Downey recalls, "Andy verbally leveled Botha. Andy brought up the sins of apartheid, the history of the apartheid regime, and the fact that its current manifestation was sitting before him. Andy wasn't going to give Botha any quarter. It was clear to me that this guy had never been spoken to like this—not by another white person, at least." The last straw came when Andy pointed out that the South African government had been in Southwest Africa, illegally, for fifty years, applying apartheid even beyond its own borders. At that, the South African delegation stood up.

"Botha said, 'I'm insulted,'" notes Downey. "Andy looked at him and said, 'Everything you've done is insulting.'

"It was fabulous! You could say Andy was being *abrasive*. Yes, he was—to somebody who richly deserved it."

SOMEBODY'S GOT TO DO SOMETHING: Making the Case against Bob Sikes

Bergen Record, August 25, 1978: "From the start, the 39-year-old Ridgewood Democrat made it clear he was not going to follow the usual route to congressional success—by shutting up, listening to the party leadership, voting like a good scout, and waiting his turn for power."

If any action typified Andy's determination to speak out of turn—from the start—it was his leadership in bringing down a corrupt colleague, Robert Sikes, the eighteen-term Florida Democrat who chaired the powerful Military Construction Subcommittee of the Appropriations Committee, which handed out largesse in the form of defense contracts to many members' districts.

In mid-1975 the good government group Common Cause sent damning information on Sikes to House leadership, to the House ethics committee, and eventually to all 435 members. The charges alleged that:

- In 1961 Sikes sponsored legislation to develop a parcel of Florida land he partly owned—that bill, added to another he'd introduced in 1948, enabled him to turn a $58,000 investment into a $442,000 profit.
- In 1974 he lobbied and voted for a $73 million contract for an aircraft company in which he owned a thousand shares.
- He lobbied for the siting at Pensacola Air Station of a private bank in which he held stock.
- He served on the board of a company selling life insurance to service members through the Non Commissioned Officers Association; the arrangement allowed that company to evade regulations restricting the work of insurance salesmen on military bases.

Neither the ethics committee nor the House leadership responded to Common Cause; only four House members answered, all declining to take action. Andy was not one of the four—he apparently didn't see the letter—but on March 28, 1976, *60 Minutes*, the CBS News investigative television show, reported on the allegations.

"I was at home in New Jersey watching *60 Minutes* one night," Andy recalls. "Common Cause had done an investigation. It was the most classic example possible of a guy in a powerful position legislating items that translated immediately into his personal financial gain. It was outrageous. My reaction sitting there was, 'My God, this is unbelievable. Somebody's got to do something about it.' And then I said to myself, 'Well, you're a member of Congress. *You* do something about it.'

"It was that simple."

Despite the charges, Sikes seemed untouchable. Members of Congress did not want to cross the man able to shovel Pentagon money into their districts. Members of the New Jersey delegation were grateful to Sikes for his help in ending an Army plan to close Fort Dix and other bases located in the state. "He's our protector," one New Jersey member said of the powerful Floridian.

The brash freshman from Ridgewood was undeterred. In April, he wrote a letter to the House ethics committee (formally the House Committee on Standards and Conduct) calling for an investigation of Sikes. Forty-four members co-signed the letter—none of them from New Jersey.

"The trick about the ethics committee," says Andy, "was that they never did anything, because the only way they could open an investigation was at the request of a member. What Common Cause had to say didn't matter—there would be some press coverage, but the ethics committee would not be triggered. The only way to trigger it was to have a member file an action. Formally. On paper.

"Which I did."

House leadership was not amused. Majority Leader Tip O'Neill made known his opinion that, according to the *Record*, "pursuing such an investigation is not the best way to win friends on Capitol Hill."

But Andy pressed on, as did the committee. In July, the body's findings caused the House to vote 381–3 to reprimand Sikes.

That result, however, didn't satisfy Andy, who argued that the job wouldn't be done until Sikes lost his chairmanship. In January 1977, as the Democratic caucus was selecting committee chairs for the Ninety-Fifth Congress, Andy pushed for Sikes to be demoted.

Although O'Neill, newly elected Speaker, said Sikes had been "punished enough," Andy didn't back down. O'Neill's preference for preserving Sikes's chairmanship, said Andy, was "inconsistent with what he [O'Neill] wants in the way of a tough code of ethics and a tough enforcement of it."

When the issue came to a vote in the Democratic caucus, the vote was 189–93 to oust Sikes—an "embarrassment," as the *Record* noted, to O'Neill and Majority Leader Jim Wright, who had also opposed the move.

"When Andy took on Bob Sikes," says Tom Downey, "a thoroughly detestable and corrupt individual, that was particularly courageous."

Certainly, Andy wasn't making friends for himself when he took to the House floor to berate his colleagues. "The House," he said at one point in the Sikes affair, "too often has sidestepped disciplinary action because of the operation of the buddy system or the reluctance of individual members to criticize colleagues."

In early 1977, in a profile of New Jersey's entire congressional delegation, the *Record* noted that Andy "could claim much of the credit" for Sikes's downfall. Predictably, the article went on to describe the attitude of Andy's in-state colleagues: "The action by Maguire, who has gained a reputation as an effective but abrasive House upstart, tells something about the present standing of the New Jersey delegation. Generally disliked by his New Jersey colleagues, Maguire worked with little assistance from them—even though six of the other ten Democrats from New Jersey voted with him in the end."

The *Record* went on to cite two sources of the enmity toward Andy: "Veteran members—and a couple of younger members as well—dislike Maguire, partly because of his pushiness and partly because of jealousy over his ability to attract newspaper and television coverage."

The representatives had reason to be jealous—Andy did draw the attention of the press. First and foremost, Andy generated coverage because of the causes he pursued and the ardor and incisive language with which he pursued them. But he also learned early on that ink and airtime came most often to those who weren't shy about seeking them.

One day, just as Andy was beginning his first term in the House, he was among a group of new members interviewing committee chairs. Exiting the meeting room to make a phone call, Andy was stopped in the hallway by a television correspondent, Roger Mudd, of CBS News. Mudd wanted to know what was going on inside; Andy replied that the new members had agreed to keep the discussions confidential, and kept walking to a phone booth. A couple of minutes afterward, Andy learned later, Toby Moffett came out. When Mudd asked him for information, Moffett said, "Sure." Mudd's brief interview with Andy's friend appeared that night on *CBS Evening News*.

"Lesson learned," says Andy.

Andy's hometown paper, the *Bergen Record*, employed a crack political reporting staff, publishing a comprehensive, day-by-day account of the doings of local House members and New Jersey's two US senators. Even though Andy didn't employ a press secretary until his second term, the *Record* kept readers familiar with his work, and the *New York Times* reported on the unconventional young lawmaker, as well. Were Andy serving today, with twenty-four-hour cable stations eager for articulate, opinionated elected officials to populate their panels, he would be a national presence—at least to viewers of MSNBC. Even though MSNBC, CNN, and Fox News hadn't come into existence during Andy's tenure in Congress, he did appear on national television from time to time—on the *Robert MacNeil Report* discussing energy or debating tax policy with Jack Kemp, on ABC's *Good Morning America* to talk about a campaign finance bill he was cosponsoring.

Some in Congress considered Andy a showboat, but the fourth estate recognized his worth. During his second term, the *Record* named him one of New Jersey's best members of Congress, saying,

> Sophomore Andy Maguire, 39, will never just fence politely when he can go for the jugular. . . . He is abrasive and frequently arrogant.
>
> But even if you don't like him—and if you know him, there's an even chance you don't—you've got to admire his courageous battles with General Motors, Gulf Oil, and the congressional establishment."
>
> When Maguire is at his best, he is truly exceptional.

WE WANT TO BE PROUD AGAIN: Ford, Reagan, Carter, and the Campaign of 1976

Although he was the incumbent president, Gerald Ford had to fight for the 1976 nomination of his party to a full term in office. Ronald Reagan challenged him for the nod, and came within a whisker of capturing it.

Reagan had found success as a Hollywood actor but never ascended to the top tier of stardom—his anodyne face and buttery voice were not enough to compensate for the wooden delivery that rarely conveyed any semblance of real emotion. Reagan had achieved some notoriety as president of the Screen Actors Guild during the 1950s, when he'd cooperated with the House Un-American Activities Committee in its campaign to purge Hollywood of artists tainted by alleged Communist affiliation. His experience with HUAC, as well as with the high marginal tax rates of the era, turned the onetime Democrat into a hard-right conservative, with a distrust of the federal government, an aversion to progressive taxation, and a bellicose stance toward America's cold war rival, the USSR.

Well before he entered politics, his face and voice inhabited American living rooms. With his film career petering out in the '50s, Reagan signed on to host a weekly TV anthology series, *General Electric Theater*. The job also involved speaking to audiences at General Electric facilities across the country, giving the actor the opportunity to hone his skill as a public speaker. He later hosted a Western-themed anthology series, *Death Valley Days*, introducing and summing up each episode, which reliably carried the theme of flinty individualism.

In 1964, it was television that ignited his political career. With many well-known Republicans refusing to support the GOP's hard-right nominee, Barry Goldwater, Reagan delivered a speech containing an enthusiastic endorsement of the Arizonan and his ideology. Reagan attacked social spending, welfare cheats, and the very idea of government, charging that the Democrats wanted to "solve all the problems of human misery through government and government planning." And he derided the socialists at home who coddled the socialists abroad. "Those who would trade our freedom for the soup kitchen of the welfare state have told us they have a utopian solution of peace without victory. They call their policy 'accommodation.'"

Goldwater lost big in the 1964 election, but Reagan was a winner. He parlayed his speech into a successful bid for governor of California in 1966, besting Democratic incumbent Edmund "Pat" Brown, whose defeat of Nixon four years earlier had inspired the former vice president to tell the press they wouldn't "have Nixon to kick around anymore."

Reagan's attempt to govern according to his far-right philosophy collided with reality when he had to renege on his campaign promise to cut taxes—while he cut property taxes, he raised sales, income, and other taxes. But he found another issue to ride to national prominence: campus unrest. Reagan had promised during his 1966 campaign to "clean up the mess at Berkeley"—the University of California at Berkeley, home to the first of the mass student protests that would intrude upon the peace of American college campuses during the mid to late 1960s. He placed new members onto the UC state board of regents; the newly constituted board forced Berkeley's president to resign. And he sent the California Highway Patrol and the National Guard to the campus to quell uprisings. The moves proved immensely popular in the state, whose politics at the time were still dominated by Republicans.

Harboring ambitions beyond Sacramento, Reagan declared his candidacy for the 1968 presidential nomination at that summer's GOP convention; the delegates, already set on Nixon, mostly ignored the late bid. By 1975, however, Reagan saw an opportunity to bring his emphatic brand of Republican conservatism to bear against the more moderate strain represented by Ford. Ford's lackluster performance on the economy, particularly his inability to get control of inflation and unemployment, added to his embrace of détente with the Soviet Union, opened a path for the Californian. Announcing his candidacy in November 1975, Reagan not only criticized Ford's economic record and beat the drum for a more confrontational foreign policy but also dispensed a generous dose of his suspicion of the federal government: "We created government as our servant, beholden to us and possessing no powers except those voluntarily granted to it by us. Now a self-anointed elite in our nation's capital would have us believe we are incapable of guiding our own destiny."

Establishment political observers didn't take Reagan seriously: He was a lightweight, an actor, a cowboy, a warmonger, an extremist. But Reagan won the balloting in nearly two dozen states against the accidental president who had never before run a race in anything larger than his Michigan congressional district. The candidates entered the convention in Kansas City with Ford enjoying a slight, but not conclusive, lead. The gathering was, and no doubt will continue to be, the last major party nominating convention to open with the winner of the race still in doubt.

Just before the convention, Reagan did something no one was expecting: Aiming to win the support of uncommitted delegates not comfortable with his hard-right views, he named as his prospective running mate Senator Richard Schweiker, a known moderate from Pennsylvania. The move failed to gain Reagan votes from the moderate wing of the party and provoked anger from the right. It was a curious and rare misstep, reeking of desperation and a compromise of principles, by a normally sure-footed political operator.

Ford dealt with issues concerning his own vice presidential choice. In the face of the challenge from Reagan, Ford had months earlier seen the need to cut loose Nelson Rockefeller, the liberal former governor of New York whom Ford had appointed vice president according to the Twenty-Fifth Amendment. Long the whipping boy of GOP conservatives—he'd been booed at the 1964 convention when he'd dared to speak up against Goldwater's extremism—Rockefeller was replaced as the nominee by

Robert Dole, the Kansas senator with a sharp tongue, chosen by Ford to mollify the party's right wing.

When the convention's delegates cast their votes, Ford took the nomination by a margin of only 117 delegates out of more than 2,200 cast. On the last night of the convention, Ford delivered his acceptance speech and was then joined on the rostrum by his family, his running mate, and assorted GOP dignitaries. The delegates applauded, the band played, creating what was normally the closing tableau for a national convention. All that was needed to complete the picture was the runner-up. Ford beckoned Reagan and his wife, Nancy, watching from the balcony, to join the group—to raise hands, observers presumed, with the nominee in the traditional gesture of party unity. But when the couple reached the stage, Ford asked Reagan to address the crowd. As the audience cheered and the band played "California, Here I Come," Ford escorted Reagan to the microphone, introduced him, and stepped aside. Reagan delivered a generous extemporaneous endorsement of Ford mixed with a helping of the Californian's anti-government boilerplate, denouncing "the erosion of freedom that has taken place under Democrat rule in this country; the invasion of private rights; the controls and restrictions on the vitality of the great free economy that we enjoy."

The delegates hung on every word from the losing candidate who somehow had become the convention's closing act.

Gerald Ford had won the nomination of the Republican Party. Ronald Reagan had won the party's future.

Ford's Democratic opponent in the fall would be James Earl "Jimmy" Carter, an evangelical Christian who had recently served a single term as governor of Georgia.

One of the most unlikely presidential candidates in US history, Carter, a graduate of Annapolis, owned a peanut farm and taught Sunday school in his small hometown of Plains, Georgia. He was a prime example of what were called New South governors—a group of state chief executives then emerging with the mission of transcending the region's ugly racial history. Carter's winning the Georgia governorship marked a sea change in the state's politics: Elected in 1970, he'd succeeded Lester Maddox, a clownish segregationist who had made his name by refusing, even after the passage of the 1964 Civil Rights Act, to allow Blacks to eat at his fried-chicken restaurant. In his campaign for the office, Maddox had passed out miniature versions of the life-sized axe handles he'd brandished to keep out the unwanted customers. Carter vowed change. "The time for racial discrimination is over," he said in his inaugural address.

Carter hoped to lead a shift in national Democratic politics, as well: Moderate in his governance, as any Democrat needed to be to serve as governor in a Southern state, he represented a departure from the forthright liberalism of George McGovern, whose forty-nine-state loss in 1972 Democratic voters and officeholders had no wish to repeat. But Carter's most important appeal in this first election after Watergate was his professed honesty: "I will never lie to you," he pledged. The contrast with Nixon was stark: Where Nixon was shifty, Carter was earnest; Nixon corrupt, Carter clean; Nixon foul-mouthed, Carter a Sunday school teacher; Nixon a lawyer, Carter a peanut farmer; Nixon a creature of Washington, Carter a lifelong resident of a small town.

Carter's campaign was based less on ideology than on ethics and on overcoming a generalized distrust of government. In September 1975, noting that he'd already taken his campaign for the White House to forty-two states and over two hundred cities and towns, he cited two questions voters asked him "again and again." The first was: "Can our government work?" People wanted to know if government could be "competent, well-organized, efficient, economical and well-planned." Second, "Can our government be decent?" Can government "be a source of pride, instead of shame and embarrassment"?

Washington was the problem this outsider was running against. "Interminable Washington hearings," he said, "and neatly typed staff reports can never explain the consequences of unfair taxes, a disgraceful welfare system, bureaucratic incompetence and indifference, or economic mismanagement half so clearly and unforgettably as the average American who suffers from them."

Competing against a field of better-known candidates—Senators Scoop Jackson and Frank Church; Morris Udall, the droll representative from Arizona; and, in his final campaign, George Wallace—Carter managed a narrow win in the Iowa caucuses then went on to take most of the states in the Northeast, Midwest, and South, pulling into the national convention at New York's Madison Square Garden as the presumptive nominee.

After balancing the ticket with a Northern liberal senator, Minnesota's Walter F. Mondale, as running mate, Carter in his acceptance speech promised "a complete overhaul of our income tax system. I still tell you: It is a disgrace to the human race." He called for a "nationwide health program," and an end to discrimination by race or sex.

But the center of his appeal, as it had been throughout his campaign, was a promised pivot from the years of Nixon. Lawbreaking, especially by the powerful and the rich, needed to be punished: "It is time for our government leaders to respect the law no less than the humblest citizen, so that we can end once and for all a double standard of justice. I see no reason why big-shot crooks should go free and the poor ones go to jail."

But retribution alone, the nominee argued, would not solve the nation's ills. A moral rebirth was in order: "Our country has lived through a time of torment. It is now a time for healing. We want to have faith again. We want to be proud again. We just want the truth again." Carter was running against Nixon more than he was running against Ford.

And he was running against Washington. "It is time for the people to run the government, and not the other way around," he said—a formulation that could just as easily have been spoken by Ronald Reagan.

At the beginning of the fall campaign, Carter led Ford—by 33 percentage points, according to one poll. Through September, Ford employed a "Rose Garden strategy": campaigning by not campaigning, staying in the White House to show people he was busy doing his job.

The two candidates agreed to hold four debates: three between the presidential contenders, one between their running mates. At the vice presidential debate, Dole did not do his ticket any favors when he referred to the Americans who had died in the "Democrat wars" of the 20th century—a curious statement for the Kansan, a war hero whose right arm was disabled during his service in one of those wars, World War II.

But Dole's debate misstep was minimal compared to Ford's, who shoved his foot deep into his mouth during the second meeting of the presidential candidates. The topic the evening of October 6 was foreign policy. One of the journalists posing questions was Max Frankel, a longtime foreign correspondent for the *New York Times*. Asking Ford about US relations with the Soviet Union, Frankel mentioned the Helsinki Accords, which, he said, recognized Russian "dominance in Eastern Europe." Toward the end of a long answer, Ford defended the agreement by noting that the pope had signed it. The candidate concluded by saying,

"There is no Soviet domination of Eastern Europe and there never will be under a Ford administration."

The moderator called upon Carter to speak, but before he could, Frankel interrupted. Incredulous that Ford had seemed to deny the existence of the USSR's satellite states, Frankel said, "I'm sorry, I—could I just follow—did I understand you to say, sir, that the Russians are not using Eastern Europe as their own sphere of influence . . ."

Given a chance to climb out of the hole, Ford kept digging. "I don't believe, uh—Mr. Frankel that uh—the Yugoslavians consider themselves dominated by the Soviet Union. I don't believe that the Rumanians consider themselves dominated by the Soviet Union. I don't believe that the Poles consider themselves dominated by the Soviet Union. Each of those countries is independent, autonomous: It has its own territorial integrity and the United States does not concede that those countries are under the domination of the Soviet Union. As a matter of fact, I visited Poland, Yugoslavia, and Rumania to make certain that the people of those countries understood that the president of the United States and the people of the United States are dedicated to their independence, their autonomy, and their freedom."

According to post-debate reporting, Ford apparently had meant to say that despite Soviet domination of Eastern Europe, the people of that region retained their spirit and sense of nationhood. But that's not the way the words came out. Ford went days before he corrected his statement.

Political gaffes are especially damaging when they reinforce a preexisting image of the gaffe maker. In this case, Ford's error confirmed his image as a likable dunderhead, out of his depth in the job making him the most powerful person in the world.

The results on November 2 were close. Carter took the entire deep and border South, except for Virginia but including Texas. Ford took everything to the west, as well as four of six states in New England, plus New Jersey, Illinois, and his home state of Michigan. Carter won the Electoral College 297–240 (with one faithless elector voting for Reagan), and won the popular vote by 1.7 million, or 2 percent. In the House, Democrats added one seat to their sizable majority while in the Senate the numbers were unchanged.

Two years earlier, the post-Watergate Congress had taken power. Now it was the turn of the post-Watergate president.

NO SWEAT: Andy's Reelection to a Second Term

Andy loved being in Congress and wanted to stay there. In 1976 he ran for reelection.

The GOP primary turned out well for Andy: Republican voters passed on the chance to run a moderate Republican, choosing instead James Sheehan, a right winger who had served as mayor of Wyckoff.

"The campaign for Maguire's 7th Congressional District seat," said the *Record*, "is shaping up as a classic confrontation between a staunch conservative attacking his opponent as a big spender and a liberal incumbent stressing his legislative accomplishments."

"Sheehan wasn't a towering intellect," says Andy, "but that doesn't mean he wasn't noisy. He was a caricature of a know-nothing, conservative, right-wing Republican from a small town."

Sheehan didn't come up with much original about Andy—the challenger ran a standard conservative campaign assailing welfare, affirmative action, and school busing. Andy was "more liberal than Bella Abzug," said Sheehan, referring to the Manhattan Democratic congresswoman known for her floppy hats, loud voice, and in-your-face feminist progressivism. Noting that Andy had voted against cuts in the federal food stamp program, Sheehan said that "if you're a bum, a college student, or a hippie, you can qualify for this program."

In the press and at debates Andy defended his record: "I'm going to run on the basis of what I've been doing in Washington, not against some of the astonishing things Mr. Sheehan has been saying." Andy might have considered Sheehan's charges specious, but he took one of them—that he was a profligate spender of taxpayers' money—seriously enough to rebut it at length. "It used to be that if you were a liberal, you were a big spender," Andy said. "That's no longer true. The new members have combined a liberal concern for human needs with a very hard-headed, tough-minded approach to spending based on what does and doesn't work."

Like many liberal politicians when the '60s flowed into the '70s, as the faith in government generated by civil rights legislation and the Great Society gave way to the distrust of government caused by Vietnam and Watergate, Andy felt obligated to defend himself against the charge of fiscal irresponsibility. That perceived need would only increase over the next two decades, as conservatives put liberals more and more on the defensive over their belief in the positive role government could play in American society.

As he had two years earlier, Andy made his case not only via the press but also, tirelessly, to individual constituents. He worked the neighborhoods, running from house to house in his sneakers while a phalanx of volunteers rang doorbells.

The demographics of New Jersey's Seventh Congressional District were still not making life easy for a Democratic office-seeker. "Andy can't win," said Gina Glantz, again Andy's campaign manager, "unless we turn out the Democratic vote and unless he gets some Ford-Maguire votes."

He got them. Gerald Ford won New Jersey, 50 percent to Carter's 48, and Bergen County, 56 percent to 43. Andy won reelection with 56.5 percent of the vote to Sheehan's 43.5.

"I buried him," Andy says.

CHAPTER 7

UNEASY ALLIANCE: A Second Term, a Frustrating President

Jimmy Carter was unquestionably the most moral president of my lifetime, but he wasn't much of a president.

—MOLLY IVINS

TONE DEAF: The Carter White House and the Congress

"I was optimistic," Andy recalls, describing his mood as Jimmy Carter entered the White House in January 1977. "I thought he had a set of perspectives and sensitivities that could make him a fine president. I thought he had his heart in the right place and wanted to take the nation in the right direction."

The feeling was common among Andy's colleagues in Congress, who looked forward to working with a president of their own party after eight years of Republicans. "Many Democrats," says John Lawrence, "felt that

Carter's election was going to remove the barrier—veto by a Republican president—that had prevented them from doing things. But Carter had a number of policies, particularly his fiscal rectitude, that ultimately were damaging to those Democratic aspirations. He was also a strong supporter of deregulation, which was problematic for many of the consumer-oriented members. There were certainly victories with the Carter administration, but there was also a great sense of disappointment among Democrats that they did not achieve more of what they had been unable to get done under Nixon and Ford."

Carter had campaigned as an outsider, the stranger on a white horse, pure of purpose, who would restore morality to the nation's fallen capital city. But he never became an insider. He approached Washington on his terms, and Washington had its way with him.

"Carter did not do well with Congress," says Lawrence. "He didn't understand Congress, he had no experience with Congress, and he brought in a lot of people who had little experience with Congress. I contrast him with Ronald Reagan, who had never served in Congress, or Barack Obama, who had served in Congress but only in passing. They brought in skilled political operators who knew how Washington worked. Carter did not. Off the top he did several things—particularly the water project hit list—that went right at Congress without recognizing the institutional interests of the House and the Senate."

Perhaps no action taken by President Jimmy Carter better illustrates his mix of high-minded civic virtue, political ineptitude, and counterproductive self-righteousness than his actions on water projects. After only a month as president, in the budget he was submitting for fiscal year 1978, he called for the defunding of eighteen large-scale items, mostly dams in the South and West. The projects had already been authorized and funded; on many, construction had already begun. Quickly, the collection of targeted projects became known as the "hit list."

Carter's intentions were honorable. Campaigning in New Hampshire a year earlier, he'd said, "I personally believe that we have built enough dams in this country and will be extremely reluctant as president to build any more." Likewise, he'd promised, as do all seekers of federal office, to cut "wasteful spending" and balance the budget. But unlike nearly all seekers of federal office, he meant to keep his promise. Environmentalists praised him for halting projects they considered deleterious to the nation's natural resources.

But the new president seemed oblivious to the political price he would pay by picking fights with numerous lawmakers—many of his own party—who, barely knowing him, had no reason to trust him. Vice President Walter Mondale, who had just left the Senate after a dozen years in the body, had warned his boss about attacking projects in which members of the House and Senate had invested large sums of political capital. But Carter, certain he was acting in the nonpartisan national interest, saw no need to address the parochial political interests of his fellow elected officials. He proposed the cuts after almost no consultation with Congress and less than thorough consultation with Cecil Andrus, the respected former Idaho governor now serving as secretary of the interior. One Hill staffer, quoted by the *Washington Post*, described the apparent cluelessness of the new White House: "The Carter people didn't understand that a lot of political work has gone into getting projects authorized and funded. It is not something whipped up overnight. It required years getting local and state officials behind a project along with the congressional delegation."

Western lawmakers accused him of hostility to their region—"Carter Declares War on West," read the headlines—where he'd carried not a single state in the recent election. The president, the westerners said, did not appreciate the extent to which their part of the country relied on dams to manage scarce water supplies that provided irrigation, power, and drinking water.

What Carter seemed to miss, above all, was that by treating as expendable the items lawmakers considered important, he was inviting those lawmakers to treat as expendable the items *he* considered important. Carter's fellow Southern Democrat, Russell Long, the Senate Finance Committee chairman first elected to the Senate in 1948, visited Carter in the White House to make that point. Carter's stance on the projects, Long told him, would alienate "his own best soldiers." Lawmakers, Long told a television interviewer, recounting the advice he'd given Carter, "will go along with him on something they are committed to," but if a piece of legislation is "one of those things that could go one way just about as easy as the other, they [will] tend to slough off and vote against him."

Democrats in Congress would show the president of their own party deference early in Carter's term. Before he left office, their loyalty would run out.

"The people around the president were hostile to members of Congress," says former representative Tom Downey. "There were lots of stories about members not being invited to things."

Carter couldn't afford to sacrifice friends. "Even though the majorities were very large for the Democrats," Downey says, "remember, this was before the Republican takeover of the South. So a good number of the Democrats from the South never voted with Carter. They were basically Democrats in name only."

Carter seemed to believe his policies would gain support on their own merits, with no need for the horse trading and side deals that made Congress work. In April 1977—again, in the administration's early days—New Jersey governor Brendan Byrne and four members of the state's House delegation met with the president at the White House to plead for a reversal of the Pentagon's plan to cut seven hundred jobs from Fort Monmouth, the Army base near the Jersey Shore. After the visitors had their say, Carter said he'd refer the matter to the secretary of defense.

"But Mr. President," one of the representatives said, "it's already been to his attention, and that's why we're here."

Carter, according to the press account, "glared" at the congressman and said, "Would you prefer that I not bring it to the secretary's attention?"

Democrats in Congress were expecting more from a president of their own party. A Republican House member from New Jersey noticed their discomfort: "It really seems disconcerting to them to hear Carter say how open he is to people when he doesn't talk to them very much at all." One lobbyist with ties to Democrats put it this way: "They kind of shake their heads a lot. They look for excuses for him; they say surely it can't be Carter's fault for he's one of ours."

"I think the universal view about him," Andy says now, "which I agree with, was that he staffed the White House with his one-dimensional limited-view-of-the-national-interest cronies from Georgia. Why do presidents so often make that mistake? Clinton did the same thing.

"Carter didn't know how to work with Congress and didn't have people who did. Carter wasn't good at dealing with Congress. That was the case over his whole four years in office. That's a big strike against any president."

Early in Carter's tenure, Andy's view of the president was more favorable. "I think that Carter's natural allies in the Congress are people like me," he said in May 1977. While confessing that he was uncertain whether the White House was even aware of his support, Andy said he felt an affinity toward Carter. "People I feel close to here play the game differently," said Andy. "We're not playing the old boy game, and I don't think Carter is either." Andy liked the president's inflexibility: "I'm not a trader myself, and I respect a guy who doesn't trade off on issues."

Today, however, Andy backs off such praise. "I saw Carter's approach as a reflection of my own," he says, "which had its plusses and minuses. I didn't trade my vote on this for somebody else's vote on that, which you can describe as either a strength or a weakness. Carter was like that. I initially regarded that posture as a positive, but he ultimately was so ineffective that it didn't much matter whether he wanted to trade something or not.

"As a crusading member of Congress, you don't necessarily have to trade and make compromises. As president, you do."

RIGHT AND WRONG: A Principled Practice of Politics

"Andy was not a big schmoozer," says Michael Levin, "he didn't have the patience for it. He was happy being on a basketball team and talking to people about substantive issues and putting coalitions together. But he wasn't big on going out for drinks with people or having people to his house for dinner."

"That's exactly right," says David Dreyer, "but he wasn't a solo artist. He lived for creating coalitions. He lived for needing more chairs in his personal office because a meeting had ballooned to larger than originally anticipated. That's when he knew there was good chemistry.

"He hated the *trappings* of politics, he didn't hate politics—he was a good politician. But he could see the ticking clock. He wanted to accomplish as much as he could in the time he'd been granted."

"Andy was a bit more uptight than some of the people in Congress," says John Lawrence, "even the people he ran with. I don't want to oversell it—he had a propriety, maybe a combination of maturity with standoffishness or rectitude. You didn't see Andy Maguire getting down and messing around the way others did. He was moralistic—I don't mean he was a conservative moralist. I mean that he had a certain view of who he was and what was right and what was wrong."

Andy displayed his rectitude—politics be damned—during the campaign for House majority leader in December 1976. "It was a hugely consequential race," says Lawrence.

The contest took place as Democrats were selecting leadership for the new Congress to begin in January. Tip O'Neill, majority leader in the ending Congress, was moving up to take the Speaker's gavel in the next, after Carl Albert's retirement. Several members announced their candidacy for leader, but before long the field narrowed.

"The fight," Lawrence recalls, "came down to Phil Burton, from California, a reform leader—a hard-line pro-environment, pro-labor, pro-civil-rights liberal—but a problematic, unpleasant person, and Jim Wright, from Texas, who had been pro-war and had voted against the '64 civil rights bill, an old bricks-and-mortar transportation guy earmarking his way to popularity with his backslapping Southern drawl. Almost a caricature of the Southern pol.

"Careful maneuvering was going on that ended up having real significance in the New Jersey delegation, which was at that point chock-full of interesting characters—Frank Thompson and Eddie Patten and Bob Roe and Jimmy Howard. These were old-line Democratic politicians. Some of them would vote for reform measures, but you would not confuse them with flower children. They were tough guys.

"You would have thought that if you looked at the range of people in the delegation, most would have been with Phil because they were pro civil rights. But everything's connected in Congress. Frank Thompson was a big pro-labor liberal reformer—you would think, 'Boy, there's a natural guy to support Phil Burton.' But Thompson had vied to be chairman of the House Administration Committee, losing out to a buddy of Burton's. Phil had naturally favored his friend, not Thompson, for chair, so now Thompson was a sworn enemy of Phil. Plus you had people like Bob Roe and Jim Howard, high-ranking members on the Public Works and Transportation Committee. Jim Wright was on that committee. If he left to become majority leader, slots on the committee would open up for Roe and Howard to move up in seniority and eventually become chairmen, as both of them did.

"So in the New Jersey delegation, because a member either was Thompson, who was still nursing the grudge of having been defeated by

Burton's guy, or was friends with Thompson, or was pursuing his self-interest on the Public Works Committee, nine of the eleven Democrats wound up voting for Wright.

"Maguire refused to, even though a lot of freshmen, even freshmen reformers, did. That infuriated the senior members of the New Jersey delegation. 'I got everybody but that son of a bitch Maguire,' was the feeling. I'm sure Andy would point to that vote as indicative of his independence and his unwillingness to be cowed by the higher-ups. But it also illustrates that it's problematic to function within a delegation if you're voting against its senior members. Not to mention that you voted for the guy who lost—that doesn't help, either. Fortunately, he already had a good committee assignment.

"Maybe that vote was not the smartest thing to do politically, but it demonstrated Andy's sense of—I don't know if I'd say self-confidence. His sense of principle."

Burton's loss to Wright—by a single vote—was not Andy's only disappointment during the Democrats' organization of the Ninety-Fifth Congress. The caucus also voted down a series of procedural reforms that would have built upon the changes implemented two years earlier.

"Yes, I was low," Andy said later, pointing to the defeated reforms, "I was low for several days."

AN UNPLEASANT CONVERSATION: Carter's 1977 Energy Proposals

From the beginning, Jimmy Carter made energy the central issue of his presidency. He laid out the basics in a televised speech on February 2, just two weeks into his presidency. Explicitly trying to evoke the informality of Franklin Roosevelt's famous "fireside chats," he spoke while seated in an armchair, aside a blazing White House fireplace. Wearing a cardigan to highlight his request that Americans save energy by lowering their thermostats, he reassured the public that "in order to solve our energy problems we need not sacrifice the quality of our lives." But in two speeches that April he conveyed a different message.

He delivered the first from the Oval Office. "Good evening," he began. "Tonight I want to have an unpleasant talk with you about a problem unprecedented in our history. With the exception of preventing war, this is the greatest challenge that our country will face during our lifetimes. The energy crisis has not yet overwhelmed us, but it will if we do not act quickly."

In contrast to his soothing forecast two months earlier, Carter now warned that his plan would require "sacrifices and changes in every life. To some degree, the sacrifices will be painful—but so is any meaningful sacrifice. It will lead to some higher costs, and to some greater inconvenience for everyone." Even more striking was that he not only asked people to change, but also found fault with them. "Ours is the most wasteful nation on earth," he said, referring to Americans' consumption of energy. He came down especially hard on people with big cars: "Those citizens who insist on driving large, unnecessarily powerful cars must expect to pay more for that luxury." Solving the energy problem was imperative, the "moral equivalent of war."

In that speech, as well as in his address to a joint session of Congress two days later, Carter emphasized the need to use less oil, not because of concerns about global climate change—Carter would later that year be briefed on the danger, but the issue was still virtually unknown at the time—but because importing oil not only was expensive but also made the United States dependent on foreign suppliers. Moreover, the president said, oil was a finite resource. If the world's population didn't alter its habits, "we could use up all the proven reserves of oil in the entire world by the end of the next decade." Carter laid out ten principles that would guide US policy. "The first principle," he said, "is that we can have an effective and comprehensive energy policy only if the government takes responsibility for it and if the people understand the seriousness of the challenge and are willing to make sacrifices." Other principles concerned the need for fairness and economic growth. "The cornerstone of our policy" was found in number six: "reduce demand through conservation."

The specifics of Carter's plan covered every conceivable aspect of energy policy, addressing nuclear power, coal, and the pricing of oil and gas, as well as the efficiency of cars, appliances, and furnaces. The proposals included incentives for people to exchange their "gas guzzlers" for compact cars, a tax on gasoline if its usage continued to rise, and controlled raising of the price of oil and newly extracted natural gas.

With this comprehensive array of proposals, and the personal authority he assigned to it—three nationally televised speeches during his first three months in office—Carter was saying something no previous president had: America needed to recognize limits, not just on how much oil the nation could safely consume but also on the very postwar prosperity that Americans assumed would never stop expanding. And by calling for limits on the use of that avatar of American freedom, the automobile, he was telling the nation that it could no longer afford its cult of unchecked individualism.

At first, Carter's plan drew widespread praise. James Reston, a columnist for the *New York Times* and as much as anyone the barometer of Washington establishment opinion, wrote that the president's "attack on reckless waste, his insistence on conserving energy, his willingness to face some of the most powerful industrial forces of the nation, and his solemn appeals for cooperation in the long-range interests of the country, have impressed the capital and won the respect even of many men and women who disagree with his proposals."

Henry Kissinger added his kudos, calling the plan "overwhelmingly in the national interest."

In August, the House of Representatives approved legislation that, for the most part, accorded with Carter's proposals, including allowing the price of natural gas to rise to no higher than $1.75 per thousand cubic feet. In early June, under intense corporate lobbying, a Commerce subcommittee approved broad deregulation of that price. But at the end of the month the full committee opted, by a one-vote margin, to keep the $1.75 ceiling. Leading the effort to protect that ceiling was Andy, who employed a variety of parliamentary maneuvers to force a vote before the deregulation side could muster the support to defeat him.

"Representative Maguire prevailed on all counts," reported the *Times.*

The Senate was another matter. In October, the upper chamber passed a bill that decontrolled the price of natural gas and included other provisions called for by industry lobbyists.

As the two bills went to a House-Senate conference to come up with a final package, the struggle over the legislation was just beginning. In late October, Andy and sixty-six other House liberals met with Carter. The representatives insisted that the price of natural gas be set no higher than $1.75. Andy said afterward that Carter "specifically agreed with a point I made, that oil companies have so much at stake in the existing House bill that they would rather have it as it is than have no bill at all. That gives him leverage."

Fearing that the raft of proposals on which he'd staked his presidency might fade away without yielding a single piece of legislation, Carter accused the oil companies—many companies known primarily for oil production also extracted natural gas—of "potential wartime profiteering." That same day, however, the secretary of the newly created Department of Energy, James Schlesinger, and some White House aides were offering industry representatives compromises that would bestow upon their companies billions in new profits.

The legislation remained in conference. After Thanksgiving, Andy and Toby Moffett set up a meeting in which House liberals urged House conferees to avoid excessive concessions. Andy warned the administration not to take the liberals' support for granted. "I don't think they'll be able to save it [the bill] simply by waving the flag and saying we have to have a bill," he said. Andy met with Schlesinger, too, and didn't mince words. "We are engaged in a political struggle," he told the new secretary. "We need to know where you stand. It isn't good enough to have the administration restating its preference for the House bill and compromising everything away. What will be left? Why doesn't the president say, 'We just won't accept any more garbage in this bill'?"

Andy secured what he thought was a commitment from Schlesinger that the administration would not accept any price limit higher than "a dollar seventy-five, and at most a minor adjustment in that." Andy took Schlesinger's words to mean an absolute ceiling of $1.85 and announced that apparent promise in a press conference immediately afterward. But three days later he heard that Schlesinger was making different offers to the Senate.

Andy and Toby Moffett then had a meeting, proposed by the White House, with the president and Stuart Eizenstat in the Oval Office. "I told Carter and Eizenstat," Andy recalls, "that $1.75 or, as Schlesinger had implied, as much as $1.85, would provide an enormous windfall to producers compared with what it cost to produce the gas and with the prices that producers had been satisfied with for decades. Furthermore, I said that raising the price higher would have a negative overall effect on the economy. I said these costs were unnecessary, since a price cap was available in the House legislation and could be insisted on with the Senate.

"The president listened attentively but made no counterargument other than to state that a year had gone by and a conclusion was needed. In due course, via a device that is well known when a senior official wants to stop talking about something, Carter ended his part of the conversation: An aide walked in with a note for him. Carter read it, said he was needed elsewhere, and said we should continue to talk with Eizenstat—which we did.

"Of course, the entire meeting made no difference; a courtesy had been extended, period. Without a commitment from the White House to even try to hold the line on pricing, Toby and I came away from the encounter with nothing to show for having talked directly with the president."

At year's end, the conferees still had not come to agreement. According to the *Record*, "the entire energy question—along with its impact on Carter's prestige—is very much in doubt."

Asked by the paper to grade Carter's first year in office, Andy gave it "a high B."

"People want to finish this energy bill," said Andy in January. "They are perplexed about how something like this could take so long."

Deadlocked over the price of natural gas, the conferees met only once before mid-April. Andy was losing hope that Carter would hold fast on pricing. "The president has said, in effect, that he will accept anything as long as it has the title 'energy bill' on it," Andy said. Carter, a year after presenting his proposals, was losing patience. "We have wasted twelve months of precious time," he said. "I call on Congress to fulfill its duty to the American people."

Late in April, the conference completed its work, fashioning a bill that included a compromise on what had been the main sticking point, the price of natural gas. The bill would allow that price to rise to almost two dollars immediately, with a gradual rise adding another two dollars, until the lifting of all controls at the beginning of 1985. Carter pronounced himself "pleased and gratified" that the conferees had settled on a bill, even though he conceded it wasn't the bill he preferred. "This agreement," he added, "represents a long overdue step toward the creation of a truly national market for natural gas as well as a crucial breakthrough toward enactment of the nation's first and long delayed National Energy Plan."

Andy was neither pleased nor gratified. "It's a capitulation by the House to the Senate," he said.

The legislation limped along until finally, in October, Congress passed the National Energy Act. Exhausted by the long process, most liberals in the House and Senate—although not the one named Andy Maguire—gave their final assent to a bill they and their president could point to as they campaigned in the approaching midterm elections. Despite the rise in the price of natural gas, the bill included many components of Carter's original plan: anti-gas-guzzler incentives; tax credits for renewable energy like solar and wind; encouragement of power plants to use coal, nuclear power, and alternative fuels; and other measures to encourage energy conservation.

Carter had gotten his bill. But he was losing Congress.

RIDICULOUS: Andy Calls Out the President

He was certainly losing the representative from New Jersey's Seventh Congressional District.

In August 1978, the American Medical Association released a new report on smoking. Based on nineteen years of research, the report found, according to the *Times*, that smoking "can cause irreversible heart damage and might be responsible for medical maladies ranging from indigestion to cancer." That same day, addressing an audience of tobacco farmers in North Carolina, Carter called for a continuation of federal support of the price of tobacco and for "an enlightened education and research program to make the smoking of tobacco even more safe than it is today."

Andy sent the president—of the United States, of Andy's own party—a handwritten note asking him to provide evidence of tobacco's safety. "Dear Mr. President," the note began, "I'm sure you must know how utterly ridiculous your statement on smoking actually was."

In May 1980, Andy said of Carter, "In the first eighteen months he made decisions which took a great deal of guts and courage. In the last eighteen months, it has been a complete about-face on the political courage index." Andy offered a literary comparison to explain Carter's governance: "It's like the description of some modern writing as protean. The work is constantly evolving and shifting its facts and its focus. You end up with a mishmash that doesn't give any direction or consistency."

Andy talks with a constituent during a day long "neighborhood tour," 1978.

THE SECRETARY OF STATE
WASHINGTON

October 10, 1980

Dear Andy:

Some time ago you and several of your colleagues made a special effort to achieve passage of the full amount of emergency food assistance in a supplemental appropriation requested by the Administration. Much has been achieved as a result of your fine efforts and I would like to take this opportunity to let you know precisely how the supplemental PL 480 funds were used.

As a result of your action, more than 300,000 tons of American food have reached Africans and Asians who might otherwise have suffered crippling malnutrition or even starvation. Emergency grant assistance under PL 480 Title II made possible by the supplemental was concentrated in three crisis areas. The first, Kampuchea, requires little in the way of explanation. It is certain that without an additional 23,000 tons of emergency food supplies the suffering both in Cambodia itself and in the refugee camps along the Thai border would have been much worse than has been the case.

Approximately 46,000 tons of food went to Afghan refugees, now numbering more than one million, in camps in Pakistan. Pakistan of course has assumed primary responsibility for these refugees. The US has contributed nearly one half of the total aid from other countries reaching these victims of Soviet aggression, and it is safe to say that without our assistance their plight would be desperate.

The Honorable
Andrew Maguire,
House of Representatives.

Letter from US Secretary of State Edmund S. Muskie.

Almost half the money expended on emergency food supplies -- $33 million out of the $73 million -- was devoted to Africa. (These sums do not include an additional $49 million required for transportation costs, increasingly a major part of any relief effort.) As you know, Africa now has three million refugees, more than any other continent. In past months chronic shortage has been greatly worsened not only by refugee needs but also by severe drought in parts of eastern and southern Africa. The result has been a spectrum of suffering unsurpassed anywhere in the world.

Our emergency food aid was used for the following purposes, among others:

-- to help feed refugees in Somalia, which as a result of the fighting in the Ogaden has about half of the African refugee total;

-- to alleviate massive human suffering in Uganda where there has been starvation in the Karamoja region as a result of drought and the chaos left by the previous regime of Idi Amin;

-- for humanitarian food aid to Ethiopia, whose people have been among the hardest hit by the African drought;

-- to help Tanzania meet emergency needs and to establish a strategic grain reserve, part of an ongoing effort to eliminate drastic fluctuations in food supply.

In addition to these grant programs the supplemental provided $16 million under Title I for highly concessional food aid loans to Liberia, Mozambique, Sudan and Tanzania.

These are only the highlights; more complete details regarding the emergency relief effort made possible by the supplemental are spelled out in the attached table. More important perhaps than the individual programs is the fact that this appropriation enabled the US to maintain its leading position as the foremost food aid donor in the world. Based on this record and on plans for the coming fiscal year we were able to take the lead, together with the FAO, in stimulating further international action to address Africa's food problems, an effort which was launched at a conference held in Rome on September 19.

-3-

In closing, I would like to thank you for your support of this worthwhile program. Nothing more effectively demonstrates the combination of skill, strength and compassion that has made the United States an effective world leader. I deeply appreciate the role you have played in making this vital contribution possible.

With warm best wishes, I am

Sincerely,

Edmund S. Muskie

Enclosure:
As stated.

Refugee camp in Somalia visited by Andy, 1980.

Refugee woman and child, Somalia, 1980.

WORKSHOP ON

ASIA NETWORK FOR SMALL SCALE AGRICULTURAL BIOTECHNOLOGIES (ANSAB)

March 30 - April 01, 1992, Kathmandu

JOINTLY ORGANIZED BY: APPROPRIATE TECHNOLOGY INTERNATIONAL, WASHINGTON & NEW ERA, KATHMANDU

Honorable Ms. Shailaja Acharya, Minister for Agriculture, Nepal and Honorable Andrew Maguire, President of A.T. International with joint commitments to serve resource - poor farmers of Asia through ANSAB (March 30, 1992). First ANSAB Workshop held in Kathmandu.

As CEO of EnterpriseWorks Worldwide, Andy introduces a new program in Nepal, 1995.

REORIENTATION: Transforming the Federal Government's Response to Cancer

One of Andy's most long-lasting and farsighted contributions to the nation's well-being was his raising of the government's awareness of environmental causes of cancer and his insistence that government research dollars go to finding not only a cure for the disease but also ways to prevent it.

Andy's involvement in the issue began when tests by the Environmental Protection Agency revealed that the air and water in and around a DuPont chemical plant in West Virginia were contaminated by nitrosamines, a known class of carcinogens. At a hearing in May 1976, Andy heard workers report that fifty-four plant employees had recently been diagnosed with cancer, and that twenty-eight of them had died. Calling for an investigation of the plant, Andy had DuPont turn over to the committee the company's two decades' worth of records regarding cancer among all its workers.

Andy found the discovery in West Virginia impossible to ignore in large part because of DuPont's presence in New Jersey: Not only did the chemical giant operate eight facilities *in* the Garden State; it also operated a variety of facilities just *outside*, in Delaware just across the Delaware River.

"New Jersey had among the worst toxic dumping in the country," says Andy. "The famous toxic site was Love Canal, in Niagara Falls, New York. But in New Jersey we had lots and lots of energy, chemical, and pharmaceutical companies, and for decades they dumped stuff everywhere. The Ford Motor Company polluted the Ramapo Mountains in a way that took decades to overcome."

Indeed, the chemical industry was New Jersey's largest employer at the time, with 130,000 workers and a $1.2 billion payroll. The omnipresence of polluters in the state seemed unavoidably linked to a conclusion reached after a twenty-year study by the National Cancer Institute: New Jersey's cancer mortality rate was one of the highest in the country.

"My state," said Andy in September 1976, "has both of the prime ingredients for accelerating the cancer rate—a multitude of chemical plants and industrial polluters, and the densest concentration of automobiles in the nation."

"The Sierra Club and other environmental activists in the state were on to all this," Andy says today. "The newspapers were on to all this. I asked for and got a tutorial with Dr. Irving Selikoff, an epidemiologist who lived in my hometown and practiced at Mount Sinai Hospital in New York. He was the person who discovered the link between asbestos fibers and mesothelioma, a great leader among scientists on the health consequences of environmental failures. And I worked hand in glove with another farsighted specialist, David Rall, the director of the National Institute of Environmental Health Sciences. I thought that contamination of air, water, and soil was the sort of thing that was extremely damaging, not only to the environment itself but also to the health of my constituents and of people across the state and country. I liked nothing better than to combine something that was important to the State of New Jersey with something that was important to the nation as a whole. All of that converged into my becoming a spokesperson on the issue."

It was Andy who drove the issue in Congress. In September 1976, at his request, the Oversight and Investigations Subcommittee of the House Commerce Committee convened hearings on the topic.

"We have scientific evidence that links pollution with cancer," Andy told the press the following month. "We may never be able to tell precisely what amounts of any single pollutant are likely to produce cancer in human beings. We must act to be on the safe side."

Perhaps Andy's most consequential step was his redirecting of federal research funds.

"My view," he says now, "and the view of those of us who were active on the issue was that an enormous amount of money was being spent at the National Institutes of Health and the National Cancer Institute on figuring out how to treat cancer once you had it. But the insight of the Selikoffs of this world—and he was far from the only one—was in tracing the relationship between cancer and polluted air and toxic chemicals, whether the chemicals were introduced into the environment via agriculture or the dumping of toxic waste or in consumer products.

"It goes with the larger strategy of how excellence in health care has to involve preventive strategies. You eat the right food, you get the right exercise, you don't smoke. Another thing you do is you don't pollute the environment that is interacting with people and their health. I gave a speech at the National Cancer Institute urging them to include more fully in their agenda and in their expenditure of funds preventive strategies with respect to environmental threats to health."

"It is clear that we're not going to deal with cancer simply by treating people once they get it," Andy said in December 1977. "We've got to prevent them from getting it. Cancer experts say that between 60 and 90 percent of all cancer is caused by environmental elements, and yet only 15 percent of the National Cancer Institute's $815 million budget is delegated to this area."

Nearly half a century later it may seem that the nation has always monitored environmental causes of cancer. It hasn't. As much as anyone, Andy changed how the government of the United States approaches the disease. "The late 1970s was when all that began to come into focus," he says. "It wasn't an add-on to something that was already there. It was a big move."

On October 15, 1978, both houses of Congress approved legislation funding health research. The bill included provisions, sponsored by Andy, ordering that:

- the National Cancer Institute "expand and intensify research on the carcinogens—cancer-causing chemicals—which people are exposed to on the job and through air, water, and food"
- five of the eighteen members of NCI's advisory board be "experts on occupational or environmental carcinogens"
- the National Cancer Institute report to Congress annually "a list of all known or suspected carcinogens, and estimate of the number of people exposed to these chemicals, and an evaluation of the effectiveness of government controls—if any—aimed at reducing the dangers"

The NCI still provides that annual accounting. It is no longer widely called the "Maguire Report," but for years it was.

Andy tackled the regulation of carcinogens in a number of household products, such as hair dye and pesticides. More prominent was his advocacy of a nationwide ban on the artificial sweetener saccharin.

A chemical derived from coal tar, saccharin had been in use as a substitute for sugar since the early 20th century; by the 1970s, it was ubiquitous, especially in low-calorie soft drinks. However, researchers at that time found that laboratory rats fed large amounts of it tended to develop bladder cancer.

Enter Andy Maguire. "We brought the experts before the committee," he says. "They said, 'Look, the animal testing on this is pretty clear and there's no reason not to be careful; find some other sweetener to put in people's food.' But we could not assemble a majority either in the committee or on the floor. Eventually there was a vote of the full House where just about everybody and their brother lined up in favor of keeping saccharin."

First, Andy fought for a ban; realizing a ban was impossible he fought for availability only by prescription; when that suggestion went nowhere he called for a warning label on any product containing saccharin. His colleagues in Congress approved none of it.

The federal government did ban saccharin, in 1981, as a potential carcinogen. However, after subsequent studies suggested that fears of bladder cancer in humans were not as well founded as previously thought, the government reversed the ban. Saccharin today is a frequent additive to processed foods, although not as common as the sweeteners sucralose and aspartame.

In response to his colleagues' refusal to restrict the sweetener, Andy suggested it be sold with a special warning label: "Saccharin does not cause cancer in the opinion of your congressman, despite scientific evidence that it does."

"That," says Andy today, "is why I was so popular with some of my colleagues."

WHETHER THEY LIKED HIM OR NOT: Countering Special Interests

"Andy was a visionary," says Ed Markey, the Massachusetts Democratic colleague of Andy in the House who later went on to the Senate. "He had a longer view of where we had to go as a country, and what it was that was stopping us from getting to that better place. He knew the special interests that we had to fight. The Commerce Committee had a conglomeration of special interests that lobbied on a daily basis."

"The lobbyists always wanted to meet," says Andy. "They always wanted to have their experts talk to my staff. They always wanted to modify whatever it was that we were trying to do, or get us to sign up for something we thought was inappropriate.

"During the 1970s, though, we were not dealing with the huge proliferation of special-interest lobbyists you have on the Hill today, and have had over the last several decades. There was a huge explosion in the '80s and '90s of not just the XYZ association—the corn producers, the steel manufacturers, the textile mills—but all the law firms that began to pull in the direction of 'strategic consulting.' They would hire one important former member of the House or Senate after another to work both sides of the aisle on behalf of major corporations and major corporate groups. We had relatively little of that in the '70s. It was a short list: the phone company, which didn't want to be broken up; the auto manufacturers and the United Auto Workers, which, after Leonard Woodcock took over from Walter Reuther as president, didn't want to toughen mileage standards or cut exhaust emissions."

"Andy was fearless," says Markey. "He stood up for the truth. He stood up for what we should aspire to as a country. For some people, that's difficult to accept, but it was an important, valuable role he played in laying out the long-term goals we should have for our country. And he was indifferent to whether or not those special interests liked him or not."

"The Clean Air Act was up for revision in '76," says Bob Kerr, "and was finally revised in '77. Andy was engaged with the whole thing, but the two issues he focused on were PSD—prevention of significant deterioration—and auto emissions."

Although Congress had in the 1950s and '60s passed several laws aimed at reducing air pollution, the Clean Air Act of 1970 was the first to outline national standards for air quality. However, that bill lacked teeth. The Clean Air Act Amendments of 1977 added important improvements to the 1970 statute: The new legislation gave the Environmental Protection Agency the authority to regulate industrial pollution in order to prevent significant deterioration of air quality and also to set new standards for vehicle emissions. Andy was key to the amendments' passage in the House and then to the composition of the final bill.

Hearings on the bill at times grew heated. "Leonard Woodcock was no Walter Reuther," says Andy. Reuther, president of the UAW from 1946 until his death in a plane crash in 1970, earned acclaim not only for his stewardship of the union but also as a champion of liberal causes, especially the civil rights movement. "Against the background of the

UAW always having supported me, Woodcock probably didn't expect to be cross-examined when he merged his position on emission controls with that of the auto companies."

"Andy absolutely grilled him," says Bob Kerr. "Andy felt this was a critical issue of health. I think Woodcock was shocked that someone the UAW was supporting had questioned him that way."

After the House and Senate passed different versions of the law, the legislation went to conference. Normally, junior members do not serve on conference committees; senior members favored by the relevant subcommittee chair are rubber-stamped by the full committee chair. But in this unusual case—where subcommittee chairman Dingell, who represented Detroit, did not favor the strong auto emissions provisions of the bill that Andy and his like-minded colleagues had secured both in committee and on the House floor—an interesting maneuver changed the traditional arrangement. Outside environmental groups, led by Rafe Pomerance of Friends of the Earth, persuaded Harley Staggers, the full committee chair, to appoint Andy and another pro-environment junior member, Henry Waxman of California, to the conference committee to safeguard the provisions of the House-passed bill, which was closer to what the Senate wanted than what Dingell and the auto companies desired. Assigned to the conference committee, Andy argued for maintaining the most stringent standards in the two bodies' bills. He succeeded in large part.

The negotiators gave ground on the timing of vehicle emission standards after automakers threatened to halt production if controls on hydrocarbons, carbon monoxide, and nitrogen oxides were implemented for their 1978 models. Standards on hydrocarbons and carbon monoxide were delayed until 1980; the standard on nitrogen oxide would wait until 1981. However, the conference adopted the Senate's more stringent version of the nitrogen oxide regulation, which mandated that emissions be cut in half. "The latter standard," said the *Times*, "was especially important to Representative Maguire, who contends that the nitrogen oxides may be a major contributor to New Jersey's high cancer rate."

In early 1978 Andy recognized serious inequities in the federal Guaranteed Student Loan Program, which, under strict limits, subsidized the interest rates banks charged students and their families for qualified student college loans. He reached across the aisle to a popular colleague, Bill

Steiger, a moderate Republican from Wisconsin to join him in addressing the issue.

The initial Maguire-Steiger bill, the Capital Availability for Higher Education Act, which built on an earlier bill introduced by Andy in 1975, was widely circulated and extensively revised based on input from state guaranteed-loan agencies, higher-education associations, and other affected parties, and on information developed during a packed public debate at the Brookings Institution between Maguire staff and staff of the Senate Health, Education and Labor Committee chaired by Ted Kennedy.

Tragically, Steiger, only forty years old, died of a heart attack in December. In March 1979, Andy introduced the new Fair Access to Higher Education Act, soon informally called the Bill Steiger Memorial Bill. Despite this emotional connection, the legislation received a notably cool reception from the turf-conscious House Education Committee, on which Andy did not serve.

Nevertheless, many of the bill's key provisions eventually did become law through a variety of legislative initiatives. Among them:

- income-based loan repayment to minimize needless defaults and reduce burdens on less affluent students or those who choose public service
- extending loans to freshmen, half-time students, and minority or out-of-state students
- barring banks from discriminating against applicants who lacked existing banking relations
- establishing loan referral, loan packaging, and loan refinancing mechanisms
- measures to increase access by boosting loan market liquidity

PEACEMAKER: Egypt, Israel, and Jimmy Carter

Foreign policy issues provide most presidents respite from dealing with a recalcitrant Congress. Jimmy Carter was no exception.

Carter notched several impressive achievements in foreign policy during his four years as president of the United States. He recognized the need for the United States to surrender the Panama Canal to the nation of Panama and—working with Congress—accomplished the transfer.

Here again, Andy played a role on a crucial close vote: Working directly with Secretary of State Cyrus Vance, he brought members of the large incoming class who did not pay much attention to foreign policy into the yes column.

After years of realpolitik, Carter reintroduced concern for human rights to America's international posture, although his application of that principle was selective—holding to account nations of little geopolitical import to the United States, like Somoza's Nicaragua and Pinochet's Chile, but turning a blind eye to abuses in key strategic allies like Marcos's Philippines, the shah's Iran, and Park's South Korea. He opposed apartheid in South Africa and helped bring about the end of white rule in Rhodesia, which the new Black-led government renamed Zimbabwe. He signed the SALT II arms control treaty with Soviet leader Leonid Brezhnev in June 1979, although prospects for Senate ratification of the agreement foundered after the USSR's invasion of Afghanistan six months later. And, on his first full day in office, he helped the nation heal from the wounds of Vietnam by granting amnesty to the young men who evaded the draft.

His most celebrated foreign policy success dealt with the Middle East. Upon taking office, Carter commenced an effort to forge peace between Israel and all its Arab neighbors. Talks in Geneva made little progress toward a comprehensive settlement, but a bilateral agreement between Israel and its most powerful Arab adversary, Egypt, seemed possible. In November 1977, Egyptian president Anwar Sadat, who had prosecuted the Yom Kippur War that had punctured Israel's feeling of invulnerability, announced that he would visit Israel if invited; Israeli prime minister Menachem Begin issued an invitation; ten days after his initial offer, Sadat became the first Arab leader to visit the Jewish State. Scenes from the Egyptian leader's three days in Jerusalem—an event deemed unthinkable only weeks before—opened new possibilities for peace between Israel and its bitter enemy.

By summer 1978, negotiations between the two nations were stalled, so in September, Carter brought Sadat and Begin to Camp David, the presidential retreat in Maryland. Before long, the two leaders could barely stand to be in one another's presence, so Carter undertook a campaign of shuttle diplomacy, talking to each leader separately, back and forth between their cabins. Begin was amenable to Egypt's demand that Israel return the Sinai Peninsula, captured from Egypt in the 1967 Six

Day War, but balked at allowing the establishment of an independent Palestinian state in the West Bank and Gaza. After thirteen days at the presidential retreat, the three leaders reached an understanding and went to the White House, where Sadat and Begin signed the Camp David Accords with Carter as witness. In the document, Begin issued vague promises about elections in the occupied territories and Sadat committed Egypt to become the first Arab country to formally recognize Israel's right to exist.

The accords did not constitute a peace treaty, so, the following March, Carter journeyed to the Middle East, where he conducted another round of shuttle diplomacy, this time not from cabin to cabin but from country to country. Carter wrestled agreement between the two nations on a formal peace treaty that established mutual diplomatic relations and returned the Sinai. Once more, Sadat and Begin signed the agreement at the White House. In return, Carter committed the United States to an ongoing program of foreign aid to both countries—dollars that flow to this day.

In an interview years later, Carter said:

> When I was elected president nobody asked me to negotiate between Israel and Egypt. It was not even a question raised in my campaign. But I felt that one of the reasons that I was elected president was to try to bring peace to the Holy Land.

Dealing with difficult personalities—Begin had been especially vexing—Jimmy Carter had coaxed into existence the first peace treaty in the history of the Arab-Israeli conflict. But this triumph was not the foreign policy episode on which America's voters would judge him when he sought reelection.

POLITICS VS. POLICY: Dealing with Competing Pressures

"In the '70s," says Andy, "when considering any controversial issue, there was a rough equivalence between what corporate interests, represented by individual trade groups and/or national organizations like the Business Roundtable, were able to deliver by way of muscle and support and what labor could deliver. Labor unions were much stronger then, and much more important in the overall scheme of things. If you wanted to improve bargaining or wages or training or opportunities or health care for working- or middle-class people, the leverage of labor and that of management were about the same.

"But there was also a third element, which was critical to me, because this was where I always went if I wanted what I regarded as an objective progressive opinion: the not-for-profit lobbying groups. Friends of the Earth, the Children's Defense Fund, and the like. I worked closely with them, because I regarded myself as someone who was committed on behalf of my constituents and my country and my prospective grandchildren to get important things done without respect to what special interests thought about them. So I would work with the Natural Resources Defense Council. I would work with pediatricians. Yes, there was a pediatricians' association, but pediatricians wanted to improve health care for kids. Those were the people I worked with.

"The oil companies were well decked out with lobbyists, but I don't remember meeting with oil company executives or representatives. My positions on energy issues were so clear that they must have felt there were more wobbly people they could make more progress with. Why waste time talking to me? I spent a whole lot less time meeting with bevies of lobbyists than did some of my colleagues who were not necessarily clear about how they were going to vote on a bill until the last minute. I saved myself a lot of hours.

"For example: We were the first out of the box on improving cleaner standards for autos. Once during that time, when a committee meeting broke up, a representative of one of the major auto companies approached me and asked if he could meet with me. My response was, 'You know where I stand. There's no point in our having a meeting, because nothing is going to change my view about the need to move on these environmental requirements. The companies, for decades, have opposed any progress on this. So the answer is no.'

"Another example was the Clinch River Breeder Reactor, which was supposed to transform our ability to produce electric power using nuclear breeder technology. Masses of money were poured into that. The plant was in Tennessee, in Congressman Al Gore's district.

"It turned out that the major engineering consultants on the Clinch River Breeder Reactor, Burns and Roe, were headquartered in Bergen

County—in Oradell, not in my district, but adjacent. So the CEO of Burns and Roe wants to come and talk to me. I've already decided I'm going to vote no on the project.

"'Yes,' I told them, 'have him come and talk to me.'

"The CEO and his associates arrive. They had their slide presentation and they had all the stuff about the Clinch River Breeder Reactor and why it was so important and how it was going to be a breakthrough in electricity production. I'm certain they felt that since I was a congressman from the county where their national headquarters were located, and the CEO had come and talked to me, and they had shown me this presentation about how this was the future of energy, they could count on my vote. But I voted against them. I'm sure they were surprised.

"The next election campaign, I'm going door to door in my district and I'm in the town that's right next to the town with the headquarters. A lady comes to the door and says, 'There's some reason I'm not supposed to support you.' And so we chatted. Eventually it turned out that her husband worked for Burns and Roe.

"Lesson: If you're going to put yourself out there, there are costs.

"The Clinch River Breeder Reactor was a lemon. It fell apart after hundreds of millions of dollars were poured into it. We were right, it wasn't going to work—even though we didn't have the votes to kill it.

"But you see, I was willing to put myself out there, even if it was clear that it would be in a losing cause."

LOSING AND WINNING: Campaigns for the Senate and the House

"I definitely had state ambitions. My career goal was to become a US senator of note and importance.

"I had grown up in years when there were giants in the Senate in both political parties. Harrison Williams and Clifford Case of New Jersey, Margaret Chase Smith of Maine and Everett Dirksen of Illinois on the Republican side. William Fulbright of Arkansas, Wayne Morse of Oregon, Gaylord Nelson of Wisconsin, Phil Hart of Michigan, Vance Hartke of Indiana. Scoop Jackson of Washington, for whom I interned. Hubert Humphrey of Minnesota—certainly. He was one of my idols. I explicitly thought about Humphrey in terms of fighting the good fight and knowing that whatever criticism you might get for being upfront on this or that issue can be dissolved if people have the feeling you're working on their interests, that you're independent-minded, that you care, and that you're going to make a difference.

"The Senate. That's where I hoped I was headed."

Clifford Case was known as one of the most liberal Republicans in the US Senate since his election to the body in 1954 after a campaign in which right-wingers called him "Stalin's choice for senator." Over his four terms in office, Case had compiled a record of solid support for civil rights legislation, as well as for laws favored by organized labor and environmental advocates. While Case might have lived on the leftward edge of the GOP Senate conference, he was by no means an anomaly. Liberal Republicans had been among the most prominent US senators in the '50s, '60s, and '70s—from Jacob Javits of New York to Charles Percy of Illinois, from Leverett Saltsonstall of Massachusetts to his successor, Edward Brooke, the first Black senator since Reconstruction. Margaret Chase Smith of Maine denounced Joseph McCarthy from the floor of the Senate less than four months after his speech in Wheeling, West Virginia, flung him into the national spotlight. Charles Mathias of Maryland warned against Richard Nixon's "Southern Strategy." Mark Hatfield of Oregon persevered as one of Washington's most outspoken opponents of the Vietnam War.

But by 1978, as the GOP was becoming more defined by its burgeoning Southern wing, liberal Republicans were being squeezed out of their party. Case, seeking a seventh term, would struggle in the GOP primary. In the meantime, New Jersey Democrats were holding a primary of their own. Andy was interested in competing.

"I didn't look forward to running against Clifford Case," he says, "which would have been difficult, but I did think I was ready to mount a statewide campaign. I thought the state was trending Democratic and that Case, as much as I liked him, was vulnerable."

Andy hoped for a repeat of the dynamic that had carried him to victory over William Widnall. "Recent polls show that Mr. Case has the classic profile of an incumbent who has stayed too long," Andy told the *Times* in December 1977. "My theory of this campaign is that we must have a candidate who is young, attractive and who can hit voters with gut issues."

"I never shied away from risk," Andy says today. "I thought I was ready and that I had a breadth of support in other key counties. And then there were the statewide groups—women's groups, environmental groups, labor—that supported me. Who would have a better shot?"

His name was Bill Bradley—and his shot at the Senate came about because of the shots he'd taken at Madison Square Garden.

Unlike Andy, who was a stranger in many parts of New Jersey, Bradley—the recently retired star forward for the championship New York Knickerbocker basketball teams of 1970 and 1973, and the hoops legend at New Jersey's contribution to the Ivy League, Princeton—needed little introduction. Bradley, who had campaigned for Andy in 1974—he was one-fourth of the infamous tennis match after which Andy tumbled trying to jump the net—had for some time looked to enter politics.

As the campaign to oppose Case started to take shape, Andy met with the former athlete. Andy recounts the get-together: "I said, 'Bill, don't you think you could start by running for the House? There's a seat waiting for you with a Republican incumbent. Why don't you knock him off?' He politely thanked me for my thoughts and went ahead with his Senate race."

As the *Times* noted in December 1977, "While there may be several contenders in the Democratic primary [Maguire] sees Bill Bradley, the former basketball star, as his major opponent. But he believes that Mr. Bradley will 'fall short because he is depending on his celebrity status' rather than discussing the issues."

Andy hoped for the endorsement of Brendan Byrne, the Democratic governor of New Jersey first elected to that post in 1973. Byrne's successful backing of New Jersey's first income tax, enacted in 1976, had earned him the nickname "one-term Byrne." But while he faced a tough primary in his 1977 bid for reelection, he crushed his GOP opponent that November to emerge as the undisputed leader of the state Democratic party.

When Andy met with Byrne in January 1978, the governor affirmed his public neutrality in the race for the party's Senate nomination. However, Byrne was known to privately favor Richard Leone, who had managed his '73 campaign. "Leone was Byrne's candidate," says Andy. "Byrne had appointed him state treasurer. Leone was a really good guy, and he lined up David Garth, the political consultant who had worked so closely with Lindsay and others. I guess Leone thought he could enter elective politics via Byrne's popularity. Leone later told me that at one point he and Garth had talked about his getting out of the race and supporting me. But that never happened."

By January, although Andy hadn't officially entered the race, he'd raised $57,000 of the half million he estimated he'd need to run an effective primary. The *Record* covered a fundraiser thrown for him by a "big-league Democratic hostess" in her twentieth-story apartment on New York City's swanky Central Park South. Attended by "several dozen guests," who snacked on smoked turkey and cheese and crackers, the affair featured Parren Mitchell, a member of the Congressional Black Caucus from Maryland, who came to vouch for his friend. Andy, discussing his rivals for the nomination, said Leone was "a fine fellow . . . but without a base." Bradley? "A fine basketball player." (Elsewhere, Andy joked to the press that Bradley "shoots only 50 percent from the floor.")

On January 22, the three candidates fought through a snowstorm to debate at a Manhattan television studio. Andy pointed to his accomplishments in Congress, Leone emphasized his knowledge of government finance, and Bradley, according to the *Record*, said that "his inexperience doesn't matter, because he understands the issues and knows how to work with people."

Two weeks later, after failing to meet interim fundraising goals, Andy bowed out of the race he'd never formally entered.

"Once Bradley entered the picture," Andy says now, "there was no route forward for me. The celebrity culture in American politics—don't get me started on that."

Running for the Senate would have meant giving up his seat in the House; now he would run to keep it. The *Record* praised Andy's decision as a "timely and statesmanlike move." If Andy lost the primary, or won the primary and lost the general, "he'd be out of a job, and his constituents in Bergen County would be out of a first-rate congressman." The editorial closed with:

> He's headstrong, ambitious, and impatient, which is why he aspired to the Senate, and he is unlikely to have another shot at that for at least six more years. Too bad; he'd probably do as good a job in the upper house as he has done in the lower. But the line from Longfellow has probably already been quoted to him: "All things come round to him who will but wait."

As it happened, 1978 proved to be the end of the line for Clifford Case. He fell victim not to Bradley's celebrity but to the changing GOP, losing the primary to a hard-core conservative, Jeffrey Bell, previously an aide in Ronald Reagan's 1976 presidential campaign. Bradley doubled Leone's vote tally in June, then trounced Bell in November.

"Bradley had the great good luck that Bell won the primary against Case, and off he went," says Andy.

Bill Bradley would go on to be an effective US senator but hardly a standout. "I remember a conversation with Susan Thomases," says Andy, "who was Bradley's alter ego, about how important it was to him to be selective in the issues he took on. She added that I would benefit from being more selective.

"Bradley was very, very careful in what he chose to work on. He was not much into tackling issues that would cause trouble for him with any measurable constituency. He was always thinking about running for president.

"If you're famous for any unrelated reason, it doesn't matter whether you've had political experience or have anything in particular to offer. Bradley was unusual in that, potentially, he had a lot to offer. But in the Senate he delivered a lot less than he might have. Bradley was famously slow and, for many, overly patient with himself about making decisions; often it seemed he was on the basketball court working to find the open shot. The same was true of his presidential race in 2000, when he ran in the primaries against Al Gore. It's not that he wasn't right on the campaign's big issues—he was right to emphasize health care—but he was a wooden speaker. He lacked the necessary pizazz and effectiveness to become a national leader. Nevertheless, he sure as hell was able to ride his celebrity to the US Senate, upending everybody, like Leone and me, who had dedicated our lives to public service.

"I try not to be angry about it every day. Just when somebody brings it up."

Andy faced a more formidable challenger to his reelection in 1978 than he had two years earlier. Marge Roukema, a resident of Ridgewood, had never run for anything more exalted than the board of education, but she easily won the endorsement of the state party apparatus and then breezed through the GOP primary.

Andy's opponent in 1976 had been a self-styled, unapologetic "conservative." Roukema, showing a better understanding of the district's independent-minded voters, billed herself as a "moderate." However, the difference was less substantive than stylistic—despite her more agreeable personality, she barely deviated from standard GOP dogma. She chose as the centerpiece of her campaign the Kemp-Roth tax cut, a proposal, then all the rage among Republican candidates across the country, to slash income tax rates across the board by some 30 percent over three years, although, to establish her bona fides as a moderate, she adjusted phase-in to five years.

Named for its two chief sponsors—Jack Kemp, a Republican congressman (and retired pro quarterback) from Buffalo, and William Roth, a Republican senator from Delaware—the proposal previewed the "supply-side" tax cut that Congress would pass in 1981, during the opening months of the Reagan administration. Proponents of the plan claimed that the sharply lower tax rates would not add to the federal budget deficit: The lower rates would juice the nation's economic output, thus generating not merely *as much* tax revenue as before but *more*. Abracadabra, free money!

Running in the 1980 Republican presidential primary, George H. W. Bush derided the magical economic theory, which Ronald Reagan supported, as "voodoo economics." In 1978, Roukema preached the voodoo. "This will not increase the deficit," she said.

(It did.)

Newspaper accounts from 1978 suggested that Andy had been caught off guard by the strength of Roukema's campaign, but today Andy denies it. "She was a much better candidate than Sheehan," he says. "We knew the demographics and the voting behavior in the district. We knew we had a huge job."

Andy asked Elgie Holstein to manage the effort. "Gina Glantz had run the '76 reelect but was not interested in doing a third campaign," says Holstein. "We were executing a model we were familiar with. We knew who our supporters were. Andy had developed a limited but impressive base of donors in both New Jersey and Washington. Again we had the personalized letters, the neighborhood walking tours. We had all the things we knew how to do from the previous two campaigns."

Andy put on his sneakers and went to work. "I went to ten thousand doors," says Andy, "just as I had earlier." ("I like his red shoes," said a woman behind one of those doors.)

Andy's supporters in this campaign included a movie star known for his devotion to environmental causes. Not long after President Carter signed the Clean Air Act amendments Andy had labored so effectively to shepherd through Congress, Robert Redford attended a fundraiser. The announcement of his presence triggered a minor frenzy among the residents of northern New Jersey.

"We had the event at the posh Ridgewood Country Club," recalls Glantz. "Lots of Republican donors and rich businessmen called Andy to say they were contributing to ensure there was room for their wives and daughters to attend. Others had dinner in the nearby section of the club and sent their wives and daughters through the room divider to get a free look at Redford. Big Democratic donors called to ask that their wives and daughters be chosen to pick him up at the airport. Eventually, Andy settled on Meg and me. Meg, of course, had an abiding interest in the environment. I had a title with entitlement (campaign manager). So no one could complain.

"We invited the press to a pre-event at Andy's house. We arrived and Redford wanted to 'freshen up,' so I took him upstairs. On the way he asked where he should throw away his gum and a reporter said she would take it. I swear this happened!"

"It was highly unusual for Redford to endorse candidates," says Andy, "but he headlined fundraisers for me twice: In this congressional campaign and again in my Senate race, in May 1982."

Roukema did not enjoy Andy's name recognition, but she had the backing of the national Republican Party—owing to the district's history and population, the GOP had put Andy on its "hit list" of vulnerable incumbents. The party supplied money and expertise; pros from Washington ran Roukema's campaign. She even paid for three days of TV ads—a rarity in New Jersey congressional races. Candidates did not normally advertise on television, considering the inefficiency of buying time in the costly New York City media market to reach a district containing less than 1 percent of that market's twenty million people.

"Marge was very involved in civic events and very attractive," says Holstein, "with a husband who was a respected member of the medical profession in Ridgewood. But she was not a seasoned campaigner. Had she been more aggressive and knowledgeable, I'm not sure whether the result would have been the same."

For all the favorable press Andy had received during his two terms in office, Holstein and others in Andy's campaign found the coverage in the *Record* that year to be biased toward Roukema. When Holstein confronted a reporter with that perception, the reporter told him, "Marge is the new face. Everybody knows who Andy Maguire is. I want to show who Marge Roukema is."

The tables had been turned in the four years since Andy had sold voters on his newness to topple the long-serving, elderly incumbent, William Widnall.

"Roukema brought energy to the campaign," says Ted Hoff, who worked on the campaign while on leave from his job as the transportation specialist in Andy's DC office. "She was out and about, talking to people."

For most of the fall campaign, a pressmen's strike shut down New York City's major daily newspapers—the *Times*, *Daily News*, and *Post*. Andy's challenger took advantage of the situation, publishing a daily she called the *Roukema News*. "She would stand at train platforms in Bergen County and hand out copies," says Holstein. "The paper would feature some combination of pro-Roukema political stuff and some anti-Maguire stuff, but pretty gentle. The reason many commuters eagerly accepted it was that it had lots of national and world news in it, too."

Roukema took her messaging from the standard GOP playbook for that year—indeed, for every year: Andy loved taxes, hated the military, and wanted to spend every penny in every taxpayer's pocket.

"Andy Maguire votes for higher income taxes," she charged, "higher Social Security taxes, and higher energy taxes—and for higher domestic government spending at nearly every opportunity."

"It was the usual claptrap about spending," says Andy, "notwithstanding that the National Taxpayers Union had awarded me a top ranking because I'd voted against so much federal spending. I always voted against the omnibus public works bill because it was full of pork. I would offer my amendments, which would be defeated, or I would join somebody else who was offering amendments, which would be defeated. Same for the military budget. I would support sensible amendments that said, 'No more B-1 bombers. No, we don't need five new battleships of ancient design.' And then, unlike most of my colleagues who supported such amendments, I always voted against the final bill. Discussing the defense budget with me, Tom Downey, a member of the Armed Services Committee, once said to me, 'It's fine and right on the merits for you to vote against it. I would vote against it if I could, but I can't.'

"So Roukema said I was anti-defense when, in fact, I was pro the right kind of defense. I thought building something in somebody's congressional district was far less important than giving the troops the training and hardware they needed."

"Time after time I have moved against wasteful spending," Andy told a Chamber of Commerce meeting in Montvale that October. He pointed out that he was one of only twenty-eight members of the House to oppose a highway and transportation bill stocked with $16 billion worth of "wrong-headed and ill-conceived" pet projects. He was one of only thirty-seven Democrats and twenty-two Republicans, he said, to vote against a $10.2 billion "pork-barrel" public works bill.

"Mr. Maguire believes in more government regulation, I believe in less," said Roukema. "Mr. Maguire believes that only he and his like-minded friends in Congress have the answer to the nation's problems. I believe the people have the best answers, if they are only allowed to apply them."

In debate, Roukema even went after Andy on the issue he'd brought to Congress practically single-handedly, the environmental causes of cancer. Suggesting that the prevalence of environmental carcinogens had been exaggerated, she called for greater research emphasis on the disease itself rather than on efforts to limit contamination.

The *Record* weighed in, endorsing Andy as "one of the brightest, hardest-working, and most articulate members of Congress," noting his work as a champion for "consumers against big business" and defending him from Roukema's charge that he was a liberal big spender. The editorial concluded: "We can think of few public officials who are as worthy of reelection as Andy Maguire."

Roukema came closer than Sheehan did. Andy won with 52.5 percent of the ballots to his challenger's 46.6.

"In 1978 Carter was losing his popularity," says Hoff, "so we had to work pretty hard to win. Andy's margin was down, but at least he got over 50 percent. It was a thrilling victory."

Although Andy had won by 14 points in 1976, he pronounced himself happy with this year's closer result. "I was targeted [by the GOP]," he said on election night. "To win by a six- or seven-point margin is excellent. I'm very pleased."

So was his opponent. "To come from nowhere and give Andy Maguire the political scare of his life is something in itself," she said.

Two days later, Roukema told the *Record* of her intent to run against Andy in 1980. "It will be a presidential election year," she said.

It would indeed.

CHAPTER 8

POTENTIAL UNFULFILLED: Jimmy Carter, Andy Maguire, and the Will of the People

Tony Conigliaro lived that dream for six years in the 1960s before tragedy cut the dream short.

—**ROCCO CONSTANTINO** (on the Red Sox slugger whose career was cut short by a fastball to the face)

It was a shame he got hurt when he did. With a few more years, he could have made the Hall of Fame.

—**JOHNNY PESKY**

WEIRD: Carter, Camp David, and the "Malaise" Speech

By the summer of 1979, Jimmy Carter's luck seemed to have run out. Despite his having appointed an "inflation czar" the previous October, an oil shock triggered by revolution in Iran boosted inflation to double digits and once more forced Americans to wait in long lines at the gas pump. Unemployment hadn't risen, but, at around 6 percent, neither had it fallen. Interest rates were soaring, the stock market sinking. The president's approval rating according to Gallup had collapsed, sinking from 50 percent in January to 28 percent at the end of June.

In Tokyo for a seven-nation economic summit, Carter hoped to get a vacation in Hawaii on the way back to Washington. But his aide Stuart Eizenstat, in a memo describing the deteriorating circumstances at home, told the president, "I do not need to detail for you the political damage we are suffering from all of this." Carter skipped his vacation and flew to DC, where he prepared to address his anxious fellow Americans.

At the request of the White House, the television networks reserved time on the evening of July 5 for a presidential address. Carter and his wife, at Camp David, read the draft his speechwriters had produced—an unremarkable listing of a variety of options to deal with the oil crisis—and were not satisfied. Carter then telephoned his aides in the White House and ordered them to call off the speech, setting off one of the weirdest episodes in presidential history. The nation, Carter felt, was afflicted by something more profound than lines at the Exxon station. "There's more to it than energy," he told his staff. "I just don't want to bullshit the American people." The press reported that the administration had provided no explanation for the cancellation. The White House was forced to assure the nation that the president had not nixed his speech because of ill health or an undisclosed national emergency.

And then the president of the United States disappeared.

He remained at Camp David for ten days, canceling all previously scheduled appearances, such as a trip to Louisville for the National Governors Association. He conducted intense consultations not only with his staff but also with some 130 other Americans—"business and labor, teachers and preachers, governors, mayors, and private citizens," he would say—whom he had invited to help him take the nation's temperature. He also traveled by helicopter to Pittsburgh to meet with a dozen ordinary citizens at the nearby home of a machinist and his wife. Asked about his visit with the president at the Maryland retreat, Otis Bowen, the governor of Indiana and a physician, took pains to report that he thought the president looked "well and healthy. And I know for a fact that he ran a couple of miles this morning."

His work done at the presidential retreat, Carter returned to the White House on Sunday, July 15. That evening, he spoke to the nation from the Oval Office. The speech dealt with the energy emergency, but in an unusual context. He opened with criticisms of him he'd heard during "an extraordinary ten days." Among the "typical comments" he received were:

- "Mr. President, you are not leading this nation—you're just managing the government."
- "Some of your cabinet members don't seem loyal. There is not enough discipline among your disciples."
- "Don't talk to us about politics or the mechanics of government but about an understanding of our common good."
- "Mr. President, we're in trouble. Talk to us about blood and sweat and tears."
- "If you lead, Mr. President, we will follow."
- "Our neck is stretched over the fence and OPEC has a knife."
- "Be bold, Mr. President. We may make mistakes, but we are ready to experiment."

Carter went on to say that the nation was suffering not just from a flawed energy system but from "a crisis in confidence."

"It is a crisis," he continued, "that strikes at the very heart and soul and spirit of our national will. We can see this crisis in the growing doubt about the meaning of our own lives and in the loss of a unity of purpose for our nation."

America, said its president, was turning its back on what had made the country great: "In a nation that was proud of hard work, strong families, close-knit communities, and our faith in God, too many of us now tend to worship self-indulgence and consumption. . . . But we've discovered that owning things and consuming things does not satisfy our longing for meaning. We've learned that piling up material goods cannot fill the emptiness of lives which have no confidence or purpose."

He did propose several energy solutions that addressed, well, energy: "Beginning this moment, this nation will never use more foreign oil than we did in 1977—never." To achieve this end he set import quotas for oil and announced a plan to develop synthetic and renewable fuels. Among the proposals was a mandate to shift oil-fueled electricity plants to coal.

The task ahead would not be easy, he said. "There is simply no way to avoid sacrifice."

He ended the thirty-two-minute speech with:

> I will do my best, but I will not do it alone. Let your voice be heard. Whenever you have a chance, say something good about our country. With God's help and for the sake of our nation, it is time for us to join hands in America. Let us commit ourselves together to a rebirth of the American spirit. Working together with our common faith we cannot fail.

Early reaction to the speech was positive, at least among members of his own party. Speaker Tip O'Neill called the talk "the best speech he has made," adding, "I am confident the American people will respond with the necessary responses and that Congress will pull together in this time of crisis." A *New York Times*/CBS poll saw the president's approval rating jump from 26 to 37 percent in a single week. Three quarters of that poll's respondents agreed "that there is a moral and spiritual crisis, that is, a crisis of confidence, in the country today."

But then Carter began a series of inexplicable personnel moves. He appointed his longtime political adviser, Hamilton Jordan, the most reviled person in Washington, White House chief of staff. He asked all the members of his cabinet to offer their resignations. Jordan distributed several hundred "staff evaluation forms" to senior officials and ordered them to grade their subordinates. Andy, like most of Washington, no fan of the president's new chief of staff, said, "It's utterly appalling to many of us that the White House thinks that the answer to its problem is giving more authority to Hamilton Jordan. Members have joked in the past that it is easier to get Carter himself on the phone than Jordan."

And then began the bloodletting. Jordan demanded that transportation secretary Brock Adams fire his deputy and send another aide to the White House for a chewing out. Adams resigned in anger, as did the two aides. Carter fired his energy secretary, James Schlesinger, and his secretary of health, education, and welfare, Joseph Califano. Both men, the president believed, not only were insufficiently enthusiastic in supporting Carter's proposals on the Hill but also undercut his initiatives in the press. Carter also dispensed with his attorney general, his secretary of the treasury, and his secretary of housing and urban development.

Whatever goodwill Carter had generated with his stated determination to tackle the nation's problems was lost. Andy was among the critics. "Carter has obliterated the positive new beginning he made on Sunday," he said. The Speaker was also unhappy, telling Jordan, according to the *Record*, that "the best thing he and press secretary Jody Powell could do for the president was get on a bus back to Georgia."

"I found it difficult," Andy says today, "to make any sense out of the entire episode. Califano was doing a terrific job at HEW."

Somehow, Carter's address became known as the "malaise" speech, even though that word appeared nowhere within it. And while the country had initially approved of Carter's call for national purpose, as the speech sunk in and the cabinet firings multiplied, anger mounted over Carter's seeming to blame the country's woes on the public, not on his own inadequate leadership. The problem, Americans believed, wasn't their "worship" of "self-indulgence and consumption," as he'd contended on July 15. The problem was their president—an incompetent chief executive who couldn't set an energy policy without embarrassing himself and the nation by his ludicrous management of his cabinet and staff.

Carter's approval ratings dropped again. But they rose in November, influenced by events in Iran.

LONG MEMORIES: The United States, Iran, and Mohammad Mossadegh

Jimmy Carter owed his failure to win reelection to any number of factors—a skilled and appealing opponent, persistent inflation, a primary challenge. But he could be said to owe the loss to Dwight Eisenhower, Allen Dulles, and Kermit Roosevelt, as much as to anyone.

In 1951, Shah Mohammad Reza Pahlavi of Iran, responding to the will of the parliament with which he shared power, appointed Mohammad Mossadegh prime minister. An advocate of social reforms and increased democratization, Mossadegh in May 1952 nationalized the Anglo-Iranian Oil Company, the British-controlled firm that dominated Iran's sizable oil industry. In response, the United Kingdom mounted a naval blockade that prevented Iran from exporting its oil, effectively idling production. Jockeying with the shah for power, Mossadegh was forced to resign in July but, after hundreds of mass demonstrations in his support, was reinstated and given control of the nation's military. Parliament then granted him broad emergency powers, which he invoked to institute land reform and limit the powers of the shah.

The following year, America intervened. Spurred by a British government unhappy with the loss of its oil interests, new president Dwight Eisenhower agreed to CIA chief Allen Dulles's plan to overthrow Mossadegh. The CIA operative on the ground who engineered the coup d'état was Kermit Roosevelt, grandson of President Theodore Roosevelt.

In on the plot, the shah followed the coup by enhancing his power, eventually emerging as a dictator. The shah did much to modernize Iran, building infrastructure, instituting literacy programs and land redistribution, liberating women. But as he brought the nation up to date, he tightened his grip on its political dissidents, using as the instrument of his repression his dreaded secret police, SAVAK.

Throughout the '60s and '70s, American presidents relied on the shah, whose sizable army they generously supplied with American-made weapons, as a cold war ally who would protect US interests in the oil-producing Persian Gulf region. "We welcome you here as not only an old friend," Nixon told the shah as the monarch visited Washington in 1973, "as a progressive leader of your own people, but as a world statesman of the first rank."

Carter followed in this tradition. Toasting the shah in Tehran in December 1977, the president said, "Iran, because of the great leadership of the shah, is an island of stability in one of the more troubled areas of the world.

"This is a great tribute to you, Your Majesty, and to your leadership and to the respect and the admiration and love which your people give to you."

Carter also said, "The cause of human rights is one that also is shared deeply by our people and by the leaders of our two nations."

The victims of SAVAK torture chambers could not have appreciated this statement by an American president who styled himself a champion of human rights around the world.

Barely a year later, the shah would flee his country. And in that former "island of stability," the name Carter would be reviled.

In January 1978, a wave of anti-shah street demonstrations began in Iran; as the year went on, the protests got bigger and more frequent. In response, the shah introduced measures aimed at increasing democracy and lessening the influence of SAVAK. But those steps did not stem the tide of popular revolt, so in the fall he declared martial law in a dozen of the nation's largest cities. In October, workers around the nation staged a general strike. Directing much of the action was a cleric exiled in Iraq, Ayatollah Ruhollah Khomeini. Protestors targeted their wrath not just on government offices but also on Western establishments like movie theaters and department stores. Foreign policy personnel within the Carter administration argued over how to respond to the unrest overtaking America's ally.

But events overtook both the shah and the American president. In January 1979, the shah departed Iran for Egypt, where he was welcomed by President Sadat. The shah left the government in the care of a prime minister, who disbanded SAVAK. But on February 1, Khomeini arrived in Tehran; in a March referendum, the nation's citizens declared an Islamic republic.

Carter's recent embrace of the shah did not sit well with the young revolutionaries who had brought down the Peacock Throne, but the White House might have avoided further consequences had the deposed monarch not asked to be admitted to the United States for medical treatment. Suffering from lymphoma, he hadn't stayed long in Egypt; after wandering from country to country, he had arrived in Mexico in June. Carter realized the need to distance himself and his administration from this now-disgraced former partner, but he faced pressure from two powerful individuals: David Rockefeller, chair of Chase Manhattan Bank, which had done much business with his friend the shah, and Henry Kissinger, who threatened to withdraw his support from the SALT II arms treaty if Carter did not admit the former ruler. Told, incorrectly, that the shah could not receive the treatment he needed in Mexico, Carter on October 20 reluctantly gave the go-ahead for him to be treated at a hospital in New York City.

Anti-US protests erupted in Iran, carried out by demonstrators aware of America's role not only in bolstering the shah in recent years but in the original sin of his empowerment amidst the toppling of Mossadegh a quarter century before. On November 4, a group of radicalized students overran the US embassy in Tehran, taking fifty-two Americans prisoner. The students demanded that the United States both repatriate the shah to stand trial in Iran and apologize for the 1953 coup. The

Carter administration, seeing the students' action as a violation of the ancient tradition of diplomatic immunity, would not yield. Iran's leader, Ayatollah Khomeini, backed the holding of the hostages. "Death to America," demonstrators chanted day after day. "Death to Carter."

At first, as Americans rallied 'round the flag, Carter's public approval ratings rose, from 32 percent according to Gallup just before the hostage-taking to 58 percent in January. But as the crisis continued, the number sank back to the low 30s. Carter was not helped by Walter Cronkite, the "most trusted man in America." Cronkite had always ended his nightly CBS newscast with "And that's the way it is," followed by the day's date. Starting in December he added a running count of the days the hostages had been held in Iran.

That month, Carter, realizing that the stalemate would never be resolved with the shah on American soil, arranged for him to be flown to Panama. The shah eventually returned to Egypt, where he died on July 27, 1980.

The shah's expulsion did nothing to soften Iran's determination to hold onto the captives. For months Carter resisted a military solution, figuring that any attempt to free the Americans by force would result in the death of some or all of them. But on April 24, he sent eight US helicopters from the aircraft carrier USS *Nimitz* to conduct a rescue.

Their first stop was a landing zone in eastern Iran. There things began to go wrong. Dust storms disabled two of the helicopters; a third was also found to be unusable. The operation's planners considered six aircraft the minimum for success, so the commander on the ground aborted the mission—a decision Carter approved. Before the service members could return, an accident with a refueling airplane killed eight of them. News of the failure only made Carter look weaker.

America and its president had been humbled by a much smaller country, led by religious fanatics. Carter would stand for reelection on November 4, 1980, one year to the day after the fall of the embassy. After the election, negotiations intensified with the Iranians for the hostages' release. The captives were freed on January 20, 1981, the day Carter's successor as president was inaugurated. The Iranians timed the release so that the liberated Americans didn't exit Iranian air space until after Ronald Reagan had taken the oath of office. In 2023, a former Texas lawmaker publicly confirmed what some had long suspected: The Reagan campaign had secretly approached the Iranians, offering them arms sales in a future Reagan administration if they held the hostages until after the election.

KEEPING CLOSE TO HOME: A Liberal Survives in a Swing District

Throughout his time in the House, Andy was profiled as one of the body's most liberal members—certainly the most liberal among the New Jersey delegation. In January 1976, he was the only representative from the state—and one of only twenty-seven members nationwide—to win a 100 percent rating from the liberal advocacy group Americans for Democratic Action. The following year the ADA scored him at 95 percent, still the highest for any New Jersey representative. The ADA continued to rate Andy at or near the top of its list until the end of his tenure.

Commenting on the perfect ADA score in 1976, Andy denied that his views were out of step with those of his constituents. "I'm voting my suburban district," he said. "The political attitudes of my district changed over the years, and think I reflect them now."

Andy's protestations notwithstanding, the 1976 presidential balloting made clear that Bergen County retained a Republican tilt. What enabled Andy to win two reelection campaigns was not the similarity of his ideology to that of his constituents. He won because he focused on issues of immediate importance to voters and stayed close to his district.

Andy adopted energy as his signature issue—its cost and availability, which voters confronted every month when they paid their utility bill and every few days when they stopped at a gas station. He also worked to curb pollution, including carcinogens that contributed to New Jersey's high incidence of cancer—a statistic well known, and viscerally felt, by his constituents.

He also advocated for a television station in New Jersey.

The Garden State was split between two media markets: northern New Jersey tuned into stations broadcasting from New York City, southern New Jersey watched programs beamed from Philadelphia. Aside from a public UHF station based in Trenton, barely accessible to most TV watchers, no station—no VHF station, appearing on one of every TV's standard channels from 2 to 13—called the state home.

"The point of that initiative," Andy says, "was that TV news coverage of New Jersey came out of the stations in New York and Philadelphia, and the coverage was lousy. This issue was another one in which I identified a huge gap that needed to be addressed. New Jersey is a major state. It needed to be properly covered by television news." Andy worked the issue from 1976 through the end of his time in office. He introduced legislation to require that each state in the Union be home to at least one commercial VHF station and pushed steadily for the bill's passage. But since the measure would have had no effect on forty-eight states—Delaware and New Jersey were the only states without such a station—members of Congress were not motivated to lend their support. The bill failed to become law.

Even so, what Andy started came to a happy conclusion after he left office: In 1983 an independent station, WOR—Channel 9—moved its headquarters across the George Washington Bridge, from New York to Secaucus.

Andy also made sure he was seen in his district—week in and week out. He gave speeches to every group, he appeared at every event. He spoke on "The Relationship of Religion to Government" at the Bergen County council of churches. His topic at a nurses' dinner was "Health Care, Right or Privilege?" At Ramapo College he talked about "Government, Science, and Health," at Bergen Community College about Medicare. He spoke at a Man of the Year brunch for the local chapter of B'nai Brith, talked about the Middle East to a group of Jewish singles, and addressed those gathered for the ground-breaking of a new synagogue.

He made himself even more visible by sponsoring a series of forums around the district. Some sessions involved no more than his listening to constituents and answering their questions. More than once his forums provided information to New Jersey business owners hoping to sell goods and services to the federal government. Another forum's topic was bicycling.

But he also hosted prestigious guests at forums designed to bring his constituents up to date on matters of national importance. At a forum on nuclear energy, three scientists, one who'd come all the way from Texas, traded their conflicting views. At a forum on environmental cancer, Dr. Irving Selikoff, the epidemiologist from Ridgewood who had previously advised Andy, debated a former top scientist at E. I. du Pont de Nemours & Co. on the potential dangers of carcinogens. At a forum on energy, a high-ranking Washington official appeared along with the vice chairman of the Allied Chemical Corporation. Joe Papp, the impresario behind New York's Public Theater, hosted a half-day forum on the arts.

Andy also kept his constituents informed on international affairs. Clifford Case, then in the Senate, came to discuss America's foreign policy; at the session Andy called him the nation's most influential voice on foreign policy after Henry Kissinger. Andrew Young, the US ambassador to the United Nations, spoke about human rights around the world. A forum on the Middle East drew 1,100 spectators, was interrupted for five minutes by a hundred demonstrators, and made the *Times*. The Egyptian and Israeli UN ambassadors spoke, but not in each other's presence and without shaking hands. US assistant secretary of state for the Middle East Alfred Atherton, presented the official American view. "The history of peace efforts in the Middle East," he said, "has been called a series of lost opportunities."

"I built a reputation," says Andy, "as a very, very independent guy who would not be beholden to even my own political party—look at the Sikes affair. I was going to represent the people of my district, I was going to represent the State of New Jersey, I was going to do whatever it took to be helpful to people, not only in my state but across the country. That was more important to people than whether I took a 'liberal' position on this or that issue. In the forums, I brought people from all over the country, whether it was Andy Young or a nuclear scientist, to talk to hundreds of my constituents. The forums underlined that I was looking for the right answers."

FOOD FOR FURNITURE: A Creative Solution to an Urgent Need

In 1980, after the previously appropriated foreign assistance account had been exhausted, Bill Gray, the Pennsylvania House Democrat who chaired the Congressional Black Caucus, challenged the White House to take action to assist needy citizens in the developing world, people such as Cambodians in Thailand, Afghanis in Pakistan, Somalis in Kenya, and residents of famine-stricken states in sub-Saharan Africa. Why, Gray wanted to know, was nothing being done while tens of thousands of children were dying of starvation? The response he got: Find us the money.

The result was emergency food aid provided through what would be dubbed the "Food for Furniture" amendment to the Foreign Assistance Act.

"My staffer, David Dreyer," recalls Andy, "generally made it his business to follow issues and actions that would likely interest me but that fell outside the jurisdictions of my committees. David noticed a proposal put forward by Senator Jim Sasser, a Tennessee Democrat, to cut funds for the purchase of new furniture by the General Services Administration, since GSA warehouses were already full of surplus furniture.

"The Sasser GSA funding reduction proposal had drawn no sponsors in the House, but Dreyer drafted for me a 'Dear Colleague' letter outlining an initiative to switch the excess GSA furniture funds Sasser had identified to America's depleted foreign assistance account. I reached out to my Democratic classmate Floyd Fithian, from Indiana, an agriculture-heavy state whose farmers would produce some of the needed food. I asked Floyd to join me in supporting the hybrid proposal, and he did. We quickly gained bipartisan support from leading internationalist Republicans Ed Derwinski, of Illinois, and Silvio Conte, of Massachusetts.

"Our proposed House legislation cut the GSA budget by $100 million with most ($73 million) going to refugee and famine relief but leaving a smaller portion ($27 million) to reduce federal spending. This combination was attractive to members of both parties.

"Because there was no precedent for the transfer of appropriations from the jurisdiction of one House authorizing committee to that of another, we had a serious procedural problem with the Appropriations Committee, on which neither Fithian nor I served."

Andy and Fithian called on Massachusetts Democrat Ed Boland, a senior member of the House Appropriations Committee and chairman of the House Rules Committee. Boland signed on to their unusual proposal and had the Rules Committee allow the Food for Furniture amendment to be in order; the full House then approved the measure 346–47. Another Democratic classmate of Andy's, upstate New York's Matt McHugh, a junior member on Appropriations, then shepherded the proposal through the House-Senate conference committee. Final passage of the bill, which authorized 300,000 tons of American food to be sent overseas, soon followed in both the House and the Senate.

On October 10, 1980, just after the close of the fiscal year, then Secretary of State Ed Muskie wrote a "Dear Andy" letter that described how the supplemental monies had been spent:

It is certain that without an additional 23,000 tons of emergency food supplies the suffering both in Cambodia itself and in the refugee camps along the Thai border would have been much worse. . . .

Approximately 46,000 tons of food went to Afghan refugees, now numbering more than one million, and it is safe to say that without our assistance the plight of these victims of Soviet aggression would be desperate. . . .

Almost half the money expended on emergency food supplies was devoted to Africa:

- to help feed refugees in Somalia, which as a result of fighting in the Ogaden has about half of Africa's three million refugees
- to alleviate massive human suffering in Uganda, where there has been starvation in the Karamoja region as a result of drought and the chaos left by the previous regime of Idi Amin
- for humanitarian food aid to Ethiopia, whose people have been among the hardest hit by the African drought
- to help Tanzania meet emergency needs and to establish a strategic grain reserve

In addition to these grant programs the supplemental monies provided $16 million . . . for highly concessional food aid loans to Liberia, Mozambique, Sudan, and Tanzania.

Nothing more effectively demonstrates the combination of skill, strength and compassion that has made the United States an effective world leader. I deeply appreciate the role you have played in making this vital contribution possible.

With warm best wishes, Edmund S. Muskie

A LOST CAUSE: Giving Up on Jimmy Carter

"I am very, very disappointed with Carter," said Andy in May 1979. "But I am not yet part of any draft-Kennedy group—not yet."

On April 5, 1979, the president announced his intention to lift all controls on the price of oil by September 30, 1981. Expecting that as the domestic price rose to world levels the oil companies would reap handsome returns, Carter proposed a "windfall profits tax" that would direct some of that bounty to public purposes such as mass transit and aid to the poor.

At the end of May, House Democrats held a vote within their caucus on the president's decontrol plan. Majority Leader Jim Wright warned his members that voting to maintain controls "would be deeply embarrassing to the president and to the Democratic Party." But the troops didn't listen, voting against Carter's plan by a 2–1 margin. "This is a complete and total repudiation of the president's position," said Andy's friend Toby Moffett. "This is the first clear indication that the president's party is rejecting him." Andy weighed in on Carter's assertion that decontrol would lead to conservation and greater production. "This is a fantasy," he said, "and House members are beginning to realize it."

In August, a couple of weeks after the "malaise" speech, Andy observed that congressional Democrats no longer felt obligated to back their president. "You have the incredible situation," Andy said, "where a member of Congress can receive a personal call from the president of the United States, and then go right in and vote against him." Andy's Democratic colleagues in the New Jersey delegation were no less brutal in their criticism. Carter, said William Hughes, from Cape May, "proved that it is not enough just to be a decent man." Newark's Peter Rodino said, "He took on a very onerous task. But he failed to understand that he cannot do it alone."

In September, Andy was talking openly about denying Carter the party's nomination the following year. "If Kennedy wants it, it's his," said Andy. "Carter can't turn it around."

In October, Andy's years of effort to maintain federal control over the price of oil ended in defeat. Although the Democratic caucus had opposed the president's plan in May, the full House now approved it. The tally was lopsided enough at 257–135 that Andy finally threw in the towel. Asked if he would continue the fight, he replied, "That was it. People are getting tired of this."

In mid-March 1980, Congress passed the windfall profits tax. But around the same time, Carter took action to further increase the price of oil, imposing a hefty tariff on each barrel the United States imported. He pitched the fee as an anti-inflationary measure: The revenue raised would decrease the budget deficit that was, he said, causing higher prices throughout the economy. In May, four representatives, Andy and Moffett, along with two Republicans, filed suit to block the fee, which was expected to add 10 cents to the cost of a gallon of gasoline.

In other words, two Democratic congressmen were suing their own president six months before he was to stand for reelection.

"He was doing the wrong thing," Andy says today. "This was one anti-sensible-economics, pro-oil-companies step too far. It was inconsistent with everything that I—and I thought Carter—had been working for."

Andy's colleagues in the House, Democrats and Republicans, soon passed legislation to block the tariff. Carter vetoed the bill, but both houses of Congress voted to override with well over the two thirds required by the Constitution.

The vote was bipartisan, but Democrats dominated both the House and Senate. So now it was not just two Democrats but the majority of Democrats in Congress who were handing their standard-bearer a stunning embarrassment shortly before Election Day.

The overwhelming majorities for the override also demonstrated appalling political malpractice by the White House: Had Carter and his aides counted the votes, they must have known the veto wouldn't hold up. And what candidate with any political sense imposes a brand-new tax in an election year?

AN ETERNAL DREAM: Ted Kennedy Challenges Jimmy Carter

Incumbent presidents who face strong challenges to their reelection from within their own party rarely win a second term: Lyndon Johnson withdrew when confronted by Eugene McCarthy and Robert F. Kennedy; Gerald Ford lost to Jimmy Carter after Ronald Reagan took the nominating contest to the convention; George H. W. Bush had to fend off Patrick Buchanan before falling to Bill Clinton. In 1980, the incumbent was Jimmy Carter, and his primary challenger was the man millions of true believers had long looked to as the last best hope for a revival of forthright American liberalism.

Edward Moore "Ted" Kennedy might have run for, and captured, the Democratic nomination for president in 1972 or 1976 but for the scandal he never shed. Just before or just after midnight on July 18–19, 1969, the senior senator from Massachusetts and last surviving son of Rose and Joseph Kennedy was driving on the Cape Cod island of Chappaquiddick when a wrong turn led him to an unlit bridge. Losing control of the car, he drove off the bridge and into Poucha Pond. Kennedy managed to get out of the submerged vehicle and swim to shore, but his passenger, a twenty-eight-year-old campaign worker named Mary Jo Kopechne, drowned inside the car. The senator, who later claimed he tried and failed numerous times to extricate Kopechne, did not notify the police of the accident until after 10:00 a.m. He would plead guilty to leaving the scene of an accident, but otherwise suffered no legal consequences.

Kennedy addressed the nation a week after the incident, but many doubted his account. What had he been doing with Kopechne? Ted Kennedy was known as a playboy—was there a sexual angle to the story? He was known to enjoy a drink—had he been driving under the influence? Had he really swum down, seven or eight times, to try to rescue Kopechne without success? Why hadn't he reported the incident immediately?

Chappaquiddick—the scandal encompassing what happened and the questions he never convincingly answered—had kept him out of the running for two presidential elections. But in 1979, dissatisfied with the presidency of Jimmy Carter and recognizing Carter's flagging popularity within the Democratic Party, he decided to make the run his family's acolytes had been urging on him since the death of his brother Robert in 1968.

Kennedy had clashed with Carter over the senator's signature issue, health care. Carter had campaigned in 1976 on introducing a national health insurance system similar to the system Kennedy had proposed; in office, the president tried to work with Kennedy on a bill. But ultimately, Carter's cautious approach to the federal budget, his preoccupying focus on energy, and the diminution of his political power as his term went on killed any effort to enact such legislation.

Kennedy, long the nation's leading Democrat, seemed a sure shot to unseat the arriviste from Georgia whom the party faithful had never fully trusted and now seemed ready to abandon. Carter, however, did not flinch. At the White House in June 1979, discussing the senator's as-yet-unannounced intentions, Carter told a pair of junior Democratic congressmen, "If Kennedy runs, I'll whip his ass." Walking away from the White House, the young representatives surmised that they had been given the quote in order to leak it to the press. They did, inducing general delight over the language used by the nation's most famous Sunday school teacher.

Unintimidated, Kennedy declared his candidacy on November 7. "I say it is not the American people who are in a malaise," he said that day. "It's the political leadership that's in a malaise." Echoing Andy, he also criticized Carter's lifting of price controls on domestic oil as "the single most inflationary step."

Unfortunately for the senator, however, he had sabotaged his candidacy before it started. In a lengthy interview televised by CBS News on November 4, the reporter Roger Mudd asked, "Senator, why do you want to be president?" A simple enough question, but Kennedy could not give a simple, direct answer.

Even more damaging was the senator's answer to Mudd's next question: "What would you do different from Carter?"

"Well, in which particular areas?" said Kennedy.

When Mudd named particular areas, the senator had virtually nothing of substance to say.

The criticism was immediate and scathing. The interview, pundits charged, showed that Kennedy expected to win the presidency not by offering a well-defined vision for the country but by trading on his last name. (Politicians ever since, if they or their handlers are at all competent, begin their candidacy prepared with an answer to the why-do-you-want-to-be question.)

Carter did whip Kennedy's ass, winning the lion's share of states and delegates in the nominating campaign, although Kennedy did take California and New York. However, the senator did not formally withdraw his candidacy until the second day of the August convention, again at New York's Madison Square Garden, when he failed to win a rule change that would have created an "open convention"—one in which delegates were released from the obligation to vote as their states' voters had directed them.

On the third night of the gathering, it was Kennedy's turn to speak—and he stole the show.

He criticized the Republicans, praised Carter, and mentioned a few specific initiatives, including health care. But mostly his speech was a hymn to the classic Democratic cause:

> The commitment I seek is not to outworn views but to old values that will never wear out. Programs may sometimes become obsolete, but the ideal of fairness always endures. Circumstances may change, but the work of compassion must continue.

After a recounting of his campaign and of people he met along the way, he closed with:

> And someday, long after this convention, long after the signs come down and the crowds stop cheering, and the bands stop playing, may it be said of our campaign that we kept the faith.
>
> May it be said of our party in 1980 that we found our faith again.
>
> And may it be said of us, both in dark passages and in bright days, in the words of Tennyson that my brothers quoted and loved, and that have special meaning for me now:
>
> *I am a part of all that I have met*
> *Though much is taken, much abides*
> *That which we are, we are,*
> *One equal temper of heroic hearts*
> *Strong in will*
> *To strive, to seek, to find, and not to yield.*
>
> For me, a few hours ago, this campaign came to an end.
>
> For all those whose cares have been our concern, the work goes on, the cause endures, the hope still lives, and the dream shall never die.

The speech, whose final draft was written by two veterans of Camelot, Ted Sorensen and Arthur Schlesinger, Jr., was pure Kennedy magic. Here was the last brother, the bearer of the flame, assuring the faithful that the dream lived, though it had seemed to perish in Dallas in 1963 and Los Angeles in 1968. Half an hour went by before the audience stopped cheering and the convention could complete the day's business.

This was the act Carter had to follow the next and final night of the gathering.

Carter's speech was forgettable except for two things:

One, as he was naming great Democrats of the past, he called Hubert Horatio Humphrey "Hubert Horatio Hornblower."

Two, amidst the dropping balloons after he finished talking, Carter invited Kennedy to join him on the rostrum. Kennedy did and shook Carter's hand. Carter then tried to raise Kennedy's hand in the traditional gesture of party unity.

Kennedy wouldn't let him.

Just after Ted Kennedy formally entered the race in November 1979, the press reported that "sources close to" Andy said he was about to endorse the senator. But, for all Andy's dissatisfaction with Carter, he never did.

"I met with Kennedy along with some other members," says Andy, "and I decided it wasn't in my interest to get into that one. I had great admiration for Kennedy, particularly his leading on health care issues. I sponsored in the House some of the legislation he was putting forward in the Senate, and vice versa. I don't know the answer except that I thought it was something the Democratic Party was going to sort out without my help.

"I also felt that as a presidential contender he would have Chappaquiddick hung around his neck.

"I literally didn't know what to do."

Andy continued to withhold his endorsement—from both candidates. Oddly, in January 1980, he told the press that he preferred Walter Mondale, Carter's vice president, as the presidential nominee.

"Mondale didn't have any minus points attached to his name," Andy says today.

In the New Jersey primary, which took place on the last day of primary voting, June 3, Kennedy crushed Carter by a hundred thousand votes. But by the time the returns came in that night from California, Carter had amassed the delegates needed to capture the nomination. Even so, two weeks before the party's August gathering, Andy added his name to those calling for an open convention.

"Imagine if Teddy had held off seeking the nomination until now," Andy said a week later. "He'd be drafted." And again, he repeated his wish that Mondale head the ticket.

The pipe dream of an open convention ended when the delegates voted down the necessary rule change on the convention's second day.

Carter would be the presidential nominee. Walter Mondale would remain on the bottom of the ticket.

UNDERESTIMATED: Ronald Reagan, 1980

Ronald Reagan, after his near miss in 1976, was running once more for the Republican Party's nomination, and this time he was unstoppable. He faced several capable, credentialed opponents—former congressman, ambassador to China, ambassador to the UN, GOP party chair, and CIA director George H. W. Bush; Howard Baker, the Tennessee senator famous for asking "What did the president know and when did he know it?" at the Watergate hearings; Kansas senator and GOP vice presidential nominee four years earlier Bob Dole; John Connally, the former secretary of the treasury and former Democratic governor of Texas best known for being in the limousine with JFK in Dealey Plaza; as well as a couple of congressmen from Illinois, John Anderson and Phil Crane.

After Bush won a straw poll in Iowa to start the primary season—and boasted of his "big mo[mentum]"—the candidates moved to New Hampshire. With Bush and Reagan the only candidates scoring beyond single digits in the polls, the *Nashua Telegraph* arranged a debate between the two of them. Reagan, however, looking to dilute the strength of Bush's campaign, decided to foot the bill for the event from his own campaign funds and invited the other candidates. The night of the debate, the lesser candidates all showed up and walked onstage looking like third-grade boys hoping to play in a softball game run by their high school–age brothers. The editor of the *Telegraph*, Jon Breen, ordered his sound man to turn off Reagan's microphone. "I'm paying for this microphone, Mr. Green [*sic*]," said Reagan before the technician could follow Breen's order. The crowd, and Republicans around the country, swooned over Reagan's display of anger and bravado attached to a virtuous assertion of the favorite rights of all good Republicans: property rights.

Eventually the other candidates left the stage to Reagan and Bush for a debate that was far less memorable than its preface.

After Reagan won in New Hampshire, the field turned to South Carolina. Reagan's camp identified John Connally, who had entered the race with substantial fanfare and sacks of money, as its biggest threat in the Palmetto State. After campaign operative Lee Atwater, a South Carolina native, spread a rumor that Connally was buying the Black vote, Connally was done—his campaign ultimately spent $10 million to win just one delegate. Atwater would be a master at racial dirty tricks. In 1988, working for George H. W. Bush, he pinned Willie Horton on Michael Dukakis; in 2000, Atwater won the South Carolina primary for Bush's son by spreading salacious rumors about John McCain's nonwhite adopted daughter.

Dole, Baker, and Connally withdrew in March, the two Illinois congressmen withdrew in April. Bush did not formally withdraw until late May, well after the contest had been decided.

To reach out to the chamber of commerce wing of the GOP, Reagan chose Bush—George Herbert Walker Bush—the exemplar of high WASP, country-club Republicanism, as his running mate. Bush quickly recanted the (accurate) description "voodoo economics" he'd pinned on his new boss's tax plan.

Reagan, in his speech to the convention, hit the familiar GOP notes, opposing high taxes and excoriating Carter for his "mediocre leadership." But the GOP nominee set forth another theme, which would win him the election. Carter and the Democrats, said Reagan,

> say that the United States has had its day in the sun, that our nation has passed its zenith. They expect you to tell your children that the American people no longer have the will to cope with their problems, that the future will be one of sacrifice and few opportunities.
>
> My fellow citizens, I utterly reject that view.

On the issue that dominated Carter's presidency, he said:

> Those who preside over the worst energy shortage in our history tell us to use less, so that we will run out of oil, gasoline, and natural gas a little more slowly. Well, now, conservation is desirable, of course. We mustn't waste energy. But conservation is not the sole answer to our energy needs. America must get to work producing more energy.
>
> The Republican program for solving economic problems is based on growth and productivity.

The American people, Reagan said, did not have to sacrifice. Instead:

> I believe it is clear our federal government is overgrown and overweight. Indeed, it is time our government should go on a diet.

And he asked Americans to look at the previous four years:

> Can anyone look at the record of this administration and say, "Well done"?

The Republican Party had found its hero. And he faced a hobbled opponent.

Maguire & Co. knew that Carter's unpopularity would damage Andy's shot at reelection in 1980. Rob Esposito, tapped to manage Andy's 1980 campaign, said as much all the way back in June 1979. "The motivation just may not be there to go to the polls," said Esposito. "And we have to gear up, raise money, and organize for turning out the vote." A Bergen County Democratic freeholder counseled patience. "A year is a long time," he said. "Before you make judgments, you have to see who the other side puts up. If the Republicans put up Ronald Reagan against Carter, that could be like Johnson against Goldwater. I'll just cross my fingers."

The election would indeed be like Johnson against Goldwater, although not in the way this official was expecting.

The freeholder wasn't alone in underestimating the eventual GOP nominee. In February 1980, Andy told a gathering of Democrats, "I've been sort of secretly hoping they have Reagan at the top of the ticket."

"If it's Bush, we're in trouble," said Bergen County's Democratic chair.

Today Andy says, "I just couldn't believe that the United States of America would elect someone who was known principally as an actor, someone as thin in his ability to think about what the country needed as this guy, someone who had, I would say, an indifferent, retrograde tenure as governor of California. I couldn't see it being replicated on the national stage.

"He was also downright dumb. He had this wonderful persona which everybody loved, right? But he didn't understand much of anything. He was a shill, a convenient shill. He also was the one who first began to eliminate the highest levels of professional civil service in the agencies and in the State Department, instead appointing major donors. And he began the process of turning regulatory agencies over to former lobbyists.

"Insufficient attention has been given to all the ways he undermined our democracy."

Tom Downey also misjudged Reagan's appeal. "I never credited him for the eight years that he was governor of California," Downey says. "To me he seemed a simpleton, unable to answer questions. Trump is a nastier version of Ronald Reagan, but Reagan was equally inept. At least Reagan was genial and followed the norms of government. I don't think he was a particularly good president, though he is a Republican icon. But I was wrong, like many of my colleagues, in thinking that he was a simpleton who would be easily defeated.

"He was comfortable in his beliefs and expressed them clearly. He kept his pitch optimistic. And he had a great voice. And he looked good. As president, when the economy started to recover, he could rightfully take credit, though Paul Volcker, the Fed chair, probably deserves more credit than Reagan. But the fact is, Reagan did play a role.

"The other thing about Reagan is that he did listen to good advice and at the end of the day would compromise. We did the Social Security amendments in 1983, which undid much of the Reagan tax cuts. He showed a capacity for both accommodation and leadership.

"He did the dog whistles on race, the welfare queens, the campaign opening in Mississippi. He was a traditional Republican race baiter, but he did it with a smile."

Andy would again face Marge Roukema in 1980, but it was Reagan who beat him.

HOTHEAD: Confronting an Oil Company President

In 1979, on the radio and in newspapers, Andy requested that constituents send him letters and postcards with their opinion of efforts to decontrol the price of oil. Thirteen thousand such communications had arrived by the time the president of Mobil Corporation, William Tavoulareas, came before Andy at a hearing on Capitol Hill.

As Andy began his questioning, his press assistant held up a poster with the simplest, and most common, message he'd received: No Decontrol.

The captain of industry did not seem pleased to be there. "Tavoulareas was moaning and groaning," says Andy, "as they do, about how difficult their jobs were, and how important it was for the country, and how they needed all these tax breaks, and the free market should decide the price of oil and blah, blah, blah."

In response, according to the *Record*, Andy "proceeded to flail Mobil and other oil producers for price gouging, profiteering, and deserving the public's distrust.

"Tavoulareas defended Mobil for a few minutes, then lost patience and stalked out of the hearing room with his aides, leaving the congressman declaiming to an empty table."

"Andy was tough on witnesses he disagreed with," says Elgie Holstein. "He bore in relentlessly, often with very aggressive questioning. That's not at all uncommon in Congress. Tavoulareas was a hothead. Walking out of a congressional hearing because you don't like how you're being questioned is almost never done—it's frowned upon even by people who may have sympathies for the witness. It wasn't like Andy was calling the man a liar or besmirching his parentage. It wasn't personal. It was about the fact that Mobile was making outsized profits thanks to the continued run-up in international oil prices and that Andy had begun a campaign to get people to send him postcards and letters in which they would express their opposition to price decontrol.

"Andy was the leader on the no-decontrol campaign—he had many colleagues who supported him. Speaker Tip O'Neill, though not a fan of decontrol, was a guy who did not believe in rocking the boat with the Democratic president, Jimmy Carter. If Carter was going to allow decontrol to happen, or quietly support it, Andy wasn't going to stand for it. But O'Neill didn't believe in having his Democratic caucus embarrass the Democratic president.

"I would say that if Andy, being from the kind of district he was from, were in the Congress today, the leadership of the House of Representatives would be falling all over itself to ensure that he got campaign contributions, that he got support, that he was given opportunities to shine and to stand out, all for the sake of maintaining a Democratic majority. But at that time, people like Tip O'Neill and his predecessor as Speaker, Carl Albert, rested comfortably on their large majority, which included many conservative Democrats. So Andy was taking on these fights without the benefit of strong support from leadership."

"Andy understood," says Michael Levin, "that every institution is a center not only of conservatism, but also of possible resistance. Institutions all start out resisting anything that changes the status quo, because they've reached all these balances within themselves that fiercely resist change. Change is disruptive and painful and uncertain. But institutions also can be great ways to propagate change if you can harness them in the right way."

"Speaking of Andy," says Ed Markey, "I would say that liberals are usually right, but too soon. The things for which he was criticized at the time—when people look back, they will see that he was almost always accurate. He had a swing seat, but he was courageous every single day. I admired that in him. Because others shied away from doing what he did.

"He did so at his political peril. He paid the ultimate political price in the loss of his seat in 1980."

INEVITABLE: Reagan Defeats Carter

Jimmy Carter had plenty going against him as he entered the fall campaign: rampant inflation, unemployment that had begun to rise, hostages in Iran, a Democratic Party fed up with him. What he had going for him was his opponent's reputation, outside the Republican Party, for extremism and recklessness.

Complicating the race was a third candidate running as an independent. John Anderson, one of the Republican congressmen from Illinois who had briefly run in the GOP primaries, had been considered a conservative when he'd arrived in the House in 1961, but in recent years had moderated his profile. While he never seriously vied for victory in November, his candidacy served as a landing site for Republicans and Democrats unhappy with their party's choices. In polling over the summer, Anderson drew as much as a quarter of the electorate's support, although that number shrank as the election neared.

Like Nixon a dozen years earlier, Reagan did not make explicit appeals to white racism, choosing instead to send signals that were hard to miss but easy to deny. Carter had captured most of his native Dixie four years earlier, but his unpopular presidency left the region free to continue its changeover from Democrat to Republican. Reagan pressed that advantage, kicking off his campaign with a speech at Mississippi's

Neshoba County fair, just a few miles from Philadelphia, Mississippi, site of one of the most notorious atrocities of the civil rights movement. During Freedom Summer 1964, white terrorists murdered three young men working to register Black voters: two white Jews from New York City, Michael Schwerner and Andrew Goodman, and one African American from Mississippi, James Chaney. Of course, Reagan rejected the suggestion that he was sending a coded message to racist whites by opening his campaign at this location. But the subject of his speech told a different story: He spoke of "states' rights," which of course had been the rallying cry of segregationists as they fought the demise of Jim Crow. And throughout the campaign, the nominee was happy to spin made-up yarns about "welfare queens" who used a twenty-dollar food stamp to buy a quart of orange juice, then spent the change on a fifth of vodka.

After the conventions, polling showed a close race, but by October, the incumbent had opened up a substantial lead. Carter's main line of attack was that his opponent was unstable—even worse, a warmonger. Reagan fed this description. Earlier in the year, he had proposed a military blockade of Cuba as a response to Soviet aggression in Afghanistan. He also expressed doubt about nuclear arms control deals with the USSR, vowing to scrap the SALT II treaty in order to negotiate one with better terms. And he suggested that the key to reaching an improved agreement was renewing the very competition such agreements were designed to end. "One card that's been missing in these negotiations," he said, "has been the possibility of an arms race." Carter, professing to find these statements "shocking," said, "I'm not insinuating that Mr. Reagan wants war. I'm not insinuating that he's a warmonger"—much as Richard Nixon, at every campaign stop in 1960, had loudly promised not to talk about his opponent's Catholic religion.

Ronald Reagan—at least, the Ronald Reagan that Carter and his team painted—scared people. But then came the debates.

The third candidate confounded plans for the encounters. Carter refused to participate in any debate that included John Anderson, so the first debate included only the president's two opponents. Carter and Reagan finally squared off, without Anderson, on October 28, seven days before the balloting. Live on television, Reagan was anything but frightening—his smooth voice was calming, his demeanor reassuring. This was not the monster Carter had been conjuring.

Reagan won the debate, and the election, with two memorable moments. When Carter pointed out (accurately) that Reagan had stood against the creation of Medicare in 1965, Reagan smiled and said, "There you go again." The explanation that followed—his whitewashed explanation for opposing the popular program—was not nearly as important as his successful portrayal of the president as a pedantic scold, aligning with perceptions held by large numbers of voters.

And then, in his closing statement, Reagan posed the question at the center of any presidential reelection contest: "Are you better off than you were four years ago?"

After four years of Carter's uneasy public persona, after four years of inflation and almost a year of humiliation at the hands of the Iranians, after four years of a president telling Americans they would have to live in colder homes and drive smaller cars, here was an amiable uncle who promised that Americans could continue being Americans—people who knew no limits.

In 1964, the Republican Party had gone down to disaster with Barry Goldwater and his proclamation that extremism in the defense of liberty is no vice. Reagan stood as the inheritor of Goldwater's hostility to government and the Russians, but said his piece with a gentle off-center nod of his head and a million-megawatt smile perfected by the miracle workers known as Hollywood dentists. Reagan put his extreme views into language that made them seem like common sense. After all, what citizen who'd ever waited two hours at the DMV would say a word to defend government bureaucracy?

The race was over. Reagan cruised to a landslide victory, winning over 50 percent of the popular vote to Carter's 41 percent and Anderson's 7 percent. Even more humiliating to Carter was the score in the Electoral College: Reagan won forty-four states to finish with 489 electoral votes to Carter's six states and the District of Columbia, yielding 49 votes. Key to Reagan's victory were white working-class voters, a demographic that had been reliably Democratic since the New Deal. Stan Greenberg, a Democratic pollster, conducted a study of such voters in Macomb County, a working-class area north of Detroit, populated in large part by immigrants and the descendants of immigrants from Eastern Europe. Greenberg's label for them, "Reagan Democrats," stuck, and was applied to similar voters nationwide. Reagan Democrats would transform American politics, leading to further whitening of the GOP's electorate and further diversifying of the coalition that elected Democrats.

Reagan also achieved a breakthrough with white evangelicals. Well-known preachers, such as Billy Graham, had dabbled in politics for years, although Graham, while conservative, had tried to maintain influence with politicians of both parties. In 1976, most white evangelicals had supported Jimmy Carter, one of their own. But in 1980, evangelical leaders, most prominently Jerry Falwell, head of an advocacy group called the Moral Majority, began to take an active role in electing conservative Republicans. The issue at the top of the agenda for what was becoming known as the "religious right" was abortion. Although evangelical Protestants had not, overall, reacted in horror immediately after the Supreme Court's 1973 decision in *Roe v. Wade*, right-wing preachers, along with Republican politicians and activists, realized that opposition to abortion could be the central issue around which conservative Christians could be organized to vote Republican. The year 1980 marks the beginning of the GOP's capture of the allegiance of "pro-life" voters.

The identification of white evangelical Christians with the Republican Party has since then become so complete that in 2016 they gave overwhelming support to Donald Trump, a lying, thrice-married adulterer so ignorant of religion that he can't recite a single verse from the Bible. Four years later, even his separation of children from their parents at the nation's southern border, and the holding of those children in cages, barely dented the support of these millions of Americans who call themselves pro-life but worship white identity first, the Golden Rule second.

The New Deal coalition—whites from the South, added to liberals, blue-collar workers, and minorities in the North—had collapsed. Democrats would need to find other ways to win elections.

ONCE MORE UNTO THE BREACH, DEAR FRIENDS (AND DON'T FORGET YOUR SNEAKERS): The Maguire Campaign, 1980

The rematch between Maguire and Roukema followed the contours of the original, although at a higher temperature. Andy, claimed Roukema, was a liberal ideologue: "I say he is not representing the economic interests and the individual thinking of people in the district." Roukema, claimed Andy, was a tool of big business: "I wonder from her approach whether she is representing Texas or Bergen County." Roukema again enjoyed the financial largesse of the national party and this time started with the name recognition she'd had to build last time. Andy's campaign saw Roukema for the threat she was, opening its headquarters earlier than it had in 1978 and combing through transcripts of that year's debates looking for advantages. Andy brought Gina Glantz back to advise the campaign. Angie Martin, an experienced operative who earlier ran a tough but successful campaign for Toby Moffett, managed the reelection effort in the still Republican-leaning district. Of course, Andy once again put on his sneakers as he and his volunteers hit the streets.

Tempers flared at the candidates' second debate:

"Marge," said Andy, "you don't understand how things are done in Congress."

"Don't patronize me," said Roukema.

Through all the debates, Roukema went hard at Andy for his votes against military appropriations bills. Andy explained that he opposed not defense spending but wasteful defense spending and actually called for increasing the Pentagon budget to pay for needed items like additional maintenance, training, and cruise missiles. (A brilliant analysis of the defense budget, researched and written by Andy's then-chief of staff Kathy Rae, buttressed Andy's argument in the debates and in the Congressional Record that the Pentagon budget actually should be increased to pay for such needed items.) But that explanation made no difference. At the third encounter, Roukema escalated her attack on the purported peacenik. "Andy," she said, "what credibility can you possibly have with that talk of defense? If it were up to Andy Maguire, we wouldn't have an Army, Navy, or Marine Corps." That last sentence earned boos from Andy's partisans among the audience of five hundred at Bergen Community College in Paramus.

Andy tried to tie Roukema to the industry he'd spent six years fighting: She was "the Republican darling of oil and gas." To emphasize that he was on the side of people who bought gasoline, not those who produced it, he and consumer champion Ralph Nader manned the gas pumps together at a filling station in Lodi. Gerald Ford came to the district to campaign for Roukema; Walter Mondale came to boost Andy. Andy's reelection race was the cover story, with photos, in the *Congressional Quarterly*. Andy again defended himself against the false charge that he was a big spender and asked voters to trust him, even if they didn't agree with him on every issue. "Stick with me," he said to one citizen. "You know how hard I work."

The *Bergen Record* delivered its usual glowing endorsement. "Mr. Maguire is as independent-minded and hard-working as ever," it said. Criticizing Roukema for the heightened negativity of her campaign compared to her tone in 1976, the editorial argued that her "rhetoric can't hold a candle to Mr. Maguire's record." The endorsement concluded by conceding that "there is no reason to believe Mrs. Roukema would be a less-than-adequate congresswoman. But why settle for adequacy when excellence is available? Andrew Maguire is, quite simply, an excellent congressman. We wholeheartedly endorse his reelection."

Andy had all the elements that had won him reelection the last time: the same opponent, the same energetic campaign, the same reputation as a tireless champion of consumers, the same extravagant level of praise from the local newspaper. But this year he had an anchor around his neck: the candidate at the top of his ballot.

"I would say that nine days before the election, Andy would have won handily," recalls Ted Hoff. "But I was up in the district that whole last week and I had a lot of volunteers telling me that they were feeling something different.

"The Reagan-Carter debate was on October 28. It was heavily watched because people were thinking about change but were wary of Reagan. That's when the shift happened. October 28. And then Reagan came to Lodi for a rally on the thirtieth."

If many in Andy's campaign were expecting to lose, the candidate wasn't among them. "I didn't see it coming," he says. "I thought we were doing well."

On Election Day, Andy campaigned from dawn to dusk. At breakfast time he went to Hackensack, where he stopped at McDonald's then swung around to Dunkin' Donuts. He next drove to Teaneck, where he hopped from table to table at The Cedar Lane Grill, Louie's Charcoal Pit, and the International House of Pancakes. He visited his lucky Shop-Rite, in Rochelle Park, as he had every election day. Another round of restaurants for lunch, then door to door. In Lodi at 5:45 p.m. he was still knocking, still talking: "Please vote. I need you. I need you. We've got a real tight race. The oil companies are pumping millions into my opponent. We can't let the oil companies take this district."

Some three hundred of Andy's supporters filled the Knights of Columbus hall in Hackensack after the polls closed.

"It was a terribly painful evening," remembers Ted Hoff. "Although I had felt the ground shifting before the election, on election night itself, as the votes were coming in from key towns, I still couldn't believe it. I had trusted that in the end, because Andy was such a terrific congressman, he was going to prevail.

"I was up in front of the crowd, and people were calling out for me to give results. Initially I was reluctant."

The *Record* reported that the volunteer putting up numbers was so upset that he didn't give any information for an hour and a half. "Finally," said the paper, "he chalked up the partial results and some in the crowd shook their heads silently while others gasped."

"There were lots of tears," says Hoff. "I know I was in tears. It was an intensely painful evening for all who cared about Andy."

When the result was known, Andy entered the room. "Let me tell you what the problem was," he said to his supporters.

"Carter!" someone yelled out.

"We had to run well ahead of the president," Andy continued.

Keeping a smile on his face, he said, "I hope that we have served the people of the Seventh District well. I believe that we have." And he added, "There was an awful lot of ticket-splitting. There wasn't enough."

"Andy was strong," says Hoff. "He was looking to strengthen people, to have people see that we would continue to make progress. He emphasized how deeply he appreciated how much everybody had done, how much they had tried to do all the right things. He was speaking to people about *them*. He was not in any way wallowing in his own pain. I remember how gracious and grateful and strong he was, as many of us were crying."

Marge Roukema beat Andy by nine thousand votes, with 50.7 percent to Andy's 46.5. Ronald Reagan scored higher, romping in New Jersey with 52 percent to Carter's 39 percent and Anderson's 8 percent, and in Bergen County with 56 percent to Carter's 34 percent and Anderson's 9 percent.

In the Seventh Congressional District, Reagan's margin was even higher, with Carter barely topping 30 percent. "How the hell do you deal with 30 percentage points?" said Angie Martin.

"I was defeated by proxy," says Andy. "I was devastated. I ran nearly sixteen points ahead of Carter. You can argue that I ran more strongly relative to the Democratic and Republican field in my county and state than ever before."

"That 30 percent figure," said Martin, "just made it impossible as it did in election district after election district all over the country. A lot of good people were lost."

Indeed, they were. The Democratic Party retained its majority in the House, but at a cost of thirty-four seats. Democrats suffered a rout in the Senate, however, losing a dozen seats and the majority. Fixtures of the nation's politics—Frank Church of Idaho, George McGovern of South Dakota, Herman Talmadge of Georgia, Birch Bayh of Indiana, Gaylord Nelson of Wisconsin, and others—succumbed to the bloodbath.

"I expect to be part of a new alignment," Roukema said on election night.

She would be.

SAYING GOODBYE: A Congressman Leaves Office

Andy finished his service in Congress "in his frenetic style," as the *Record* said in a final profile in December. One last minor controversy arose as a result of a report in a gossip column in the *Washington Star*. Andy's staff helped arrange a tour of the White House for Bruce Springsteen's E Street Band, pride of the Garden State, in Washington for a pair of concerts. The gossip columnist suggested that Andy himself was searching high and low for a ticket so that he could attend one of the sold-out shows. Andy's staff defended their boss, saying, "He didn't even know who Bruce Springsteen was. We had to explain it to him."

While not ruling out a bid for higher office, Andy talked down the idea. "I have no ambitions at all—right now," he said. "I would say the odds are that it will not happen." And he reiterated the reason he was soon to clean out his desk: "I lost because Reagan crushed Carter. I've always said Carter had many more accomplishments to his credit than people recognize, but it is also clear that Carter completely failed to understand the importance of broadening his inner circle. To have kept Hamilton Jordan and that crowd tightly around him—these guys he had picked up off the road somewhere in Georgia—showed the narrowness and insecurity of Carter. That was evident through his presidency in his inability to deal on their own terms with congressional leaders."

The election of 1980 marked the end, once and for all, of the 1960s liberal consensus. Ronald Reagan later said that people mistook him for wanting to undo the New Deal when all he wanted to undo was the Great Society. He wouldn't be able to undo all of Lyndon Johnson's majestic social architecture—not Medicare, the wildly popular program Reagan had condemned as "socialized medicine" before its passage in 1965. But he would do what he could to undo the rest.

On January 20, in his inaugural address seventeen days after Andy became a private citizen once more, Reagan said, "In this present crisis, government is not the solution to our problem; government is the problem." While he later tried to qualify the statement—noting the phrase "in the present crisis"—people rightly understood him to believe that government was the problem at any time, crisis or no. If there was any ambiguity to his statement, he dispelled it a few years later in a joke: "The nine most terrifying words in the English language are: I'm from the government, and I'm here to help."

It's not hard to see the direct line from those comments to George W. Bush's catastrophic mishandling of the response to Hurricane Katrina in 2005 and from there to Donald Trump's criminal mishandling of the coronavirus in 2020.

Reflecting on his six years of service, Andy told that profiler in December, "The record is full. I was able to do far more of significance than I thought was possible."

"One of the great tragedies," says Tom Downey, "was Andy's exit after only three terms. I think he would have had a profound impact on the institution had he stayed longer.

"He was like a great ballplayer who gets injured early in his career. You spend your time wondering what might have been."

CHAPTER 9

HIGH STAKES: Working to Avert Generations of Trouble during the Age of Reagan

Ronald Reagan is the first modern president whose contempt for the facts is treated as a charming idiosyncrasy.

—JAMES DAVID BARBER

TRÈS SHEIK: A Senator Falls

"Obviously, I had to regroup," says Andy Maguire.

First things first, the now former congressman needed a job. He accepted an offer from Mitchell Fein, a backer of his who ran a consulting company called Improshare. The name signified the theme of the firm's work with corporate clients: how to share a company's wealth with employees according to improved productivity. "I never regarded that job as a terribly important part of my work," says Andy. "It was just to keep money flowing for my personal expenses. Nonetheless, Mitchell Fein had developed a sensible approach, which deserved to be much more widely replicated than it was. A then-common corporate incentive structure involved profit-sharing. However, in some cases workers upped their performance but received no reward if their company had blown the opportunity and not made a profit. Mitchell, by contrast, charted productivity through a number of indices and based employee rewards on those measurements, whether the company made a profit or not.

"It harkened back to the work I did during my year with the Ford Foundation before I ran for Congress. I had focused on the workplace, studying blue-collar workers who had walked off the Lordstown, Ohio, General Motors assembly line because they viewed their jobs as boring, repetitious, and meaningless. So Improshare was comfortable for me. I was grateful to Mitchell for his offer to join him."

In mid-1981, Improshare was hired by the Singer Sewing Machine plant in Elizabeth, New Jersey. Confronted with withering foreign competition, the company had stopped manufacturing household machines, firing over half its 1500-member workforce. Those who remained made industrial machines. With Improshare measuring productivity week by week, the firm achieved gains that led to bonuses for both workers and management. "Improshare is a very powerful motivator," Andy told the *Record*. "We have found that productivity gains that can be achieved range anywhere from 10 to 60 percent within a few months."

The job at Improshare paid Andy's bills for about a year. But the job was too one-dimensional for someone whose interests in Congress ranged from oppression in South Africa to the absence of a TV station in New Jersey to the environmental contamination that caused cancer. "When I left Congress," Andy recalls, "I knew I was going to miss the array of domestic and international issues I was able to work on as a member. Almost anything else one might do requires focus and concentration on a particular set of goals. The overall opportunity in Congress was remarkable."

But Andy got one more shot at elected office, because an esteemed US senator fell for the act of a phony Arab sheik.

Abscam began as an FBI sting operation to combat small-time fraud in and around New York City. At the center of the operation was Melvin Weinberg, a convicted con man who had convinced the Bureau to reduce his sentence for real estate fraud from three years to probation if he turned his talents and connections from crime to law enforcement.

The Bureau created a phony company, Abdul Enterprises—hence the "Ab" in the operation's name—headed by a fake Arab sheik looking for devious ways to invest his yachtload of petrodollars. The scam pursued cases involving stolen and fraudulent financial instruments—securities, certificates of deposit—then focused on stolen works of art. Agents posing as the sheik's representatives soon recovered two paintings worth a combined million dollars.

But the sting shifted its attention after Weinberg received a tip about Angelo Errichetti, the mayor of Camden, New Jersey. It seemed that Errichetti, a heavyweight in South Jersey politics, often looked for ways to enhance his modest municipal salary. Sure enough, when Abdul Enterprises came calling, the mayor accepted the bribe the agents offered in exchange for his help in achieving their ostensible goal: obtaining a license to operate a casino in Atlantic City. "I'll give you Atlantic City," Errichetti told the undercover G-men. "Without me, you do nothing."

"He was a nice guy," Weinberg said later. "But he was just an unbelievable crook. He had no fear."

Errichetti told his new friends of several congressmen who would be pleased to join in the fun; soon, the operation was snagging US representatives from as far away as Florida and South Carolina. The operation then moved on to a bigger fish, the senior US senator from the State of New Jersey, Harrison "Pete" Williams.

Williams got his nickname when his grandfather, informed that his newborn grandson would be called Harrison Arlington Williams Jr., said, "For Pete's sake, that's a long name." Elected to the Senate in 1958, Williams had established a solid liberal record—he was a reliable friend to the civil rights movement and organized labor, and he wrote the Occupational Safety and Health Act. Popular among New Jersey voters, Williams, sixty years old, might have remained a senator for another two decades.

The FBI learned that Williams had a financial interest in an idle titanium mine in Virginia. A second pretend sheik, played by an agent of Lebanese descent, offered to invest $100 million in the mine if Williams agreed to secure government contracts for it. At first, Williams turned down the offer, but in a meeting five months later, he agreed to undertake the effort. "If this can be put together," a hidden camera recorded Williams telling the undercover operatives, "in my position . . . within the government here, which goes back decades, and knowing as I do the people that make the decisions . . . when we've got it together, we move."

At another meeting, the senator offered the apparent sheik help in obtaining permanent US residency status. The sheik offered Williams a personal cash payment as thanks. Williams declined that sum but reaffirmed his interest in the sheik's mining investment.

Williams was indicted on October 30, 1980, just five days before Andy's loss to Marge Roukema. On May 1, 1981, a jury convicted the senator on nine counts of bribery and illegal use of his office. Sentenced to three years in prison, Williams appealed, pointing to his initial refusal of the scheme as proof he'd been a victim of entrapment. Although some legal observers agreed, the appeals court did not. Williams served two years in a federal prison in Newark, then the third in a halfway house. Altogether, twelve government officials were convicted in the Abscam scandal, including six members of the House of Representatives.

In the closing days of Bill Clinton's presidency, Williams petitioned Clinton for a pardon. Clinton denied the request. Harrison Arlington "Pete" Williams Jr. died in 2001, after spending the last two decades of his life not in the Senate but in disgrace.

BIG MONEY, BIG PROBLEM: Running for Senator, 1982

Pete Williams remained a senator until March 1982, resigning only when his colleagues were on the verge of expelling him. But the end of his political career had been in sight since his indictment. The next full term for the seat was scheduled to be decided in November 1982; now that term was up for grabs.

Andy's bid for the Senate in 1978 had been aborted by Bill Bradley's celebrity, but the '82 race looked like a fairer fight. "It was always my goal to reach for the Senate," says Andy. "By the beginning of 1981, it was pretty clear that Williams wasn't going to be able to continue in office. Very soon after I lost my congressional race, I looked at 1982 and decided that I would go for it, that I was as well positioned for the race as anyone in the state. I zeroed in on it right away."

Andy activated his network around New Jersey. "I had, of course, a long list of organizations and individuals who had supported me in my congressional campaigns," he recalls. "I went to work on that base. William Winpisinger, head of the machinists' union, signed up right away and gave me my first five-thousand-dollar PAC contribution. I was then able to go to others and say, 'Winpisinger thinks this is real and important. We'd like to talk to you about becoming involved.'"

Andy prepared a fifteen-page brochure listing his strengths as a candidate; he handed it to party leaders throughout the state. Andy, the document boasted, was "unmatched in terms of personal energy on the campaign trail," retained the loyalty of a "huge, unsplintered geographic base," and had compiled "a record of raising the money it takes to win." During the fall 1981 state campaign, he collected chits he hoped to cash in during the following year's Democratic primary: He stumped for Democratic state legislative candidates and for the Democratic nominee for governor, his former colleague in the House, James Florio, who would be defeated by Republican Thomas Kean. Andy also began to rack up endorsements from outside the party—notably from not only Winpisinger's International Union of Machinists and Aerospace Workers but also the League of Conservation Voters. He promised potential supporters that he wouldn't drop out before the primary, as he had in the race against Bradley. "In contrast to 1978," said Andy's brochure, "he can say firmly and early that he's in this one for the duration." And he touted his ability to win over voters not considered reliably Democratic: "Everyone knows that this was a very Republican district that no Democrat ever won, except for me. I won by getting independents and suburban voters, and I damn near did it again in the face of Carter's extraordinary poor showing."

On December 8, 1981, Andy declared his candidacy in three places: the Stadium Club in the Meadowlands Sports Complex, the State House in Trenton, and a hotel in Cherry Hill. In the statement he read at each event, he assailed Reaganomics and the recession caused by Fed chairman Paul Volcker's determination to rid the US economy of the inflation it had suffered for a decade. "Those who are at the center of power have followed the ideas of an outworn past," he said, "and they have brought our economy to the dead center of recession and stagnation. The American dream of buying a home is out of reach, hope is dying in our inner cities and waning among the families of our suburbs, and millions are out of work. And the leaders who have misled us this far are out of ideas. They tell us to wait, to hold on—that the answer to their shortcomings is more of the same."

At this point, Andy's only announced rival for the Democratic nomination was Howard Rosen, a Millburn lawyer with no experience in public office. However, more formidable potential candidates, including Florio and the Essex County executive, Peter Shapiro, had not ruled out joining the race.

Andy's candidacy picked up steam. Unions for auto workers, teachers, communications workers, and hospital workers all announced their backing. At Leonia Middle School in January 1982 he joined the then-leading GOP candidate, Jeffrey Bell, who had lost to Bradley in 1978, for a debate on supply side economics. A poll showed Andy's name recognition in New Jersey at 39 percent, a number needing improvement but still not bad for a candidate running his first statewide campaign. To counter the perception that he was too liberal to win, Andy pointed to his endorsement by the Eastern European Democratic Leadership Caucus, a conservative group focused on the plight of nations dominated by the USSR. Calling for a renewal of the Soviet grain embargo, Andy said that the caucus's backing was "clearly an endorsement which was not predictable based on these stereotypes."

By the beginning of March, other candidates had joined Andy in the Democratic race: Angelo Bianchi, a former state banking commissioner and aide to Brendan Byrne; Cyril Yannarelli, a Passaic County freeholder; and Frank Forst, mayor of Jamesburg. Rosen, who had developed a significant war chest, started advertising on television. But Andy's fundraising was fruitful, too. An event in Boston hosted by a former House colleague netted $10 thousand. Planned visits by Ed Asner and Andrew Young were expected to draw not just more money but also more press. Andy would eventually gather a sum normally considered more than adequate to fund a statewide primary race in New Jersey. "I raised half a million," says Andy, "which was as much as Bill Bradley had raised in '78 or Florio had raised running for governor—as much as any statewide Democrat had ever raised for a primary."

But then another contender threw his hat into the ring and changed everything.

Frank Lautenberg was not a billionaire, as some tycoons-turned-pols have been—his net worth didn't come close to the fortunes Michael Bloomberg and Ross Perot amassed from exceptional companies. But, thanks to his long employment by Automatic Data Processing (ADP)—starting as a salesman, ending as CEO—he'd banked tens of millions. By 1982, he'd become one of New Jersey's most generous and reliable contributors to Democratic campaigns.

"He was one of the big Democratic moneybags in the state," says Andy. "He had donated to all of my previous congressional races, probably to every Democratic member of Congress. But he had never shown any interest in running himself until well after I had taken the post position in the race.

"I did not feel good about his entry."

Lautenberg's lavishly self-financed campaign was made possible by a recent Supreme Court decision. In its 1976 case *Buckley v. Valeo*, the Court invalidated a variety of campaign-finance limits, including the ceiling on funds candidates could contribute to their own campaigns. The decision enabled a long list of "We need a businessperson to run the government like a business" candidates throughout the country, including in New Jersey. "There had been a $35,000 limit on what candidates could spend on their own races for Senate before *Buckley* overturned it," says Andy. "This race was the first time New Jersey experienced this phenomenon, which then became a pattern. Jon Corzine, a Goldman Sachs multimillionaire, won a US Senate seat then became governor. Today we have Governor Phil Murphy. He's a fabulous guy; we would see eye-to-eye on the issues. But he's another Goldman Sachs multimillionaire doing the same thing Lautenberg did. He plastered his personal money all over the state in the two-year lead-up to his run for governor. It works." Lautenberg had served as chairman of the Port Authority of New York and New Jersey but otherwise had no experience in public office.

Ideologically, Lautenberg was a strong liberal; he and Andy had little to argue about on policy. "The big disagreement we had," Andy says, "was whether somebody who had spent six productive years as a member of Congress was more qualified to be senator than someone who had never run for office before but had the money to bankroll his own campaign. He looked around and said, 'I can buy this race.' And buy it he did.

"I met with city officials around the state who, based on their views and organization, should have been inclined to support me. If Lautenberg hadn't been in the race, they would have. I'm thinking about the mayor of Camden, the mayor of Newark, the mayor of Jersey City. But Lautenberg poured money into stuff those guys wanted.

"I went to see the mayor of Elizabeth, Tom Dunn. He was one of the people Lautenberg bought off. Dunn did me the courtesy of having me sit for an hour and a half outside his office before he saw me. But I'm a persistent sort. I wasn't going to let him do that to me and not have a chance to see him; I was going to stay there until I got in. Eventually I did.

"Greeting me, Dunn said, 'You're an orange man, aren't you?' Meaning that I was Protestant as opposed to Catholic (green). 'You're a Scottish Presbyterian. I know about you.' Still fighting the wars from the old country.

"It was a difficult meeting. Dunn was superficially cordial, but it was clear I was not going to deliver him into my column."

Florio and Shapiro did not enter the race. Congressman Joseph LeFante did, but his arrival did not do much damage to Andy's prospects; LeFante's base was Hudson County, which Andy was not counting on for substantial support. However, the last candidate to join the contest posed a threat.

Barbara Sigmund, the mayor of Princeton, was running in a House primary but pulled out of that race at the last minute to compete for the Senate. Her candidacy impinged on Andy's in two ways. First, she became the only woman in a multi-candidate race. Andy had been endorsed by women's groups, including the New Jersey chapters of NOW and NARAL. Even though those organizations remained behind Andy, Sigmund's presence couldn't help but lessen his prospects among female voters.

Second, in addition to his base in Bergen County, Andy was strong in Mercer County, where Princeton was located. "That was the other major county where I could have collected significant votes," he says. "I had tremendous support in Princeton. In fact, when the Princeton Democratic Committee held its endorsement meeting, Sigmund beat me by only one vote. People were outraged that she had gotten into the race."

Andy's campaign considered bringing legal action against Sigmund's. "We had a decision to make," he says. "Do we challenge her signatures? Because, entering the race on the last day of eligibility, there was no way she could have gotten the requisite number of true signatures to get on the ballot. We weighed the pros and cons—we had well-known leaders in Princeton ready to mount the challenge. But my advisory group, which included Gina Glantz and my father, and I decided not to do it. We thought the costs of a challenge might outweigh the benefits: 'Here's Maguire going after the only woman candidate.' The fact that she'd lost an eye to cancer brought her lots of sympathy.

"Looking back, I think we should have challenged; it was a moment for hardball. But my advisory group felt she wouldn't have much effect on the final result anyway, that the race boiled down to Lautenberg and me.

"I don't know whether that was a wise or unwise decision. But that's the one we made."

Andy notes that with Lautenberg running, the architecture of the race posed another concern. "Frank's home was Essex County," Andy says, "the second largest in the state after Bergen." Andy had ties to Essex County: He was close with Shapiro, the county executive, and Shapiro's top aide, the same Gina Glantz who had managed Andy's successful campaigns in 1974 and 1976. "Along with Bergen and Mercer, Essex was where my supporters and I anticipated crucial support and votes. But we received fewer votes there than we would have had Lautenberg been from anywhere else in the state."

The *Bergen Record* reported that Lautenberg spent some $2 million on the race (with later estimates ranging up to 3.5 million). In the end, Lautenberg won the multi-candidate primary with 26 percent of the vote, edging Andy, who took 23 percent. LeFante followed with 20 percent, ahead of Sigmund with 11 percent. Andy trailed Lautenberg by 11,000 votes statewide, out of nearly 400,000 cast.

Election night, Andy and his supporters gathered in the ballroom of the Meadowlands Hilton Hotel in Secaucus. "You were the most formidable candidate," one staffer said to Andy.

"We didn't quite formidable-ize ourselves to the last ten thousand votes," Andy replied.

Some in Andy's campaign and in the press pinned Andy's loss on Sigmund. Andy cites Lautenberg and his money.

"My weakest part of the state was the south," Andy says, "because I was not well known there. Lautenberg was able to spend an enormous amount of money on media in that region, and that expenditure operated as the defining variable in the race. One would assume that were Sigmund not in the race, Lautenberg's buy in the southern part of the state, including Mercer, would have prevailed."

On election night someone asked Andy if he would stay active in Democratic politics. Andy answered that "of course" he would. But he knew that any future he had in politics would not include service as an elected official.

"I couldn't see a way forward," he recalls, "because Bradley and Lautenberg had both just been elected." Andy's old congressional district in western Bergen County had been reapportioned to make it even more Republican—opposing Roukema for a third time made no sense. The seat in eastern Bergen County offered better prospects—Harold Hollenbeck, the Republican incumbent who had ousted Henry Helstoski in 1978, was a weaker candidate than Roukema. "In '82," says Andy, "Bob Torricelli ran against Hollenbeck and won, just as I could have. I wouldn't have been the only person to rebound that year after losing in the awful election two years earlier.

"But the opportunity for the Senate was there. I had let it go by in '78, for good reasons. When Lautenberg entered the race, I suppose I could have exited and switched to the House race. But I believed that Lautenberg's not being known would make him beatable. I believed I would win."

No Senate seat in New Jersey would open up until 1996, when Bill Bradley retired. Frank Lautenberg retired in 2000—he was succeeded by Corzine—but remained a private citizen for only two years: In October 2002, he became the emergency Democratic senatorial nominee when Bradley's successor, Bob Torricelli, withdrew at the last minute after confessing to ethics violations. Lautenberg, winning that race and another in 2008, remained a senator until his death in 2013.

Twice, years after his final campaign, Andy briefly considering running again for elective office—in 1999, for the Senate seat to be opened up by Lautenberg's approaching retirement, and in 2013, when some urged him to run the following year against the Republican who in 2002 had won Andy's old seat following the retirement of Roukema. The demographics made sense: Through prior redistricting, the district had trended more Republican, but the most recent redrawing had returned to the district several communities that had once been Maguire strongholds. Even so, too much time had passed for the Maguire Magic to work any more miracles. Andy had lost his political base and his place in the news, notwithstanding a column from the *Bergen Record*'s top political editor, Jim Ahearn, touting Andy's congressional service and suggesting that Andy, "if he could find a way to do it, would make a first class Senator for New Jersey." In 2000, facing Corzine, he would have run into the same buzzsaw that had felled him eighteen years earlier: a rich person's self-financed campaign. In 2014, the midterms were taking place in the sixth year of Barack Obama's presidency—historically nearly a sure bet to result in congressional losses for the president's party. Andy's name still resonated in Bergen—he was backed by all four Democratic county chairs for a return bid. If successful, he would have set a record for longest span of time between tours of congressional service. But, says Andy, "I would have lost in 2014 because it was a bad Democratic year. The Republican incumbent won 55 percent to 43 percent. I would have run five points ahead of the Democrat who made the race, but I still would have lost."

Andy's aspiration to become a long-serving, consequential US senator would go unfulfilled. More years as a congressman marveling at the sight of the US Capitol as he walked home from work under its dome—gone. A presidential appointment to an executive-branch job might have been a possibility, except that the GOP would hold onto the White House for another decade. "With my record," says Andy, "the State Department, the Harvard PhD, the job in New York City, the three terms in Congress, I would have been an appropriate appointee to State or Health and Human Services or Housing and Urban Development or wherever—had there been a Democratic president."

Today, some former members of Congress stay in the public eye with frequent appearances on cable television. But in 1982, cable TV was in its infancy, not yet carrying three news networks that require knowledgeable, personable talking heads at every hour of the day and night.

Andy needed to make a career change.

A NEW SHERIFF: Ronald Reagan and His Revolution

By the time Ronald Reagan brought his zealous distrust of the federal government to the White House, the nation was primed for it. Until recent years, Americans had expected leaders to solve problems and tell the truth, but that trust had turned to cynicism after the lies and frustrations of the Vietnam War and the lies and corruption of Watergate. Lyndon Johnson's Great Society, the most ambitious attempt in the nation's history to establish justice, spread fairness, and protect the vulnerable, had foundered on the rocks of that same president's unpopular war in a small country in Asia. Johnson's successor, Richard Nixon, a man who preached peace and progress, had revealed himself to be a crook and a thug. Jimmy Carter, a Democrat, had run for president by running against Washington—an outsider come to clean up the mess made by the professionals. Carter did seek government intervention in one sector of the economy, energy, but otherwise did not attempt new large-scale initiatives that assigned to the federal government the responsibility to alleviate large-scale problems.

But while Carter may have discomfited official Washington, it was the former movie star who set the nation's capital, and the nation, on a decidedly new course. Americans already had lost confidence that the federal government could do big things well; now the public was asked to believe that activist government was not only ineffectual but oppressive, that freedom and collective national action, at least on domestic issues, were incompatible. American government, insofar as it tried to do anything significant, was, Reagan wanted Americans to believe, un-American.

For all of Reagan's famous "optimism" about America and its future, his million-megawatt grin masked a corrosive cynicism about the ability of human beings to work together for the common good.

March 30, 1981, was a lucky day for Ronald Wilson Reagan, in office just over two months. First, five shots from would-be assassin John Hinckley's six-shooter missed the new president. Second, riding away after the sixth shot ricocheted off the side of the presidential limousine and into the side of the president, the Secret Service agent who'd thrown him into the car recognized that his charge had been injured and directed the driver to change his destination from the White House to George Washington University Hospital. The bullet had pierced Reagan's lung; before being stabilized, he would lose half his blood supply. The timely intervention of the doctors saved the new president's life—and just in time: Had he first gone to the White House instead of speeding directly to the hospital, he would likely have died.

John Hinckley nearly killed Ronald Reagan, but the would-be assassin saved the new president's legislative agenda.

After Reagan took office, people realized that he was serious about implementing the plans he'd proposed during the campaign—plans that only a few years earlier would have been widely dismissed as "crackpot." Reagan's signature domestic initiative was a massive tax cut, with all taxpayers seeing their rates drop but the most generous reductions going to the wealthy. Evaluated by budgetary and economic standards that had guided Washington for decades—i.e., non-voodoo economics—the proposal was likely to add tens of billions of dollars annually to the federal budget deficit. Reagan coupled the tax decrease with calls for cuts to government programs Reagan deemed unimportant bordering on immoral—Medicaid, food stamps, job programs, aid to education. The budget Reagan proposed for fiscal year 1982 slashed nearly three hundred domestic programs—even expenditures once thought sacrosanct, such as veterans' benefits and aid to farmers.

Lane Kirkland, president of the AFL-CIO, promised in late February that a coalition of 157 unions, civil rights organizations, religious organizations, and not-for-profit social welfare advocacy groups would "carry out a fight against the unnecessary and unwise destruction of social and economic advances in the past fifty years."

But Reagan's being shot a month later—after addressing the very same AFL-CIO at the Washington Hilton Hotel—and, even more so, his behavior just after the shooting, endeared him to the American public. His wife, Nancy, had been at the White House at the time of the attack; when she met Reagan at the hospital, he quoted the words said over half a century earlier by prizefighter Jack Dempsey to *his* wife after he'd lost the heavyweight title to Gene Tunney: "Honey, I forgot to duck." On the operating table as he was about to receive general anesthesia, he pulled down his oxygen mask to joke to the team of doctors and nurses surrounding him, "I hope you are all Republicans." The team laughed. "Today, Mr. President," a Democratic doctor said, "we are all Republicans."

The public would naturally feel sympathy for a president who'd been shot. Just look at this remarkable specimen of American pluck and manhood—at death's door, with half his blood out of his body, yukking it up with his beloved wife and with the medical professionals working to save him.

What advantage could Democrats derive by opposing this man? How could they discuss his policies for what they really were? Could such a great guy, not to mention a seventy-year-old man who had survived a wound that would have killed most people half his age, really be so heartless as to deprive children of their lunches? Could this fearless man, alive thanks to the prompt intervention of a grade-A medical team, really be so callous as to deprive poor people of *their* medical care?

"What happened to Reagan on Monday is the stuff of which legends are made," the esteemed *Washington Post* political columnist David Broder wrote as Reagan recovered. Broder later said that Reagan "was politically untouchable from that point on. . . . He became a mythic figure."

Speaker Tip O'Neill and President Ronald Reagan got along famously—numerous photos show the two jovial Irishmen drinking toasts together on St. Patrick's Day and laughing at each other's stories. The Boston ward heeler did find the former Hollywood star personally charming. But the Massachusetts liberal had no use for the California conservative's presidency. Later in Reagan's first term, O'Neill would assail the president's governing philosophy: "The evil is in the White House at the present time. And that evil is a man who has no care and no concern for the working class of America and the future generations of America, and who likes to ride a horse. He's cold. He's mean. He's got ice water for blood."

Yet when Reagan's tax bill came up for a vote at the end of July 1981, 48 members of the Speaker's 243-strong Democratic House caucus supported the cold, mean man, the man who, on the edge of death, had laughed off the attempt on his life.

No John Hinckley, no Reagan Revolution. "Honey, I forgot to duck"—who could have guessed on September 23, 1926, that the words of the loser of that night's fight would change the course of American history?

Perhaps Ronald Reagan's most consequential intervention in the American economy and in the American way of life did not come in the form of tax or budget cuts. Rather, it came in an executive action that told the labor movement that a new sheriff was in town—and was not friendly.

On August 3, 1981, the nearly thirteen thousand members of the Professional Air Traffic Controllers Organization (PATCO)—the union representing the federal employees who ensured that airplanes took off and landed safely and efficiently at America's airports—went out on strike. Air travel in the United States came to a virtual standstill. Reagan responded in force: He declared the action illegal and gave every striking controller forty-eight hours to return to work or be fired. No recent president had ever played such hardball with a federal employee union.

Reagan made good on his threat. On August 5, he commenced the process that would leave 11,359 controllers jobless. Furthermore, the union-busting president announced a lifetime ban on the rehiring of any controller who had been fired. In October, the Federal Labor Relations Authority decertified PATCO as the representative of federal air traffic controllers. The union was finished.

Union membership among US workers had already been dropping since its high point, in the mid-1950s, when better than one in three American workers belonged to a union. The relocation of factories from union-friendly states in the North to right-to-work states in the South, as well as from the high-wage labor market of the United States to the low-wage labor market in developing countries, had already eliminated union jobs and weakened unions. Reagan's handling of the PATCO strike accelerated the trend. Since FDR, the federal government had helped to safeguard the right of unions to organize and to strike. Those days were gone.

In 1983, one in five US workers belonged to a union; today the number is one in ten. It's no coincidence that as American union membership has dwindled, American economic inequality has surged.

There is no denying that Ronald Reagan remade this country.

SCHOLARLY PURSUITS: Work at Harvard and a Think Tank

Out of office, out of work, out of luck, Andy needed a break.

"The first thing that happened," Andy says, "was that I got an opportunity to go to the Kennedy School, at Harvard, as a fellow. That was a wonderful way to return to where I'd done my graduate work. The fellows at that time were terrific. One was Madeleine Kunin, who had just left office as lieutenant-governor of Vermont and would be elected governor two years later. She and I became close because we shared strong views about where the country needed to go and what the role of government needed to be. I thoroughly enjoyed that semester.

"I led a seminar on policy issues affecting children—I enjoyed putting it together and I loved mentoring students. The experience took me back to when I led the YMCA-YWCA Summer in Washington program for college students, where I met the remarkable Margaret Lydia Green, whom I later married. And I enjoyed interacting with distinguished professors of this and distinguished professors of that.

"After Congress and after a political campaign, my time teaching at Harvard was relaxing—enjoyable in terms of the lack of pressure and not having to do everything on my list every day. I noticed that I got way fewer phone calls than I had before. When I was in Congress the calls came in nonstop from other members, from outside actors in the news or elsewhere, and from constituents. Suddenly I led a much quieter life.

"And then, after this sojourn in academia, the opportunity came to take my first real post-congressional job."

"The World Resources Institute," says Andy, "was the first international, not-for-profit think tank dedicated to addressing natural resources and changing environmental conditions and their connection to economic change and development the world over. Other organizations had focused on the environment itself, but WRI focused on the entire resource space of the planet."

Funded by a grant from the MacArthur Foundation (of the "genius" awards), WRI was founded in 1982 by Gus Speth, who had run the Council on Environmental Quality in the Carter White House. Rafe Pomerance, an environmental activist and lobbyist who had recently served as president of Friends of the Earth, recommended Andy to Speth.

"I suggested that Gus talk to Andy," Pomerance recalls. "Former members of Congress are often seen as only ex-pols, has-beens, rather than people who have a lot to contribute on their own." Pomerance himself would soon join WRI, working in the organization's initiative on climate change—one of the first such efforts in the world.

"They were looking for somebody to head up this US Stake in Global Resource Issues project," says Andy. "Rafe recommended me and I got the job."

As the project's director, Andy worked to formulate policy that recognized the effect of the world's environment on American economic, political, and security interests.

"Our headline undertaking in this global resources project," he says, "was the book I edited with a colleague from WRI, Janet Welsh Brown."

Bordering on Trouble: Resources & Politics in Latin America (Adler & Adler 1986) included contributions from thirteen well-known experts on Latin America—journalists and academics—as well as commentary and a chapter by Andy and Brown. The book surveyed a broad range of short- and long-term issues regarding Latin America and its resources, and the attendant concerns and responsibilities of the United States.

"You can't look at these issues in terms of the environment alone," says Andy. "You have to look at them in resource-space, economic, and development terms if you are going to get a grip on what is going on out there and what's important for the future of the human race.

"These concerns are crucial for any broad understanding of US security interests—not just the narrowly defined problems of the spotted owl or desertification in sub-Saharan Africa. Such issues will affect the long-term interests of the United States economically, as well as in terms of our standing in the world, our long-term security, and the world's long-term security. It's all bound up together. Our job was to demonstrate why that was the case and how that was the case, and to make clear what was at stake.

"Our organization was at the forefront of these discussions—that's why the MacArthur Foundation created WRI. A lot of these concepts have been accepted as obvious over the last forty years. In 1982, they were anything but obvious."

Bordering on Trouble covered issues ranging from the urbanization of Mexico around its capital to Venezuela's dependence on oil exports, from the cost of economic development in Brazil to pressures on the Amazon rainforest. Walter LaFeber, a professor of history at Cornell, contributed a chapter that presented a revisionist appraisal of the Alliance for Progress. Initiated during the Kennedy administration, the alliance was ostensibly designed to transform traditional heavy-handed US commercial exploitation in Latin America into cooperation that benefited both North and South America.

Mainly, however, it didn't. For a worldwide perspective, Andy's US Stake in Global Resource Issues unit funded the research for what became historian Richard P. Tucker's *Insatiable Appetite: The United States and the Ecological Degradation of the Tropical World* (University of California Press).

"Everybody thought the Alliance for Progress was a great program," says Andy. "In fact, it quickly became coopted as an extension of US anti-Communism and the narrow cold war view of US security interests in Latin America.

"In other words, the idea was to talk a good line about balanced economic growth and how we have to deal with poverty and all the rest of it, but in reality, the money went to the elites—as it always had. Money went to the interests oppressing indigenous peoples. Money went to the death squads. There's not much of the Alliance for Progress worth praising, after you look at it closely. We recruited LaFeber, one of our country's foremost experts on Latin America, to write this chapter and I edited his work."

Writing the final chapter, Andy and Brown summed up the history of US-Latin America interaction: "In extensive relations with Latin countries we [in the United States] are often patronizing, possessive, and prescriptive. But little do most of us understand the intimacy of those relations, the predominant power of the United States for over a century, and the resulting ambivalence that today still figures in Latin-U.S. interaction. Our ignorance amounts to arrogance—potentially dangerous arrogance."

They concluded: "But the Latin countries will not succeed without the consistent, firm backing of the United States. The United States is so rich, so powerful and so dominant in this hemisphere that no large enterprise can move forward effectively without its support. When the United States drags its heels, even the next largest and most powerful countries can accomplish little without the greatest extra energy. The colossus of the North can say aye or nay. If it merely acquiesces, history will register a no vote, and the United States will be bordering on generations of trouble."

A STRAIGHT PATH: Reagan, Trump, and the Degradation of a Major American Political Party

The Republican Party of Donald Trump, a party that denies science, venerates an obviously unfit leader, treats fantasy as truth and truth as fantasy, and is horrified by the demographic trends that foretell the end of white preeminence, did not spring from thin air. The maladies of the GOP may certainly be traced back to Joe McCarthy, William F. Buckley, and Barry Goldwater. But the party of Lincoln could not have become the party of Trump without the person and presidency of Ronald Reagan.

Not that Ronald Reagan was Donald Trump—unlike Trump, Reagan did not expect the presidency to yield personal enrichment; unlike Trump, Reagan filled a number of key positions with qualified, dedicated public servants—the likes of James Baker and George Shultz either didn't serve in the Trump administration or served only briefly; unlike Trump, Reagan didn't cheapen public discourse by personal vulgarity.

Nonetheless:

- Like Trump, Ronald Reagan said preposterous things: Trees cause pollution. He was present for the liberation of Buchenwald. (He spent the war years in Hollywood, working for the First Motion Picture Unit of the Army Air Corps.)
- His supporters laughed off the fact that the president of the United States was either delusional or a serial fabulist, but the president's personal delusions engendered policy delusions, leading administration officials and Republican lawmakers to ask the American public to believe obvious nonsense. Exhibit A: The 1981 tax cut that he and his aides contended would increase tax revenues. In only a year's time, the exploding deficit caused Reagan the tax-cutter to impose what to that point was the largest tax increase in American history. Yet Republicans to this day have not given up on the notion that tax cuts for the wealthy and powerful pay for themselves. And despite their self-description of the GOP as the party of "fiscal responsibility," Republicans are horrified by the deficit when a Democrat is president but unfazed by it when one of their own occupies the White House.
- Reagan's unwillingness to be persuaded by facts affected his foreign and national security policy as well. Against the findings of government scientists and engineers, he believed that the United States could quickly develop an impregnable missile defense system. "Star Wars," the nickname given the technology by the press, denoted the general awareness that the system, as Reagan perceived it, belonged to the realm of science fiction, not science fact. In October 1986, at a summit meeting in Iceland with Soviet leader Mikhail Gorbachev, Reagan's insistence on retaining America's ability to test and implement missile defense derailed an agreement that would have eliminated both countries' stockpiles of nuclear weapons.
- Like Trump, Reagan didn't let the world's toughest job burden him. "He only works three to three-and-a-half hours a day," said Tip O'Neill in 1983. "He doesn't do his homework. He doesn't read his briefing papers. It's sinful that this man is president of the United States." His backers on Capitol Hill didn't mind until, toward the end of his term, a blue-ribbon commission blamed the Iran-Contra scandal on Reagan's lax "management style."

- Trump confined children in cages; Reagan did nothing so immediately cruel. But he blithely cut government programs that helped the poor while he pared the tax rates of the rich. One public relations misstep came when officials in the Department of Agriculture, looking for ways to cut the costs of the federal school lunch program, suggested that relish and ketchup could, for nutritional purposes, be considered "vegetables." "Ketchup as a vegetable" became shorthand for the creative callousness of the new administration. Senator John Heinz, Republican of Pennsylvania, heir to his family's ketchup fortune, commented, "Ketchup is a condiment. This is one of the most ridiculous regulations I ever heard of, and I suppose I need not add that I do know something about ketchup and relish, or did at one time." Realizing the beating his administration was taking in the press, Reagan promptly scotched the idea.
- Trump, the thrice-married adulterer who paid big money to conceal his one-night stand with a porn star, inspired blind devotion from the majority of Christian fundamentalists. Again, Reagan did nothing so egregious—he was, from all accounts, devoted to his wife. But in its fealty to Ronald Reagan, the religious right was following a man who went to church as seldom as he saw his grandchildren. In the 1980s, conservative Christians established themselves as the GOP's voting and organizing backbone; since then, party leaders have relied on cultural issues—abortion, homosexuality, prayer in schools, guns, white resentment; more recently, critical race theory, LGBTQ+ rights, library books—to provide cover for their primary agenda: slashing taxes and regulations objected to by the wealthy Americans and big corporations that fund Republican campaigns.
- Like Trump, Reagan conducted a blatantly illegal foreign policy. Trump withheld congressionally mandated aid to Ukraine in order to pressure that country's president to mount a phony investigation of Joe Biden and his son. Reagan's breaking of the law came in the service of ideology, not domestic electoral advantage.
- Two years before Reagan took office, leftist rebels in Nicaragua—calling themselves Sandinistas in honor of Augusto Sandino, who fought US occupation of Nicaragua seven decades

earlier—overthrew the regime of Anastasio Somoza, a kleptocrat friendly to the United States. The Reagan administration did its best to terrify Americans over the small country's new government. Much as leaders a generation earlier had warned of Communists hopscotching their way from Hanoi until they washed up under the Golden Gate Bridge, Reagan & Co. measured the distance from Managua, Nicaragua's capital, to the closest US city, Brownsville, Texas (1250 miles).

- Reagan's solution: Support of the Contras, right-wing rebels seeking to bring down the Sandinistas. Congress at first authorized aid to the Contras but in 1984 prohibited further assistance. Administration officials devised ways to get around the ban. First, they secured funds from other sources—from governments in Saudi Arabia and Taiwan and from private individuals—to replace the US aid and staged a covert operation to ship the US arms purchased with those funds to the Contras. Then they came up with what Lt. Col. Oliver North, the Marine running the operation on the National Security Council, called a "neat idea." Separately, the Reagan administration had begun to sell arms to Iran in exchange for that government's help in freeing US hostages held by Hezbollah in Lebanon. The sales violated the Reagan administration's own stated embargo on arms sales to Iran and Reagan's firm public refusal to negotiate with terrorists: "We make no concessions, we make no deals," he'd said. North's neat idea was to use the profits gained from the arms sales to pay for weapons to send to the Contras.
- The affair became public after the crash of a plane supplying the Contras. A joint Senate-House panel followed with hearings broadcast gavel to gavel by all major broadcast networks. Just as nearly every GOP member would justify Trump's illegal conduct three decades later, nearly every Republican in the Iran-Contra hearings justified Reagan's illegal conduct. The two-headed scheme surely merited Reagan's impeachment and removal from office: If the executive branch is free to ignore the legislative branch's power of the purse, what good is the Constitution? But Reagan was too personally popular and Democratic leaders too frightened to take him on, preferring to wait for the nearing end

of his administration. Unlike Trump, Reagan was not impeached. Unlike Trump, Reagan testified about the scandal under oath. And unlike Trump, Reagan showed contrition: "A few months ago I told the American people I did not trade arms for hostages. My heart and my best intentions tell me that's true, but the facts and evidence tell me it is not." In light of his subsequent diagnosis with Alzheimer's, this pleading of the senility defense may have been entirely appropriate.

- Nevertheless, like Trump, Reagan and his administration got away with breaking the law and violating the constitutional order.
- Trump's mishandling of the COVID-19 pandemic cost the nation hundreds of thousands of lives. During the 1980s, as another epidemic, AIDS, killed thousands of Americans, the president of the United States had nothing to say about it. After all, the disease wasn't ravaging the people he and his kind cared about: Gays, Haitian immigrants, and heroin addicts didn't vote for or contribute to Republican politicians. Only Reagan's surgeon general, C. Everett Koop, refused to look away from the devastation. Why do you care about those people? administration officials asked Koop. Because, Koop replied, they're my patients, too. Reagan acknowledged the existence of the disease only when it afflicted his old Hollywood pal, Rock Hudson.
- Trump sabotaged the work of federal agencies, reversing long-standing policies and regulations and putting in charge people opposed to the core missions of those agencies. Reagan's head of the Occupational Safety and Health Administration was a construction company executive who ended OSHA's health warnings to workers in the textile industry. Reagan reoriented the Consumer Products Safety Commission and the National Labor Relations Board away from the consumers and workers those organizations were designed to protect. When public outcry kept the administration from abolishing the Legal Services Corporation, which provides legal representation to indigent Americans, Reagan appointed as head of the organization a man with a history of opposing its work. Ronald Reagan's Department of Justice changed the regulations for the Foreign Corrupt Practices Act, making bribery of foreign companies harder to prosecute.

Under the leadership of President Ronald Reagan, the United States retreated on civil rights, aid to the poor and weak, protection of consumers, and education. Franklin Roosevelt's reorientation of the United States government toward protection of the vulnerable and toward the interests of the broad majority of the population was gone. Republican presidents Dwight Eisenhower and Richard Nixon might have resisted additional reforms, but neither tried to do away with the New Deal consensus. Reagan and his acolytes, on the other hand, sought a return to the nation as it had existed in the decade before FDR, a time when an American president, Calvin Coolidge, would say, "After all, the chief business of the American people is business."

Laissez-faire economics and automatic suspicion of any major federal program aimed at protecting vulnerable Americans would prevail for four decades. Even the two Democratic presidencies during that time—headed by two relatively progressive-minded politicians, Bill Clinton and Barack Obama—would be hamstrung by the assumptions that Reaganomics and Reaganism had fastened to American ways of governance. "The era of big government is over," declared Bill Clinton in 1996. Even Barack Obama, who in 2010 succeeded in bringing about the most significant expansion of the social safety net in decades, the Affordable Care Act, followed up that accomplishment not by crowing about it but by preaching a return to deficit cutting.

It would take the election of Joe Biden in 2020—after widespread revulsion over the person and presidency of Donald Trump, after the realization by many previously unconvinced Americans that the crises threatening the nation and the world could not be addressed without "big government"—to begin the return of America's public sector to the vision established by Franklin Roosevelt nine decades earlier.

GIVE INDUSTRY A BREAK: Reagan's Environmental Appointees

Reagan's penchant for hiring foxes to rule chicken coops was nowhere more evident than in the agencies dealing with the environment and natural resources. His appointees to the Department of the Interior, to the Environmental Protection Agency, and elsewhere agreed: their job was to get out of the way of industry, leaving it free to extract and pollute. "It just seems as if they have carefully searched the country for people with good credentials and for opposing the environment," said the president of the National Audubon Society.

To head the Bureau of Land Management, the agency responsible for administering more than 340 million acres of public lands, Reagan appointed a man who, as speaker of the Colorado House of Representatives, sponsored a bill to transfer those acres to private and state ownership. The White House Council on Environmental Quality gained one appointee who, as the chief environmental official in Ohio, called for lowering air-quality standards in order to permit the burning of soft coal, and another who stated that the pendulum had "swung too far toward the environmental protection side" and that it was time to give "industry a break to get this country moving again."

Worst of all were Reagan's appointments to the two senior-most positions dealing with the environment: secretary of the interior and administrator of the Environmental Protection Agency. To head Interior he appointed James Watt, a Wyoming lawyer whose most recent job had been heading an advocacy organization concerned with private property rights. In the department of you-just-can't-make-this-stuff-up, Watt, at a hearing shortly after his confirmation by the Senate, was asked about conservation of natural resources for future generations. His reply seemed to state that conservation was not important because End Times were approaching: "I do not know how many future generations we can count on before the Lord returns," he said.

He advocated increased mining and oil drilling on public lands and public waters. He called for the abolition of the Land and Water Conservation Fund, whose purpose was increasing the acreage of land protected by wildlife refuges, and pulled thousands of acres from possible designation as wilderness area. (At the Interior Department during Carter's presidency, Andy's wife, Meg, had managed the Land and Water Conservation Fund and expanded its reach into urban environments.)

Anne Gorsuch, at EPA, was even less qualified for her job than Watt was for his, with no environmental credentials other than being an ultra-conservative Colorado state legislator. During her twenty-two months heading the agency she cut its budget by more than a fifth, curbed legal action against polluters, and weakened air pollution regulations.

Watt and Gorsuch both left their posts in 1983. Gorsuch resigned after confirmation of reports that she had withheld some $6 million in federal funds designated for the cleanup of a toxic waste dump in Los Angeles—at the time former California governor Jerry Brown, a Democrat, was running for the US Senate; she didn't want to dispatch funds that might help his campaign. Watt resigned after a controversial statement in a speech to the US Chamber of Commerce: Mocking affirmative action, he said that on a commission reviewing an Interior program, "I have a Black, a woman, two Jews, and a cripple. And we have talent."

A SNOWLESS NEW ENGLAND: America's First Attempts to Reckon with Climate Change

Since the 1950s, if not earlier, American scientists have been analyzing the climatic consequences of burning fossil fuels. In 1955, a researcher working for General Electric told a meeting of the American Institute of Electrical Engineers that the excess carbon dioxide generated by human activity might be "having a greenhouse effect on our climate." The unnamed author of the *New York Times* report on the speech noted that "glaciers are melting more rapidly and fish are caught off Greenland that were formerly seen only in waters far to the south."

The oil industry has long been aware of the problem: In 1958 and 1968 the American Petroleum Institute conducted studies that predicted, in the words of the later report, "serious worldwide environmental changes."

During the 1960s, the administration of Lyndon Johnson commissioned a study of the phenomenon. The study's report, as the *Times* later noted, "warned of the rapid melting of Antarctica, rising seas, increased acidity of fresh waters —changes that would require no less than a coordinated global effort to forestall." Without such action, the United States "could see a snowless New England, the swamping of major coastal cities, as much as a 40 percent decline in national wheat production, the forced migration of about one-quarter of the world's population"—and not in centuries but within the lifetimes of those reading the report in 1965.

In 1977–78, a group of government scientists known as the Jasons (after the leader of the Argonauts) again studied the subject and reported to the US Department of Energy that if the production of greenhouse gases was not checked, the world could see a rise in sea levels as much as 16 feet, along with severe worldwide disruption to agriculture and the availability of drinking water. The authors of the report sent copies to scientists around the world, to energy industry organizations, and to a variety of civilian and military government agencies, including the White House.

Still, the issue did not pierce the national and congressional consciousness.

That ignorance would change thanks to a non-scientist, Rafe Pomerance. Reading an EPA report on coal, Pomerance noticed what seemed to be almost a throwaway line: The continued use of fossil fuels, the report said, could cause "significant and damaging" changes to Earth's climate within twenty or thirty years. Pomerance wanted to know more. He contacted Gordon MacDonald, one of the Jasons, for more information.

Alarmed by what MacDonald told him, Pomerance arranged for the two of them to brief officials at numerous government agencies. After the two men met with President Carter's science adviser, the adviser called on a senior government meteorologist to convene a meeting of top scientists to analyze the issue. Like the previous reports, the report from this gathering warned of dire consequences should global temperatures rise.

Exit Carter. Enter Reagan. The White House Council on Environmental Quality issued another report, warning of "a warming of the Earth, possibly with very serious effects." The Reagan administration considered doing away with the council.

Despite the apparent indifference at the White House, some members of Congress were beginning to show interest—the House held hearings in 1981. But the problem seemed too theoretical, the catastrophic consequences too far in the future, for the issue to jolt the public imagination or spur more than a few elected officials to action. Besides, scientists warned of a 2°C rise in world temperatures—how much damage could be done by a couple of measly degrees?

But then scientists found something more immediately frightening: a hole in the ozone layer. The hole was not a literal hole, but rather a thinning of stratospheric ozone, the gas that protects life on Earth from the danger of excessive exposure to ultraviolet light from the sun. Experts warned that a reduction in ozone could result in an exponential increase in rates of skin cancer. The "hole" was manmade, caused by a class of chemicals called chlorofluorocarbons, or CFCs. CFCs were used in plastic foams, in air conditioners and refrigerators, and as propellants in cans of everything from hair spray to insecticide.

Here was a problem the public could visualize—a giant hole in the air miles above the ground. The cause of the hole was a particular class of chemicals—widely used but hardly the foundation of the world economy, as were (and still are) fossil fuels. CFCs were also potent greenhouse gases. But skin cancer represented a more urgent danger than the warming of the planet, no matter how much more disruptive climate change would be in the long term.

"Part of what I did," says Pomerance, "was trying to interest Congress in the issue. To do that you have to work with staff, you have to brief members, you have to propose hearings, organize witnesses, get to the media—all of that. The first culminating event was the hearing in June 1986. There were a lot of preliminary pieces that got it to that point.

"I had convinced a staffer named Curtis Moore to hold a hearing on climate change." Moore advised Pomerance that pairing the two issues—global warming and ozone depletion—would do more to attract the attention of Congress than continuing to focus on warming alone.

The staffer had another piece of advice for Pomerance: "Curtis said to me, 'You need a champion. You need a horse on this issue. You gotta get Chafee onboard.'"

Few US senators have been more respected than the late John Chafee, the moderate-to-liberal Republican of Rhode Island. During the 1960s he was his state's governor before Nixon appointed him secretary of the Navy. Elected to the Senate in 1976, he remained in the body until his death in 1999 at age seventy-seven. A Marine veteran of Guadalcanal and Okinawa in World War II, he led a rifle company in Korea. In the book *The Coldest War*, a memoir of the Korean conflict written by James Brady, one of the Marines the Rhode Islander commanded (and no relation to the press secretary and gunfire victim in the Reagan White House), the author calls the future senator "the only truly great man I'd yet met in my life."

Curtis told Pomerance that John Chafee, chair of the Senate Subcommittee on Environmental Pollution, was holding a meeting to decide what to do with his environmental agenda. "So," Pomerance says, "I went to Gus Speth, who went to that meeting and convinced Chafee to do the climate issue. We built into one of Chafee's speeches that he would hold hearings, then we organized the hearing and got the media there." The hearing, on June 10, 1986, chaired by Chafee, addressed both "the greenhouse effect" and "ozone modification." "The hearing made all the front pages," Pomerance recalls, "*Washington Post*, *New York Times*, magazine covers. Chafee did a great job and blew the thing open.

"We had big-name scientists on the first panel that day; Andy was a witness on the second panel. That was an important moment for him and for the issue."

Andy had recently been promoted to WRI's vice president for policy affairs—he became the organization's chief liaison to relevant international agencies, whether headquartered in the United States or around the world. "The main thing," he says, "was to relate to all of the key institutions—UN agencies, nongovernmental development agencies, the World Bank—that intersected with the concerns we had at WRI. Along with Speth, I would go to meet with senior people at such institutions and try to get them to devote a greater percentage of their time and money to issues combining stress on the environment with concerns of security and development. And I worked to create joint arrangements between them and us—we engaged in all sorts of collaborative activities, such as a tropical forest initiative with the UN agencies based in Europe."

Now the agency he would try to influence was the US Senate. "As you are hearing at this very important session this morning, Mr. Chairman," said Andy to begin his testimony, "we have reached a dramatic moment. Apart from nuances, the international scientific community has reached a consensus: mankind's activities are changing the atmosphere in ways that could profoundly affect the habitability of the Earth. The magnitude of the risks is unprecedented. The question is: What do we do?"

Andy outlined the scope of the problem: The entire climate system—precipitation, winds, storm patterns, soil, and temperature—would be affected on a scale unprecedented in human experience. He cited the devastation to be inflicted upon US agriculture, and referred to retreat in European glaciers and warming in the southern hemisphere. He mentioned the increase in skin cancers likely to result from depletion of stratospheric ozone.

Scientists on the panel explained technical details. Andy, the former lawmaker and diplomat, filled in the human context and the domestic and international political imperatives.

"As you and others, Mr. Chairman, suggested today," he continued, "some problems are almost too overwhelming to comprehend in terms relevant to our daily lives. Nuclear war is the classic example. Because it is so frightening, there is a tendency to avoid talking about it. Likewise, the profound changes implied by climate and ozone change can lead us to look away or seek excuses for delay."

Climate change was not only a clear danger, said Andy, but a present one, with consequences already apparent: drought in the Sahel of Africa, extreme weather events in the United States, a rise in water levels of the Great Lakes that threatened to "displace entire communities."

Andy urged that "active collaboration between scientists and policy-makers begin immediately." He called for every relevant arm of the US government to assess climate and ozone change as it affected that agency's jurisdiction. He called for international cooperation, suggesting that the topic be on the agenda at the next US-USSR summit and that the United States bring up the issue with China. Far from the economic powerhouse it is today, China was by 1986 just beginning to emerge from three decades of a centrally planned system. Andy noted that China's expected economic growth would require a dramatic increase in the country's burning of the most problematic of the fossil fuels, coal.

There was no time to waste. The United States, Andy testified, needed to "adopt incentives and controls that increase our options and buy time for solutions." Steps to be taken promptly included reduction of the use of CFCs, energy conservation through more efficient technologies, faster development of renewable energy sources, and the curtailing of deforestation. He described specific actions to be taken to reduce levels of each of four harmful gases: carbon dioxide, CFCs, nitrous oxide, and methane.

Andy closed with this piece of advice: "Finally, Mr. Chairman, we should begin now to examine the technical aspects and to fashion a political consensus for more aggressive policies such as a carbon tax on fossil fuels, since such approaches may soon prove necessary."

Andy and other witnesses had elucidated the phenomenon threatening the planet and described the beginning phases of a plan to save it.

Would anyone listen?

LANDSLIDE: Reagan's Reelection, 1984

By the time Ronald Reagan stood for reelection in 1984, inflation had been wrung out of the economy and unemployment was headed downward. "It's morning again in America," said the narrator of the incumbent's most effective campaign ad as the screen filled with images of hardworking Americans getting back to the jobs and lives that had been interrupted by the economic malaise of the Carter years. The Democrats didn't stand a chance.

Their party flirted with nominating Gary Hart, a relatively unknown senator from Colorado who billed himself as the bringer of "new ideas." But in a primary debate in Atlanta, front-runner Walter Mondale, who had inherited his timeworn liberalism from the New Deal via his mentor Hubert Humphrey, successfully framed his opponent's reason for running as an empty pretention. Referring to a contemporary Wendy's commercial in which an elderly woman inspects the scanty hamburger offered by a rival, Mondale said to Hart, "When I hear your new ideas, I'm reminded of that ad, 'Where's the beef?'"

Hart, a long shot to begin with, didn't recover from the insult. He finished the nominating process a distant second to Mondale, whose long and visible career as a liberal and a party stalwart earned him strong support from organized labor, party leaders, and the rank and file. Mondale made history by choosing as his running mate a woman, Geraldine Ferraro, a previously unremarkable US representative from Queens, New York. As slim as Mondale's chance of beating Reagan was to begin with, the Minnesotan narrowed it even more at the Democratic convention by making a crucial mistake: He told the truth. Promising to cut the swelling "Reagan budget deficit" by two thirds, Mondale said, "Let's tell the truth. It must be done, it must be done. Mr. Reagan will raise taxes, and so will I. He won't tell you. I just did."

The choice for November was set: Americans could choose morning in America or they could eat their spinach. Issues aside, Mondale, an exceptional public servant, was running against an exceptional personality. Reagan looked marvelous on a horse—had Mondale ever ridden one? Reagan's good looks and winning smile had lit up movie screens; Mondale was presentable but not even remotely a screen idol. Reagan spoke in a deep voice lubricated by honey and platitudes; Mondale's voice was high-pitched and nasal, his uncomfortable truths spoken in a pronounced Minnesota accent.

An underdog victory seemed possible at only one point in the campaign: At the first candidates' debate, in Louisville on October 7, Reagan seemed disoriented and disconnected—likely an early sign of the Alzheimer's that would be made public in 1994, five years after he left office. But in the second debate he reassured voters by knowing where he was and seeming alert. At seventy-three years the oldest person ever to occupy the Oval Office to that point, Reagan disarmed the issue when one of the panelists asked him the inevitable question about his age. Reagan came back with the line he had prepared: "I will not make age an issue of this campaign. I am not going to exploit, for political purposes, my opponent's youth and inexperience." The fifty-six-year-old Mondale, who had served a dozen years in the Senate and four years as vice president, laughed along with the studio audience and the public watching at home. But the Democrat knew at that moment that the contest was decided.

People liked Ronald Reagan and they liked the direction of the economy. Twelve years after George McGovern had won just one state and the District of Columbia, Mondale did the same—although, unlike the senator from South Dakota, this time the candidate carried his home state. Reagan won the popular vote 59 to 41 percent.

Would American liberalism ever prevail again?

GENTLEMAN DEMAGOGUE: George Bush and the Campaign of 1988

What was left of the plausibility of liberalism as a defining theory of American governance was incinerated by the campaign of George H. W. Bush in 1988. Then Vice President Bush, by all accounts a generous, kind, thoughtful man in his personal dealings, ran a racist, demagogic presidential campaign the likes of which most voters had never seen. But Bush, a gentleman of impeccable manners, maintained a safe distance from the worst of it, leaving the dirty work to the hired help.

In May 1987, Gary Hart, the presumed front-runner for the Democratic nomination, withdrew from the race after revelations of marital infidelity, including an embarrassing photograph showing a young woman (not his wife) sitting on his lap on the deck of a cruise ship aptly named *Monkey Business*. A large field of candidates not implicated in sex scandals yielded as the party's nominee the governor of Massachusetts, Michael Dukakis, a moderately liberal pragmatist, more technocrat than revolutionary, a genial man of bland personality. To balance the ticket Dukakis chose as his running mate the lordly senator from Texas, Lloyd

Bentsen, who, as it happened, had originally won his seat by defeating a former congressman named George H. W. Bush.

Bush, essentially promising a third Reagan term, steamrolled his competition for the Republican nomination—including the oleaginous television preacher Pat Robertson and the acerbic Kansas senator Bob Dole. After Bush won the New Hampshire primary he was interviewed on NBC by anchor Tom Brokaw. At the end of the conversation, Brokaw told Bush to look at the monitor and see Dole, who was waiting for his turn on air. Brokaw asked Bush if he had anything to say to the man he'd defeated. "No," said Bush, "just wish him well and meet him in the South."

"And Senator Dole, is there anything you'd like to say to the vice president?"

"Yeah, stop lying about my record."

Months later, to a crowd gathered along the riverfront in New Orleans, not far from the hall hosting the Republican National Convention, Bush introduced his running mate, Dan Quayle, a forty-one-year-old senator from Indiana. The baby-faced Hoosier rushed to the stage as though he were assistant head cheerleader at a junior high school pep rally. His reputation only went down from there, with verbal missteps and awkwardness that gave Americans the impression that God had run out of brains to pass out the day Quayle was born. Quayle's lampoonable persona gave Democrats their only enjoyable moment of what turned out to be a dismal fall campaign. When questioned about his youth, Quayle would regularly note that he was more or less the same age as John F. Kennedy had been during the 1960 campaign. When he raised the comparison in his debate with Bentsen, the tall, white-haired, stentorian-voiced Texan was prepared: "Senator, I served with Jack Kennedy. I knew Jack Kennedy. Jack Kennedy was a friend of mine. Senator, you're no Jack Kennedy." Quayle seemed ready to weep. Modern American political history has not seen another putdown as withering or as memorable.

Like most speeches accepting a party's nomination, Bush's convention address was mostly forgettable. Two moments, however, stood out. He called for a rebirth of volunteerism across the country—"a thousand points of light," in words written by his speechwriter, Peggy Noonan. Translation: He wanted to see the harsher aspects of Reaganism soften, as long as neither he nor the government he sought to lead had responsibility for supplying the theretofore missing compassion.

Also, Bush vowed that as hard as people would press him to raise Americans' taxes, he would never give his consent. "Read my lips," he proclaimed. "No new taxes!"

Early polls gave Dukakis the lead—Bush lacked Reagan's charisma, and the public seemed ready for a change in government, especially after the previous year's exposure of the Iran-Contra scandal. Bush and his campaign decided they had only one option if they wanted to win: Tear Dukakis apart. They focused on two issues as irrelevant as they were incendiary.

In 1977, Dukakis had vetoed a bill prohibiting Massachusetts teachers from refusing to join in the saying of the Pledge of Allegiance—the law reflected not the governor's disrespect for the flag but rather his adherence to the Supreme Court's 1943 ruling on the issue.

In 1986, Dukakis had approved a weekend furlough, in accordance with the regular practices of the Massachusetts prison system, for a convicted African-American murderer named Willie Horton. Horton did not return when his furlough expired. Ten months later, he victimized an engaged couple in Maryland, stabbing and tying up the man and raping his fiancée.

An independent political action committee ran an ad featuring Horton's mug shot, criticizing Dukakis over the furlough. Bush disavowed any connection to the ad, but the Bush campaign itself soon ran its own ad on the topic: The spot showed a shadowy line of dark-skinned men passing through a revolving door as they were released from prison.

Dukakis, Bush's campaign was saying, was an unpatriotic coddler of Black criminals—and, by the way, he opposed capital punishment. But Bush & Co. didn't stop there. A natural-born American citizen, Dukakis was proud to highlight his history as a son of Greek immigrants. But that profile allowed the GOP to paint him as a foreigner. At a visit to a General Dynamics factory in Michigan, Dukakis took a brief spin in an Army tank. The helmet on his head accentuated the size of his prominent nose, his half-smile looked like a goofy grin—the Bush campaign included the footage in an ad that painted the Massachusetts governor as an untrustworthy steward of America's defense.

Real Americans believed in the death penalty, the flag, and protecting well-behaved white people from violent Black people. They had American-sounding names. In short, Bush charged, Dukakis was a "liberal." Dogged by the accusation, Dukakis, late in the campaign, finally admitted to being one. He was the last presidential nominee to cop to what became known as "the L word."

Bush swamped Dukakis, who improved on Mondale's performance, but only barely. He carried ten states and the District of Columbia, winning only 46 percent of the popular vote to Bush's 53 percent.

George H. W. Bush had made "liberal" a dirty word. This wealthy scion of a patrician New England family, a man never trusted by movement conservatives, a man of no identifiable ideology aside from his personal ambition, had finished what Reagan had begun: Bush had driven a stake in the heart of American liberalism as a respectable theory of US governance.

A BLOWN OPPORTUNITY: George Bush, John Sununu, and the Fate of the Planet

"I am an environmentalist," George Bush had declared during the 1988 campaign. He'd also said, "Those who think we are powerless to do anything about the greenhouse effect are forgetting about the White House effect." By contrast, Dukakis had claimed that coal could meet the country's energy requirements for three hundred years. The energy industry seemed to accept the need for action on climate—or, at least, the inevitability of action. The greenhouse effect, said a coal spokesman, was no longer "an emerging issue. It is here already, and we'll be hearing more and more about it."

Other countries—Germany, Norway, the United Kingdom, Sweden, and Canada—had begun to tackle the issue. Ten days into the Bush administration, the new secretary of state, James A. Baker III, hosted at Foggy Bottom an international meeting on the warming planet. "We can probably not afford to wait until all of the uncertainties about global climate change have been resolved," he said. "Time will not make the problem go away."

The statement earned Baker a call from Bush's White House chief of staff. Baker didn't know what he was talking about, said John Sununu, the former governor of New Hampshire now running the White House. The secretary should avoid the issue. Sununu, a man of immense self-regard, had a PhD in mechanical engineering from MIT that, in his opinion, gave him the knowledge and credentials to judge the science on climate change and find it lacking. Bush's EPA administrator, William Reilly, urged Bush to seek a global treaty that would curb the emission of carbon. But Sununu argued that scientists had been alarmist and wrong before; they were alarmist and wrong now. The restrictions urged by climate scientists would impinge on that golden calf of Republican ideology, free enterprise, and cause immense, needless damage to the US economy.

In November 1989, representatives from more than sixty countries met in Holland to discuss moving forward with a global treaty on climate change. Bush, just a week before, had promised that the United States would "play a leadership role in global warming." But when an agreement was hammered out, the US delegate, after consultation with Sununu, refused to sign because the document called for a freezing of the rate of carbon emissions. "Your government," the Swedish delegate said to an American observer, "is fucking this up."

The United States did move ahead with support of a treaty that called for a reduction in CFC emissions by 50 percent within a decade. And Bush did support and sign the 1990 Clean Air Act, which mandated a cap-and-trade mechanism that greatly reduced the problem of "acid rain," the sulfuric acid released into the atmosphere from coal-fired generating plants. But in the conflict between Reilly and Sununu over climate change, Bush backed his chief of staff.

The commitment to fight global warming had sounded good in Bush's campaign; in reality, it was a throwaway line, a promise he was no more sincere about than he was about his tax pledge—a pledge, Bush told Dukakis during the customary post-election winner-loser meeting, he would hold off on breaking until after the 1990 midterm elections. No president would take significant action on climate change for two decades. And while in the late 1980s a Republican officeholder, John Chafee, had played a key role in bringing the issue of climate change to the public's attention, and in the 2000s Senator John McCain co-sponsored a major bill on the topic, at this writing, well into the 21st century, nearly every key Republican officeholder continues to deny that the problem exists.

"We did get half a loaf," says Pomerance. "We negotiated the Framework Convention on Climate Change"—agreed upon at a UN conference in Rio de Janeiro in June 1992—"which was given advice and consent by the Senate unanimously in 1992. But it had no real requirements to reduce emissions. The argument is that had George H. W. Bush decided to impose emissions reductions, he might have succeeded.

He succeeded on acid rain. So it's conceivable that we could have acted with greater urgency in climate than we did. We don't know, because we didn't get that far. We were trying to get the treaty negotiations to include a commitment to the United States to reduce emissions, but we never got there.

"Sununu was a curmudgeon. As an MIT engineer, he thought he knew best. I don't think he was put up to it by the oil industry or anything. I think that's just where he was.

"Now, let's say that H. W. Bush had proposed serious emission reductions. Would that have passed Congress? I don't know, that's hypothetical. But there certainly was a moment, with a Republican president, who could have succeeded when he went that way on the environment because he could bring Republicans with him. That's the only time that moment has existed. It was a brief window. W. was sort of interested in doing something, but Cheney scotched it.

"With a Democratic administration, the Republicans automatically aligned themselves against climate action. You need bipartisan work to get this done. If there's a Democratic president, they're going to have to work with Republicans. If there's a Republican president, they're going to need the cooperation of Democrats. It's not an easy path.

"Here's the thing: To decarbonize the energy economy is the largest task ever invented for government and for the economy. That's a huge lift.

"There was a chance. If H. W. had put on a carbon tax at that point, the US and the world would be a lot farther along than we are now. No question."

A POOR FIT: A Job in the Securities Industry

Andy's reputation earned him consideration from the Wilderness Society when it was looking for a new director—he was one of two finalists but did not get the job. An offer did come from the North American Securities Administrators Association. "They called," he says, "because I was on the Commerce Committee, where we had jurisdiction over securities law as well as health and energy and all the rest of it. This association looked after the interests of the 'small investor.'

"The association included securities regulators from the Canadian provinces, which is why it was called the North American as opposed to the US. The members had historically always had a chair appointed for a one-year term from among themselves. They had never had an operation in Washington. They had never had an executive vice president who put together legislative initiatives at the federal level.

"When they recruited me I thought, Well, this will be an interesting change. I was positioning myself on behalf of small investors and consumers who needed to be protected from the big players. And they doubled my salary—that was an additional reason it was an attractive opportunity."

As executive vice president of the North American Securities Administrators Association, and first executive of its DC headquarters, Andy structured and staffed the new office. He worked to get Congress to reform laws governing securities markets, he worked with the Securities and Exchange Commission and the National Association of Securities Dealers on policy and enforcement strategies, lobbied to increase the uniformity of state regulation, and sought to educate investors.

In short, Andy set up the association's Washington lobbying operation. But the members of the association didn't cooperate. "There was a lot of internal conflict," he recalls, "among the officials who wanted to support the Washington office and really make something important out of it versus the guys who mainly looked forward to a week off at an all-expenses-paid annual conference. There were limits to what I was going to be able to do there.

"It wasn't working. So I left."

Once again, Andy needed a new job and a new challenge.

CHAPTER 10

MCKINSEY MEETS THE PEACE CORPS: A Businesslike Approach to International Development

It is quite wrong to assume that poor people are generally unwilling to change; but the proposed change must stand in some organic relationship to what they are doing already, and they are rightly suspicious of, and resistant to, radical changes proposed by town-based and office-bound innovators who approach them in the spirit of: "You just get out of my way and I shall show you how useless you are and how splendidly the job can be done with a lot of foreign money and outlandish equipment."

—E. F. SCHUMACHER,
Small Is Beautiful: A Study of Economics As If People Mattered

TECHNOLOGY ON A HUMAN SCALE: E. F. SCHUMACHER AND THREE INVENTIONS

Andy Maguire's next job existed because of the work of a European scholar who challenged mainstream thinking on economics and development.

Born to an educated German family in 1911, Ernst Friedrich Schumacher studied at Oxford, then taught at Columbia in New York before returning to Berlin. In 1936 he left Hitler's Germany for exile in England, where he was arrested as an enemy alien after war broke out. Sent first to an internment camp, he was soon put to work on a farm in Northamptonshire, where his daily work in the fields helped give the young intellectual a lifelong appreciation of simple rural toil. Soon Schumacher was back at Oxford, developing plans for postwar reconstruction. His distaste for conventional economics—and conventional economists—was clear. "Give me farm labourers," he wrote, "or factory workers—even shop assistants—I am certain they will talk more intelligently and more to the point than some of this scum of the earth, called Oxford post-war Reconstruction Planners." That attitude would fuel his professional outlook as a leading British writer on economics after the war.

Schumacher rose swiftly in the ranks of UK economists, serving as chief statistician for the British Control Board, which worked on the reconstruction of Germany, and from 1950 to 1970 as the chief economic adviser of the British National Coal Board, where he contributed planning considered to have been instrumental in returning Britain to the prosperity it had sacrificed in the fight against Hitler.

In his postwar writings, Schumacher sought to humanize economics, to shift the discipline's focus from statistics to the people's lives behind them. Then, during a three-month sabbatical in Burma, in 1955, his worldview deepened further, giving him a novel insight: Bolstering a nation's economy by adding massive new factories and infrastructure, while useful in wealthy countries—and in the formerly wealthy countries of Europe then redeveloping after the devastation of World War II—was ineffective in improving lives in the poorer nations of Africa, Latin America, and Asia.

"Wisdom demands a new orientation of science and technology toward the organic, the gentle, the elegant and beautiful," he wrote in his bestselling book *Small Is Beautiful: A Study of Economics As If People Mattered*, published in 1973. Instead of infusions of "advanced technology," Schumacher argued, poorer societies required the implementation of "intermediate technology," technology that employed local resources and local labor at scales "appropriate" for non-industrialized, agriculture-based economies.

"Schumacher was a British philosopher who went to Burma in the '50s and fell in love with the concept that technology is not neutral," says

Valeria Budinich. Budinich, a native of Chile with a degree in engineering from the University of Texas, would work closely with Andy during the 1990s. "Technology needs to be appropriated by local communities, and it needs to be relevant to people's daily lives in ways that do not disrupt whatever the culture, the practices, and the traditions are. You can picture Gandhi and his spinning wheel."

To implement his ideas, in 1966 Schumacher, with the support of the British government, founded the Intermediate Technology Development Group. "Any intelligent fool can make things bigger, more complex, and more violent," he wrote in *Small Is Beautiful*. "It takes a touch of genius—and a lot of courage—to move in the opposite direction."

"The Intermediate Technology Development Group," says Budinich, "based in London, was the baby of Schumacher. *Small Is Beautiful* was an incredible bestseller because he pointed to a very different way of looking at development." Some members of the US House of Representatives, reading Schumacher's book, decided to form an American counterpart to the British firm. Called Appropriate Technology International, the agency would receive its funding, $3 million per year, through the United States Agency for International Development (USAID).

"The spirit of the new organization," says Budinich, "was that you needed a different type of innovation. You needed a group that was dedicated to connecting with grassroots development groups, with small producers and artisans, in ways that contrasted with the way the World Bank and USAID saw needs."

"It's fair to say," says Budinich, who joined the organization in 1986, "that ATI was established with this spirit of needing an alternative way of innovating to complement what was already happening in international development. But also, to fulfill the promise that small can be beautiful, impactful, and relevant—the promise of Schumacher's book.

"In the post–Second World War period, development had a bias toward massive investment, toward big-is-better. Politicians in countries around the world endeavored to attract resources to their countries, without necessarily ensuring the relevance of those resources for local communities. That's what was needed in places after the war as countries tried to recover. Some efforts were amazing successes. Obviously, when you build a road through a rural area, you can transform the area for good—*if* the road is accompanied by other types of interventions. But many efforts were terrible failures, involving rampant corruption and with little relevance to people's lives. That was the thinking for large international multilateral organizations: massive infrastructure development projects. In the process, they were forgetting the people and their needs. By the 1970s, a shift was needed, and ATI was a pioneer of that shift. In the first ten years of ATI, before Andy and I arrived, you had hundreds of projects funded through small grants and partnerships with institutes and local investors from around the world."

During that first decade, ATI's most successful projects involved the introduction of simple technological improvements that changed lives in the developing world. The two most significant inventions were a manually operated oilseed press and a treadle water pump, both devised by Carl Bielenberg, an MIT-trained engineer who to this day continues to work on developing energy and agricultural technology appropriate to the needs of Africans.

Oil formed an essential part of people's diet in much of sub-Saharan Africa, but despite the abundance of oilseed crops—rapeseed, sesame seed, sunflower seed—conversion of the seeds into oil used for cooking was difficult and expensive. Bielenberg devised a press, manually operated by one person, that enabled small producers to harvest the oil themselves.

"ATI transformed the way that cooking oil, which is a basic everywhere in the world, was obtained by small holders in Africa," says Andy. "Before ATI was there, they either didn't have the cooking oil, or they had to pay high prices for imported oil from India. They had several different oil-seeds that could be processed locally on their own homesteads. Carl Bielenberg, ATI's engineering consultant, invented the oilseed press, which could be used even by people of small stature, including women and children."

Bielenberg likewise invented a treadle water pump, operated by a single person treading on two foot pedals, that enabled farmers to more effectively irrigate their fields. "We used the treadle pump in multiple African countries to increase production of vegetables and fruit," says Andy. Eventually, these seed presses and treadle pumps improved the lives of millions of Africans.

Another inventor was Ralf Hotchkiss, who as an Oberlin undergraduate lost the use of his legs after a motorcycle accident. "Ralf Hotchkiss developed an affordable wheelchair that could be manufactured in a metalworking shop anywhere in the world," says Budinich. "ATI paid for the training of artisans. That was one of the technologies that was spread to at least twenty different countries."

But as successful as innovations like the seed press, treadle pump, and wheelchair were, ATI's approach began to show its limitations. "It was necessary to go beyond technology," says Budinich.

IT'S ALL ABOUT THE VALUE CHAIN: An Organization Refocuses

To chart a new direction, ATI needed a new leader.

"A year before Andy came, there was a crisis in the organization," says Budinich. "The chairman of the board was forced to resign. The board brought in a new chairman who had the support of Congress: Bill Drayton." Drayton, a former employee of the management consulting giant McKinsey & Company, had served as assistant administrator of the Environmental Protection Agency during the Carter administration. In 1980 he founded Ashoka, a nonprofit organization dedicated to encouraging "social entrepreneurship," that is, using entrepreneurial methods to effect meaningful social change. Budinich would later work at Ashoka. "Bill was a friend of Andy Maguire," she says. "They had worked together because both were firm believers in the need for better environmental policies. When Bill Drayton came on board, he started looking for a new CEO."

"Bill Drayton came after me to take the job," says Andy. "He had become, probably, the world's leading spokesman for social entrepreneurship. Among the things that made me attractive to them were my experience, worldview, and understanding based on my work at the State Department, in Congress, and at World Resources Institute.

"Also, I was connected to Capitol Hill. ATI's funding at the time was from USAID only, and there was always a battle, because the people running USAID would rather have had that $3 million a year to do what they wanted with it, as opposed to having Congress siphon it off to this little appropriate technology organization. In addition, I had demonstrated a strong commitment to the environment through my work in Congress and afterward.

"I also had grassroots development experience in New York City, and had demonstrated an ability to build coalitions to define and pursue objectives for significant change within that complicated array of government departments and competing interests.

"I think all of that played into Drayton's interest in me."

In 1990, Andy took over as chief executive officer of an organization ready for change.

"Before me," says Andy, "ATI was basically just handing out small, short-term, one-off grants. The theory back then was: There are local organizations, nongovernmental organizations, public interest organizations, working on development—they need a little bit of extra help. But there was no master plan. There was no strategic thinking about what to do at the grassroots. It was 'appropriate' in the sense of small and local: If we can just get the right technology in the hands of people it will change everything. Which was not a thorough understanding of change. And by and large, it had less impact than it should have. Some money went to organizations that definitely were adding value in their localities or in their nations. Some money went astray, to outfits that really weren't doing anything important, other than appointing themselves to do this or that."

"There were inherent limitations," says Budinich, "in the idea that you produce a new technological design, you prototype with local investors, and then it was going to spread like hot cakes because of how brilliant the idea was and because it was locally manufactured. The reality was that you needed to think about it. Among the new group of people at ATI, we said, 'Yeah, that's true. But you need to create a market-based approach, otherwise you are going to benefit very few people.'

"The hardcore, the traditionalists, were saying, 'The hell with it. Let's give away these things. Maybe they cost a hundred dollars or twenty dollars or fifty or three hundred. It would be better to benefit as many people as possible up front—because they are poor, they have a need now—than wait for years to create a for-profit approach.'

"For me, the way forward was obvious, but the traditionalists had a strong argument: ATI was created to help the poorest of the poor. And by imposing on them costs—with no or limited subsidies for purchase of the technology—you'd delay addressing these people's urgent needs.

"However, the progress wasn't happening. We did an initial evaluation of how many people ATI was benefiting, and the number was ten thousand. We had an annual budget on the order of $3 million with the USAID cooperative agreement.

"It amounted to a huge subsidy with minimal payback. By 1995, after switching to the integrated approach, ATI was benefiting more than 150,000 people. By the end of the '90s, the number was half a million. And we could count, and knew how to count, millions of others who had been involved in some way and positively affected. That increase happened because the market-based approach to international development took off. We were pioneers."

The change in focus involved applying a management-consultant approach to international aid, addressing not only the technology but how it was used, seeking not just to make work more efficient for individual farmers and workers but also to integrate their efforts into a larger whole that could be nurtured and transformed through careful analysis of production and markets. ATI detailed the advantages the organization sought to instill as follows: "Skillful business management, cohesive producer groups (which allow small producers to band together for maximum effectiveness), savvy product development, processing techniques and marketing, and access to credit."

"ATI started recruiting more MBA types," says Budinich, "as opposed to hard-core inventors like Hotchkiss or Bielenberg. We started thinking about new questions, like: Okay, if people cannot afford the technologies, how can you create a financing program? Or: How can we build partnerships with companies to manufacture locally at a larger scale and multiply the impact?

"Many with the more traditional approach resigned in protest because they thought we were deviating from the original mandate. But we were able to make the transition without negating the value of all the contributions the amazing inventors made. Instead, we built on their achievements."

ATI even applied its redesigned approach to what had been to that point its most successful technology, the seed press. Now, giving farmers the device would be just the first step. ATI's new plan, named the Regional Oils Project, aimed to transform the African oilseed industry, which had been "historically controlled by the state and dominated by large urban firms," in order to create "a new rural industry" that would benefit hundreds of thousands of small producers. Begun in Tanzania and Zimbabwe, then rapidly expanding to other African countries, the project swiftly increased demand for oil, leading to a quadrupling of oilseed production. In Tanzania, the program initially supplied a thousand presses. On average, twenty farmers grew seed for each press in operation; thus, ATI was enabling some twenty thousand farmers to tap into new, lucrative markets. The key to the improvement was "an assessment of each step in the value chain—from the producing of oilseeds through processing and marketing of the final products—and the identification of an integrated set of value-adding interventions." The regional approach developed expertise that could cross state borders, creating "a mechanism for enhancing south-south exchanges," as opposed to the customary arrangement of expertise flowing from the developed north to the supposedly unskilled laborers of the undeveloped south.

"Carl Bielenberg," Budinich recalls, "the inventor of the seed press and many other gadgets in Africa, learned about the arrival of Andy and the new approach and decided that he didn't want to work with us anymore. He'd had it with ATI.

"I didn't see him for twenty years. And one day, I'm at my Ashoka office and I see him passing in the corridor. I invited him in, even though I didn't know how he'd remember me, because we hadn't been in touch. I had a profound respect for the pioneering work he had done as an inventor, so I was very reverential to him. To my surprise, he said, 'I came to apologize. I remember what you and Andy did. Twenty years later, I see that you guys were right.'"

"When I was hired," says Andy, "Drayton wanted us to reorient ATI to the McKinsey consulting concept of a value chain."

Harvard Business School professor Michael Porter first conceptualized the theory of "value chain" in his 1985 book *Competitive Advantage: Creating and Sustaining Superior Performance.* Simplified, a value chain is the collection of steps through which a product or service is formed to deliver value to customers. ATI aimed to help poor producers in Africa, Asia, and Latin America participate in and profit from the string of actions involved in product creation, from the harvesting of raw materials to the manipulation of those materials to the marketing of those materials for sale. In the then-prevailing dynamic, small farmers produced raw materials, which were then processed and sold by others; those others reaped the lion's share of the total profits.

"You have a certain resource," Andy explains. "You have a certain number of people trying to exploit that resource. Typically, the small producers would not be able to do it at scale; they would sell it to middlemen for pennies. So there was no connection between the labor harvesting the resources and the development of high-quality products that would eventually be sold regionally, nationally, internationally. The idea of the value chain was to capture as much as possible of the value and the income from the hard work of the original producers."

"Porter's book," Budinich adds, "said that value is not only in the product, value is generated through all the steps, from production all the way to processing, to marketing. And that any company needed to examine the value creation at each step. Because at the end of the day, your competitiveness and your success in the market were going to depend on that. Today, that is established truth. But in the '80s, it was a major breakthrough.

"Porter had used the concept only in the context of value-added steps within a single company. We took the idea and applied it to development. We said, 'Look at, say, the production of sunflowers in the field, to the collection of the sunflower seeds, to the preprocessing. All of that is done by different people in Africa. But if you look at the value chain over the entire industry, you can create a much more impactful development project. Let's get the small producers first of all to create as much value as possible. And then to capture as much of that value along the way for themselves. In the process, we needed to redefine their relationships with intermediaries."

"Before Andy came to ATI," says Susan Swift, who left a job as a congressional staffer to become ATI's director of communications, "the organization was focused on technology, not on the value chain for these groups of low-income people. Andy thought through the value chain, right on up to the marketing. Sometimes, marketing might not seem to be called for—when, say, people were the sole consumers of the vegetables they grew. However, given technological improvements, those farmers might produce a whole lot more and be able to sell the additional crop. They could earn more income so they could send their kids to school—get a uniform for their kids, get shoes, get books. It was a good deal."

"We looked at value chains for entire small producer industries," says Budinich. "We thought about transforming small producers' economies by helping those producers generate and capture as much of the value-added steps in their industry as possible."

"We looked at every stage of the development of a final product," says Andy, "starting with the resource, starting with the people. There are a whole series of economic steps—management requirements, technology applications, overcoming bottlenecks—which are inevitable and have to be overcome. Identifying enhancements to the quality of what is being produced so that it's more attractive to a wider range of buyers. Making the marketing connections, depending on the product, to the cosmetic industry or to clothing manufacturers or to coffee shops. That's the value chain."

"It's the same for a big company that supplies copper," says Swift. "They're going to turn it into a product for sale. These folks had tree crops or dairy milk or fibers or vegetables. A value chain is, you take a raw product and the hard work of someone who's willing to transform that product through a variety of interventions—the word 'intervention' is always brought up—into intermediary products that might actually then be improved and sold as part of a greater inventory. Then ultimately, it goes to the consumer.

"Value is added at each stage of the production. That's why people want to be doing it. They get more money. But that very first step is the hard work and ingenuity of people who might otherwise be dismissed, not counted as economic actors: 'Oh, that's just a poor farmer. He's not relevant.' But if you get enough of them working together, then they're influencing the market. I come from a small farm. It made so much sense to me."

"A bean doesn't just become a cup of coffee," says Andy. "It has to be washed. It has to be dried. It has to be processed. And normally, the poorest people, who did the work with the resources at the beginning of the process, were unable to work through all of the steps in a value chain to secure maximum return. There were all sorts of middlemen and traders who would reap the bulk of the benefits. We all know about European countries exploiting the resources in the tropics all over the world, and poor people not getting a piece of the action.

"Most economic development work talks a great game about alleviating poverty, but it doesn't actually address the specific ways that low-income people can advance themselves. Typically, development has not figured out how to do that. We were in the business of figuring out how to do that."

WAR IS NOT THE ANSWER: George Bush, Desert Storm, and the 1992 Election

George H. W. Bush had won the White House in 1988 by contrasting his lily-white persona with two darker-skinned foils: a black rapist/murderer, Willie Horton, and a swarthy Bostonian with a foreign-sounding name, Michael Dukakis. In early 1991, his actions to check another swarthy villain seemed to guarantee his reelection a year and a half later.

Bush's posturing in the face of Iraqi strongman Saddam Hussein's August 1990 invasion of Kuwait—"This will not stand," the US president proclaimed—earned strong public support as America prepared for war in the Middle East. With impressive diplomatic skill, Bush assembled a thirty-five-nation coalition to evict Iraq from its smaller, oil-rich neighbor, although American forces would do the bulk of the fighting. The coalition's action, taken in response to one nation invading another across a recognized international frontier, aligned with the post–World War II consensus incorporated in the peace and security language of the UN Charter. However, the intervention foreshadowed a later, unjustified, American invasion of Iraq based on lies and resulting in devastating consequences for Iraqis, for Americans, and for US leadership in the region and around the world. Victory in Operation Desert Storm was swift and, for the US military, relatively pain-free—a punishing air campaign was followed by a ground war of a mere one hundred hours that saw fewer than 150 US service members killed in action. Bush, presenting himself as a paragon of hypermasculine WASP rectitude, had protected the West's oil supply from a marauding tyrant, whom he publicly referred to by the dictator's (mispronounced) first name.

Flags flew, trumpets sounded, television news networks reveled in the "shock and awe" of the US-led liberation of the beleaguered petro-kingdom. America had flexed its military muscle without apology, rendering Vietnam at long last a distant memory; in March 1991, as the war ended, Gallup measured Bush's approval rating at an astronomical 89 percent.

That number dissuaded the heaviest of the Democratic hitters—New York governor Mario Cuomo, Tennessee senator Al Gore, Missouri representative Dick Gephardt—from running to unseat Bush, leaving the field to lesser-known figures, among them the governor of out-of-the-way Arkansas who had been embarrassed in 1988 when his speech seconding Dukakis's nomination at the Democratic National Convention had bombed.

Bush seemed unbeatable.

Bush made two politically fatal mistakes after his triumph in the Gulf War. First, he violated his read-my-lips-no-new-taxes 1988 campaign pledge—a promise he'd known he'd betray even as he'd made it but had hoped to delay doing so until after winning a second term. In not only raising taxes but also raising them in a form that couldn't be disguised—Reagan had been able to camouflage the tax increases he'd supported after the profligate tax cuts of his first months in office—Bush contravened not only the centerpiece of the campaign that elected him but also the cardinal rule of performative GOP politics.

The ascendant Southern, hyper-conservative wing of the party didn't trust Bush to begin with, this representative of the old Republican Eastern elites, this investment banker turned senator's son who couldn't live down his preppy New England upbringing no matter how many pork rinds he ate. From the party's right wing came a primary challenger, Patrick Buchanan, the cable-TV firebreather and onetime Nixon polemicist. Buchanan did not win a single primary or caucus in the 1992 GOP nominating race, but his challenge gained enough momentum that Bush felt forced to grant him a prominent speaking role at that summer's Houston convention. Buchanan had never held elective office and thus had never needed to temper his take-no-prisoners rhetoric in order to build coalitions or pass legislation. His embrace of angry cultural themes in his prime-time speech—"There is a religious war going on in this country," he bellowed—followed by a no less aggressively reactionary speech by Marilyn Quayle, wife of Bush's running mate, Vice President Dan Quayle, helped sink Bush's chance of attracting the centrist voters he'd need to stay in office.

Second, Bush had no follow-up to his foreign policy successes. "In January of '92, when President Bush had a stratospheric approval rating after Desert Storm, we didn't go up to the Congress and put on the table a domestic economic program," said James Baker, who in the summer of 1992 left his job as secretary of state to take over Bush's floundering campaign. Most analysts have credited Bush and his foreign policy team—especially Baker and National Security Advisor Brent Scowcroft—with skillful managing of the fall of the Berlin Wall and the dissolution of the Soviet Union. But as the US economy fell into recession in mid-1990, Bush was clueless. He did try to brand himself the "education president," convening a White House "education summit" as empty of achievement as it was of political value. But as the economy leeched jobs, he seemed incapable—by temperament, ideology, or skillset—of taking meaningful action. He had assembled an unprecedented international coalition to save the job of the emir of Kuwait, critics charged, but took no action to save the job of the average American worker.

Weakened within his own party, seen as out of touch by the nation as a whole, the hero of Desert Storm couldn't save his own job, either.

President Bush couldn't believe his reelection was threatened by the glib governor of a small Southern state who hadn't been born when Bush was flying missions in a torpedo bomber over the Pacific in the Second World War. But Bush underestimated his opponent's political skills.

Bill Clinton became one of the youngest governors in US history when he was elected at age thirty-two in 1978. Political missteps and unfortunate circumstances—a decision to raise fees for vehicle license plates, an influx of Cuban refugees, President Carter's unpopularity—doomed the boy wonder's first bid for reelection, in 1980, but two years later he reclaimed the office and had held it ever since.

Despite his serving in a backwater, Clinton's electoral chops surpassed those of nearly every big-name national pol. A dazzling intellect enabled him to grasp the minutiae of every policy imaginable, from rural sewer systems to nuclear weaponry. His preternatural ability to project empathy enabled him to persuade everyone he met—from the cashier at the McDonald's where he stopped for coffee after his morning runs to, later, heads of state—that he understood them as no one ever had. During Middle East negotiations in 2000, Israeli and Palestinian negotiators were amazed the American president knew the geography of Jerusalem, block by block, as well as they did, and could explain every inch of the political minefields leaders on both sides would need to navigate in order to sell a peace deal to their citizenries.

He was also able to talk himself out of most trouble, usually by diverting focus from his own shortcomings to the needs of the voters whose support he sought. Twin scandals nearly strangled his presidential bid in its cradle. Just before the New Hampshire primary, Gennifer Flowers, a Little Rock lounge singer with whom Clinton had had a brief fling, claimed that she and the governor had carried on a passionate twelve-year affair. Worse, a letter surfaced to provide evidence of Clinton's slippery avoidance of military service during the Vietnam War. Clinton's explanation for his draft dodging was risible, but voters in the Granite State and elsewhere largely gave him a pass: With the Cold War at an end, voters didn't mind a president with substandard national security credentials as long as, unlike the incumbent, he seemed intent on taking action to unchain the gates of closed factories.

Clinton was a stalwart of the Democratic Leadership Council, a group of Democratic operatives, theorists, and politicians—disproportionately from Southern states—who saw the resounding defeats suffered by traditional Democratic liberals like George McGovern, Walter Mondale, and Michael Dukakis as a sign that American voters were no longer in the mood for traditional Democratic liberals. If Democrats wanted to capture the White House again, the DLC reasoned, the party needed to move rightward, away from its identification as the party of ethnic minorities. No issue better exemplified this strategy than welfare. Democrats believed they had been losing the culture war over this issue, enabling the GOP to convince white voters that the Dems were the party of handouts to lazy Black people. Clinton, brilliant at the formulation of slogans that could mean whatever a voter wanted them to mean, vowed to "end welfare as we know it."

While Clinton did signal in 1992 that he was "a different [i.e., less liberal] kind of Democrat," he also called for a range of investments, in physical and human infrastructure, that accorded with traditional Democratic notions of social spending. Moreover, he promised massive reform of the national health care system—a goal that had eluded progressive presidents since Theodore Roosevelt. But 1992 did not offer a simple choice between Clinton's moderate liberalism and Bush's moderate conservatism, because an independent candidate arrived to muddle the decision. Ross Perot, the billionaire owner of Electronic Data Systems, self-financed a candidacy animated by empty platitudes purporting to be common sense—all that a broken Washington needed, he argued, was for this salt-of-the-earth tycoon to "get under the hood" and do the needed repairs. But Perot's making the federal budget deficit his signature issue would shape the race and Clinton's presidency.

As the campaign entered autumn, the sixty-eight-year-old incumbent seemed old and out of touch, and an object of pity when, during debates, his two rivals ganged up on him. During the decisive second encounter, set in town-hall format, Bush fumbled a voter's question about his personal experience of the sluggish economy. "I don't think it's fair to say, 'You haven't had cancer,'" he sputtered. "'Therefore, you don't know what's it like.'" Clinton then walked downstage and turned on the empathy, talking about the Arkansans he knew who had lost their jobs.

Late in the campaign, with defeat inevitable, Bush barked, "My dog Millie knows more about foreign affairs than these two bozos"—these two bozos being Clinton and his running mate, fellow DLC-er Al Gore. The president's desperation—this warrior/congressman/party chairman/diplomat/CIA director/vice president/president/world statesman was about to lose to this callow nobody?—was warranted. Bush went down to defeat in the three-way race, winning not even 40 percent of the popular vote.

After Republicans had occupied the presidency for a dozen years, and twenty of the previous twenty-four, a Democrat had won the White House. As imperfect a champion as Clinton was of America's liberal project, that project could now resume.

TAKING CHARGE: Andy as New CEO

Andy moved quickly to put his stamp on the organization he'd been asked to lead. Valeria Budinich recalls her first meeting with him, before his official hiring. "The day-to-day leadership of the organization," she says, "was basically six people: four regional directors, and two directors of specific areas of expertise. Andy met with each one of us. I was the director of Latin America, and I was very young—thirty-two years old. All the other guys were forty, forty-five, or more. The Africa director and I were the last to meet with Andy. I knew that all the other directors were very disappointed with the organization—I knew that in talking with Andy they'd be focusing on scarcity, complaining that ATI needed more money, that the prior president hadn't been effective in renegotiating the cooperative agreement with USAID. One complaint after another.

"When we got in to see Andy, the Africa director monopolized the conversation for the first forty minutes, again with all these complaints and what needed to be fixed—basically, saying we should be pumping

Congress for more money. But when my turn came, I shared with Andy what I saw as the opportunity emerging, and that the organization was positioned to do much more and have a deeper impact throughout the world. He got incredibly excited, and said, 'I want to learn more about that. Let's figure out how we can take it to the next level.' A month later, he was officially chosen, and one of the things that he did when he arrived—in his first two, three months—was ask for a strategic review, where, again, all six in the leadership group were interviewed.

"By the end of that process, Andy decided to name me chief operating officer. On that day, four of the six directors resigned. They said I didn't have the seniority. The bottom line is that Andy's decision was bold. In fact, it was pretty stressful to me—a bit overwhelming—because I had no ambition to take that role. But it's fair to say that it proved to be the right decision, because the future of the organization was in finding a new path forward."

Of course, the directors who resigned were all men.

"It was my age," says Budinich, "and it was the fact that I was woman, yes. Also, I'm gay. So the combination of all of that proved to be too much. Oh, and I was the only foreigner."

"Andy is a really dynamic leader," says Susan Swift, whose work with ATI included liaison to Congress. "He can put this kind of thing across to anybody. I went with him to a number of congressional members' offices—some of them he knew from his time in the House. He always gave a wonderful presentation: 'You want to help poor people. Here's a way. We're treating people with respect, like they're a client coming to McKinsey saying they want to improve their business, they want to tap into a wider economy.'"

"Andy's a bold thinker," says Budinich. "He created a dynamic in the organization in which he invited all of us to think big. He was also not afraid to make carefully assessed bets."

On taking over as ATI's CEO, Andy instituted a thorough review of the organization's activities. "We looked at how to redeploy our resources more effectively," recalls Budinich. "So what we did between 1990 and 1995 was reimagine the organization based on the insight of value chains and transforming small producers' economies. The first step was to review all the programs. There were on the order of sixty grants, and it was everything under the sun, even radio stations. We had a program in Vanuatu—I had to look on the map: Where in the world is that?

"ATI was a very decentralized operation and people were funding grants from $50,000 to $250,000 in a sometimes chaotic way. But there were also gems in the portfolio. The key was to find the most promising and focus on those. For six months or more, we did a review. And from the sixty grants we prioritized twenty, which became ten. As Andy says, 'The idea was to pick those areas of economic activity where tens or hundreds of millions of people and families across the world were working hard every day in those product sectors.' But that meant discontinuing forty or fifty ongoing relations, and figuring out a way to accelerate the closing of those grants. That made a lot of people unhappy.

"We had many people who had been Peace Corps volunteers, and there was a part of them that was fantastic. They were incredibly committed. They had lived with the type of beneficiaries whose lives we wanted to improve. They were the right resource, but some of them weren't ready to embrace this market-based approach. They had trouble navigating that delicate balancing act between overprotecting a community and helping it transition to a more market-based economy, away from dependency. Many of those people left the organization. We started hiring more MBAs. And then we started changing the new project approval process and requiring the adoption of this value chain approach, which meant addressing a series of questions about an industry, not just a technology.

"We also needed to learn, as an organization, how far each region of the world was ready to go. Because the needs of Asia were different from those of Africa, different from those of Latin America. I'm sure in the process we made some mistakes. But ultimately, the numbers proved us right, because in the impact evaluation framework that we built, our beneficiaries—and we didn't call anybody a beneficiary unless we saw his or her income increase by a factor of at least 20 percent—went from 3,000 to roughly 160,000 in a matter of two or three years. Five years later, it was half a million. We achieved that increase through the new approach."

Andy recalls that USAID's evaluation experts complimented ATI for having designed and implemented the most robust impact tracking system of any of USAID's contractors. The stats—carefully compiled by Budinich and ATI's in-house expert, Eric Hyman, an economist who later revolutionized evaluation at the African Development Foundation—demonstrated doubling and tripling of client incomes and a widening circle of direct and indirect beneficiaries reaching into the millions of small-scale farmers and entrepreneurs.

Budinich gives Andy credit for the program reevaluation. "That shift," she says, "from sixty grants on topics that were almost all different, to an integrated program with about ten product lines central to the economic lives of broad swaths of low-income people across countries and regions—that was his thinking. The other thing is that he created performance rewards and public recognition within the organization. It was to make all of us see ourselves as a cohesive team. Two years after Andy came on board, we were like a big family. We went from like forty people to sixty people, and then three years later to 120 people in five different countries.

"The staff was growing, but it was a core group that was very, very integrated, very supportive of one another. Andy created that kind of climate of deep collaboration. This is not minor, because NGOs tend to get into a mindset in which all the different program directors are competing for the same resources. The last thing people do is collaborate.

"He was also remarkably supportive of women—I wasn't the only woman he supported. Systematically, he would make sure we were a diverse team. And he didn't tolerate situations that were discriminatory of women. We had situations in which he reacted in a matter of hours, firing somebody. There was zero tolerance. The part that was always harder with Andy is that he's impatient. This stuff takes time. I'm sure he often felt frustrated because of how long things took. That part of navigating the daily life of ATI wasn't easy for him, or for many of the people on the team.

"He and I developed a very, very close relationship. When he had something important to discuss, he would meet me in the corridor and say, 'Step into my office.' And we would end up talking for five or ten minutes, discussing something that needed to be discussed right there, which was good."

Andy recalls his mission when he was hired: "To make ATI more relevant and powerful to the real objectives of helping low-income people in the Third World. And provide them with the tools to do it themselves. We saw ourselves, if you will, as consultants to our clients. We weren't there to tell them what to do. We were there to work with them on solving the issues and problems that prevented them from capturing value. We were looking to transform economic sectors that were critical to low-income people in these countries and across the world, and we wanted especially to develop women leaders, known to spend money wisely on behalf of education for their children and better health care for their families. And so we became installed client partners."

To do big things, Andy needed to expand ATI's resources beyond the $3 million allocated annually by Congress. "We didn't answer the typical RFPs, requests for proposals, from big international organizations," he recalls, "which had already decided what they wanted to do. We produced unsolicited proposals. And for the decade we were at work, those were welcomed. People were looking for ideas. And we were able, with our connections and with the power of our models, to go into the United Nations Capital Development Fund or the World Bank or wherever. We would say, 'We can put a dollar on the table if you'll put ten dollars on the table.' And they would sign up for these projects.

"We identified people within these organizations who were sympathetic to what we were trying to do, and we worked with them on developing proposals. There are always people in these organizations who are looking for innovation and for opportunities to make a name for themselves by moving to the next level, as difficult as that is in big, bureaucratic operations. We would find those people through our networks. And then we would work with those individuals on refining the proposals and making them as impressive as possible. Look at what Valeria did with the UN Capital Development Fund. We had never before had any UN agency support. She put that together, and then I went with her to meetings in New York. I went as the CEO, and my background was always impressive to people we were dealing with: 'Here's a former member of Congress. Here's a former State Department guy. And look at this Valeria person, she's an engineer out of Latin America. So this is attractive to us.'"

Prior to becoming CEO of ATI, Andy had not been in charge of a large corporate structure. Nevertheless, his background had prepared him well for the job. "There's a tendency to say, 'Let's appoint a businessman to run this thing,'" he says. "But the learning and the experience that you get from being a member of Congress, organizing a successful campaign—people underestimate what kind of a management job that is and how you achieve remarkable results in the process of tackling a congressional race or, say, trying to innovate in some of New York City's most difficult neighborhoods. My first full-time job was for the State Department—I learned how you make your presence felt inside a massive bureaucracy, by working with the right people to get the right twist on any complicated objective. ATI was both in my comfort zone and a challenging assignment for me.

"We had at first maybe thirty-five people in DC, some of whom traveled back and forth on a regular basis to all of these countries where we operated. And then we had hundreds of people from the countries in which we were working, people on the payroll of the projects full-time or part-time, working closely with nonprofit organizations. It was a much bigger management job than it appeared, not just thirty-five people trying to change the world from Washington. I didn't do all that myself. I hired absolutely superb people, Valeria being one example. Smart and savvy people. The Latin America director who took over when Valeria became COO was from Honduras. Our director in Zimbabwe was a local African leader. We were always as close to the grassroots as we could get."

NEW NAME, NEW BOARD, NEW MONEY: ATI Becomes EWW

USAID's $3 million annual subsidy was hardly enough, by itself, to support all of ATI's ambitions. And by the mid-1990s, even that amount seemed about to be withdrawn. Rob Esposito, Andy's former political aide who would replace Budinich as ATI's chief operating officer, recalls a 1995 meeting with USAID representatives: "I'll never forget the guy saying, 'You will have to close your doors.'" Seeing the writing on the wall, ATI had to reimagine its fundraising.

Step one was a new board of directors. "I said to Andy, 'We have to completely refabricate the board,'" says Esposito. "'We need a major Democratic pillar and a major Republican pillar.'

"Former congressman Tom Downey, a Democrat, was Al Gore's best friend and a key lobbyist in Washington during the '90s. You need something from Al Gore, you go to Tom Downey, and everybody knew Al would run for president after Clinton left. Tom Downey was his guy on the street in terms of the lobbying community.

"So Andy goes to Tom, one of his class of '74 colleagues, and says, 'Tom, look. As the years go by and Clinton can no longer serve, you become more and more of a force. We're going to reconstitute the organization; I need you to serve as co-chair.'"

To find the Republican co-chair, Esposito drew on another personal connection. "I'd kept in touch with [Andy's former aide] Elgie Holstein," Esposito says. "In Washington I was seeing Elgie and his girlfriend, Penny Eastman, socially all the time. So, of course, I'm telling them what's going on with the organization. And at some point, when I'm describing all this, Penny says, 'I used to work for this guy Rich Williamson. He's now the state chairman of the Republican Party in Illinois. He was assistant secretary for international development projects during the Reagan administration.' Lo and behold, Rich Williamson becomes our Republican co-chair.

"There's a web of relationships among people who worked for Andy. There were connections among a lot of us that have lasted our lifetimes."

As the new board was taking shape, Andy realized that another change needed to take place: the organization's name.

"Why did we change the name?" asks Esposito. "We did some surveys on the name Appropriate Technology International. People thought: 'Is that a phone company? Is that related to computers?' As we were going out to fundraise, as we were transforming the organization and wanting to give it more of a public face, changing the name became important. Within the international-development community people understood what Appropriate Technology was, but that was a narrow band of specialists.

"Through market research, we came up with EnterpriseWorks Worldwide. Everybody's into free enterprise: 'Fight poverty with profit'—that kind of stuff. After a very thorough and market-research-based set of data points, the new name arrived, and it was good."

"Andy was dying to be more businesslike in our presentation, and less NGO," says Susan Swift. "Because people take you seriously if you are more like a business. NGOs—let's face it, they've got this problem. They say, 'Isn't this awful? Help us help.' As opposed to: 'Here's a practical strategy. We're changing the world—or at least the world in which this group of people lives. Work with us. Partner with us.' See the difference in language? NGOs are dependent. Businesses provide for themselves, and they're there for the long term."

"First of all," says Andy, "we wanted to emphasize enterprise, as opposed to technology. Because technology is only one of maybe ten critical factors. Whereas enterprise—building sustainable, profit-making enterprises—encompassed our entire mission. We wanted to shift to a name that represented what we were really doing in this new installment of this tiny organization, a name that represented a commitment to profit-making, to enhancing the value chain, as opposed to just doling out gifts. So we used EnterpriseWorks—you get the double meaning, with *Works* doubling as both a noun and a verb. And then we added Worldwide, because we were all over the world. It was a marketing and branding opportunity for us, too, because the new name helped us raise money."

"It was '97," remembers Esposito. "I said to Andy, 'Let's have an opening event to unveil our new name, with Gore, whom Tom Downey can get, and Jack Kemp, whom Rich Williamson can get.'" Gore had just been reelected vice president; Kemp had run against Gore and lost.

"Then," Esposito continues, "Tom gets a major big-time Democratic Party donor couple, Ronald and Beth Dozoretz, to give us their home for the event, an incredible mansion in northwest Washington. As a matter of fact, it's their newly remodeled home, so all the glitterati wanted to see what the new Dozoretz house was like. Also at that point in the office there was this talented intern. Guess who her uncle was? Ed Asner, the actor. So she tells Asner about this great organization and what we're doing. Andy gets on the phone with Asner. Asner comes out as a special guest for the event, along with Gore."

"I can't imagine Al Gore and Jack Kemp agreeing to do a joint fundraiser for something called Appropriate Technology," says Andy. "It was a terrible name. But EnterpriseWorks resonated with them. Mary Matalin and James Carville did a joint event for us, too. We built out a board that involved people in both parties because we wanted to have that imprimatur. This was nonpolitical. This was economic development. This was business development. This was transforming economic sectors for poor people.

"Here's our board at the time of the rebirth: Tom Downey; Rich Williamson; Carter Bales, from McKinsey and Company. Some other Republicans. A major fundraiser in Washington. Look at our advisory council: David Bonior, who was the Democratic whip in the House. The president of Iceland. A major Wall Street guy, John Hurford. Oliver Stone, the film director."

With the organization reoriented and renamed, with a new, more influential board, it was time to address the funding. "We privatized," Andy remembers. "We abandoned the annual $3 million from USAID—their bureaucrats were always trying to get out of that congressional requirement—and convinced USAID to give us a one-time-only departure grant.

"Privatizing the organization was the only route forward. I was sick and tired of trying to get my $3 million out of USAID every year. It was awful. It was stupid. I had been able to secure a couple of million dollars extra from Congress, endorsed by Republican and Democratic appropriators, to help us make deals with large funders—If you put in $100,000, we'll contribute $10,000—but it wasn't nearly enough."

"Throughout the existence of ATI," says Budinich, "and later EnterpriseWorks, there was a dark cloud. The congressional resolution that had created ATI forced USAID into a cooperative agreement with our organization. The USAID people at the level of the program officers loved what we did. They were supportive. They understood our work. But at the next level up, it was like, 'Why in the world do we have to transfer part of our budget to you guys every year? Isn't it time you grow up and find your own funding?' They were disrespectful and exasperating. Andy and Bill Drayton played that game, going back to Congress repeatedly for more support and more pressure on USAID. It got to a point where it was hard to sustain."

In the face of USAID's threat to pull funding, Andy & Co. made a countermove. "'We went back to AID," says Esposito, "and said, 'Look, you're going to throw away all these years' worth of investment in this organization? Give us a chance to privatize ourselves. Give us a transition grant.' So, working with some consultants I brought in, I went to write a proposal for AID to give us $15 million to privatize ourselves over time. It took a year and this board to get AID to say, 'Okay, we'll give you the $15 million.'"

"The negotiations," says Andy, "involved a big meeting on the Hill with Brian Atwood, who had been a congressional liaison for Carter and was now Clinton's USAID administrator. The gathering was hosted by Senator Tom Harkin. David Bonior, the Democratic whip on the House side, came over to the Senate for this meeting. There aren't that many meetings for which members of Congress will walk across to the other side. We had the chairman of the Congressional Black Caucus, we had members from major committees, including the chair of House International Relations. We had this proposal saying, 'You guys hand us over $15 million and we'll go away.' That worked. That was one instance where my relationships on the Hill figured importantly."

PEAKS AND VALLEYS: Liberalism During the Clinton Administration

Just two weeks before Bill Clinton took office, his economic plans met with a dose of reality: a report that the federal budget deficit was in fact much larger than Bush had admitted to. After the Perot campaign, Clinton could not ignore that number. Fed chairman Alan Greenspan threatened Clinton with a refusal to lower interest rates unless the deficit was reduced. Complaining that he was being forced to govern like a "Rockefeller Republican," Clinton decided to postpone his program of investments; someday, he hoped, he would return to the idea.

He never did. With substantial majorities in both houses of Congress, Clinton did institute substantial progressive reforms during his first two years in office: He raised taxes on upper income brackets and got Congress to pass the Family and Medical Leave Act—a baby step compared to the social safety net practices of Western Europe but nonetheless a major improvement in the United States. He persuaded Congress to pass long-overdue gun-control legislation.

But the progressive endeavor on which he staked his first two years in office, a reform of the US health care system, failed. He made the mistake of placing his wife in charge of the initiative—although a woman of formidable intelligence and organizational talent, Hillary Clinton was not up to the political job of reformulating so large a portion of the American economy against the determined opposition of the Republican Party and corporate interests. After months of hearings and study, with too many people and groups involved, she came up with a plan that was too complicated to explain and too easy to poke holes in. Andy's sister, Marjorie Shultz, an award-winning professor of law at the University of California, was among the experts recruited. "From the get-go," she says, "it was clear the process was dysfunctional." The Clintons failed to embrace help from Republicans who might have provided it—most notably John Chafee, the immensely respected senator from Rhode Island (who had worked with Andy and WRI to hold a hearing on climate change)—and were eaten alive by a host of sophisticated Washington operators out to deny a Democratic White House any hint of a victory.

Bill Clinton made it possible for gay Americans to serve in the military, although not openly and not before he was played on the issue by Chairman of the Joint Chiefs Colin Powell. The issue of gays in the military was a lose-lose for the White House—liberals considered the policy Clinton eventually landed on, "don't ask, don't tell," insufficient, while the GOP tarred the draft-dodging Clinton as a backer of the "gay agenda." But ultimately, Clinton's standing with voters might have suffered most grievously from his successful backing of the North American Free Trade Agreement. Liberals and labor hated NAFTA, which passed only with substantial GOP support. Whatever the merits of the agreement, Clinton's identification with it aligned him in the public mind with the multinational corporations Americans blamed for their jobs being transferred to lower-paid workers in Latin America and Asia.

In the 1994 midterms, Democrats faced multiple headwinds. NAFTA, guns, gays, and the failed attempt at health care had soured the country on the Democrats they had just elected. Republicans in the House of Representatives, led by Newt Gingrich of Georgia, produced a party-wide campaign platform called the Contract with America. In content little more than a hodgepodge of bromides about limited government and balanced budgets, the contract served as a vehicle to unite voters discontented with Clinton and the louche, elitist culture he seemed to represent.

The 1994 midterms were a wipeout for the Democrats in Congress—even the sitting Speaker of the House, Tom Foley of Washington, lost his seat. The carnage spread to state capitals, too—among the top-shelf Democratic governors who lost their jobs were Mario Cuomo of New York, defeated by the unknown mediocrity George Pataki, and Ann Richards of Texas, felled by President Bush's son, George W. Bush, the underachieving front man for the ownership of a baseball team. Republicans gained eight seats to win control of the Senate. Their net of fifty-four seats in the House gave them a majority in the lower chamber for the first time in forty years.

No substantive liberal legislation would pass Congress during the remaining six years of the Clinton presidency.

The rise of Newt Gingrich stands as a milestone in the long-term decline of the American liberal project and, indeed, of American democracy. For Gingrich, the end—reversing decades of Democratic control of the House of Representatives—justified any means, including ad hominem attacks and intemperate language with little modern precedent in so prominent an American politician. The immodest Gingrich, whose brief stint as an instructor in history at the University of West Georgia in his mind qualified him as a world-class intellectual, considered himself a "defender of civilization" while members of the opposition party were "sick" and "corrupt." Compared to the wreckage of American politics perpetrated by Republicans during and after the Trump presidency, Gingrich's words and deeds seem almost moderate, but they represent a giant step toward the definition of the GOP as a party with no ambition toward policies that might actually solve problems.

The more Americans saw of Speaker Gingrich, the less they liked him—his outsize self-regard and vituperative rhetoric didn't wear well as he conducted a daily battle in the media with Democrats in Congress and the White House. Gingrich's actions came to alarm Bob Dole, the Kansas senator and Senate majority leader, who intended to challenge Clinton in the 1996 election. Toward the end of 1995, Gingrich, to Dole's dismay, forced a government shutdown over Clinton's proposed budget, calling for cuts to, among other programs, Medicare and Medicaid. In Medicare, Gingrich had picked the wrong issue on which to force a confrontation—no federal program is more popular, and Clinton was able to draw a near one-to-one correspondence between Gingrich's proposed health care cuts and the upper-income tax cuts he likewise favored. Gingrich, impervious to the idea that he could be wrong about anything, misjudged who would be blamed for locked national parks and delayed Social Security checks. Dick Armey, the Texas congressman who, as House majority leader, was Gingrich's first lieutenant, warned Gingrich at the time: "It is incongruous to the general public political awareness to think that Democrats would shut down governments; Democrats love government. It is perfectly reasonable for them to understand Republicans shut down government; Republicans don't like government. If there's a government shutdown or anything that looks like it, we're going to get the blame."

Clinton, with a personality as likable among voters as Gingrich's was detestable, capitalized on Gingrich's mistakes: Practically every day, Clinton and/or his White House aides called Gingrich, his colleagues in Congress, and their agenda "radical" and "extreme." In the end, Gingrich & Co. backed down—the Medicare and Medicaid funding stayed in the budget.

Yet despite Clinton's apparent triumph over Gingrich in the shutdown, the president's wings had been clipped. "The era of big government is over," he proclaimed in his 1996 State of the Union address.

Thus did the leader of the Democrats formalize the party's surrender to Republican assumptions about government, abandoning the proposition, forged by Franklin Roosevelt six decades prior, that the federal government had a large and indispensable role to play in advancing the general welfare of the American populace. Certainly Clinton, facing the reality of a Republican Congress, had no choice but to lower expectations as to what he could accomplish. And over the next year, he did advance smaller goals—school uniforms, "V-chips" in televisions to help parents control their children's viewing, youth curfews—in order to re-accustom Americans to the positive role government could play in their lives. But his acceptance of the Republican governmental framework would dog liberalism for years.

Dole's most daunting obstacle as the 1996 GOP nominee was the US economy. Contrary to GOP predictions that Clinton's 1993 tax hikes would devastate the nation, the economy had entered what would turn out to be a record-setting boom. Dole, then the oldest-ever major-party presidential nominee, made a grievous error in his convention acceptance speech, promising to take the country back to an idyllic past: "Let me be the bridge to an America that only the unknowing call myth. Let me be the bridge to a time of tranquility, faith and confidence in action. And to those who say it was never so, that America's not been better, I say you're wrong. And I know because I was there."

Clinton's campaign team pounced, coining for their campaign the phrase "Building a Bridge to the Twenty-First Century." Tomorrow, goes the cliché, always beats yesterday in American politics. Dole had handed Clinton the contrast on a silver platter.

Clinton's campaign also made sure to tie the unpopular Gingrich around Dole's neck at every opportunity. By the summer, Gingrich, as well as Trent Lott, the Mississippian who had taken over as Senate majority leader after Dole had resigned his seat to run for the White House, recognized that their party's nominee was doomed. Gingrich and Lott cut a deal with Clinton to pass welfare reform, giving the president a win on one of his signature issues—the last thing Dole wanted as he sought to unseat him. The Republicans in Congress needed the legislation more than Clinton did—he led Dole comfortably in all campaign polls, but the GOP's retention of Congress was no sure thing. The legislation was far less supportive of the poor than Clinton's earlier proposals had been—in the years that followed the bill's passage, welfare rolls diminished but

American poverty did not. Nevertheless, Clinton had what one critic called his "election insurance," and the GOP Congress had a high-profile legislative accomplishment to point to.

Clinton sold out the poor; Gingrich and Lott sold out their nominee. In November, both sides got their desired results: Clinton crushed Dole to win reelection and the Congress remained in Republican hands.

Of course, Clinton's second term was blown up by his dalliance with an intern. Once his misadventure leaked to the press in January 1998, Republicans in Congress moved to extract a maximum price, but they seemed to overplay their hand. Their investigation, and the lurid report filed by their handpicked special prosecutor, Kenneth Starr, wound up costing the GOP House seats in November of that year—a virtually unprecedented outcome for the out-party in an administration's sixth-year midterms. Gingrich lost his speakership—and resigned from Congress—in the wake of those results, but the GOP was determined to bring Clinton down, and so they impeached him on charges that mostly amounted to his lying about a tawdry affair he was desperate to keep from the public and his family.

Just after the Lewinsky scandal came to light, the embattled president scored a coup when, delivering his State of the Union address, he pledged to use the new federal budget surplus to "save Social Security first." Bringing the federal budget into balance was Clinton's most touted domestic achievement during his second term. And the surplus, a product of Clinton's tax hikes and a hot economy, was no small achievement for a government that hadn't seen black ink since 1969 and hasn't seen it since. The surplus also made a vital political point, disproving the GOP's never-ending smear of the Democrats as the party of "fiscal irresponsibility."

But Clinton's focus on the surplus essentially once again embraced a GOP framing of government finance: that government expenditures were illegitimate until proven otherwise, that a president could not use all available tools, including deficit spending during a time of minimal interest rates, to achieve essential ends. Even Barack Obama, after Democratic losses in the 2010 midterms, felt compelled to recite the fact-free cliché that the federal government, just like the average American household, needs to "live within its means." Of course, the GOP hates deficit spending when a Democratic president is bolstering social programs but loves it when a Republican president is cutting taxes of the Republican donor class. No Democratic president has managed to explain to the American people the shortsightedness of resistance to prudent deficit spending in the face of urgent need.

In 2000, the Republican Party nominated as its standard-bearer George W. Bush, the personable but vacuous governor of Texas and son of the man Clinton had defeated eight years earlier. Bush had little rationale for his campaign, besides his ostensible belief in "compassionate conservatism"—an implicit rebuke of the harsher elements in his party but of little practical governing import aside from the fig leaf it provided for regressive policies. His main selling point was that he promised rectitude after Clinton's moral laxity, ending each stump speech with a faux inaugural oath in which he swore "to uphold the honor and the integrity of the office to which I have been elected, so help me God."

Clinton left office with record popularity. But the sex scandal that got him impeached elected a Republican successor. Many things had to take place to give Bush the White House in 2000 over Gore by a margin of just three electoral votes—confusing ballots in two Florida counties, a third-party vanity candidacy by Ralph Nader, Gore's ineptitude as a campaigner, the disgust that prevented Gore from calling on Clinton to campaign for him in Arkansas and elsewhere, and five Supreme Court justices willing to stop the counting of votes in Florida to award the White House to the candidate of their choice. The absence of any one of those factors would have given the White House to Gore. But every one of them would have been without consequence had the Democrat been able to run on a simple pledge to continue eight years of peace and prosperity—a pledge uncomplicated by the incumbent's flawed behavior.

Clinton's effect on liberal governance will be endlessly debated. He notched many progressive accomplishments during his eight years as president—family leave, a fairer tax code, gun control. But his most sweeping effort at reform, his attempt to remake US health care, crashed and burned. His reform of welfare, while neither as helpful as proponents have claimed nor as punitive as critics have charged, did remove the issue as a racial cudgel Republicans long wielded against Democrats. His deregulation of financial markets contributed to the 2008 meltdown. And his embrace of free trade agreements, like NAFTA, still earns him scorn among the left wing of his party.

Nonetheless, Clinton did keep alive the plausibility of at least moderately liberal governance and showed that a Democratic president could maintain strong public support. Still, when a randy young intern flashed her underwear at him, he lacked the self-control to ignore her.

And so he saddled the country with an unqualified, unenlightened successor.

AT ALTITUDE: Addressing Poverty in the Highlands of Nepal and Bolivia

By the late 1990s, EnterpriseWorks Worldwide was working to transform production of:

- dairy and livestock in Bangladesh, Nepal, India, and Zimbabwe
- coffee in El Salvador and Guatemala
- household energy, through provision of a low-cost charcoal stove, in Benin, Mali, and Senegal
- market gardening, i.e., small-scale farming, in Benin, Mali, Niger, and Senegal
- oilseeds and other staple foods in Benin, Mali, Mozambique, Senegal, Tanzania, Uganda, Zambia, and Zimbabwe
- coconuts in the Philippines
- alpaca fiber in Bolivia
- other natural products, such as silk, honey, bamboo, rattan, resins, and essential oils variously in India, Indonesia, Nepal, and the Philippines

The essential oils project in Nepal involved production of the jatamansi plant, which yields oils used in the manufacture of cosmetics. "Jatamansi is a plant that grows at high altitude—fourteen thousand or sixteen thousand feet," says Andy. "It requires that low-income people go way up into the mountains to pick these plants and bring them back down. Before we got involved, Indian traders would come through the Nepalese towns and buy up these plants, which they would take to India for processing. These traders would make all the money selling the processed material to cosmetics manufacturers in Europe.

"We designed a program so that the people who picked the jatamansi on the hillside could take it to a nearby processing facility, which we built to extract the oil and make it ready to be shipped to Europe, thus cutting out the intermediary traders. Meanwhile, our marketing people talked to the cosmetics people in Europe, saying, 'We can provide this to you directly for less than you've been getting it from the traders.' Of course, that was attractive to the manufacturers. So the value was captured in Nepal by the people who brought their jatamansi to be processed at the local facility."

What Valeria Budinich calls "the most iconic project in ATI/EWW's history" was first suggested by ATI's director of Latin America before she held that post. "He wrote the concept of the alpaca project," says Budinich, "like a three-page sketch. Later, I and this guy named Richard Bowman, one of the most colorful people in ATI, worked on it. Richard Bowman was among the new generation of Peace Corps volunteers who arrived at ATI—he'd been named Peace Corps volunteer of the year in Honduras. A farmer from Idaho with an MBA. A serious cowboy—he'd arrived in DC wearing a cowboy hat. A year after that, when the UN finally said they would be interested in a full proposal, we went to the Andes, to the Bolivian highlands, met the farmers, and developed the full proposal. I took charge of the industrial engineering part and Richard Bowman did the animal husbandry and the field parts. Together we produced what was like a book, maybe a hundred pages.

"The UN Capital Development Fund needed to approve close to $5 million to do a massive transformation of alpaca fiber production in the Andes. At that time, 90 percent of the alpacas in the world were in Bolivia. Most of the Bolivian population lives in the highlands; they are indigenous people who depend on this fiber.

"Alpacas are the piggy bank of this community. When the people need money, they shear the animals, collect the wool, and make garments. So if you help them do it more effectively and at higher quality, you can double or triple their income, connecting them with many possibilities. Otherwise they are subsistence farmers. With the exception of the fiber, they eat what they produce.

"Five years before we got there, there had been a grant from the Inter-American Development Bank of half a million dollars to a national cooperative of camelid producers. Camelids are alpacas, plus llamas and a couple of other alpaca-looking animals found only in that part of the world. Camelids are the only kind of animal that survive at that altitude, over ten thousand feet. In fact, some of the regions of the project were at fourteen thousand feet, in the highest Andes, a beautiful area. Andy and I were there a couple of times; it was a fascinating thing to sleep under the stars in the middle of nowhere.

"Where they raise the animals, there is a huge Andes plateau that you can access via La Paz, the capital of Bolivia. It's like a three-hour drive on dirt roads, in a Range Rover, from La Paz. You ascend a bit, but you start high—La Paz itself is at twelve thousand feet.

"With the support of the Inter-American Development Bank, the farmers had built a cooperative that organized more than a hundred thousand of them. That provided some level of credit to a small percentage of members. But by the time we came, the most valuable resource, the animals themselves, had serious health issues, with a high mortality rate. And to give you a sense, you are talking about families that would earn like a $200 aggregated income monthly, and each alpaca would be worth like $700. So one of them dying would be a massive blow to your finances.

"The goals were first of all to create as much value as possible. And then to capture as much of that value for the farmers themselves. To start, there was a need for massive upgrading of all the veterinary and animal husbandry practices. For example, if 3 percent of your animals die, versus 20 percent, you're talking about a massive gain. So in the middle of this semi-desert, semi-arid area, we created a medical bath for the animals.

"And then, they were shearing the fiber of the alpaca with opened tin cans. This fiber is like cashmere—the longer the better. It grows long on the animal, but if you shear it with a tin can, it's going to be multiple lengths. And then, at the end of the value chain, you have a fashion designer in Milan who wants to make this gorgeous alpaca coat which he's going to sell for several thousand dollars. But in the process of exporting the fiber, you have an incredible percentage of rejects, because of the uneven lengths.

"So we needed to introduce new technologies for how people were not only caring for the animals, but also managing the harvesting of the fiber. The other thing that nobody had in the Andes was the ability to sell uniformly high-quality bales of alpaca fiber. The question was: How could you do preprocessing in-country, compact the fiber, and then sell the premium, certified-quality fiber to the Milan-type market?

"That's what the project did. It improved the fiber quality and the animal husbandry practices. It improved the harvesting process. And we needed to do that with technologies that could be readily available in the middle of nowhere. We're talking about people at very high altitudes, removed from electricity, because when you go to the high Andes, you have a horizon of miles and miles and miles, with no infrastructure. Nothing. So you needed shearers that did not depend on energy facilities that you find for sheep-shearing in, say, New Zealand. And that's what we created there, with the help of the local cooperative. We established small centers to shear the wool and do the grading depending on the length and the color."

An understanding of the fiber's color proved to be another key to the project's success. "Alpacas come in eight or ten natural colors," says Budinich. "When we did the design of that project, we consulted with people in Peru, a neighboring country where they have a lot of llamas. The Peruvians were state-of-the-art camelid veterinarians. They recommended that we introduce a breeding element in the program to make all the alpacas white.

"But our team said, 'Before we propose this $5 million project to the UN, let's go to Milan and do some research.' In Milan we were told, 'Natural colors are a major plus, drawing a premium price. Forget about making all your alpacas white.' We stopped that idea, and it ended up being a major differentiation for Bolivia to compete with Peru, because only Bolivia kept the natural alpaca hues. There are even blue alpacas. You are in the middle of nowhere and you see these blue animals—it's a dark blue that's like a variation of the black. But it does look blue, not black.

"When we started this project, the price per kilogram paid to the farmers was less than $1.50. By the end of the project, it was higher than $10.00.

"The beautiful concept of this project is that it served as a bridge to accelerate the development of a national asset. Alpacas are critical to the development of Bolivia—you are talking on the order of 700,000 people whose livelihoods rely on the production of alpaca fiber (plus some camelid meat). The farmers were capturing a small fraction of that value. The project touched on all of their needs with an approach that improved the animal husbandry in remote locations and also had a centralized, state-of-the-art facility to package the fiber and make it ready for the export market.

"My happiest moment with this project was one day in 1992, when the project was already underway. I visited the representative of the UN Capital Development Fund in Bolivia who told me, 'We have a problem, but it's a good problem. This morning, I had in my office all the exporters of alpaca fiber in the country, and they were basically complaining that the UN was using subsidies to unfairly compete with them. This is an indication to me that this project is working at a scale that is remarkable, because these buyers can feel the pain.'

"We changed the dynamic by bypassing the intermediaries. And we got higher prices because we helped create a better-quality alpaca fiber that nobody else could produce. In 1992 and 1993 this program was chosen as the best UN-funded program in the world."

"The organization's mission had expanded," says Rob Esposito, "beyond the introduction of appropriate technology to looking at the whole gamut of interventions, from production to processing to marketing, of whatever the commodity that was being grown or herded or manufactured. We would enable small-scale producers to increase the value of their products—and, subsequently, their income—two or three times beyond what it would have been without these often simple interventions. The *Washington Business Journal* wrote about ATI and EnterpriseWorks; they called it 'a Peace Corps with a business plan.' And that's what it was."

"The point was, we were change agents," says Andy. "We built teams and got important stuff done."

While much of Andy's job centered on navigating the corridors of power in Washington, he also logged thousands of miles traveling to distant locations.

"In his first year at ATI," Budinich recalls, "Andy said to me, 'If we're going to push this forward, we need to identify who in the world has done the closest thing to what we want to do.' We identified two projects. One was in Turkey. 'I want to go there with you,' he told me, 'and meet with the founders, so that we understand what we're getting into.' We met with a Turkish development foundation that had helped transform the Turkish poultry industry, turning the country from an importer to an exporter of chickens and eggs.

"The industry in Turkey was based on more than two million small farmers with a few chickens each but with centralized facilities, similar to the arrangement we would install in the Andes, for the processing of the meat and eggs.

"On the same trip, we went to India to see the other project we identified. The National Dairy Development Board of India, the largest cooperative in the world, involved ten million farmers. They controlled the entire value chain of dairy production in India. We met the founder at a dinner he hosted at his home for Andy, myself, and several other people. He told us how in 1960 he'd had the courage to say to Nehru, 'Cancel the imports of powdered milk in India, because that's going to be the only way small producers will have control of the local market. And if you do that, I will organize these producers and I will create this massive industry,' which he did, to the tune of several billion dollars. It continues to operate today. Those trips were, in typical Andy fashion, a bold idea: Let's figure out where in the world something was happening that resembled our plans. It felt like research into our future."

Andy recalls other travels. "Our Republican co-chair," he says, "Richard Williamson, was intent on getting out in the field, so he and I went together to the coffee program in El Salvador—we met with all the people involved. Not long after that he and I went to India and later to Senegal. It was very exciting.

"I would go out to many places and I would meet with our teams, and with whatever local nongovernmental organizations were involved with us, and with producers themselves and with relevant government officials.

"It was all great. I hiked up to a very small town in northwest Nepal, which you couldn't get to except by foot, and met with the whole team of people doing the jatamansi work. It was up there, at fourteen to fifteen thousand feet. I was there to be a cheerleader while our team and Nepalese partners put the particulars together for a brand-new processing facility—the only industrial facility of any kind in that northwestern corner of Nepal.

"There are people in all countries who are trying to move the needle. There are community leaders, there are young people who want to rise to the challenge. There are people who want their friends and relatives to increase their incomes so that their kids can have a better education, so that they can live in a more healthful community. One of the things you discover when out on the ground is that these are very, very hardworking people.

"The whole notion that, oh well, all those people in Africa, Asia, and Latin America are poor because they don't work hard is nonsense. They're working from dawn to dusk to provide for themselves and their families. They are very bright. They are doing absolutely everything that they can do within the context that they inhabit, in terms of preserving resources, working in an environmentally sensible way, producing the highest-quality products they can. But to get to the next level, they need a McKinsey-type analysis of the potential. That's what we brought to the table.

"They were our clients, for whom we had enormous respect. We weren't there to dole stuff out. We were there to empower people, to help them get past a particular bottleneck, which might be technological, might be managerial, might be a lack of access to talk to potential buyers internationally. We would help with all that.

"We were not helicopter parents, it was the opposite. It was looking for what was going on, on the ground, that could be magnified and enhanced. What was it going to take for these smart, hardworking people to get to the next level?"

For Budinich, the most memorable trip of her tenure with ATI/EWW was to Zimbabwe. "Andy knew much more about Africa than I ever did," she says. "And he understood that in Africa we could achieve a large impact. I remember going with him to Africa to visit the project in Zimbabwe. We saw the blessing of sunflower seeds, with African female farmers singing.

"And then the famers put on a theater presentation, a play, in which they showed us, in their local language and with mime, the value chain of sunflower oil before and after they acquired the press. For example, at one point someone played the role of a truck driver, and there was money exchanging hands. The difference was that the farmer at the end of the first vignette—showing the 'before'—would end up with little money. The farmer in the second vignette—the 'after'—would end up with three or four times more and everyone was smiling.

"It was a beautiful way of capturing the fact that the community understood it had been possible to change the system by participating in this project and taking the risk of buying a press. They understood that it wasn't good for them to sell the raw seeds for a fixed amount—doing so yielded only a fraction of the real value. They were much better off taking those seeds, pressing them, and selling the oil. I wish we would have filmed that play, because it was such a powerful moment, showing a community that truly understood that they could shape their own destiny."

BITTERSWEET: Andy's Departure from EWW

For all the success ATI/EWW enjoyed under Andy's leadership, the organization fell short in effecting change on the scale its approach merited. "We were on the forefront of how to strengthen the whole fabric of social culture and values and economic transformation for the low-income people of the world," says Andy. "And building leadership that is indigenous. That's what Drayton was all about. That's what Valeria was all about. That's what I was all about.

"By the 1990s, organizations were starting to shift. Most organizations understood that to be sustainable and to be scalable, something more than the dole was needed. But it's interesting that there were no organizations that I know of that had our exclusive focus on value chain and profit-making enterprises. CARE, for example, was doing education. They were doing health care. They were doing whatever. And they would have a little piece that related, say, to getting local handicrafts marketed worldwide. Not the way we were thinking about it, but there was definitely an interest in having things make economic sense, so that the gains lasted, so that when you left town, or the project was completed, the activity could have a continuing life.

"CARE had a small entrepreneurship program that wasn't well put together. We went to CARE and said, 'Look, you have this little piece over here for encouraging entrepreneurship, but you don't do it well. How about giving us ten or twenty million dollars to do it for you and really make it sing?' We made more or less the same suggestion to various large do-good organizations. But people typically continue to do things the way they're used to doing them. And there would always be people in the organization who saw us as a threat to their own standing there.

"Our model should have been adopted, big-time, by people like CARE and other nongovernmental actors, by the World Bank, which, with its vast resources, its economists, and its engineers, spent most of its time on big infrastructure projects. Even USAID, instead of being possessive about the few million dollars that went our way, could have incorporated our approach more broadly. It was one of Drayton's objectives to convince larger actors that they needed to do more of this. We were successful in getting individuals within these organizations to work with us and to help fund the jatamansi or the coffee or the alpaca fiber or whatever. And we succeeded a hundredfold in reaching our objectives on the ground in multiple countries in Africa, Asia, and Latin America. We measured the results in very sophisticated ways. We demonstrated that we were doubling and tripling and quadrupling people's incomes. But in spite of the almost uniform success in everything we touched, we were not able to achieve a big breakthrough in funding. I would have loved to have had a hundred million dollars from the World Bank. That would have been peanuts for them. Look at what we did and how we did it and what we accomplished. But the orders-of-magnitude levels of support didn't arrive."

The work of ATI/EWW has been compared to that of Muhammad Yunus, founder of Grameen Bank, who received the Nobel Peace Prize in 2006 for his work in extending microloans to individuals in developing countries. "Yunus had a laser-like focus on microloans," says Andy. "Our feeling about that was, well, that's all very nice, but microloans for what? You can set up any number of seamstresses with their sewing machines. And people are paying the money back and they are getting a leg up, at least within the context of their own families and communities. But are you transforming an economic sector?

"We regarded ourselves as change agents and we certainly changed the lives and the livelihoods of hundreds of thousands of low-income people we worked with over the years in those many projects. But it was hard getting major development institutions to shift gears."

ATI/EWW saw some success in working with larger organizations. But, says Andy, "by the end of the decade, the whole way that foreign development was administered by the US government went through a period of change. Creativity was lost. USAID became, basically, a paper-pushing bureaucratic outfit. It didn't do or supervise or dream up its own projects, as it had originally. What it did was put out requests for proposals (RFPs) to what we call 'Beltway bandit' consulting firms, which, indeed, were all around the Beltway. These firms would answer these enormously complex RFPs because they were the only outfits with the staff to cover the multiple objectives of typical omnibus RFPs. These firms would helicopter people in and out of wherever they were working. It was like the people who went over to Russia after the collapse of the Soviet Union, all these mega consultants who were going to create American-style capitalism there. It doesn't work.

"It was a long-term trend and it became more and more pervasive. Well into the '90s, we were able to design unsolicited, innovative proposals and convince decision makers in donor organizations here and abroad to pay attention and become our partners. But by the end of the decade, there was no opening for any of that anymore.

"I was at ATI/EWW twelve years. That was long enough. I turned it over to a very able thought leader I'd come to know through the Aspen Institute. But she faced all the same problems. After I left EWW as CEO, I continued to serve on the board. We did arrange a strategic alliance with a larger outfit called Relief International, and some of our expert staff went to work for them. Ultimately, RI bought us out, with the aim of moving beyond giving immediate relief to people in crisis situations. They saw us as an outfit that knew how to anchor such people for the longer term in their lives and their economic futures.

"This part of my professional life is a bittersweet story, because I really threw myself into it. And I got fabulous people involved. Surely what we accomplished on a limited budget offers a premier example of my putting teams together here and around the world to pursue hugely popular grassroots, sustainable, income-producing development agendas, often empowering women as key economic actors with all the attendant social benefits that brings. Where we did have problems, was in scaling. Ultimately, despite tripling our revenues from a hundred new donors, we were disappointed that we couldn't leverage the work at the higher levels of funding that Bill Drayton and Valeria and I had hoped could and should have been possible. I'm disappointed that our work wasn't immediately multiplied tenfold or a hundredfold.

"The good news is that EWW did have a continuing influence in the development community and in the theory of how you work with low-income people to surmount challenges and capture value. But institutionally, in the bigger picture, it wasn't reaching the level we had hoped. I hate to admit that, but it's the case.

"Still, we can look back and say, yes, we did make a difference. We influenced those who followed us."

CHAPTER 11

FRUSTRATION: A Variety of Pursuits, 2003–2014

It is common sense to take a method and try it: If it fails, admit it frankly and try another. But above all, try something.

—FRANKLIN ROOSEVELT

OTHER PEOPLE'S AGENDAS: Consulting

Once again, Andy Maguire needed employment. For the time being, he would freelance.

From 2003 to 2006, he became what many veterans of government become: a consultant. Andy is quick to point out that he did not work as a lobbyist. "If you're lobbying, you're trying to influence a piece of legislation or modify proposed regulations," he says. "What I did was more small-bore. I helped people sell stuff."

Still, Andy sought opportunities where he could assist in environmental initiatives or elevate people's health and well-being—'stuff' with social as well as economic benefit. He worked with a variety of clients. One such firm was the International Metalizing Corporation. "I was brought in by the chairman," Andy recalls, "a wealthy guy out of Philadelphia who had made his money in the financial industry." Based in New Jersey, the organization naturally turned to the former Bergen County representative for help in marketing its wares to the public sector.

The company had managed to score some profits before Andy came on board, selling its wares as far away as the Panama Canal. But management envisioned a big future for the firm and for the process the firm's CEO had invented. "Metalizing" aimed to transform the maintenance of large pieces of infrastructure. "With bridges and the like," Andy says, "every couple of years you have to scrape them down and repaint them. Continuous cleaning and painting, especially of large structures, exposes workers to toxic substances, including heavy metals, while emitting volatile organic compounds that are air pollutants. But the process developed by this company's founder made it possible to essentially spray a silver-colored coat of metal onto major structures—a much simpler and more environmentally sound procedure. The company had done it in various places, working for various private and public entities, but they wanted to expand."

Andy recalls his work pitching the company to two governmental agencies. One was the US Navy. "Company leaders," he says, "wanted to establish a relationship with a major arm of the US military, and they felt their metalizing process could be useful on ships. Of course, in the Navy, as in other organizations, people in technical positions with influence over the purchase of goods and services are usually locked into the people they work with—for example, the painters they've employed for the last fifty years." Nonetheless, Andy was able to get a foot in the door. "We set up a demonstration on a ship, and the demonstration went well: We showed that the process worked. But the Navy didn't buy it. They thought the stuff would inevitably flake off—or maybe they just didn't want to change. We met with the top technical people. They said, 'That's nice. But we'll continue doing things the way we've always done them.'"

The other public entity to which Andy connected International Metalizing operated the ferries that ran in and out of Seattle. "Think about ferryboats," says Andy. "They're exposed to water and erosion all the time." Andy approached his friend Norm Dicks, the longtime congressman from Washington State with whom Andy had played basketball in the House gym during Andy's time on the Hill. "Dicks set me up with the ferry people in Seattle—remember, we're just a little outfit from

New Jersey." But ultimately, Andy was no more successful with the ferry operator than he'd been with the Navy.

Andy undertook other initiatives for International Metalizing. "I talked to the people building a big bridge in Tacoma," he says. "I went to four or five different places on the company's ticket but made little progress. Their process was a technological innovation that people generally weren't interested in, because they felt they already knew what they were doing.

"Accessing the right people in those places was not that easy to do, and I was able to do it. But in terms of upping sales, I was not as successful as I expected. I quarterbacked opportunities and demonstrations, but the founder/CEO was limited in his ability to close deals with his own product.

"I worked for them a couple of years; they paid reasonably. But when, despite all my frenetic activity, I wasn't able to jump-start a noticeable uptick in sales, the chairman—who had made his money in finance but was untutored in infrastructure and naive about the CEO—ended our relationship."

Andy also chaired the board of The Global Livestock Group, Inc., a company that managed programs in India and Uganda seeking to reduce methane emissions from ruminants through a change in their diet. The aim of such reduction was to produce tradeable, verifiable international carbon credits for use by energy companies. "The effort was a spin-off from EnterpriseWorks Worldwide," says Andy. "We privatized our existing programs to improve the feeding of mainly cows, but also buffalo, to cut levels of methane, a significant greenhouse gas. Shell and other multinationals were trying to design ways they could convince the world they were offsetting their fossil fuel emissions. We set up GLG on the theory that there would be a market for measurable carbon credits, making this company profitable. Richard Bowman, the EWW livestock specialist who was instrumental in upgrading alpaca fiber production in Bolivia, led this new company.

"TransAlta, the second largest utility in Canada, funded the effort for several years. The company aspired to become carbon neutral, so they scoured the world and got a variety of partners who would work with them on X, Y, or Z. Meanwhile, we proved our methane reduction project's worth to the EPA, which looked at our results and said, 'You guys have done it! You've definitely got it together.'

"Bowman and our technical consultants had figured out a way to put a simple harness around the neck of a cow eating an enhanced diet. Trace chemicals on the harness were activated as the cow exhaled, showing how much methane was emitted, allowing comparisons between the levels of improvement with different mixes of diet additives. At scale, such a provable reduction in methane emissions from simple additions to ruminants' existing diets could be hugely important to corporations and governments alike.

"I've often felt I was ahead of the curve on this, that, or the other thing. Well, this initiative was such a case. Our finance expert, Ken Locklin, a former banker, predicted it might be five years before carbon credits would be fully bankable, so we felt our timing with our successful experiments in place was about right and we'd be ready. It turned out Locklin underestimated the time frame—it took a couple of decades.

"Ultimately the carbon capture aspect of the project fell away, though a private company created by our Ugandan partners continued to produce the feed additive we'd formulated especially for African cattle, since it improved the cattle's overall health. At the time, scholars, researchers, and institutions around the world were trying to assess how carbon credits might be gleaned from forestry and agriculture. Indeed, the Waxman-Markey climate bill that passed the House years later tiptoed into this arena. Livestock all over the world are significant emitters of methane. But this was like the metalizing of bridges and ferryboats and naval vessels: It just wasn't there yet.

"For it to work for TransAlta and others going forward, there would have to be some accrediting agency saying, 'Yes, this is what you did and we recognize it.' That was not yet in place. TransAlta was trying to show the world that it was a progressive corporation, but despite TransAlta's alignment with the Canadian government's longer-term objectives to combat climate change, the government wasn't eager to help, either. After a couple of years, the company no longer subsidized what we were doing.

"And so, that was that."

Andy then had an opportunity with the AFL-CIO to head its international operations, but after a series of promising meetings with the president and other top officials he found the union's compensation package insufficient. He worked briefly on fundraising for People for the American Way, then designed marketing strategies for two international companies, one based in Australia selling ergonomic computer keyboard products, the other in Dubai focused on upgrading security and infrastructure in conflict-ridden locations like Sudan. "I worked hard at these jobs," he recalls. "I thought I gave good value. But as you might imagine, I found the work intensely boring and decided I did not want to make the rest of my life about consulting—in other words, working on other people's agendas. I certainly did not want to become a lobbyist. I had no inclination to go to former colleagues in Congress to prod them to manipulate wording in legislation in order to please private interests."

Andy then turned down a full-time offer from the Dubai-based international firm, Unity Resources Group (URG), to take a newly created position with a challenging multilateral not-for-profit institution.

He was recruited after answering a want ad.

VACCINES AND A TURF WAR: GAVI

"There are always ads in the front of the *Economist* for all sorts of international postings," Andy says. In 2006, he read a notice advertising a new Washington-based position for the Global Alliance for Vaccines and Immunization (GAVI). "I submitted my papers."

Founded in 1999, and underwritten in large part by the Bill and Melinda Gates Foundation, GAVI is an international consortium of governmental and nongovernmental organizations that provides vaccines to children across the developing world. Based in Geneva, GAVI has been an immensely successful enterprise: By 2022, it had vaccinated nearly half the world's children.

"The US government contributed to GAVI through USAID on a limited basis," says Andy, "but the organization had only a minor presence in Washington—one former congressional staffer who worked on maneuvering the USAID contribution each year through the House Appropriations Committee, somebody else who handled finances. Geneva headquarters brought me in to create a US entity we called the Immunize Every Child Campaign."

"The Gates Foundation has a very rational way of looking at how they spend their money," says Susan Swift, Andy's former colleague at EWW, whom he hired at his new job. "They looked across the developing world and said, 'What's the one intervention that could save the most children from dying?' They landed on immunization, because lack of immunization kills immense numbers of kids zero to five. They die from diseases that most everybody in the United States has been vaccinated against.

"GAVI has a governing council—more like a secretariat—based in Geneva. This council works with a whole bunch of donor countries—all the rich countries participate. And then the council works with a whole bunch of recipient countries, especially the big ones, which are also putting money into it, like a Nigeria, an India. GAVI has programs to go out and vaccinate all these kids."

The Immunize Every Child Campaign, says Swift, "was designed to raise money from private individuals, the highly affluent as well as donors who may not have been at the uppermost levels. Andy put together a council of notable people. Somebody might not be inclined to meet with us about a midsize donation. But if we said, 'We're going to have a reception and somebody important's going to be there . . .'"

"We would bring in luminaries to up the profile," says Andy. "We had a big fundraiser in New York. Madeleine Albright spoke. The former head of USAID attended. Others."

"Chairman of that council was Dwight Bush, who was married to Vernon Jordan's daughter," says Swift. "Dwight Bush had been an ambassador, he'd worked at Sallie Mae. A really cool guy. Alice Albright was head of our Washington office; her mother, the former secretary of state, would come to events. Andy taught me: 'Okay, these people are famous. But if you approach them with the right argument, they can become a part of what you're doing, and be grateful for the opportunity.' We would plan events with headliners to attract others who could give significantly."

"My team and I did two crucial things," says Andy. "One, and this is where Susan Swift became critically important, we improved our online presence. She came up with a sumptuous, absolutely beautiful website, which got rave reviews from headquarters in Geneva, to serve as an anchor and a central place through which money would flow."

"Andy was figuring out what the strategy should be," says Swift. "I came up with the communications and helped design the website, in partnership with a very good outfit in Washington called Blue Spot. We were also doing some social media, where we would tell stories. We had to come up with campaigns where we would say things like 'Hundreds of people died in this country from this disease, which is vaccine-preventable.'"

"The other thing we did," says Andy, "was put together as many events as we could. I brought in a professional fundraiser, who worked under my direction. Those efforts paid off. For example, at one event we got a $1 million commitment from a hedge fund heavy out of Boston. However, such cases were not as many as we hoped to achieve."

Andy was pleased to have joined GAVI. "This outfit was one of the most important international health operations on the planet," he says. "It had a tremendous track record in terms of accomplishing its mission, which was to vaccinate as many kids as they could, all over the world. It was absolutely fabulous."

He assembled a skilled team that began to establish a fundraising presence in the United States. But turf wars and personality clashes hampered his ability to do the job. "I did not end up having much respect for the CEO," he says.

"Julian Lob-Levyt, kind of a Hugh Grant–looking British guy, headed GAVI," says Swift. "He was likable, but a huge ego preceded him through every door. That aspect of him was not inclined to make Andy like him, or vice versa. Because let's face it, Andy has an ego, too."

The main source of friction between the two men was the scope of Andy's operation. "My beat was supposed to be the United States," Andy recalls, "but I saw myself as somebody who could do more. One of the ways we tried to demonstrate such capability was reaching out to Americans living in London. We ended up holding a terrific fundraiser there at a fashionable house donated for the event by custodians of the British royal family.

"Another opportunity was with a board member, Princess Cristina of Spain. Lob-Levyt had introduced us to her and, in turn, to CaixaBank. This bank, Spain's largest, was engaged in an effort to show the world that they were progressive, so they agreed to support vaccination on a major scale. Lob-Levyt opened the door, but it was my fundraising team that walked through it over a period of months. We shuttled back and forth to Spain putting all the pieces together with the bank's technical and money people. We did the work that confirmed a real relationship and put the specifics together for the multimillion-dollar commitment CaixaBank subsequently made to GAVI's programs.

"The bank had a broad-minded senior team that cared about what was happening not just in Spain—they had branches all over the country—but across the world. They wanted to be leading corporate actors on the good guys' side. And the princess was a part of that. She was terrific.

"But at year's end, when it came time to account for how much we had been able to do with this bank—we're talking several million dollars—Lob-Levyt would not allow us to include it in our report to the board of directors. His view was that because he had opened the door to the princess, he should get all the credit. If we had been able to put that number on our books, it would have added to the dynamism of what we were doing and could do in the future, including in the United States. We were the ones who did all the work, but I was supposed to keep my nose in the United States."

Despite the friction with the home office, Andy did his best to maintain a positive working environment for his team. Swift remembers the atmosphere—and the perks, which included an unlikely encounter with a real-life princess. "I met her at the GAVI office in Barcelona," says Swift. "She said, 'Would you like a coffee?' She's a very down-to-earth person. I told somebody, 'I've never had a princess make me coffee before.'

"We had some fun times. The whole team went with Andy to Geneva for meetings—there was lots of camaraderie. He was a fun boss, the center of the constellation, and we moved around him. He also took us all to California for a meeting of the Association of Fundraising Professionals—that was really fun, too. He spent time with us and invested in us. I never felt as though he thought of himself as more important. He did, I think, but he didn't broadcast it. Which was nice.

"Despite the fact that Andy can be a little grouchy, he's a really good, decent person, who looks at you when he's talking to you and figures out what you're saying. And figures out who you are. Not a lot of people do that."

Andy tried to involve the Spanish princess further, but was rebuffed by Lob-Levyt. "I told my American board members," he says, "because I didn't have much direct contact with the CEO, that it would be great to have the princess on the board of the Immunize Every Child Campaign. There were two board members, Americans, who really wanted this to happen. They're basically the ones who hired me. But the answer from Geneva was, 'No. You're not going to have the princess of Spain on your board.' Can you imagine how helpful that would have been to us in the United States? She was willing to do it.

"I declined to attend the next board meeting in Europe, where I was to make my report, because I was not going to be able to include in it any part of what we'd done in Spain. I sent someone else from our office. What the CEO had done was just too blatantly idiotic a move with respect to the prospects of the DC office—an office the board had created."

"Andy refused to go to a meeting in Geneva," says Swift. "I think he felt like it was not going to be a good-news meeting. Not that he was going to be fired, but he'd have to listen to those clowns in Geneva. (That's my word, 'clowns.' He wouldn't say that.) I think not going was not a good idea. It was, in some ways, a self-fulfilling prophecy: They were going to part ways."

"Obviously, refusing to show up at a board meeting is not a perfect way to go forward," says Andy.

"Andy and the European people at the secretariat," says Swift, "weren't each other's favorite people. I feel like he did everything he could to make the US project a success. It was sad, because Andy worked really hard."

One way Andy worked hard was by connecting with deep-pocketed potential donors. "I took it upon myself to have sit-downs with a couple of people—people I'd met through the GAVI network—about making significant private contributions," he says. "In that effort I was supported by those helpful board members. But the CEO again got his nose out of joint because I'd met these people through existing GAVI relationships. They weren't people I had turned up from scratch.

"I went to Fort Lauderdale for a day with an enormously wealthy financier who had a gigantic custom-made boat he was very proud of. I asked him if he would consider a private contribution—he'd given to the AIDS Network, I pointed out to him, but hadn't yet given to GAVI. The next thing I know, I'm being told by the CEO to stand down: It was *his* territory. Another huge moneybags I wanted to approach was Carlos Slim. He's one of the wealthiest people in the world, because he had free rein from one Mexican president after another to take over that country's telecommunications industry. Through some contacts from my work at EWW we had a way of getting to him. That effort, too, was shot down by Geneva. We also had a way of getting to one of the major money titans in the Mideast, in one of the Gulf states, because he had a history of philanthropy we thought was relevant. I started down that track but got the message from the CEO: 'No, no, not your job. We will in due course pursue contacts in the Middle East. That's my turf.' Then there was Mo Ibrahim, the enormously wealthy Sudanese who brought the cell phone to much of Africa. My thesis adviser at Harvard, Robert Rotberg, knew Ibrahim well and was always willing to help, so we could have made contact. But once again, we were told not to.

"I couldn't spread my wings."

A turf war was not the entire story behind Andy's troubles with Geneva. He faced a larger clash of cultures. "One of Andy's questions was, How did Switzerland treat us?" Swift notes. "They felt we were small potatoes, which we were. Because we were only going after individuals, whereas they had hundreds of millions of dollars from the Gates Foundation and governments.

"In the United States, the way you raise money is from rich people, and that was something the Geneva group didn't like. They thought it was tawdry. They looked down on the idea that rich people would have anything to do with GAVI. Forgetting that Bill and Melinda were there—they're rich, right? Geneva looked down on us."

Andy and Lob-Levyt were an odd match, with the British CEO headquartered in Geneva unwilling to brook competition from the savvy American ex-politician. "I'm over in Madrid," Andy recalls, "for the big celebration with CaixaBank and the princess. And there's this big meeting in the huge hotel dining room. Lob-Levyt gets up and gives a perfectly adequate summary of what GAVI is doing and what it wants to do. And then I was asked to speak. I talked about coming to the party in a taxi and mentioning the work to the driver, who said, 'Oh yeah. La Caixa. They're doing such great work.' I brought the house down with that anecdote. Afterwards, Lob-Levyt's media aide came over and told me how terrific my speech was. The implication was that he wished he could get the same kind of speech out of his own CEO. All of this played into the total picture.

"For two years I poured myself into doing the very best I could for an organization with a vital, life-saving mission that was consistent with all my values and everything I'd spent my life doing. I had a two-year contract and would have been happy to stay for a third because we had a three-year plan. But they decided not to continue with me. I fared okay: I got a nice severance package. Not so the Immunize Every Child Campaign: It folded within a year from inattention and lack of support from Geneva.

"That's the way the world goes. There are going to be times when stuff like that happens and it's particularly likely to happen in a situation where I don't feel that promises to me have been kept and I don't have much regard for how the CEO I report to behaves.

"Interestingly, a couple of years after we parted company, the board terminated Lob-Levyt. Who's to know why? He seemed like a caring, mild, staff-supporting leader when he talked to GAVI's employees. But there was something else going on with him.

"My first year at GAVI was terrific. All kinds of support from all kinds of people in the organization. Year two, as I tried to become a major player, not so good. We parted amicably, although not in what I would call a satisfactory way.

"But thinking back about it, at the beginning I went to all these interviews with the US board members and with the staff person who worked on the Hill about the USAID money. This man and I had never met, but he knew Congress and had, he told me, enormous respect for what I'd done when I was there. He thought I was the right person for the job. And then they set up a video interview with the CEO. It was supposed to be for an hour and a half. I remember being struck by the fact that despite having been scheduled to be there from the beginning, he didn't join until about fifteen minutes before the end. And then he wanted me to summarize.

"I remember feeling at the time: That is not the way I would have handled this. A new person we're going to be paying north of $300,000 a year to set up a whole new initiative in the United States. If that new effort was important to me, I would have been on that call. Of course, he was dedicated to the goals of the organization, for sure, and I did like his style with his employees. They had made enormous progress in their mission, no question about that, either. But I have strong views about leadership and how I've led in my own work, and how I've seen other leaders unwilling to hire people who knew stuff the leaders didn't know or had capabilities the leaders didn't have. It's the flawed leadership model of 'surround me with people who like what I do and support what I say, with no more discussion.' He ended up being one of those, and it's difficult for me to work with people like that. He didn't have the good sense to understand how to properly support a colleague. I think he hired me only because his American board members wanted him to, plus he liked the idea of having a former member of Congress on the team.

NOT UP TO THE JOB: The Presidency of George W. Bush

From an early age, George W. Bush was in over his head, relying on his father's influence, not his own efforts and talents, to get ahead. Despite a mediocre record of achievement at the upper-crust boarding school George H. W. Bush attended, George W. was accepted at his father's college alma mater, Yale, where a C average didn't prevent his joining Skull and Bones, the ultra-elite secret society of which his father had also been a member. After W. received his diploma in 1968, at the height of US involvement in the Vietnam War, he did what his father had done during World War II: He became a military pilot. But while the father had flown combat missions over the South Pacific, the son patrolled the skies of Texas, avoiding Southeast Asia thanks to the much-coveted spot his influential dad had secured for him in the Texas Air National Guard.

After completing his military obligation, the younger Bush studied business, although he owed his subsequent success not to his Harvard MBA but, again, to his father's name. He traded on that name to make a fortune in the oil business, to be the public face of a baseball team's ownership group, and to be elected governor of Texas despite no history of elective office or substantial civic leadership. With the end of the Clinton presidency looming, leaders of the Republican Party anointed Bush, a macho-sounding Texan and son of a man thought an exemplar of rectitude, their best bet to succeed the chief executive who'd been caught with his pants down.

During the 2000 Republican presidential primary race, when Bush's bid was threatened by the "maverick" appeal of Arizona senator John McCain, the Texan did what his father had done twelve years earlier: He turned a blind eye as his chief strategist savaged his opponent with a racist attack. McCain had won the season's first contest, New Hampshire, throwing the Bush campaign back on its heels. Now the candidates headed toward South Carolina, where Bush's chief strategist, Karl Rove, employed the dark arts he'd learned as a protégé of Lee Atwater, the strategist who had engineered the elder Bush's election in 1988. Just as Atwater had demolished Michael Dukakis by tying him to an African-American murderer, Rove spread rumors that McCain, the adoptive father of a daughter born in Bangladesh, had fathered an illegitimate Black child. McCain didn't stand a chance among white voters in the first state to secede from the Union in 1860. With his win in the Palmetto State, Bush effectively sewed up the nomination.

Once the primary balloting was finished, Bush appointed Dick Cheney to head the committee recommending the ticket's vice presidential running mate. Cheney, secretary of defense during George H. W.'s war to pry Kuwait from the hands of Saddam Hussein, conducted an exhaustive search that ended in his suggesting . . . himself. The callow governor took the advice of the man who would soon lead the new president to another, more decisive war against the Iraqi villain.

Thanks to ballot irregularities in Florida, the vanity campaign of Ralph Nader, and a Supreme Court unashamed to rule according to its partisan preferences, Bush became the first candidate since 1888 to win the White House despite losing the national popular vote. Analysts who expected Bush to govern with a sense of modesty born of his narrow, disputed victory were proven wrong when Bush steered the government toward a hard right turn in a variety of domestic areas, such as worker safety, wilderness conservation, social spending, and the environment. His central domestic legislative achievement came months into his presidency, when he persuaded Congress, with a GOP majority in both houses, to pass tax cuts weighted heavily toward the wealthy. Overnight the new rates erased the federal budget surplus achieved during the Clinton years yet did nothing to restore the American economy to the Clinton boom times. On September 10, 2001, Bush seemed headed to a single term in office.

Bush's performance the next day—continuing to read a children's story to an elementary school class for several minutes after an aide had whispered in his ear that the nation was under attack; flying stealthily to military air bases, not bravely to the nation's capital—earned him few plaudits. But in the days that followed he assumed the persona of a decisive leader during a time of crisis. Three days after the attack, speaking through a bullhorn at the site of the leveled World Trade Center towers in New York, he vowed retribution against "the people who knocked these buildings down."

In his speech to a joint session of Congress six days later, he rallied a shaken nation and promised righteous vengeance. Notably, with anti-Muslim sentiment cresting, this evangelical Christian president visited a Washington mosque to demonstrate that America's quarrel was not with a religion but with a group of terrorists. But that gesture did little to quell the bigotry that would surge, in no small measure because of the wars Bush would undertake and the way he would fight them. Bush's posturing cemented his image as a manly commander in chief. His negligence prior to 9/11—it was soon documented that he had been warned that Al Qaeda was planning an attack on US soil but did nothing to prevent it—never seemed to register with the public at large.

Bush took his nation to war twice in the aftermath of the attacks—both times to disastrous effect. In Afghanistan, the US military deposed the ruling Taliban but, because of poor planning and an insufficient force level, allowed the mastermind of the attacks, Osama bin Laden, to slip through American fingers. And then he made one of the worst decisions in the history of American foreign policy when he ordered American troops to invade Iraq and topple the regime of Saddam Hussein. Why did Bush focus American vengeance for the 9/11 attacks on the Iraqi dictator, who was in no way responsible for those attacks? Perhaps because the leaders driving the early Bush administration, Vice President Cheney and the equally arrogant Secretary of Defense Donald Rumsfeld, saw the world through ideological filters that discounted the harm done by non-state actors like bin Laden and inflated that done by regional tyrants like Hussein. Perhaps because Bush believed the bogus intelligence Cheney brought before him purporting to show Hussein's massive arsenal of weapons of mass destruction. Perhaps because Bush bought into the neoconservative fantasy of making a show of American power in an important region in the world. Perhaps because Saddam Hussein had plotted to assassinate Bush's father. Perhaps because the son needed to outdo that father, who had punished the Iraqi dictator in 1991 but had stopped short of unseating him. Whatever the reason, the war did not add up as a response to the terror attacks of 9/11 or as a deterrent to future attacks.

Bush's plan for the aftermath of toppling the Iraqi regime seemed to go no further than putting the grateful population to work sweeping up the rose petals they had scattered at the feet of the noble American liberators. When the people of Iraq did not greet the Americans with adulation, and when they were not thrilled with the American plan to install as their new leaders Iraqi emigres with ties to the Republican Party, the occupiers had neither the ideas nor the resources to deal with the resulting chaos.

George W. Bush's war in Iraq was a strategic disaster, exposing flaws and weaknesses in the US government and military, branding the American president as a man who had unleashed a foreign invasion based on lies, and removing a regional counterweight to Iran, a rival more threatening than Iraq to the interests of the United States and its allies in the region. Of course, the war was a moral disaster as well, causing the deaths of some 4,500 American service members and perhaps half a million Iraqis.

As damaged as America's reputation was by the needless carnage incurred during the invasion of Iraq, Bush's approval of torture in the interrogation of suspected terrorists brought even more egregious moral infamy on a nation that saw itself as a moral beacon. The callow president, evidently swayed by the bleak worldview of his vice president and defense secretary, and in the throes of an arrogance born of insufficient understanding, seemed never to comprehend the shame he brought upon the United States of America. Nor did he even appreciate the ineffectiveness of seeking intelligence through torture when the more humane techniques of experienced investigators, people derided by torture supporters as "soft," produced more reliable information. Bush's boosters in Congress and the press praised him for bringing "moral clarity" to US foreign policy. But press reports, some including photographs, of waterboarding and stress positions, of foreign black sites, extrajudicial rendition, and enhanced interrogation techniques, made a mockery of Bush's so-called freedom agenda.

As much as any event during his time in the White House, the Iraq War displayed a president in over his head, unaware of the limitations imposed by his insecurity and incompetence.

CLEAN AIR-COOL PLANET: Working the Senate on Behalf of the Climate

Again, Andy needed a job. This time an offer came via an old friend and comrade-in-arms. "Rafe Pomerance and I had worked together since the earliest days I was in Congress," Andy says, "and then at World Resources Institute. He's also part of my men's group. We've had a fifty-year relationship." In 2009, Andy signed on as senior adviser to an organization formed by Pomerance to advocate for action on climate change. "Rafe had created Clean Air-Cool Planet as the latest iteration of his continuing involvement and leadership, and he brought me in. Unlike my time with Lob-Levyt, Rafe and I worked together hand in glove. Lots of mutual admiration and respect for what each of us was accomplishing in life."

The time seemed right for a breakthrough in the federal response to climate change. After losing the presidential election in 2000, former vice president Al Gore began touring the country with a lecture called "An Inconvenient Truth," a presentation arguing for urgency in addressing the challenge of a warming planet. A book and documentary film based on that talk came out in 2006—the book was a bestseller, the film won an Oscar. Public opinion surveys showed rising awareness of the issue and support for governmental action. Even President George W. Bush's consciousness seemed to be raised by his former rival's work. Through most of his presidency, Bush, a proud product of the Texas oil business, had minimized the existence and severity of climate change. Shortly after his inauguration in 2001 he declined to implement the Kyoto Protocol, the broad international agreement, signed by the United States during the Clinton administration, that recognized the threat of climate change and committed the treaty's signatories to reductions in emissions of greenhouse gases. Consistently, his administration parroted the climate disinformation propagated by the energy industry and suppressed honest discussion of climate change by government scientists.

In September 2007, however, with his popularity dissolving over unfinished wars and a lackluster economy, Bush finally made a public gesture toward addressing the issue: He hosted an international conference on the subject. "We must lead the world to produce fewer greenhouse gas emissions," he said. But, as the *New York Times* reported, Bush's "calls for each country to decide for itself how to rein in pollution, and his refusal to embrace mandatory measures, have set the United States apart from other countries . . . ." The world did not take seriously Bush's commitment to the effort. Sixteen nations took part in the gathering, but all sent non-senior officials as their representatives. Germany's environmental minister attended the conference but also made time for two meetings with congressional Democrats; within a year and a half, the minister noted, Bush would be out of office.

The Democratic president who replaced Bush pledged in his campaign to mount a robust effort to counteract climate change—proposed steps included investments in clean energy and mandatory limits on emissions. However, once Barack Obama took office in January 2009, two factors prevented his fulfilling that promise. First, he had to address an economic emergency. The financial panic of 2008, due in large part to lax regulation of the finance and mortgage industries and a nationwide bubble in real estate, forced the new administration to focus its attention on preventing a second Great Depression. Following up on efforts begun by the exiting Bush administration, Obama and his team averted such a catastrophe. Nonetheless, in the year and a half that followed the demise of the investment bank Bear Stearns, whose March 2008 failure presaged the full-blown financial panic that would overtake Wall Street that autumn, the US rate of unemployment doubled, from 5 to 10 percent. As the country embarked on a protracted recovery—unemployment would not return to 5 percent for another six years—action on climate seemed to many a luxury a traumatized nation could ill afford.

Second, Obama and his allies in Congress saw a historic opportunity to implement thorough reform of the US health care system, a dream of presidents and congresses for a century. The fight to pass the Affordable Care Act, nicknamed Obamacare, dominated Washington's legislative agenda for the first year of the Obama presidency. Relying on large Democratic majorities in both the House and the Senate, Obama and his allies in Congress succeeded in enacting Obamacare in March 2010 despite months of determined opposition by the Republican Party, right-wing media, conservative activists, major corporations, and reactionary billionaires, nearly all unconcerned whether the wild accusations they leveled against the plan—"death panels," "tyranny," "Marxism"—bore any resemblance to reality. After that ordeal, neither the president nor Democrats in Congress had appetite for knockdown, drag-out battles over other contentious issues, including climate.

However, early in Obama's first term, before the frenzy over the Affordable Care Act derailed most other legislative opportunities, the House of Representatives did take action on climate change. Two of the most influential and active advocates of climate action in that body, Henry Waxman of California and Ed Markey of Massachusetts, both close friends and colleagues of Andy's from his time on the Hill, sponsored far-reaching legislation. The Waxman-Markey bill, formally named the American Clean Energy and Security Act of 2009, in accordance with the wishes of the Obama administration and in a concession to the reality of what was and wasn't achievable, did not take the simplest, albeit more costly and polarizing, approach to carbon emissions: Set fixed emissions limits and mandate that industry meet them at each facility. Rather, Waxman-Markey relied on a flexible "cap-and-trade" system of controls, with total levels of emissions lowered over time to targets identical to those called for by Obama during his campaign. Those who reduced emissions more than required could sell surplus reductions at a profit to those whose reduction costs were much higher. Like the successful Acid Rain Program, this approach aimed to cut overall reduction costs in the United States by 50 percent or more. Among its many provisions, the bill also devoted funds to alternative energy technology and energy efficiency, mandated improvements in energy efficiency in various sectors of the economy, and added incentives for the use of electric vehicles.

Conservatives criticized the legislation as harmful to the economy, even as corporate behemoths like Ford, Dow Chemical, and General Electric supported the bill as a creative alternative to rigid "command and control" regulation. While many major environmental advocacy organizations favored Waxman-Markey, other climate activists cited its corporate support as evidence that the bill was a half-measure at best, with solutions not equal to the massive challenges threatening the planet. Waxman, Markey, and their allies in the House, including Speaker Nancy Pelosi, engaged in prolonged lobbying of the Democratic caucus, with a variety of inducements extended to win corporate backing of the bill and the votes such backing would bring. As one journalist put it, "By the time it was voted on, Waxman-Markey was more than 1,200 pages long, full of provisions for favored corporations, complicated offset schemes and loopholes for existing coal plants. By the end Campbell's Soup even demanded a deal for the carbon-intensive process of making soup. . . ." In June 2009, Waxman, Markey, and Pelosi eked out a victory, 219 votes to 212, securing eight GOP votes in favor to offset the forty-four Democratic votes against.

The Senate was another matter. And that's where Andy and Clean Air-Cool Planet came in.

Founded in 1999, Clean Air-Cool Planet was, as Andy wrote in a grant application, "in the business of helping to alleviate the causes and effects of global warming by educating, engaging, and mobilizing Americans to take action on climate change. A science-based, non-partisan

501(c)3 organization, CA-CP has succeeded in energizing universities, businesses, communities, citizen's groups, and institutions to reduce their own greenhouse gas emissions and to bring concern about climate change directly to their elected officials and the presidential candidates to demand action."

During Andy's tenure at CA-CP, his focus was on building public support for climate legislation in the Senate. Unfortunately, the Senate was in no mood to simply give its approval to the legislation approved by the House. "Waxman-Markey," he recalls, "was sponsored by two very good friends of mine. But to get that bill passed they had to sell every piece of the furniture to somebody or other. There would be free rides for entities like utilities and farm organizations. The bill was over a thousand pages long. It was finally brokered through on a narrow vote by Waxman giving away, free, twenty years of 'This won't really affect you.' The whole Waxman-Markey bill was worked out, in principle, with a group of utilities that wanted (a) to be on the right side of the issue, or appear to be, and (b) to somehow benefit from whatever changes were going to happen in power generation. To get the last few votes, Waxman had to include giveaways.

"So the original utilities partners, validated in turn by environmental outfits like the Environmental Defense Fund, produced a set of principles. And Waxman and Markey, bless their hearts, put it all together and decided that one of the strategies was to have international offsets available: If you planted trees or cleaned up animal waste, even in some other country, you'd get an offset to your emissions. That was part of the mix, so that international corporations could figure out how to manage this new system. And then there were the very specific giveaways to the agriculture people that had to be added into the bill at the end. It became an undigestible piece of legislation which senators, and certainly the public, didn't understand."

Andy 's role was to put into action the vision of his old friend. "Pomerance is not himself an administrator," he says. "He's always right on the cutting edge of whatever the issue is, but I was basically the implementer. I got done what he wanted to get done, He contacted Holtz-Eakin, but I put him to work." Andy partnered with Douglas Holtz-Eakin, a Republican economist, in applying for and receiving funding of $250,000 from the Energy Foundation, a nonprofit organization advocating for clean energy. "Even though Holtz-Eakin and I disagreed about pretty much every other major national issue, on this we were in total agreement. We teamed up to figure out how he could exert maximum influence by traveling to states with key senators who could be persuaded to support proposals with respect to carbon pricing. He was brilliant when he went out and made these speeches and had meals with business leaders in places like North and South Carolina, Montana, Indiana. Especially states with Republican senators who might be brought along, but also states with Democratic senators who, if left alone, would track with corporate interests. What we needed was a counterpoise to the heavy-duty businesspeople whose contributions supported these senators. To talk sense to these senators about how great it would be not just for the environment, but also for the economy, to do a farsighted yet practical climate bill."

The goal was something that could pass in the Senate, and Andy headed CA-CP's effort to influence that body. "We worked with Lee Wasserman, director of the Rockefeller Family Fund," he says, "with Hal Harvey at the Energy Foundation, with Adele Morris, a top economist at Brookings. She was one of the people outlining the approach we were advocating in the Senate, a much simpler way of moving forward than had been set up in the House bill. We understood, maybe before John Kerry did, certainly before Joe Lieberman, Lindsey Graham, and John McCain did, that there was no way on God's green earth that the House bill could ever get a decent hearing in the Senate, that what was needed was a much slimmer package, more easily understandable, a form of carbon pricing, maybe with the proceeds going directly back to citizens at large—which actually was a proposal made by Senator Susan Collins of Maine. We were all working on this together.

"We tried to avoid the word *tax*. What we needed was a thoughtful, gradual raising of the price of carbon over time, with a predesignated dollar-per-ton ceiling and a support floor, so that the financial structure would not be subject to the vagaries of economic activity. The proposal had what we called a 'safety valve,' so that the numbers on the ceiling and floor could be adjusted in the future as needed. The plan would get the job done, not immediately but over a period of years. A 'price collar' we called the plan, or 'a collar with a safety valve.' The idea was for something not as scary to politicians, or to the public, as a 'carbon tax,' which of course was a nonstarter. Ever since George H. W. Bush mouthed the words 'Read my lips: No new taxes,' everyone feared anything that seemed like a raise of taxes. The Waxman-Markey bill looked to people too much like a big, immediate tax on carbon, with giveaways to all the bad actors.

"The main thing was that you would be making progress in some way. A simple proposal along those lines, with the money raised going back into people's pockets—that's the only way the Senate could have delivered. I explained that, but it didn't help. I met with the majority leader of the House, Steny Hoyer, from Maryland, in the hope that in talking with the Senate he would send a signal that said, 'We in the House would be perfectly happy if you guys want to come up with a totally different bill, because we think you can get it passed. A simple bill that would meet the objective'—that was basically the legislation Pomerance & Co. had designed. Hoyer's response was, in effect, 'Well, we've done our job.'

"If only the Senate had chosen this approach, if only McCain, Lieberman, and Graham had understood there was a possible path and that this was roughly what that path would look like. If only John Kerry had understood it well enough—he was the point person who was trying to maneuver stuff in the Senate, because he was so committed on climate. If these senators and their staffs had read the sorts of papers that were coming out of the Brookings Institution and Resources for the Future, where we had excellent contacts. These economists absolutely supported what we were trying to do. Our approach was the most rational and practical way of getting the Senate to move forward. We were in constant touch with these people at these highly respected institutions. Getting them to write stuff, keeping them up to date on what we were doing.

"If the Senate had taken that approach, then they could have gone to conference with the Waxman-Markey bill and maybe come up with something that made sense to the public."

Andy pulled out every stop as he tried to sway senators. "I dealt with CEOs and did outreach to senior officials at two important US energy utilities, Exelon and Entergy," he says. "We designed and ran a full-page ad in *Congressional Quarterly* and in the *Hill* at the critical moment when senators and their staffs would be looking at them. I was talking to the Brookings, Resources for the Future, Energy Foundation, and Rockefeller economists who supported what we were doing, trying to put a picture together that would be attractive to the senators who were actually interested in doing something. We worked senior Senate staff people.

"But the Senate never took on the notion that they needed to come up with a much simpler vehicle that could appeal across party lines and had the support of top economists. They were mired in the Waxman-Markey omnibus legislation. They couldn't seem to step away from that in the Senate.

"We never could get there. A number of us in various institutions, in Washington and across the country, were trying to square the circle on this. But we couldn't get there. During the summer of 2010 Harry Reid, the Senate majority leader, gave up on it. He never put it on the floor, because by then—more than a year after Waxman-Markey had passed the House—there wasn't any way of assembling a large-enough combination of Democratic and Republican senators in the 111th Congress, no matter what the bill was."

Ed Markey, after his bill passed in the House, had looked forward to Senate passage. "Our thought was that it would be difficult," he recalls, "but that the Senate would find a way of getting the sixty votes that were necessary." With the GOP invoking the filibuster rule on nearly every piece of legislation short of naming post offices, any environmental legislation needed this supermajority to become law.

"What happened," Markey continues, "was that the Republicans decided to demonize the health care bill in August of 2009, as it emerged from the Energy and Commerce Committee. They decided to target it, saying it called for death panels.

"This fight sapped a lot of the political capital that we had thought would be there for both bills. And by the time the health care bill finally got over the finish line, it delayed our ability to be able to move to the climate bill. If we had started with the climate bill over in the Senate, and used all the political capital on the climate bill first, then I think there was a real chance we could have gotten to sixty. John Kerry was working very hard on that. They had fifty-five votes. There were a number of Senate Republicans who were definitely interested in working toward a bipartisan bill.

"So I do think that there was a path. But the sequencing of the consideration of those bills diminished the remaining political capital. A lot of the political capital that year was also consumed by Dodd-Frank"—legislation to curb the financial industry excesses responsible for the 2008–2009 economic meltdown. "That was an emergency situation, where we had to move in and cauterize the whole financial system in the country. From my perspective, the climate bill was passable."

But climate denialism had taken hold of the Republican Party. And even GOP senators who believed in the science of climate change saw, by early 2010, a wounded president and winnable midterm elections. The Tea Party movement had begun, formed in spontaneous response to the economic crisis and the prospect of federal health care legislation, but expanded with the determined backing of deep-pocketed contributors, most notably the reactionary billionaire Koch brothers. The Tea Party featured people acting out their white resentment and anti-government rage in noisy rallies guaranteed to dominate cable news broadcasts. What's more, support for carbon control was far from unanimous among Democratic senators, with senators from farm and coal states balking at the idea. In 1990, Congress and the Bush (41) administration had overcome regional and party differences to achieve progress on acid rain. Twenty years later, attitudes had become too polarized to bridge.

The president was not much help, either. "We were very unhappy with the Obama White House because of their inattention to this issue," says Andy. "Their unwillingness to extend themselves on it. Their unwillingness to use their chips with individual senators in any way whatsoever. It was a huge disappointment. I don't know whether you can say, 'Well, health care took up all the bandwidth.' I did think Obama was absolutely right to work on reforming health care. We'd been trying to do that for decades.

"We worked the White House hard, and all we got was a little bit of rhetoric here and there: 'Good luck. Good luck, guys.'"

Obama never applied his administration's energy to the issue, even after the largest marine oil disaster in history, the Deepwater Horizon spill in the Gulf of Mexico off the coast of Louisiana, provided a perfect pretext for climate action. He didn't deliver a major speech on climate change, he didn't make a concerted effort to counter Republican lies and obstruction on the issue.

"I'm sure it was a bandwidth problem for the Obama team," says Andy. "And despite Obama's wonderful posturing on issue after issue after issue, if you look beneath the surface, you find a centralizing president who was perfectly comfortable with corporate interests."

The demise of the climate legislation meant another career shift for Andy. "After the Senate failed to act in July 2010," he says, "we had to fold our tent. There was nothing more to do. CA-CP disappeared.

"So again, I was looking for a job."

WHITE HOUSE FAILURE: Hurricane Katrina

Bush centered his 2004 reelection bid on fear. The failures in the wars in Iraq and Afghanistan had not yet been made manifest, enabling the Bush campaign to focus on his image as the wartime leader actively protecting the nation from the global threat of terrorism. At the Republican convention in Boston, the GOP faithful trolled Massachusetts Senator John Kerry by wearing Band-Aids fashioned after the military's Purple Heart decoration to mock the wounds suffered by the Democratic nominee as a young naval officer in Vietnam—while Bush spent the war flying joy rides above Texas. Bush also managed to depict Kerry as an effete elitist, even though both men had come from wealthy families and had been members of Skull and Bones at Yale. But Bush cleared brush and mangled the English language while Kerry windsurfed—in a wetsuit!—and spoke French. The election was close, but this time Bush won the popular vote as well as the Electoral College. The balloting in 2004 marked the only time after 1988, and through 2020, that a Republican presidential candidate won the popular vote.

Bush opened his second term with an initiative to privatize Social Security; a right-wing dream for decades, the scheme was quickly shot down by officials smart enough to know that it meant political suicide for any member of Congress foolish enough to support it. Bush might have muddled through the rest of his presidency had the weather not intervened. On August 29, 2005, Hurricane Katrina struck Louisiana, Mississippi, and Alabama. The storm's worst damage was suffered by New Orleans, where waters of the Gulf of Mexico overwhelmed levees to inundate large areas of the city and render hundreds of thousands of residents homeless. Bush's response to the disaster was sluggish, tone-deaf, and inept; again, he was not up to the task. As the storm was looming, with warnings of impending catastrophe, and then as it commenced its destruction, Bush barely reacted. He waited two days before leaving his Texas vacation to return to the White House to supervise federal efforts; during his flight back to Washington he allowed himself to be photographed looking at the flooded city out the window of Air Force One, lacking the self-awareness to understand the above-it-all callousness inherent in such an image. Charged with leading the government's response to the disaster, Bush's Federal Emergency Management Agency floundered, revealing itself as a dumping ground for political hacks—a fitting product of a conservative ideology that for decades had derided competent governance. When the president finally traveled to the stricken area, he seemed more concerned with the fate of the washed-out vacation home of the (wealthy, white) Senate majority leader than with the plight of the (mostly poor, mostly Black or brown) citizens of New Orleans huddling in crowded, poorly supplied shelters. Katrina, added to the worsening fiascos in Iraq and Afghanistan, ended any hope of Bush's enjoying a productive final three years as president.

REVISITING AN OLD CAUSE: Toxic Substances and a Stint at the Environmental Defense Fund

Andy's next job came from the Environmental Defense Fund, one of the nation's oldest and most influential environmental advocacy organizations. "I learned that EDF was interviewing for a senior position leading a segment of their work that related to toxic substances and environmental chemicals," Andy recalls. EDF was seeking a revision of the Toxic Substances Control Act (TSCA), which had come out of Andy's House committee and passed in 1976. "It had become painfully clear that TSCA was basically toothless. There were too many accommodations to outside pressures in the way the thing was finally put together; it needed an update. EDF had a very interesting, very competent lead senior scientist, Richard Denison, whose responsibility had been to try to work with the Hill to make progress on that effort.

"It just so happened that Bill Bradley's former administrative assistant, Marcia Aronoff, was EDF's senior vice president for programs. She had always been one of my fans, so I wrote her a note and she brought me in to see her. She told me, 'We're pretty far along on this hire, but I'll stop the process so we can consider you.' She asked me to write something, so I produced a ten-page paper on all the stuff I thought EDF could do to forward this part of their agenda. At the time EDF was all wrapped up, as everybody was, in figuring out the next step in climate action after the Senate had bailed. I was hired.

"Meanwhile, on toxic substances, Denison and Fred Krupp, EDF's president, had just opened up discussions with the associations representing pharmaceutical and chemical companies. I was immediately thrust into those talks, which were discouraging, because the industry people wanted to do nothing. Eighty thousand synthetic chemicals had come onto the market over a period of years, being developed and bought and sold, finding their way into commerce, including into many consumer products, without having been properly tested."

Andy's pioneering work on the environmental causes of cancer had been one of the most consequential and distinguishing threads of his congressional career. "That's why Aronoff was interested in having me at EDF," he says, "because I was there at the birth of TSCA. There had been a huge bias for decades in the governmental and private sectors toward the approach that said, 'Once somebody gets cancer, how can we best deal with it?' We had tried to turn that around to say, 'It looks as if there are significant environmental inputs that produce, or assist in the producing of, cancers. We should put more emphasis on that.'"

Since the 1970s, attitudes on the subject had changed. "There was good movement on that front among specialists, scientists, and environmental organizations," Andy notes. "Among corporations, too, which took pains to explain, for a combination of genuine and public relations reasons, that particular products had been carefully scrutinized in order to provide pluses, not minuses, for consumers. A lot of progress, whereas on climate change there had been nothing but backward movement for a couple of decades. Nobody was running around denying that there were environmental causes of cancer the way people were running around denying that climate change existed or that if it did, we didn't need to worry about it."

Andy's activities at EDF started with planning the next edition of the organization's biannual two-day seminar. The topic this time would be toxic substances. "Meanwhile," he says, "discussions were continuing not just with the pharmaceutical manufacturers' association but also with an outside coalition of NGOs for which this was the biggest issue. I was in the middle of all that and at the same time I was raising money for this part of EDF's operation.

"Krupp opened a couple of doors, and we worked really hard on proposals. We worked with board members who had a particular interest in this area, but the fundraising was tough sledding. I labored on all this for a couple of years. The preliminary negotiations on the revision of TSCA, with both industry and public interest groups, ground on and on and on. Every time Richard Denison came up with what he thought was a formula that would move things forward, one or the other of these parties would object. Fred Krupp took less and less direct interest. He liked to swing for the fences. He had a major donor whom he tried to talk into dumping a couple of million dollars into this area. But Krupp wasn't able to deliver that money.

"Those were two tracks: discussions with industry and discussions with the outside environmental groups. A third track was talking with the Senate, in particular with Frank Lautenberg, ironically enough. Because it was Frank Lautenberg who was taking the lead in the Senate on reforming TSCA." To this day, Andy remains bitter over his loss to Frank Lautenberg—more specifically, to Frank Lautenberg's millions—in the 1982 New Jersey Democratic senatorial primary. "But I set all that aside for purposes of trying to bring Lautenberg as far along the curve as I could on this legislation. And it was easy because he was already there. It was just a question, as it always was, of what could be negotiated with the special interests. By this time in the nation's history, passing legislation was no longer a matter of a balance between corporate influence on the one hand and union and public interest group influence on the other. It was all very much tilted toward the corporate side for everything you worked on.

"The corporate lobbying groups had a lot more sway with senators and representatives in 2012 than back in 1976. The original bill, in '76, was definitely weakened as a result of pressures from industry. But it was that times three by the time we got to the twenty teens. Corporate contributions had skyrocketed, even before Citizens United"—the 2010 Supreme Court decision that permitted virtually unlimited corporate support of political campaigns.

"Lautenberg did the best he could," Andy continued. "We worked hard with him to bring along the Republicans on the committee, and a few years after I left EDF, a bill was passed. It wasn't a great bill. It set up a regime where EPA would within the first six months set up risk evaluations on ten chemicals; after another three years, there would be twenty ongoing evaluations." The Frank R. Lautenberg Chemical Safety for the 21st Century Act, signed into law in 2016, also established a new "risk-based safety standard" for chemicals that excluded consideration of cost and required consideration of "risks to susceptible and highly exposed populations." "Of course," notes Andy, "one of the things the EPA relied on to figure out what the targeted substances should be was the Maguire Report," the National Cancer Institute's annual status report on carcinogens, mandated by Congress in 1978.

"I left EDF after two years, again discouraged at how difficult it is to move the puck in a serious way given all the powerful interests involved. I was also feeling that I hadn't received the kind of support from Krupp that I had anticipated, that he'd promised he would provide. When he read my original ten-page paper he told me it was the best presentation he'd ever received from someone applying for a job at EDF, but during my two years there, I would say he was more notable by his absence and his inattention to my little slice of the organizational pie. In addition, Marcia Aronoff retired just a couple of months after I joined, and I didn't feel that her replacement was quite in the same league. Krupp and I agreed to part ways. So once again, pluses and minuses.

"I didn't like how meager the results were. At the same time, my beloved wife, Adele, was beginning to decline from early onset Alzheimer's, and we decided to move back to New Jersey to be closer to her family."

AN ODD PASSIVITY: The Presidency of Barack Obama

The election of a Black man to the White House in 2008 seemed to signal that the United States had finally put an end to racism as a significant societal force. Barack Obama, it was said—the person and the phenomenon—was "post-racial." His mother was white; his father, whom he barely knew, was Kenyan; he was raised in multiracial Hawaii; he'd lived in Indonesia. His stirring oratory could rouse stadiums packed with people of all backgrounds. He didn't sound particularly "Black"—at least not when talking to majority-white audiences. He seemed a product less of Black America (at least as white Americans perceive Black America) than of the upper-echelon academic and intellectual circles associated with his two Ivy League alma maters. Yet for all that the presidency of Barack Obama was heralded as proof of a new racial reality, Obama's service ultimately made clear that America's original sin was alive and well. What followed the presidency of Barack Obama was the presidency of Donald Trump, whose election would not have been possible without the presidency of Barack Obama. The core of Trumpism is racism, a backlash to efforts to normalize the presence of Black people in all aspects of American life. And what such normalization could be more hateful to racists than a Black president of the United States?

Obama can hardly be blamed for this reaction to his presidency, but he, like so many others, was over-optimistic as to the distance his election could put between old and new attitudes on race. He first gained national attention with a speech touting the unity of American purpose. "There's not a liberal America and a conservative America; there's the United States of America," he said in 2004. "There's not a Black America and white America and Latino America and Asian America; there's the United States of America." Then a state senator from Illinois running for a seat in the US Senate, he was delivering the keynote address to the Democratic National Convention that nominated John Kerry. Nearly two decades later, with as much as 40 percent of the country embracing bigotry over democracy, perhaps the best that can be said of the speech is that it was aspirational, showing the way to a more equitable society. But it's hard not to see it as tragically naive.

What gave Obama's campaign for the White House in 2008 its initial rationale among Democratic primary voters was that he, unlike his chief rival, New York Senator Hillary Rodham Clinton, had spoken against the Iraq War from the beginning, whereas Clinton had made what had seemed to be the safe move at the time in voting to authorize it. Obama survived missteps that seemed to confirm views of him as an NPR-listener elitist: Talking with Iowa farmers about falling crop prices, he noted the high price of arugula at Whole Foods. He was trying to suggest that farmers diversify their products, but he outed himself as the kind of person who would know the price of arugula at Whole Foods. Later, to counter reports that he drank only imported craft beer, he made a point of sitting down in a working-class bar and ordering, as he said, "a Bud"—no doubt appalled at the political circus that forced him to drink such swill.

While he offered a long list of specific policies and programs he hoped to pursue—most notably, reform of the nation's health care system—he based his campaign on two nonideological slogans highlighting unity and optimism: "Hope and Change" and "Yes, We Can." While Clinton proved a formidable opponent, Obama prevailed, thanks in large part to his campaign's superior understanding of the primary-and-caucus nominating system. To balance a ticket headed by the first nonwhite major party presidential nominee in the nation's history, he chose as his vice president a familiar white male, Joe Biden, whose earthy reputation as "Middle Class Joe" complemented Obama's lofty image as a brainy law professor.

In November 2008 Obama faced Arizona Senator John McCain, the war hero who, since losing the nomination in 2000 to Bush, had remade his "maverick" profile into the persona of a standard conservative Republican whom the party could trust with its nomination. In 2008, he made one mistake that above all else stains his legacy: He chose Alaska governor Sarah Palin as his running mate. McCain and his team were looking for an unconventional choice to shake up a race they knew they were likely to lose, and so the senator, on impulse, chose a woman he and his staff barely knew and had not adequately vetted. Palin soon showed herself to be woefully unqualified for national office, lacking requisite experience, knowledge, and temperament, and forming an awkward pair with McCain, the third-generation naval hero who prided himself on selfless devotion to the nation's service. Palin's ignorance and propensity for word salad made her an easy target for ridicule; even so, the press and the political system had trouble adjusting to a candidate so obviously unsuited to the job she was seeking. The media never fully appreciated the threat to the polity posed by her brand of abusive, know-nothing populism. McCain and Palin lost the election, but the example set by the Alaskan—a national candidate spewing baseless innuendo, centering her appeal on white Christian grievance—helped prepare the nation for a more adept practitioner of those arts eight years later. The GOP's embrace of authoritarianism did not begin with Donald Trump—it's certainly traceable at least as far back as Joseph McCarthy. But there were accelerants along the way to today's disdain for democracy among the Party of Lincoln. Sarah Palin, unleashed upon the nation by an otherwise honorable senator from Arizona, was one of them.

Upon taking office, Obama's top priority was clear: avert economic catastrophe. As policy-makers grappled with the real possibility of a second Great Depression, the new president called for an economic rescue package involving $825 billion in new spending. Congress worked swiftly; just three weeks after Obama took office, it enacted legislation that, at $787 billion, nearly met Obama's number. Critics charged that the sum was unequal to the task and that a more effective negotiator would have made a larger initial request in order to secure a larger result. Obama and his aides argued that he got as much as he could considering the need for votes from conservative congressional Democrats and a handful of

Republicans. Whether Obama misread the situation or his critics did, the insufficient size of the American Recovery and Reinvestment Act made the nation's economic recovery slower than it need have been.

In one area, Obama succeeded where a long list of presidents had failed: He oversaw the enactment of a massive overhaul of the American health care system. In his initial efforts to create the Affordable Care Act, he reached out to Republican legislators. Willing to incorporate their pet ideas into his to gain their support, he expected the cooperation of at least some of them. However, just as Republicans had been determined to deny Bill Clinton a victory in the health care wars sixteen years earlier, GOP legislators in 2009 and 2010 ultimately showed no interest in contributing to anything Barack Obama or the Democrats in Congress could, in upcoming midterm and presidential elections, cite as an accomplishment.

Obama—and Democrats in general—never matched the intensity and absolute commitment of the Republicans, who never allowed outdated ideas of cooperation and the public good to deter them from their pursuit of power. "The single most important thing we want to achieve is for President Obama to be a one-term president," Mitch McConnell said in 2010. From their unsuccessful attempt to torpedo Obamacare, to McConnell's unprecedented use of the filibuster to block nearly every piece of enlightened legislation, to the unwillingness of so many elected GOP officials to definitively rebut the notion that Obama was not a natural-born US citizen, to what McConnell has pointed to as his proudest moment—his denial of Obama's attempt to appoint a Supreme Court justice late in his term—Republicans remained focused on their goal: control of all three branches of government. Democrats shook their heads but rarely responded in kind.

Obama did win reelection in 2012, running on a recovering economy, his appeal to a widened electorate, and his exacting of revenge against Osama bin Laden—Navy Seals, on command of the president, had killed the architect of the 9/11 attacks in May 2011. He also ran against the competent but flawed Mitt Romney, the former governor of a liberal state, Massachusetts. Romney had governed as a moderate Republican but, bowing to the needs of running as a national Republican, now billed himself as "severely conservative." The man was in a quandary. The GOP's bugaboo was Obama's health care reform. But as governor of the Bay State, Romney had instituted a system nearly identical to Obama's legislation. How, credibly, could he oppose Obamacare? The GOP standard-bearer never resolved that contradiction. Moreover, while Obama struck many as an intellectual elitist, Romney reeked of upper-class entitlement. The son of a famous auto executive and moderate Republican governor of Michigan, Mitt Romney had amassed a fortune—hundreds of millions of dollars—as a private equity pirate. Two months before Election Day, video surfaced of his telling a meeting of wealthy donors that "my job is not to worry about" the 47 percent of the US population who paid no income tax (while not mentioning that they paid plenty in other taxes). Such Americans, Romney said, because they believed that "the government has a responsibility to care for them," were automatic supporters of the incumbent. The release of the recording sealed his loss.

Despite Obama's reelection, his failure to appreciate the changed nature of political competition cost him, his party, and the nation. After Obamacare passed in March 2010, with features guaranteed to please the public—lower premiums, a ban on denial of care due to preexisting conditions, the ability to maintain coverage even after losing a job—the president, with the midterms approaching, conceded to Republican framing of the legislation. Not that he agreed that the legislation was the last step before the nation found itself mired in socialist tyranny, but he failed to tout the landmark improvement in American life that he and his party had just delivered. Instead, he treated the ACA as the skunk at the garden party, barely mentioning it and, seemingly, hoping no one else would, either. He turned his focus to deficit reduction, the ultimate GOP sucker-punch. He even repeated the oft-spoken nostrum, debunked by economists—as he surely knew—that just as an ordinary American family has to make ends meet without borrowing money, so must the federal government. When the midterms came, the Democrats were, as he put it, "shellacked," losing their majorities in both houses of Congress along with numerous governorships and state legislatures.

Obama's passivity in the face of the long-term Republican power grab also produced disastrous consequences late in his term. Not long before Election Day in 2020, the president received evidence that Vladimir Putin's Russia was interfering in the 2020 presidential campaign on behalf of Donald Trump. He asked congressional leadership of both parties to join him in a strong public statement condemning the interference and warning Americans to be on guard against such propaganda. McConnell refused Obama's entreaty, claiming that allegations of Russian meddling amounted to a partisan attempt to swing the election toward the Democratic nominee, Hillary Clinton. Obama, rather than seizing the opportunity to confront the Russian threat, highlight the corruption of the Republican nominee, and condemn a party that didn't mind support from a foreign autocrat, opted to forgo comment on the issue. By not ringing the alarm, by not sharing publicly the proof he had of Russian interference, Obama permitted Trump and the Republicans to deny the truth. Perhaps Obama, like most other informed observers, believed Clinton would win the election and that the matter of Putin's malfeasance would be sorted out under her presidency. Or perhaps, despite eight years of Republican opposition and obstruction at his every step, he still didn't realize what he was up against. Or perhaps he lacked the temperament for bare-knuckled political combat.

Turning some 50,000 votes in three states from Trump to Clinton would have awarded the Electoral College to the Democrat and averted the nation's still-ongoing Trumpian nightmare. Would such a declaration by Obama have changed those votes?

BACK IN NEW JERSEY: Climate and Politics in the Garden State

"So, in mid-2013," Andy recalls, "I'm in New Jersey. I still wanted to do stuff, so I teamed up with former Republican representative Dick Zimmer. He didn't serve in Congress the same time I did, but we knew of each other and had a lot of mutual respect."

The project on which Andy cooperated with Zimmer arose out of Andy's prior relationship with the Union of Concerned Scientists. "They were among the people Pomerance and I worked with when I was at Clean Air-Cool Planet," he says. "We'd had sit-downs with UCS in DC about strategy in the Senate and so forth. I got to know some of their senior staff people. They came to me after they learned that I had returned to New Jersey. They wanted a response to Superstorm Sandy, which had wreaked havoc in the state the year before."

UCS paid Andy for his work on this effort, but Zimmer chose to work pro bono. "That didn't make any difference when Zimmer and I went around together to meet with people," says Andy.

"My idea," he continues, "was to get Governor Chris Christie to set up a blue-ribbon commission on extreme weather, a panel composed of top corporate leaders, top labor leaders, and top legislators. Zimmer and I ferried ourselves around the state for close to a year to line up a potential membership list for this commission. We talked to all these people, and every single one of them agreed: 'Yeah, sure, I'd serve on that.' The head of the AFL-CIO, the head of a chemical company, CEOs of telecommunication companies. The flooding from Sandy had short-circuited all sorts of activities around the Jersey shore—it was a disaster.

"Our thinking in pursuing this angle was: Christie was a candidate for president, and the only Republican running who had not slammed the door on the existence of climate change. All the rest of them had said, 'There is no such thing.' We thought, 'Here is a guy who has wide appeal both within the Republican Party and beyond. If he sets up a commission in his home state to seriously look at these issues, it would be nothing other than a plus for him.'

"We did not meet with Christie himself, but we met with his top people. Zimmer and I also met with two highly regarded former New Jersey governors, Republican Tom Kean and Democrat Brendan Byrne, both of whom agreed to co-chair such a commission if Christie set it up. We talked to Haley Barbour, in Washington, the former Mississippi governor who was a Republican with a lot of influence—he was one of Christie's top advisers. He said, 'Yeah, this makes sense to me.' He was going to talk to Christie and to all the outfits in New Jersey—the Sierra Club, etc.—that cared about extreme weather, which was a placeholder for climate change. I guess that was obvious.

"We worked on this idea for about a year and a half. But Christie and his top advisers evidently decided that he didn't want to go anywhere near this issue as a Republican candidate for president." Christie no doubt still felt burned by his party's hostility over his cooperation with President Obama in Sandy's aftermath. Sandy struck New Jersey on October 29, 2012. After the storm cleared, the president of the United States visited the Garden State to tour the destruction and promise federal disaster relief. Christie profusely thanked the president—who happened to be the Democratic candidate for the White House in the election to take place just days later. Christie defended his embrace—literal and figurative—of Obama by pointing to his own responsibility as governor of a state in distress. GOP stalwarts, however, were not willing to forgive his apostasy.

"So we did not succeed," says Andy, "even though we had two terrific co-chairs, each the most venerated former governor in the political party he represented. Even though the head of the AFL-CIO was ready to go. The heads of various corporations were ready to go.

"After it was clear that Christie wasn't going to move, we did the circuit of all the foundations in the state to try to get the commission done outside government. Zimmer knew some heads of foundations, I knew some heads of foundations. Tommy Byrne, Brendan Byrne's son, was well connected with foundations. Everybody thought it was a great idea, nobody wanted to pony up the money.

"I guess Christie and his people thought, 'Well, how helpful could this be to us?' We didn't want another study to go on the bookshelf. We wanted an action program that would mobilize top leaders in the state to get serious about preparing for the next iteration of extreme weather. It was becoming more and more clear, as time went on, that climate change needed to be a major issue, not just for New Jersey but across the country.

"But we couldn't get it done."

EPILOGUE

A PRODUCTIVE LIFE: Looking Back

I took risks. Some paid off hugely, others not. But how could it be otherwise?

—ANDY MAGUIRE

Andy Maguire formed his lifetime goal at a young age. "Here's what you're going to do: Make a difference," he told himself when only a preteen. As he grew older, he refined and expanded that ambition, adding a desire to lead. While working as an intern for a US senator, he rejected the life of a congressional staffer. "I want to be the one who helps make the decisions," he resolved. "I'm not going to Washington to hold somebody's briefcase." A job at the State Department promised a prestigious future—one that surely would have encompassed an ambassadorship or two. However, he says, "I had little desire to be an ambassador, because I thought ambassadors, except in unusual circumstances, were mostly message-runners, conveying notes between their posts and State in DC." And again that urge: "I wanted to be a decision-maker."

At State, Andy learned the basics of an elite federal government organization. In his next job, at the Office of Jamaica Planning and Development in Queens, New York, he performed his apprenticeship in community organizing and outreach. He would combine the two areas of skill in his next position, member of Congress, which remains the high point of his long career.

Sometimes Andy's colleagues criticized him as "arrogant" or overly "aggressive." He did rub some of his fellow members—especially those with less imagination and more investment in an outmoded, cramped system—the wrong way. Even as a junior member of the House, Andy demanded to be taken account of.

It was that aggressiveness—that drive to assert himself on behalf of his principles and his constituents—that made Andy an effective legislator during his six years on Capitol Hill. As a member of the Watergate class, he was among those instrumental in reforming House procedures, most notably restructuring the seniority system that had long throttled forward-looking legislation. He authored and secured passage of landmark pollution control measures. He was a leader on urging the United States to oppose the apartheid regime in South Africa. Perhaps most lastingly, he helped reshape public and governmental awareness of environmental causes of cancer, an outlook we take for granted today but not one commonly held when he began his work.

Congress was Andy's dream job. "It couldn't have been more galvanizing," he says. "It was such an exciting opportunity. For somebody coming from where I was coming from, who wanted to do what I wanted to do—to markedly improve our country and to build a better world—it was miraculous." Asked if Congress was the best job of his career, he replies, "No question. It gave me the broadest scope. I could tackle whatever set of problems and difficult issues I chose. Working with my colleagues and teams, I was able to really, really move things in very important ways."

Without being overly dramatic, we can say it was a loss to the country that Andy served in Congress for only six years. There have always been smart, serious, effective legislators in Congress to counter the doltish, frivolous, useless ones, but there have never been enough. However, conditions on Election Day 1980—an uncertain economy, a revolution in Iran, an unpopular incumbent president at the head of the Democratic ticket, an effective candidate atop the GOP ticket—left Andy jobless when the new Congress convened in January 1981.

Even while in Congress, Andy aspired to move higher, to become one of 100 legislators in the Senate, not one of 435 in the House. "My goal was to become a United States senator of note and importance," he recalls. As a youth Andy admired great senators like Everett Dirksen and Wayne Morse, Vance Hartke and Margaret Chase Smith, recognizable figures whose influence over the public life of the country spanned decades. Hubert Humphrey, he says, "was one of my idols. I explicitly thought about Humphrey fighting the good fight and knowing that whatever criticism you might get for being upfront on X, Y, or Z can be dissolved if people believe you're working on their interests, that you're independent minded, that you care, and that you're going to make a difference." To this outside eye, Andy was well suited to long tenure in what used to be called "the World's Greatest Deliberative Body." But in his only two opportunities to join that body, he ran into opponents with advantages he couldn't overcome.

In 1978, with the venerable New Jersey Republican senator Clifford Case facing trouble in his own party, Andy considered entering the race for his seat. But a political neophyte blocked his path. Andy had been a solid participant in sports as a young man—he still boasts about his achievements as a high school tennis player—but his athletic renown was no match for that of Bill Bradley, then recently retired with two championship rings from his time with the local NBA team, the New York Knicks. Bradley won the Democratic primary Andy never entered, Case lost the Republican contest. In November Bradley captured the seat.

Four years later, with New Jersey Democratic senator Harrison Williams about to resign in disgrace, Andy declared his intention to replace him but was challenged by another political newcomer. Frank Lautenberg didn't have Bradley's jump shot, but he did have the fortune he'd amassed as CEO of Automatic Data Processing. Andy's fundraising machine, though formidable, could not match the millions Lautenberg could raise by opening his own checkbook. Lautenberg edged Andy in the Democratic primary before winning in November. Bradley and Lautenberg both held their seats for multiple terms, making another Senate run by Andy impossible.

Unlike Bradley and Lautenberg, Andy had paid his dues in the House and, earlier, at State and in New York City. But who ever said life was fair? Andy recognizes the randomness in the circumstances that kept him from remaining in the House or ascending to the Senate. "Reagan,

Carter, and the Ayatollah," he recalls. "And just before I got to Congress, the Supreme Court, in *Buckley v. Valeo*, eliminated the ceiling on what a candidate for federal office could spend on his or her own campaign. I was outspent seven to one by Lautenberg, who ponied up $3.5 million out of his pocket. Those were terrible experiences." Nonetheless, as he looks back he is stoic. "On the other hand, in '74 I benefited enormously from Watergate and double-digit inflation. Politics is a blood sport.

"I'm not happy about what happened in '80 and '82, but I don't dwell on it anymore. There is lots and lots I'm so grateful for. I have four fabulous kids. Four equally fabulous grandkids. I've had wonderful family time through all of my years. I've enjoyed lifelong friendships with colleagues and many others. I've worked with amazing people in all walks of life."

A high-level administration appointment—at State, perhaps, or the Environmental Protection Agency—would have been a logical option after Andy left Congress had there been a Democratic administration. But Republicans controlled the White House for the next dozen years. Countless retired or defeated members of Congress cash in on their former office, making big money lobbying their former colleagues on behalf of deep-pocketed companies and industries and even foreign governments. Admirably, Andy eschewed that route, choosing instead to work at a series of worthy not-for-profit organizations.

At his first major post-Congress employer, the World Resources Institute, Andy co-edited and contributed to a book that deepened understanding of environmental justice issues in the Western Hemisphere. He became one of the earliest voices to speak up on climate change, testifying before the Senate in 1986, "The international scientific community has reached a consensus: mankind's activities are changing the atmosphere in ways that could profoundly affect the habitability of the Earth. The magnitude of the risks is unprecedented. The question is, What do we do?" Not enough people listened, but Andy and WRI helped begin the long, still-ongoing process to get people to recognize the dangers posed by our warming climate.

Andy considers his next job, as the chief executive of Appropriate Technology International/EnterpriseWorks Worldwide, his most consequential and satisfying position aside from his service in the House. "We were able to accomplish so much," he recalls. "What we were doing was cutting edge and it was important." Under Andy's leadership, ATI/EWW led the way in demonstrating new pathways to sustainable economic development. "Partnering with low-income entrepreneurs in Africa, Asia, and Latin America to double, triple, or even quadruple their incomes was hugely rewarding. We worked in maybe twenty countries in Africa, Asia, and Latin America on a minimal budget of six or seven or eight million dollars annually. It's astounding what we did."

Andy's subsequent work—for the Global Alliance for Vaccines and Immunization, Clean Air-Cool Planet, the Environmental Defense Fund, and his origination of an effort to shape a policy response in New Jersey to Superstorm Sandy—fell short of his goals due to internal company politics or, in the early years of the 21st century, to the rapidly gathering headwinds against progressive national policies.

And then, after his work trying to put together a commission on New Jersey's climate, Andy retired, relocating to California, where he lives today, near his sister, his children, and their families.

The liberalism that animated a young Andy going door to door with his father on behalf of Adlai Stevenson may not be dead, but it has taken a battering since the New Deal consensus broke down in the wake of the Vietnam War and the social upheavals of the '60s and '70s. Andy points to what started the decline. "Ronald Reagan was a break point—it's been downhill ever since. Jonathan Alter wrote a book about Obama called *The Center Holds*. But the center has not held. In domestic policy we've been making compromises with Republicans representing unfettered adherence to corporate goals. That's very different from when I was in Congress, when there was a rough equivalency between corporate influence and lobbying on the one hand, and labor influence and lobbying on the other. There was plenty of room for the public interest to be injected into the decision-making process. None of that is true today.

"The disasters associated with the Supreme Court—in particular, wiping out every bit of campaign finance reform—have had a huge negative effect on *all* domestic policy. And then there's foreign policy. With George W., as with Reagan, we had someone assume the presidency with little knowledge of the rest of the world. You think back to McNamara and Bundy and Rostow and that crowd vis-à-vis Vietnam—there was a repeat of that with George W. Bush and Iraq, with Cheney, Wolfowitz, et al. putting us into harm's way on the other side of the world without strategic goals that made any sense at all and doing deep damage to America and the wider world.

"Clinton also began his presidency with little knowledge of foreign policy, but he failed, on multiple fronts, in the opposite direction: After criticizing H. W. for doing nothing about Bosnia, Clinton did nothing for three years while tens of thousands of Bosnians were slaughtered. He struggled with the crisis in Somalia involving both UN and US troops. He did nothing in 1994 in response to the UN's clarion call that the situation in Rwanda required urgent international attention. Meanwhile, Rwanda spiraled down into a sustained genocide that killed eight hundred thousand people."

Beyond even those disasters, however, the country now faces the prospect, previously unthinkable, of the end of the Republic. "I'd have never thought it possible," says Andy. "In the '60s, I was definitely of the opinion, along with Martin Luther King Jr., that in time there is a bend toward justice. That we would solve the series of problems we then had before moving on to the next set of problems, approaching all these challenges in a constructive way. But that is not the record since I was in Congress. I've always been an optimist, but this doesn't look like a hiccup.

"Every one of our fundamental values has been undermined, systematically, over the last several decades. And then, with Trump, it went off the end of the spectrum to total denial of facts, of science, of counting votes. Over the last forty years, the middle part of the country has been hollowed out economically, and people are hurting big time. We've seen the rejection of civic leadership and of the democratic process that has been our touchstone since the Founding Fathers—a system that has been deeply flawed, but still moving in the right direction. All of that has been upended by Trump and his followers.

"The sense of community and shared sacrifice is gone. So most everybody says, 'So-and-so wants to cut my taxes, therefore I'll vote for him.' It's all simpleminded and narrow gauge. Self-interested, as opposed to any concept of a shared democracy, civic responsibilities, and making progress to benefit everybody."

To the surprise of most prominent political observers, Joe Biden has been a remarkably successful president, beginning the repair of the nation following the multiple catastrophes of the Trump presidency. He has presided over the passage of landmark legislation to pull the nation out of the economic doldrums forced on it by the COVID-19 pandemic, to finally commit the federal government to large-scale repair of the nation's infrastructure, and to begin to address the climate crisis. He's also rallied the world's democracies to stand up to Vladimir Putin's aggression in Ukraine. He's managed these accomplishments with razor-thin, at times recalcitrant, Democratic majorities in the House and Senate and while the nation has been plagued by the refusal of his predecessor to concede a lost election and by a right-wing mediasphere that proudly promulgates disinformation in the pursuit of power and advertising revenue.

At this writing, in early 2023, Joe Biden and the Democratic Party have beaten back the immediate threat of an authoritarian takeover of the US government. But the long-term danger remains. Donald Trump's influence seems to be on the decline in the Republican Party—not because GOP leaders have suddenly opened their eyes to the threat he poses to democracy, the rule of law, and the nation's fundamental decency, but because he has stopped winning elections for them. Still, Trump continues to hold the allegiance of most of the Republican base, making his future, and that of American democracy, impossible to predict. But even if he does lose his grip on his party, GOP leaders with similar authoritarian tendencies, but less appetite for chaos and temper tantrums—Ron DeSantis, Ted Cruz, Josh Hawley—seem poised to step into the void Trump may leave.

Biden and two other leaders in their advanced years, Nancy Pelosi and Chuck Schumer, have resuscitated, if not fully revived, American progressive liberalism. If they have not definitively saved democracy, at least they've given it a fighting chance against the illiberal forces recently gaining strength both in the United States and around the world.

Andy prides himself on his record, in Congress and elsewhere, of attracting talented people and leading effective teams. "High-functioning teams are essential to getting stuff done," he says. "It's part of my leadership model." In Congress, Andy quickly established a reputation as a member to work for, drawing capable, committed staff. "The best people found me. Bob Kerr, my chief of staff, is an example. He had worked for Ted Kennedy in the Senate and for Tom Foley, a future Speaker, in the House. At an event for new members, the chair of the meeting turned to the subject of hiring staff. He pointed to Bob Kerr and said, 'This guy is really something.' As a result, Kerr got offers from all sorts of people. He chose my office, and he told me why: He thought I was on the cutting edge and he wanted to be there, too." That opinion of Andy followed him throughout his career, as he became a boss people sought out and spoke highly of. Andy is proud to note the success people found after working for him. "Look at the career histories of these people, who went on to do amazing stuff. I enjoyed being a mentor."

Andy's success as a manager stemmed from his not thinking he knew all the answers. "I know the direction I want to go," he says, "but how are we going to do it? Bring in the experts. Figure out what's wrong. Decide what needs to be improved and get as much of it done as you can. Find the very best people who know the most about the things you yourself *don't* know."

"Respect and mutual engagement" were key, he says. "People understood from the get-go that I was going to empower them. That I would listen to their recommendations. That we would be working in an envelope of larger concerns about our society, about what needed to be improved in the world. David Dreyer just walked into my office one day and said he wanted to work for me. Same thing with Susan Swift, who had worked for Tom Harkin in the Senate and been a reporter for *Newsweek*. Susan Swift said I was the best boss she ever had. That meant a lot to me. She was able to contribute whatever she wanted to, in ways that would be valued and would make a difference."

That was Andy's priority, for himself and his staff: making a difference. Looking at his career in its entirety, Andy did make a difference, if not in the exact way he'd originally planned to fulfill that youthful ambition. But who among us follows a straight career path from start to finish? "I tackled big issues with profound implications for the future of Americans and people across the world," he says. "And often succeeded. And sometimes was frustrated by what was not possible to achieve.

"I would say that my career illustrates a number of things. One, a set of commitments. Two, an ability and willingness to take risks that not everybody would take. Leaving the State Department with a promising career ahead of me because I wanted to be a decision-maker. Most people wouldn't have taken the risk of going to economically depressed Jamaica,

Queens, to run a new program for the mayor. What former member of Congress would sign up to lead a sustainable development NGO with a minimal initial budget? Sometimes you don't succeed entirely, but you make a noticeable move in the direction things need to go. Another example: the Maguire Report on carcinogens, which accelerates our quest for healthier lives.

"All the way through, I was willing to say, 'These are my commitments.'

"I am a risk taker. I wanted in my career to change what was crying out to be changed—and move forward as much as possible on matters I cared deeply about. I was able to succeed in giving pathbreaking stuff a good push. I believe my colleagues and others saw me as someone who could make this kind of progress in challenging policy and management environments. And I did it, and kept doing it, for five decades.

"We aren't where we need to be on climate change, continuing the fight against poverty in America and abroad, working for justice wherever there is injustice, keeping our democracy as it should be while doing what we can to counter abusive authoritarians in an increasing number of countries abroad. And there is so much else."

No long life comes without disappointment. But Andy didn't wallow in regret. He relishes what he and his teams were able to do. He doesn't fixate on what could have been, what should have been. When circumstances beyond his control took from him the chance to continue serving as a public official, he pursued his goals in the private and nonprofit sectors with ardor and creativity. And he achieved what he set out to achieve: raise important issues and contribute to the well-being of people in America and around the world.

He made a difference—a distinct, compelling, pace-setting difference.

"I've led a productive life," he concludes. "When people ask me about it, this is what I tell them: 'I've lived a passionate life at work and at play.'"

Not a bad legacy.

APPENDIX

THE MAGUIRE TEAMS

Ask yourself what makes you come alive and go and do that, because the world needs more of us who have come alive.

—HOWARD THURMAN

Andy's leadership and legislative successes on multiple policy fronts in Congress were made possible through his building positive working relationships and developing networks with scores of members in both parties from across the country.

Andy's 1975 entering group of seventy-five new Democratic members voted him class representative to the Democratic Study Group, the House Democrats' strategy caucus led by respected senior members such as Don Fraser of Minnesota, Abner Mikva of Illinois, and Tom Foley of Washington. On specific initiatives, Andy teamed up with Republicans such as John Anderson of Illinois, John Buchanan of Alabama, John Heinz of Pennsylvania, Stewart McKinney of Connecticut, and William Steiger of Wisconsin, as well as Millicent Fenwick of New Jersey.

While even some respected members of the House were known for difficult relationships with their own staffs, Andy's reputation was the opposite: The outstanding individuals he hired stayed with him for years and became "go-to" mentors for the staffs of other members. Andy's people always had opportunities to move up within the team. Numerous individuals, after their work with Andy, went on to brilliant post-Congress careers.

David Dreyer, who quickly graduated from drafting constituent letters to heading Andy's policy team on off-committee initiatives and pending legislation before the full House, later became policy director for Senator Gary Hart in the Senate and then for Hart's presidential campaign.

David served in the Clinton White House as deputy communications director, working on enactment of the president's economic and health care plans. He wrote the president's keynote address for the opening of the US Holocaust Memorial Museum, cowrote his address to Congress on health care, and served as managing writer for the 1994 State of the Union address. He also worked on crisis communications. He later served as a senior adviser to Secretary of the Treasury Robert Rubin.

After leaving government, he created a consulting company, TSD Communications, to support the policy, communications, and political work of progressive clients. At this firm he worked with entrepreneurs, authors, advocates, public figures, and others, providing strategic advice to senior leaders in the fields of finance, technology, and policy development. His work has taken him around the world, on assignments that included working at the Sydney and Athens Summer Olympic Games, conducting communications audits for public and private sector organizations, advising the Ecumenical Patriarch of Eastern Orthodoxy, and providing strategic counsel for the public education campaign that helped change US policy toward Cuba during the Obama administration. TSD has received editing and writing credits on a number of books, including *Lean In*, by Sheryl Sandberg & Nell Scovell, *The Power of Progress*, by John Podesta, and *Grace Without God*, by Katherine Ozment. The firm has also prepared thought leaders for their book tours, most recently John Doerr, before publication of his book *Measure What Matters*.

Rob Esposito began his association with Andy earlier than most. While still a junior in high school, he served as director of youth operations for Andy's first House campaign, in 1974. As voter registration director in 1976 he recruited, trained, and motivated more than two hundred youth volunteers in an unprecedented and record-breaking drive that registered 11,184 new voters in targeted precincts—a key strategic objective in Andy's successful reelection bid.

Graduating from Princeton with a BA in politics, Rob worked in a variety of political, governmental, nonprofit, and private sector venues. He specialized in high-impact print communications and in what commentators described as "beat the odds," "turnaround," and "from-the-ground-up" problem-solving management.

Rob's experience includes working as manager or consultant for political campaigns and nonprofit organizations in seventeen states; staffer to two members of Congress; adjunct professor of political science at Ramapo College in New Jersey; program officer in Romania for the National Democratic Institute for International Affairs, a US-based nonprofit supporting the development of democracy during the post-Ceausescu presidential-parliamentary election in 1992; vice president of a national political media firm where his work in Indiana was instrumental in fashioning Democratic majorities in state legislative elections in 2006 and 2008; and principal author of a 140-page published "Strategic Roadmap" for the Democratic National Committee in 2008 that targeted demographic trends and Democratic electoral potential in Virginia, a presidential battleground state won that year for the first time in forty-four years.

For his political work, Rob received media accolades as "a veteran campaign manager" (*Wall Street Journal*); "mastermind of the successful effort to unseat a House veteran" (*New York Times*); and "an astute media strategist" (*Bergen Record*); "Esposito had a major impact," noted the *Herald News,* adding that "victory was seen as a phenomenal achievement." "Esposito is known to fulfill his predictions in campaigns he has worked on," reported the *Philadelphia Inquirer.*

After Andy began work as CEO of Appropriate Technology International he recruited Rob, then at mid-career, to join him as chief operating officer. Rob brought national Republican and Democratic leaders onto the board, designed a rebrand of ATI as EnterpriseWorks Worldwide, expanded a fundraising campaign that notably brought Vice

President Al Gore and former Republican vice-presidential nominee Jack Kemp together for a major event in support of the new EWW, and spearheaded a transition/privatization proposal that won a $14.25 million grant from the US Agency for International Development.

At the 1995 UN World Summit for Social Development in Copenhagen, Rob organized a "Small Farmers, Producers, and Micro-Entrepreneurs Caucus" that resulted in the conference protocol recognizing this constituency as integral to global sustainable development.

In an important congressional race, Rob identified a major error by a renowned national pollster that botched a crucial pre-election survey. The incident became a celebrated news story when then-Democratic Congressional Campaign Committee director Rahm Emanuel mailed a dead fish to the pollster.

In the private sector, Rob was director of investor financial surety bond marketing for a midsize insurance company. Most recently, he served as director of community development in Bergen County, New Jersey, overseeing operations and the distribution of $18 million in annual grants in service to a population of just under one million. Rob is grateful for the example of "humanity and good government in action" that Andy provided to him at an early age.

Gina Glantz managed Andy's 1974 primary and general election congressional campaigns and his reelection in 1976, serving in between as his district administrator. The 1974 campaign's use of computers to generate voter ID and information led to inquiries from national Democratic campaign operatives; she went on to manage, field direct, and advise on local, state, and federal campaigns. In 1985, Gina moved to California and, along with Angie Martin, founded Martin & Glantz, a firm that consulted with a broad array of progressive groups on grassroots organizing and communications strategies. Most notably, the company worked on women's reproductive health, youth violence prevention, workers' rights, and environmental justice.

Gina managed Bill Bradley's 2000 campaign for president, after which she sold Martin & Glantz to employees. She served as senior adviser to Andrew Stern, former president of the Service Employees International Union from 2001 to 2009. In 2009 Gina was a fellow at the Harvard Kennedy School Institute of Politics and later taught at Harvard's Shorenstein Center. In 2015, Gina founded GenderAvenger, an activist nonprofit dedicated to ensuring that women are always part of the public dialogue. In 2022, GenderAvenger became part of All in Together. Gina has served as chair of the Planned Parenthood Action Fund and on the boards of Oxfam America, Democracy Now, California League of Conservation, the San Francisco World Affairs Council, the Association of Colleges and Universities, and Dēmos.

Ted Hoff began his work with Andy in Washington as a volunteer in Andy's congressional office, where he focused on transportation policy, while attending Georgetown University's School of Foreign Service. He headed to New Jersey on weekends, becoming deputy director of Andy's successful reelection campaign in 1978.

Ted joined New Jersey's Department of Transportation under Governor Brendan Byrne, then rose to become Byrne's special assistant and cabinet secretary.

Motivated to learn how to better solve problems in both public and private organizations, Ted earned an MBA from Harvard Business School and was named a Baker Scholar. He taught marketing at the business school and pursued a PhD in business economics. He then founded his own education consulting firm.

Later, Ted took a senior position at IBM as vice president and chief learning officer. His award-winning work centered on leadership development; in later years he focused on broader issues of workforce development to enable IBM to deliver innovative solutions for clients.

Ted served on the board of the John F. Kennedy Library Foundation, on the Board of Visitors of the Walsh School of Foreign Service, and on the Cambridge city manager's advisory board. The Catholic Youth Organization basketball team he coached won the Greater Boston Championship in 2007. He energetically raised money for candidates and causes whose values he shared. His unique combination of exuberance, patience, intellect, selflessness, encouragement, caring for others, and sound advice made him an inspiring mentor and guide for generations of young people.

Elgie Holstein, like David Dreyer, began on Andy's staff with responsibility for constituent letters. He rapidly moved up to legislative assistant supporting Andy's work on the Energy and Commerce Committee and became the energy specialist other members of the committee looked to for guidance. Focusing on the issues, bringing other staff and their members along, designing and joining lawsuits to counteract the influence of fossil fuel companies, he was critical to Andy's success on energy and environmental issues.

After leaving Capitol Hill, Holstein created Bankcard Holders of America, a consumer education and advocacy organization to offset the influence of big credit card issuers; this position gave him national platform and media opportunities. Returning to government, he held a variety of senior positions in the federal executive branch with responsibility for a broad range of natural resources, environmental, science, energy, and economic policy issues. Those posts included: associate director for natural resources, energy and science at the White House Office of Management and Budget; special assistant to the president for economic policy, White House National Economic Council; deputy undersecretary and assistant secretary of the National Oceanic and Atmospheric Administration; and chief of staff at the US Department of Energy. In 2009, he was co-director of the DOE's presidential transition team.

As a private consultant, Elgie served as a member of an advisory committee for Sandia National Laboratories and worked as an adviser to local governments on water and energy matters. He also worked for Serco, Inc., a leading provider of professional, technology, and management services to the federal government. There he led several projects for the Department of Energy, led a workforce analysis of the FBI following 9/11, and advised the Department of Defense on military family support and benefit programs. He has also served as energy and environment staff director for the National Conference of State Legislatures.

Currently, Elgie is senior director for strategic planning at the Environmental Defense Fund in Washington, DC.

Dr. Jessica Justman was an intern in Andy's congressional office assigned to health and environmental issues.

As an infectious disease specialist and epidemiologist, she worked for over two decades to advance HIV prevention, care, and treatment and, more recently, to pioneer a precision approach to understanding the global HIV epidemic. As an associate professor of medicine in epidemiology, she has pursued research focusing on HIV epidemiology and HIV prevention studies. For example, she spearheaded the CDC-funded Population-based HIV Impact Assessment (PHIA) Project. Since 2014, the PHIA Project's national representative surveys have measured access to care and treatment and, by using novel HIV recency assays, estimated HIV incidence in fifteen African and Caribbean countries. Results from the PHIA surveys have transformed global HIV programming by highlighting the need for more effective and targeted HIV testing approaches. Jessica is also principal investigator of the TRACE initiative, a technical assistance program that helps ministries of health use HIV recency testing to strengthen the precision of HIV infection surveillance systems and guide HIV prevention programs.

Her HIV prevention research began over twenty years ago when she was the site leader for ICAP's Bronx Prevention Center Clinical Research Site. The Bronx site, along with the Harlem Prevention Center and the Eswatini Prevention Center, is part of the NIH-funded ICAP at Columbia Clinical Trials Unit, for which Jessica serves as co-principal investigator. With the advent of the SARS-CoV-2 pandemic, she has applied lessons from HIV programs and research to a wide range of COVID-19 activities, including COVID-19 surveys, vaccine trials, early treatment of COVID-19 for close contacts, and treatment trials of monoclonal therapeutics. She serves as ICAP's senior technical director and oversees the development and strengthening of ICAP's clinical, laboratory, strategic information and survey activities across a range of global projects.

Bob Kerr joined Andy's congressional office as chief of staff after working for Senator Hubert Humphrey and future House Speaker Tom Foley. After serving in that post nearly the entirety of Andy's congressional tenure, Bob accepted a senior policy post at the Environmental Protection Agency.

Cofounder and principal of Pure Strategies, Bob now works with companies and public agencies to promote environmental and social sustainability, including through initiatives on sustainability strategy, sustainable chemical programs, and climate strategy. His projects have included support for brands and retailers in building safer-chemicals programs for consumer products, an OSHA training program on reduction of hazardous chemicals in workplaces, and assisting companies in using Chemical Footprint Project tools to guide and assess progress in sustainable chemistry.

To support consumer product companies just starting on chemicals management issues, Bob authored *Sustainable Chemicals Management Software: A Pure Strategies Review of Tools for Managing Chemicals in Products*. He is a certified verifier for the Chemical Footprint Project. He has also supported development of climate and emission-trading strategies for companies and government agencies and led a congressionally mandated study evaluating the effectiveness of EPA and state emissions trading programs. Current and former clients include Ahold Delhaize, Ben & Jerry's, Best Buy, Consumer Technology Association, OSHA, Radio Flyer, USEPA, and Walmart.

Bob was appointed by EPA administrators to serve three terms on that agency's National Advisory Council for Environmental Policy and Technology. On the council, he contributed to its recommendations to broaden EPA's role in science education, in citizen science projects to engage communities in environmental sustainability, and on technical collaboration to support beyond-compliance supply chain sustainability initiatives.

Michael H. (Mike) Levin joined Andy's team as a congressional fellow, with degrees from the University of Pennsylvania, Oxford, and Harvard Law. Previously, he had served with the National Labor Relations Board, as top appellate counsel for the Department of Labor's Solicitor's Office for Occupational Safety and Health, and as deputy director of a cabinet-level Carter administration task force convened to reform OSHA. Working with Andy, Mike designed multiple policy initiatives that meshed with Andy's interests, including a bill to reform the Guaranteed Student Loan Program, legislation that for the first time advocated income-based loan repayment. He continued as fellow with, then consultant to, the Senate Judiciary Committee, then chaired by Senator Ted Kennedy, where his colleagues included Stephen Breyer (later justice of the Supreme Court) and Kenneth Feinberg (later head of the September 11th Victim Compensation Fund).

From 1979 to 1988 Mike served as the first national regulatory reform director at EPA, where he and his team developed incentive-based approaches for better environmental protection such as air emissions trading and early versions of the Clean Air Act's acid rain program. He then became an environmental/finance partner at several law firms. He founded a renewable-energy investment banking company before starting the first virtual law firm in Washington, DC. He also has been a principal in several renewable energy development firms, collectively involved in over $2 billion worth of solar energy or related transactions.

Mike has published award-winning feature articles, four poetry collections, a long series of environmental policy pieces, and two nonfiction volumes, *A Border Town in Poland* and *Firebird*, based on oral histories of tumultuous lives in Europe and the Middle East, respectively. He is the co-author and co-producer of *Two Pianos: Playing for Life,* a "concert documentary," which has been performed internationally, with live classical music about young Jewish mothers concertizing under and after the Third Reich.

Bea O'Rourke worked in Andy's campaigns and headed his district office from 1975 to 1981, when she went to Washington as chief of his transition team. Her first political campaign job was as Bergen County field director in Brendan Byrne's first bid for governor of New Jersey in 1973. Other New Jersey campaigns followed much later, for Governor Jim Florio, Congressman Bob Roe, Senator Frank Lautenberg, and her own losing effort for state Senate in 1993.

When not doing political work, she was sought after for roles in nonprofits and advisory commissions. She was chosen by Governor Christie Whitman to serve on two commissions, one on the status of women, the other on alcohol and substance abuse. Ministries, Bea's 501(c)(3), addressed institutional development needs in the Roman Catholic Diocese of Newark. She founded and developed the Department of Continuing Education at Felician University in Lodi and worked for the New Jersey Association of Student Councils and the Emmanuel Cancer Foundation. At Rutgers University, she earned her certificate in social work and then began her longest-lasting employment interest, as director of the Northwest Bergen Center for Food Action in Mahwah and Ringwood. In 2005, she was invited to participate in Leadership New Jersey's Class of 2005.

Bea is a respected experienced director in nonprofit organizations, and an expert in business and government planning, event planning, and fundraising. She is the recipient of many local and state awards.

Kathy Rae started in Andy's New Jersey office as speechwriter and issues research coordinator. Despite living in Ridgewood with her husband and three children, in 1980 she commuted to Washington to work as Andy's chief of staff, becoming one of the first women to hold that position on the Hill.

Kathy's political career began in high school in Arlington, Virginia, where she was selected to be an on-camera interviewer in a nationally syndicated television program, *Youth Wants to Know*, a Peabody Award recipient. Among the elected officials she had the opportunity to question was the legendary Illinois senator Everett Dirksen. Kathy's first post-college job was with the Metropolitan Washington Council of Governments, a regional forum of local government officials working to develop solutions for the region's challenges in housing, transportation, public safety, health and human services, and the environment.

With Andy's assistance, Kathy was hired in 1981 by the New York area's Regional Plan Association to head up its reconstituted New Jersey office. Among the initiatives undertaken during her tenure was Morris 2000, comprehensive recommendations for planning in Morris County, one of New Jersey's fastest-growing suburban-exurban areas. During her tenure at RPA, Kathy was asked by public television station Thirteen/WNET to serve as chair of the station's New Jersey Community Advisory Board.

In 1984, Kathy became director of Thirteen's New Jersey operations, beginning a nearly thirty-year career with the country's largest public television broadcaster. She was instrumental in the development of several major prime time programs including "William J. Brennan, Justice for All," a recipient of the American Bar Association's Silver Gavel Award, as well as two national Great Performances productions, "Show Boat" and "The Colored Museum," both shot live at New Jersey theater venues. Relocating to WNET's corporate offices in Manhattan in 1991, she became Thirteen's director of educational technology. In that capacity she helped develop a number of new initiatives, including the station's first web-based educational platform for schools and the Kravis Educational Multimedia Center. In 1997, she assumed responsibility for WNET's government affairs, serving as the station's liaison with elected and appointed officials at the city, state, and federal levels in the New York Tri-State area on a range of issues of concern to public broadcasting.

Since 2016, Kathy has served on the Board of Trustees of America's Public Television Stations (APTS), the advocacy and lobbying arm of public television stations nationwide. In 2000, while still at WNET, Kathy received APTS's Grassroots Advocacy Award; in 2012, she received its National Advocacy Award.

Jim Rosapepe worked as an unpaid strategist in Andy's first campaign for Congress. He designed successful strategies for an uphill campaign and continued to advise Andy during his freshman term in the House.

Jim served elsewhere as a policy assistant to members of Congress, for whom he worked on macroeconomic and competition issues. From 1979 to 1981, he served as a member of the National Petroleum Council. An entrepreneur with extensive experience in public service, since 1989 he has worked in both the private and public sectors to assist people in Central and Eastern Europe as they develop democratic institutions and market economies.

Long active in the national Democratic Party, Jim worked with President Bill Clinton and Vice President Al Gore on a variety of projects. Most recently he organized Italian Americans nationally for the 1992 and 1996 Clinton/Gore campaigns. In 1998, he took office as US ambassador to Romania.

In business, Jim has participated in financing real estate projects, commercial banks and small businesses, and has worked with American companies on projects in formerly Communist countries. He chaired the investment committee of the Albanian American Enterprise Fund, a $30 million investment fund, recognized as one of the best run in the region.

From 1987 to 1997, Jim served in the Maryland legislature, representing a multiethnic district that included the major campus of the University of Maryland. As vice chair of the Maryland House Ways and Means Committee, which is responsible for policies on taxation and local government finance, he was recognized nationally as one of the state's top leaders on economic and fiscal issues. He also championed environmental protection, education, labor rights, and private financing of transportation and real estate projects. Over the past twenty years, he has advised state governments on national and international tax and securities issues.

Many dozens of other unpaid young interns worked for shorter or longer periods of time in Andy's campaigns, in his district office, and in his congressional office in Washington. Not a few embarked on important public sector careers. **Amy Chapman**, who started with Andy's campaign while still in middle school, eventually became the political director of a major national labor union. **Thom Kleiner** and **Art Feltman**, high schoolers when they first joined Andy's effort, ran successfully for local and state offices in New York and Connecticut, respectively.

A number of people served as yearlong fellows. Two notable examples: Health policy fellows **Joelle Kayden**, a Yale graduate, and **Sam Korper**, MD, a Robert Woods Johnson–selected fellow. Despite other offers, both chose to join the Maguire team because they preferred what Andy's office was doing and how. Later, Kayden transitioned into a capital markets specialist and formed her own firm. Korper filled senior positions at the Department of Health and Human Services and the National Institutes of Health.

"Our teams were extraordinary," Andy recalls. "It was an era unusually open to genuine progress on important issues. There's no way we could have achieved the successes we did but through 'from-the-ground-up' organization and outreach in New Jersey and nationally, and through our teams' coordination of influential actors and networks that supported what we were doing inside and outside of Congress. As Elgie Holstein puts it, we maintained 'relentless pursuit' of forward-looking but realistic objectives."

Andy was fortunate also in the caliber of journalists who covered him in his campaigns and in Congress as reporters for the *Bergen Record*. These individuals went on to distinguished careers in their field. **John Walcott** became head of the McClatchy News Service. **Howard Kurtz** took the media beat at the *Washington Post* and authored *Spin Cycle: How the White House and the Media Manipulate the News*. **Dale Mezzacappa** built an award-winning career at the *Philadelphia Inquirer* covering poverty and urban education, then secured a Nieman Fellowship at Harvard. **Dick Benfield** stayed at the *Record*, becoming editorial page editor. Also at the *Record*, **Jim Ahearn** and **Bob Comstock** wrote insight-filled analytical columns. The *Ridgewood News*, despite strong Republican bias, employed a reporter, **John King**, who dealt fairly with Andy. The *New York Times* provided substantial coverage of Andy's work. Both the *Times* and the *Record* endorsed Andy every time he ran.

In his work before and after Congress, Andy was fortunate to have worked side by side with talented and devoted colleagues as they pushed to advance the public interest. Andy learned to be a contributing team member with the Department of State at the United Nations and with New York mayor John Lindsay, where he headed a regional office for planning and development and put together his first team of up-and-coming professionals. After serving in Congress, he was recruited into leadership positions with domestic and international nonprofit and for-profit organizations focused on a healthy environment, state-of-the art health care, and building entrepreneurship skills that multiplied the earnings of low-income producers. As with the members of his teams in Congress, many of his pre- and post-Congress colleagues continued into exceptional careers.

Here a few of those individuals:

Valeria Budinich worked with Andy at Appropriate Technology International/EnterpriseWorks Worldwide. Born in Chile, Valeria studied engineering at the Universidad Centroamericana in Nicaragua, then gained an MS in industrial engineering from the University of Texas at El Paso.

Upon becoming CEO at ATI/EWW, Andy elevated Valeria from Latin America director to chief operating officer; in that role, according to the Wharton School, she became "a leader in her field" of social entrepreneurship, creating and expanding businesses with social impact in dozens of countries in Africa, Asia, and Latin America.

A brilliant conceptualizer of projects, she specialized in what USAID called "unsolicited proposals" and brokered many millions of dollars from USAID, UN agencies, the World Bank, European bilaterals, and the private sector in support of EWW's initiatives.

Later, at the Endeavor Foundation, she specialized in linking entrepreneurs in emerging economies with venture capitalists in the United States. Endeavor's design for selecting high-impact entrepreneurs was developed in Chile and Argentina and has since spread to thirty countries.

At BDA, a California-based consulting firm, she developed innovative services for small and medium scale entrepreneurs and launched the first seed capital fund in Chile that exclusively finances enterprises in their start-up phase.

Valeria then became vice president at Ashoka, a pioneering organization in the field of social entrepreneurship, where she founded and led Full Economic Citizenship, a global initiative that defined and refined over fifty hybrid business models in housing, small farmer agriculture, nutrition for all, and recycling. These partnerships, combined with successive generations of new programs that have been inspired by this work, are transforming formal and informal economies by improving the lives of millions of families.

In 2012, Valeria was recognized for articulating a new vision of capitalism when she received the Harvard Business Review/McKinsey M-Prize for management innovation for her pioneering work enabling hybrid value chains and systems. This work was featured in "A New Alliance for Global Change," a *Harvard Business Review* (September 2010) article she co-authored with Ashoka founder Bill Drayton. She is co-author of *Scaling Business Solutions to Social Problems: A Practical Guidebook for Social and Business Entrepreneurs* (Palgrave, 2015), which is based on analyzing more than a thousand innovations in systems change and market leveraging. Her work exploring the worldview and leadership skills of social entrepreneurs tackling complex issues led to "Answering Society's Call: A New Leadership Imperative," an article published by *McKinsey Quarterly* (November 2019).

In 2020, Valeria joined the MIT's Legatum Center, where she is a senior adviser on innovation and entrepreneurship ecosystems and systems entrepreneurship. In announcing Valeria's appointment, MIT noted that, as a group, social entrepreneurs across the world have had a "massive impact" in their societies when partnered with corporations, governments, and non-profit organizations.

Valeria continues to be associated with Ashoka as panel chair for Ashoka selection panels around the world. She serves on the advisory boards of Danone's $120 million Ecosystem Fund, Leapfrog Investments' $1 billion impact investment fund, and the Sustainable MBA program at the University of Vermont. Her work has been recognized by the World Economic Forum and she is a regular guest lecturer at leading business schools, global conferences, and forums.

Don McHenry worked with Andy on US policy toward South Africa when Don was with the State Department, International Organization Affairs, and Andy was adviser on political and security affairs at State's US Mission to the United Nations.

One of America's most distinguished diplomats, Ambassador McHenry has for decades studied, taught, and worked primarily in the fields of foreign policy and international law and organization. After first joining the US Department of State, he served eight years in various positions. In 1966 he received the Department's Superior Honor Award. In 1971, while on leave from the department, he was guest scholar at the Brookings Institution and an international affairs fellow at the Council on Foreign Relations. In 1973, after leaving State, he joined the Carnegie Endowment for International Peace as a project director in humanitarian policy studies. He served as a member of President Carter's transition staff at the Department of State before joining the United States Mission to the United Nations.

In 1977, he was appointed ambassador and US deputy representative to the United Nations Security Council. From September 1979 to January 1981 he served as ambassador and US permanent representative to the United Nations and a member of Jimmy Carter's cabinet.

Leaving government in 1981, Ambassador McHenry became distinguished professor in the practice of diplomacy at the School of Foreign Service at Georgetown University, serving there until 2014. Upon his retirement, the university established the Donald F. McHenry Chair in Global Human Development.

During his career, Ambassador McHenry represented the United States in a number of international fora and was principal US negotiator on independence for Namibia. While at Georgetown, he undertook a number of governmental assignments, including special envoy of President Clinton for Nigeria, member of the United Nations Panel of Eminent Persons on Algeria (1998), and member of a congressional task force on the United Nations (2005). In addition, at the request of the president of Senegal, he chaired an international panel that reviewed the electoral code and processes of Senegal.

Ambassador McHenry has taught at Southern Illinois, Howard, American and Georgetown Universities. He is the author of *Micronesia: Trust Betrayed* (Carnegie Endowment 1975) and articles published in professional journals and newspapers.

Ambassador McHenry has held numerous board and trustee positions in nongovernmental organizations, and has served as a director or trustee on a broad range of corporations, universities, and foundations.

Rafe Pomerance worked with Andy at Clean Air-Cool Planet, which Rafe created as one of a variety of initiatives he took during his more than four decades of work on climate change. His early work became well known when he was featured in an issue of the *Sunday New York Times Magazine* called "Losing Earth," which described how climate change became a public issue as a result of Rafe's work in Congress and the media in the late 1970s and '80s.

Rafe's work on environmental issues began in the early '70s when he lobbied to introduce flexibility into the Highway Trust Fund, founded the National Clean Air Coalition to defend the integrity of the Clean Air Act, chaired the Board of the League of Conservation Voters, and, in 1973, cofounded American Rivers. He spent ten years on the staff of Friends of the Earth including four years as its president. He has also worked for the World Resources Institute and the US Department of State, where he served for six years as a deputy assistant secretary of state.

Susan Swift worked with Andy at Appropriate Technology International/ EnterpriseWorks Worldwide and the Global Alliance for Vaccines and Immunization.

After completing an MA in Journalism at Columbia University, Susan wrote for the International Union for the Conservation of Nature, became associate editor at *Newsweek*, then transitioned to Capitol Hill as a speechwriter for Senators Lowell Weicker and Tom Harkin.

Recruited by Andy to ATI, Susan revamped communications and was instrumental in devising and promoting strategies that expanded the international and grassroots impacts of the organization's programs in Africa, Asia, and Latin America.

When Andy's former colleague at the World Resources Institute, Mohamed El-Ashry, became president of a new organization, the Global Environment Facility (GEF), he asked Susan to join as senior editor and publications manager.

Created by the World Bank, the UN Development Program, and the UN Environment Program, GEF is a family of funds dedicated to confronting biodiversity loss, climate change, pollution, and strains on land and ocean health. GEF's grants, blended financing, and policy support help developing countries address their biggest environmental priorities and adhere to international environmental conventions. Over three decades, GEF has provided $23 billion, and mobilized $129 billion in co-financing, for more than five thousand national and regional projects.

Susan then moved to the World Bank, where she became speechwriter and special assistant to the president, James D. Wolfensohn.

As senior director, strategic marketing and communications at GAVI, Susan conceived and built an artistically beautiful, case-study based, and altruistically compelling website for the new Every Child fundraising campaign.

Later, she organized and produced for C-SPAN a staged reading of the United States Constitution at Georgetown University with the participation of leaders in government and the nonprofit sector. She built/retooled multimedia platforms, including the digital counterpart of an industry-leading quarterly. She led collaborative writing projects based on "green" ferry transportation, publishing an article titled "In Praise of Ferries," which became a series. She also created and coordinated "The Through Line," a set of articles on overcoming systemic problems from homelessness to the need for more diversity in the theater business.

Susan has worked in senior communications roles for the Children's Defense Fund, Independent Sector, and the Association of

Fundraising Professionals. She heads her own consulting firm, SDS Communications, LLC.

Carlisle Towery, who worked with Andy in Queens, came to New York after growing up in Alabama, then receiving a BS degree in architecture from Auburn University followed by an MS degree in architecture/planning from Columbia.

When he joined the staff of the New York metropolitan tri-state Regional Plan Association (RPA), Carlisle led the planning study for Jamaica, Queens, New York City "Jamaica Center." The study resulted in the establishment, by leaders from the Jamaica Chamber of Commerce—especially Joseph P. McMurray, president of Queens College, and Vincent M. Albanese, a prominent local attorney—of the nonprofit Greater Jamaica Development Corporation (GJDC). Concurrently, New York City mayor John Lindsay established the Office of Jamaica Planning and Development (OJPD) and appointed Andy to direct it.

Carlisle was hired by GJDC as its first executive director and later became the organization's president; he stayed at the agency for forty-five years. For two of those years he was also an associate professor in the graduate school of urban planning at Columbia. During his tenure at GJDC, he was guided by the plans and actions of GJDC and OJPD in transforming the older declining downtown into a multipurpose, regional subcenter as recommended by RPA. The active partnership between the two entities helped accomplish major public investments in Jamaica, including the New York College campus, regional headquarters offices of the Food and Drug Administration and the Social Security Administration, and major transportation improvements such as removal and replacement of the Jamaica Avenue El, the extension of southeast Queens subway line, and the creation of AirTrain, the light rail service from Jamaica to JFK airport. GJDC initiated extensive, major rezoning that enabled high-density, mixed-use development around the AirTrain. Jointly with OJPD, the GJDC facilitated special assessments for business improvements in four downtown districts. Collaborating with local elected officials, particularly the Queens borough presidents, notably Claire Shulman, GJDC created Jamaica Arts Center, the Farmers Market Jamaica, and the Hillside Avenue Housing Action Group, which improved several thousand apartments. With the Queens County Bar Association, GJDC helped enable the consolidation and construction of new Queens County court facilities.

Carlisle received the Person of the Year award for 2010 from the *Queens Tribune*. In 2015, he was honored with the *Queens Courier* Man of the Year Award, and touted as a "Jamaica Visionary." He was the recipient of York College's 2021 Legend Award, along with his wife Susan Deutsch, who served on the college's foundation board. He was a founding director of Partners for Livable Places, a nonprofit with the mission of promoting urban livability nationwide. He has served on the boards of several nonprofit organizations.

Dick Zimmer, a former Republican member of Congress, worked with Andy in 2013–2014 to encourage New Jersey business, labor, elected representatives, foundations, and citizen groups to establish a blue ribbon commission on extreme weather. The commission would have been chaired by former Republican governor Tom Kean and former Democratic governor Brendan Byrne, but then-Governor Chris Christie was unpersuaded.

Dick always was viewed as an exceptional campaigner and prodigious fundraiser—the kind of right-of-center Republican who was able to win elections in New Jersey.

A former Johnson & Johnson lawyer, president of New Jersey Common Cause, and Delaware Township farmer, Dick won a State Assembly seat on his second try in 1981 and moved up to the state Senate in a 1987 special election. After Representative Jim Courter announced his retirement in 1990, Dick ran for his open US House seat.

He represented New Jersey's 12th district in Congress from 1991 to 1997, giving up his seat to mount an unsuccessful run for the US Senate.

Dick has helped build coalitions of education reformers, engaged citizens, and policy leaders in New Jersey, developing important relationships with influential Democratic and Republican legislators and education opinion leaders statewide. His work has included briefings, informational forums, and support for the goals of the New Jersey Opportunity Scholarship Act, which assists students in the state's most disadvantaged districts with scholarships that allow students to choose superior schools. He has supported inter-district school choice, charter and virtual schools, online supplemental courses, education savings accounts, and studies on the positive fiscal impact that embracing Education Savings Accounts would have for New Jersey and New York.

ABOUT THE AUTHOR

Michael Takiff is the author of *A Complicated Man: The Life of Bill Clinton as Told by Those Who Know Him* (Yale University Press), awarded First Prize, Biography/Autobiography, at the Los Angeles Book Festival. His previous book, *Brave Men, Gentle Heroes: American Fathers and Sons in World War II and Vietnam* (William Morrow), was named a *Washington Post* "Critics' Pick." His writing has appeared in the *New York Times*, *Washington Post*, *Los Angeles Times*, *New York Post*, *Salon*, *The Nation*, CNN.com, and *HuffingtonPost*.

ACKNOWLEDGMENTS

Thanks to all who took time to give interviews for this volume. In alphabetical order: Jerry Breslin, Valeria Budinich, Tom Downey, David Dreyer, Rob Esposito, Gina Glantz, Ted Hoff, Elgie Holstein, Bob Kerr, John Lawrence, Michael Levin, Ed Markey, Donald McHenry, Rafe Pomerance, Marjorie Shultz, Susan Swift, Carlisle Towery, and, of course, Andy Maguire.

A special thank you to Ambassador McHenry, who went out of his way to give a tired interviewer a ride to his next appointment on a hot summer's day in the District of Columbia.

Thanks to Judy Myers, for an expert copy-edit.

Thanks to Andy, for his trust in me as the custodian of his life's story, as well as for his lifelong commitment to the betterment of our country and our world.

And thanks, above all, to my wife and son, who never complain about having to live with a writer.

Michael Takiff
New York City, October 2023

NOTE TO READERS

This book emerges from an optimistic view that history moves overall in a positive direction, and that those who commit to the public interest can advance human welfare in America and abroad.

Yet it is a long road from an inspiring Adlai Stevenson or Martin Luther King, Jr. to where we are today.

Pivoting sharply from a Rooseveltian consensus that lasted through Democratic and Republican administrations for half a century, Ronald Reagan presided over a political culture shift that elevated corporate profits over people, denigrated responsible government, maligned the poor while ignoring the effects of racial injustice, radically increased the national debt through tax cuts combined with huge increases in military spending that experts criticized as useless and wasteful, ignorantly failed to address the continuing degradation of our natural environment, and left all but the very wealthy behind.

Soon there emerged a political far right, many of whose members seem not to believe in the basic tenets of the Constitution, in the essentials of American democracy, or even in honest elections.

Along the way, George W. Bush, a candidate who lost the popular vote but became president due to the oddity of the electoral college and a transparently political 5-4 decision by the Supreme Court, doubled down on failed domestic economic policies, tolerated torture, and incompetently entangled America in disasters abroad.

Now as I write we face the continuing corrosion of our most fundamental values with the rise of the unspeakable Donald Trump and his enablers. We witness the astonishing personal and public corruption of some Supreme Court Justices. My own state's U.S. Senator, Bob Menendez, is charged with using his position as Chair of the Senate Foreign Relations Committee to act as an agent of a foreign power.

Many of our citizens are swamped with misinformation and disinformation. Too many of our leaders and citizens no longer have respect for science, for facts, for truth, for honest differences of opinion. No longer as a nation do we study and fully honor the civic virtues Americans have always before shared. No Edward R. Murrows or Walter Cronkites are heard today. Instead we are subjected to the lies and provocations of social media manipulators and bullhorn Tucker Carlsons acting out their manufactured rage at our public microphones.

As for the U.S. House of Representatives, where I proudly served at a time of institutional renewal and sweeping legislative achievements, the people's House too often is a dysfunctional embarrassment. The U.S. Senate is little better, having tied itself in knots with its own rules. The existential dangers to our democracy are heightened by the incapacity of Congress itself.

With such stunningly awful events and trends in America and around the world coming hard at us every day, I confess I feel new uncertainty about a progressive view of history. But let's all of us hope that over the next fifty years we will do better than we have over the past fifty.

Yes, there have been accomplishments over these years, but more creativity, more forward thinking, more "from the ground up" society-wide achievements are essential for America to hold secure our "of, by, and for the people" leadership role at home and abroad.

Let's take note of the millions of younger Americans who today are banding together, pushing important initiatives, working tirelessly in their communities, their states, and nationally for progressive change. Let's hope that together they will succeed in bringing a new vigor and a renewed national commitment to achieve what should be the birthright of every American.

Joined by many more leaders and citizens from oncoming generations, let's succeed in shifting our future onto a positive ascending curve once again.

This book honors the colleagues with whom I've been privileged to work at every stage of my career. They are an extraordinary group of exceptional performers who joined me in their devotion to good ideas, and in taking on the hard work of "making a difference" wherever, together, we felt we should go. Each of them did indeed make a distinct difference, and all of them gave unstintingly of their time and attention in contributing to these pages. Please look at "The Maguire Teams" appendix for the stunning shape of each of these colleagues' continued careers. I am grateful that our personal friendships have endured over the decades.

The first stop in launching this saga of what became known among all of us as "the book" was the Rutgers University Library, where my papers are stored as part of the Special Collections archive. Through their attention and good offices, Ron Becker, Albert King, and their associates unfailingly assisted me in locating what I needed. Scott Crass did early interviews and together we wrote drafts that would dovetail into the book.

The big breakthrough came when my former colleague, Congressman David Bonior of Michigan, introduced me to the historian Michael Takiff, author of major books on Bill Clinton and on World War II/ Vietnam War fathers and sons. Michael and I bonded, and off we went towards what we feel is an unusual "hybrid" chronicle of my career in the context of several chapters of America's recent progress and struggles, domestic and foreign.

Margaret "Meg" Green was an invaluable partner at the beginning of this odyssey. We met while co-leading the YMCA-YWCA "Summer in Washington" program. While only five months old, our son Jay accompanied me in a backpack as I campaigned along the route of the annual Ridgewood, New Jersey, Fourth of July parade in my first try for public office. I am convinced that Jay turned out some votes that normally would not have been mine.

Then came the incomparable threesome of Katherine, Sara, and Andrew, much to the delight of their father and mother, Alice Reed. All four kids are living jubilant lives, all are close with me, with each other, and with the parents of the mingled families. My sister Marjorie Shultz is a continuing inspiration, along with her husband Jim and their sons Steve and Matt. For the love and support of all the family—including encouragement from all of them for "the book"—I am deeply grateful.

Finally, in her absence, I embrace my wife Adele Maria DeMarco, who shared my life—including every stage of book prep—for many wonderful years.

Andy Maguire
January 2024

INDEX

Note: Page numbers in *italics* denote illustrations.

A
Abdul Enterprises, 269
abortion issue, 137–138, 261
Abscam, 268–270
Abzug, Bella, 193
Acheson, Dean, 15–16
acid rain, 301, 302, 360
activism, Maguire's devotion to, 26, 37–38, 179, *198–200*, 379
Adams, Brock, 237
Adele (De Marco, wife of Maguire), 4, 370
Addabbo, Joe, 117
Affordable Care Act, 359, 373, 374
Afghanistan, Bush and, 356
AFL-CIO, 346
Africa
- ATI in, 307
- Belgium and, 40, 47
- Bipartisan Monitoring Group, 181
- decolonization, 39–40
- history of, 39, 42
- Maguire in, 38–42, 46–49, *200, 201*
- Simba Rebellion, 47

African studies, Maguire at Harvard, 38–42, 49–50, 53
Agnew, Spiro, 15, 111, 142
Ahearn, Jim, 276, 401
AIDS, 288
air pollution
- cancer and, 215–217, 219
- climate change and, 301–302, 382
- emission standards for cars, 220, 224

air traffic controllers strike (1981), 280–281
Albert, Carl, 163, 257
Albright, Alice, 348
All in Together (nonprofit), 393
Allende, Salvador, 128
Alliance for Progress, 43, 283
alpacas, 334–335
Alter, Jonathan, 383
American Clean Energy and Security Act (2009), 359–360
American Recovery and Reinvestment Act, 373
Anderson, John, 253, 258, 259, 260, 264
Andrus, Cecil, 205
Anglo-Iranian Oil Company, 238
antiwar movement
- Kennedy, Robert F., 76
- Kent State University, 127
- Maguire and, 25–26, 73–74
- Vietnam War, 77, 112, 127

apartheid, 65, 66, 81, 181–182, 222
Appropriate Technology International (ATI), 306–313, 318–326, 382–383, 391, 401
Arab oil embargo (1973), 119, 162–163
Arab States
- Camp David Accords, 222–223
- Six Day War, 58–67
- UN Resolution 242, 59, 62–63

Arafat, Yasser, 63
Armey, Dick, 329
Aronoff, Marcia, 367, 370
Ashoka, 308, 311, 402
Atherton, Alfred, 244
ATI. *See* Appropriate Technology International
Atwater, Lee, 354
Atwood, Brian, 326
Aurelio, Dick, 122
automakers, emission standards, 220, 224

B
Badillo, Herman, 104
Baker, Ella, 34
Baker, Howard, 141, 253, 254
Baker, James A., III, 300, 315
Baker, John, 57–58
Bales, Carter, 325
Bankcard Holders of America (organization), 394
Barber, James David, 267
Barbour, Haley, 376
Barry, Marion, 34–35
Battistella, Annabel, 155

Bay of Pigs invasion, 44
Beame, Abraham, 89
Begin, Menachem, 222, 223
Belgium, in Africa, 40, 47
Bell, Griffin, 169
Bell, Jeffrey, 229, 272
Benfield, Dick, 401
Bennett, John C., 7
Bentsen, Lloyd, 298
Bergen County (NJ), 116–117, 120–125
Bergen County Sewer Authority, 122–124, 138–139
Bernstein, Carl, 141
The Best and the Brightest (Halberstam), 72
Bianchi, Angelo, 272
Biden, Joe, 147, 289, 371, 384–385, 395
Bielenberg, Carl, 307, 311
Biko, Steve, 181–182
Bill and Melinda Gates Foundation, 347
Bill Steiger Memorial Bill (1979), 221
bin Laden, Osama, 373
Bipartisan Monitoring Group on South Africa,, 181
Blackmun, Harry, 112
Boland, Ed, 245
Bolivia, 334–336
Bonior, David, 325, 326
Bordering on Trouble: Resources & Politics in Latin America (Maguire & Brown), 282–284
Bork, Robert, 142
Bosnia, 384
Botha, Pik, 18
Bowen, Otis, 235
Bowman, Richard, 334, 345, 346
Brademas, John, 158
Bradley, Bill, 147, 227, 228
Brady, James, 293
Breen, Jon, 253
Breslin, Jerry, 121, 122, 132
Brezhnev, Leonid, 129, 222
Broder, David, 280
Brokaw, Tom, 298
Brooke, Edward, 226
Brown, Edmund "Pat," 187
Brown, H. Rap, 35
Brown, Janet Welsh, 282
Brown v. Board of Education (1954), 12
Bruce, Lenny, 52
Buchanan, Patrick, 315
Buckley, William F., Jr., 89
Buckley v. Valeo, 273, 382
Budinich, Valeria, 306, 308, 310, 311, 312, 318, 319, 321, 322, 326, 334, 337, 339, 342, 401–403
Buffum, William, 55
Bunche, Ralph, 83
Bundy, McGeorge, 72, 74, 79
Bureau of Land Management, 290
Burns, Arthur, 178
Burstein, Albert, 147–148
Burton, Phil, 208
Bush, Dwight, 348
Bush, George H.W.
- about, 149, 266
- campaign of 1988, 297–302, 314
- campaign of 1992, 316–318
- climate change and, 300–302
- election (1980), 230, 253
- Iran-Contra scandal, 159
- reelection bid, 248
- "voodoo economics," 230, 254

Bush, George W.
- about, 328, 332, 354, 357, 383, 384
- Afghanistan, 356
- election, 328, 332
- environment and, 358
- Hurricane Katrina, 266, 366–367
- Iraq War, 356–357
- Kyoto Protocol, 358
- presidency, 354–357, 366
- privatizing Social Security, 366
- reelection, 366

Butterfield, Alexander, 142
Byrne, Brendan, 206, 227, 376, 393, 397
Byrne, Tommy, 377

C

CA-CP. *See* Clean Air-Cool Planet
CAFE standard. *See* corporate average fuel efficiency (CAFE) standard
CaixaBank, 349
Calabrese, Gerald, 121
Califano, Joseph, 237
California
- politics of, 189
- Reagan and UC Berkeley, 187

Cambodia, Vietnam War and, 127
Camp David Accords, 222–223
cancer
- "Maguire Report," 2, 217, 369
- saccharin, 217–218
- toxic pollution and, 215–217, 368

Capital Availability for Higher Education Act (1975), 221
Caradon, Lord, 51, 62, *196*
Carawan, Guy, 35
carbon capture, 346
carbon tax, 302, 362
CARE, 340
Carmichael, Stokely, 34, 35
Carter, Jimmy
- about, 112, 234–235, 278
- cabinet firings (1979), 237–238
- Camp David Accords, 222–223
- election of 1976, 189–191, 204
- energy proposals (1977), 209–214
- foreign policy, 221–223
- greenhouse effect, 292
- Iran and, 222, 238–241
- Maguire and, 203, 207, 211–214, 246–248
- "malaise" speech, 238
- oil crisis (1979), 235

oil policy, 210, 247–248
photo, *196*
reelection campaign (1980), 238, 248–256, 258–261, 264
on smoking, 214
on toxic waste, 215–217
water policy, 204–205
Carville, James, 325
Case, Clifford, 177, 226, 227–228, 244, 381
The Center Holds (Alter), 383
CFCs (chlorofluorocarbons), 292, 295, 301
Chafee, John, 293–295, 301, 327
Chaney, James, 259
Chapman, Amy, 135, 400
Chappaquiddick scandal, 249
Cheney, Dick, 355, 356, 384
Chetty, Shun, 40
Chiang Kai-shek, 128
Chile, 127–128, 222
China
economy of, 295
Nixon and, 128
Christie, Chris, 376–377
Church, Frank, 168, 190
Citizens Action Committee to Fight Inflation, 160–161
Civil Rights Act (1957), 71
Civil Rights Act (1964), 51, 71
civil rights movement
1950s, 12
1960s, 25, 51
Civil Rights Act (1957), 71
Civil Rights Act (1964), 51, 71
Freedom Rides of 1961, 35
Freedom Summer of 1964, 35, 259
Greensboro Four, 34
Johnson on, 70–71
Kennedy on, 69–70
King, Martin Luther, Jr., 10, 12, 25, 34, 35, 76
Maguire's activism, 2, 26, 33–37
March on Washington, 25
nonviolence, 35, 36
segregated lunch counters, 36
segregation in white churches, 36–37
sit-ins, 34
Southern Christian Leadership Conference, 34
Student Nonviolent Coordinating Committee (SNCC), 33–35
Voting Rights Act (1965), 51, 71
"We Shall Overcome" (song), 35
See also racism
Clean Air Act (1970), 219
Clean Air Act (1990), 301
Clean Air Act Amendments (1977), 219
Clean Air-Cool Planet (CA-CP), 358, 360–365, 383
climate change, 291–295, 382
Bush (G.H.W.) and, 300–302
Clean Air-Cool Planet, 358
global warming, 301
Waxman-Markey climate bill, 346, 359–365
climate denial, 365
Clinch River Breeder Reactor, 224–225
Clinton, Bill
about, 112, 289, 316, 373
avoidance of military service, 317
Bosnia and, 384
election (1992), 316–318
foreign affairs, 384
Lewinsky affair, 331
liberalism during administration of, 327–333
reelection, 330–331, 332
second term, 331
Clinton, Hillary Rodham, 327, 371, 375
The Coldest War (Brady), 293
Colgan, Howard O., Jr., 135, 150
college loans, 220–221
Collins, Susan, 362
Common Cause, 183
Communism, in Vietnam, 74
Communists, Nixon and, 128
Competitive Advantage: Creating and Sustaining Superior Performance (Porter), 311, 312
Comstock, Bob, 401
Congress. *See* US Congress
Connally, John, 253–254
conservative Christians, 286
Constantino, Rocco, 234
Consumer Products Safety Commission, 288
Conte, Silvio, 245
corporate average fuel efficiency (CAFE) standard, 165, 166
Corzine, Jon, 273, 276
COVID-19 pandemic, 288, 385, 395–396
Cox, Archibald, 141, 142
Crane, Phil, 253
Cronkite, Walter, 75–76
Cuba, Bay of Pigs invasion, 44
Cuomo, Mario, 314, 328

D

Daley, Richard J., 77
D'Amato, Al, 114
Davis, Rennie, 26
De Marco, Adele (wife of Maguire), 4, 370
Dean, John, 141–142
Deepwater Horizon oil spill, 365
Democratic Leadership Council, 317
Deng Xiaoping, 128
Denison, Richard, 367, 368
Derwinski, Ed, 245
desegregation, 12
Dicks, Norm, 344–345
Dingell, John, 163, 164, 220
Dinkins, David, 114
Dole, Robert, 189, 191, 253, 254, 298, 329, 330
Downey, Tom, 157, 174, 181, 182, 184, 206, 232, 256, 266, 323, 325

Dozoretz, Ronald and Beth, 325
Drayton, Bill, 308, 311, 340, 342, 402
Dreyer, David, 174, 180, 207, 245, 390
Dugard, John, 40
Dukakis, Michael, 297, 299–300, 301, 314, 317, 354
Dulles, Allen, 238, 239
Dunn, Tom, 273–274

E
Eagleton, Thomas, 131
Eastman, Penny, 324
Eban, Abba, 61, 62, 64
Eckhardt, Bob, 164
economics
- Appropriate Technology International (ATI), 306–313, 318–323, 324–326, 382–383, 391, 401
- laissez-faire economics, 289
- microloans, 341
- Reaganomics, 289
- Schumacher and, 305
- value chain, 311–312, 339, 340
- Volker on, 271
- "voodoo economics," 230, 254

EDF. *See* Environmental Defense Fund
education, student loans, 221
Egypt
- Camp David Accords, 222–223
- Six Day War, 58–67

Ehrlichman, John, 141, 143
E.I. du Pont de Nemours, 215, 244
Eisenhower, Dwight, 12, 15, 17, 43–44, 59, 238, 239, 289
Eizenstat, Stuart, 212, 235
Elliott, Donald H., 80, 85–86, 94, 99
Ellsberg, Daniel, 142
Endeavor Foundation, 402
energy
- Arab oil embargo (1973), 119, 162–163
- Carter's proposals (1977), 209–214
- corporate average fuel efficiency (CAFE) standard, 165, 166
- Energy Policy and Conservation Act (1975), 165
- National Energy Act, 214
- natural gas, 169–171
- oil policy, 165, 166, 210

Energy Policy and Conservation Act (1975), 165
EnterpriseWorks Worldwide, 324–326, 333–342, 391–392, 401–402
environment
- acid rain, 301, 302
- Acid Rain Program, 360
- air pollution, 215–217, 219, 220, 301–302
- Bush (G.W.) and, 358
- Carter and industrial pollution, 215–217
- Clean Air Act (1970), 219
- Clean Air Act (1990), 301
- Clean Air Act Amendments (1977), 219
- Clean Air-Cool Planet, 358, 383
- climate change, 291–295, 382
- emission standards for cars, 220, 224
- Environmental Defense Fund (EDF), 367–370, 383
- Frank R. Lautenberg Chemical Safety for the 21st Century Act (2016), 369
- greenhouse effect, 291, 292, 294
- industrial pollution, 215–217
- Kyoto Protocol, 358
- Reagan and, 289–291
- Toxic Substances Control Act (TSCA), 367
- Waxman-Markey climate bill, 346, 359–365

Environmental Defense Fund (EDF), 367–370, 383
Environmental Protection Agency, 112, 126, 215, 219, 289, 396, 397
Errichetti, Angelo, 269
Ervin, Sam, 116, 141
Eshkol, Levi, 64
Esposito, Rob, 120, 125, 133, 135, 136, 144, 146, 151, 255, 323, 325, 326, 391–392
essential oils project (Nepal), 333
Export-Import Bank Amendment Act (1978), 68–69

F
Fair Access to Higher Education Act (1979), 221
Fall, Bernard, 47
Family and Medical Leave Act, 327
Federal Reserve Board, 178
Fein, Mitchell, 267–268
Feldman, Matty, 121
Fellowship of Reconciliation, 7–8
Feltman, Art, 135, 400
The Feminine Mystique (Friedan), 18
Fenwick, Millicent, 177, 178
"fireside chats," 209
Fithian, Floyd, 245
Florio, James, 177, 271
Flowers, Gennifer, 317
Foley, Tom, 155, 328
Food for Furniture amendment, 244–246
Foot, Hugh, 62
Ford, Gerald
- about, 143, 159–160, 248, 262
- Department of Justice under, 168–169
- economic policy, 160–161
- election campaign (1976), 186–192, 194
- energy policy, 162–167
- foreign policy, 171–174
- Helsinki Accords, 172–174, 191–192
- inflation and, 160
- oil policy, 163–165
- Vietnam War, 156

Ford Foundation, 79, 122, 268
Foreign Assistance Act, Food for Furniture amendment, 244–246

Foreign Corrupt Practices Act, 288
Forst, Frank, 272
Fosdick, Harry Emerson, 7
Foxe, Fanne, 155
Frank R. Lautenberg Chemical Safety for the 21st Century Act (2016), 369
Frankel, Max, 191–192
Franklin Roosevelt (aircraft carrier), 66, 67
Freedom Rides of 1961, 35
Freedom Summer of 1964, 35, 259
Friedan, Betty, 18
Frost, David, 159
Full Economic Citizenship, 402

G

Gandhi, Mahatma, 13, 14, 34
Garber, Marjorie, 152
Garth, David, 227
Gates Foundation, 347
GAVI. *See* Global Alliance for Vaccines and Immunization
gay-rights movement, 26
GEF. *See* Global Environment Facility
gender stereotypes, 19
GenderAvenger (nonprofit), 393
Gephardt, Dick, 314
Gingrich, Newt, 328–329, 331
Giuliani, Rudolph, 114
GJDC. *See* Greater Jamaica Development Corporation
Glantz, Gina, 124–125, 133, 134, 136–138, 144, 146, 147, 150, 194, 230, 231, 274, 275, 392–393
Glantz, Ron, 134
Global Alliance for Vaccines and Immunization (GAVI), 348–353, 383
Global Environment Facility (GEF), 405
Global Livestock Group, 345–346
global warming, 301
Goldberg, Arthur J., 55, 58, 63, 68, 73, 108–109, *196*
Goldwater, Barry, 45, 71, 77, 88, 111, 143, 187, 260
Goodman, Andrew, 259
Gorbachev, Mikhail, 285
Gore, Al, 314, 318, 323, 332, 358, 392
Gorsuch, Anne, 290–291
Graham, Jack, 157
Gralla, Milton, 149
Grameen Bank, 341
Gray, Bill, 244
Greater Jamaica Development Corporation (GJDC), 95, 406
Green, Margaret Lydia "Meg," 97, 281
    See also Maguire, Meg
Greenberg, Stan, 260
greenhouse effect, 291, 292, 294
Greensboro Four, 34
Greenspan, Alan, 327
The Gulag Archipelago (Solzhenitsyn), 173
Gulf of Tonkin Resolution, 46
Gulf Oil, 171
Gulf War, 314–316

H

Halberstam, David, 72
Haldeman, H.R., 140–141, 143
Harkin, Tom, 326
Harrison, Mary Anne, 87
Hart, Gary, 296, 297, 390
Harvard University
    Maguire as fellow, 281–282
    Maguire's African studies at, 38–42, 49–50, 53
Harvey, Hal, 362
Hatfield, Mark, 226
healthcare
    Affordable Care Act, 359, 373, 374
    Medicare, 260, 266, 329
Hébert, Edward, 155
Heinz, John, 286
Helms, Jesse, 173, 174
Helmsley, Harry, 109–111
Helsinki Accords, 172–174, 191–192
Helstoski, Henry, 177, 276
Henry, Don, 135–136
Herbert, Frank, 121
Hinckley, John, 278
Hiss, Alger, 15
HIV, 394–395
Ho Chi Minh, 44, 157
Hodges, Gil, 105
Hoff, Ted, 135, 263, 264, 393
Hollenbeck, Harold, 276
Holstein, Elgie, 165, 169–170, 175, 179, 181, 230, 231, 324, 394
Holtz-Eakin, Douglas, 361–362
homosexuality. *See* LGBTQ+
Horton, Willie, 314
Hotchkiss, Ralf, 307–308
House of Representatives. *See* US House of Representatives
Howard, Jim, 177, 208
Hoyer, Steny, 363
Hughes, William, 177, 247
Humphrey, Hubert, 32, 77, 79, 129, 150, 225, 296, 381
Hurford, John, 325
Hurricane Katrina, 266, 366–367
Hurricane Sandy, 376, 377, 383
Hussein, Saddam, 314, 356
Hyman, Eric, 320
Hynes, Eddie, 133, 138, 140

I

Ibrahim, Mo, 351–352
immunization, Global Alliance for Vaccines and Immunization (GAVI), 348–353, 383
Immunize Every Child Campaign, 347, 348
Improshare, 267–268
"An Inconvenient Truth" (Gore lecture, book, movie), 358
India, 338, 345

Indonesia, 171–172
industrial pollution, Carter on, 215–217
infrastructure, ATI and, 307
Insatiable Appetite: The United States and the Ecological Degradation of the Tropical World (Tucker), 283
Inter-American Development Bank, 334, 335
Intermediate Technology Development Group, 306
International Metalizing Corp., 343–344
Iran
  Carter and, 222, 238–241
  Contra scandal, 159, 241–242, 285, 287
  oil crisis, 235
  Reagan and, 241–242
Iraq Wars, 79, 314–316, 356–357, 371
Israel
  Camp David Accords, 222–223
  history of, 60
  political parties of, 60
  Six Day War, 58–67
  United Nations Resolution 242, 59, 62–63
  Yom Kippur War, 119
Ivins, Molly, 203

J
Jackson, Henry "Scoop," 31, 73, 138, 147, 225
Jackson-Vanik Amendment, 138, 148
Jasons, 291, 292
jatamansi, 333, 338
Jaworski, Leon, 142, 143
Job, Gill, 133, 138, 139
Johnson, Lionel, 135
Johnson, Lyndon B.
  about, 32, 55, 71
  climate change and, 291
  domestic programs, 71–72
  national security team, 171
  1980 election, 248
  South Africa, 67
  Vietnam War, 45–46, 72–74, 76, 78
Justman, Jessica, 394–395

K
Kayden, Joelle, 400
Kean, Thomas, 271, 376
Kemp, Jack, 230, 325, 392
Kemp-Roth tax cut, 230
Kennedy, Edward Moore "Ted," 248–253
Kennedy, John F.
  about, 69, 139
  African feeling about in 1960s, 46
  Alliance for Progress, 43
  Bay of Pigs invasion, 44
  on civil rights, 69–70
  on colonialism, 41–42
  death, 45, 70
  Peace Corps, 43
  presidential campaign, 25, 28–31, 32
  on underdeveloped countries, 43–46
Kennedy, Robert F., 76–77, 89
Kent State University, 127
Kenya, 49
Kenyatta, Jomo, 49
Kerr, Bob, 219, 220, 385–386, 395–396
Kerry, John, 363, 366, 371
Khmer Rouge, 127
Khomeini, Ayatollah Ruhollah, 240
Khrushchev, Nikita, 44
King, John, 401
King, Martin Luther, Jr., 10, 12, 25, 34, 35, 76, 384
Kirkland, Lane, 279
Kissinger, Henry
  on Carter's oil policy, 211
  foreign policy, 74, 79, 127, 128, 129, 171–174
  SALT II arms treaty, 240
  Vietnam, 74, 128, 129
Kleindienst, Richard, 167
Kleiner, Thom, 135, 400
Koch, Ed, 113–114
Koch brothers, 365
Koop, C. Everett, 288
Kopechne, Mary Jo, 249
Korper, Sam, 400
Krupp, Fred, 367–370
Kunin, Madeleine, 281
Kurtz, Howard, 400–401
Kyoto Protocol, 358

L
labor, air traffic controllers strike (1981), 280–281
LaFeber, Walter, 283
LaGuardia, Fiorello, 87
laissez-faire economics, 289
Land and Water Conservation Fund, 290
Laos, Vietnam War and, 74
Latin America
  Kennedy and, 43, 44
  Maguire at World Resource Institute, 282
  NAFTA, 332
Lautenberg, Frank, 272–275, 369, 381
Lawrence, John, 154, 156, 162, 203–204, 207–208
LeFante, Joseph, 274
Legal Services Corp., 288
Leone, Richard, 227
Lesemann, Arthur, 121, 133
Levi, Edward, 168
Levin, Michael, 175, 207, 258, 396–397
Lewinsky scandal, 331
Lewis, John, 34, 35
LGBTQ+, gays in the military, 327–328
liberalism
  Bush (George H.W.) and, 297
  civil rights movement and, 92
  Clinton administration and, 327–333
  current state of, 383, 385
  Gingrich and, 328–329

Johnson and, 70
Lindsay in New York City, 104, 114
in Maguire household, 18
Nixon reelection and, 129–132
passing of in 1970s, 111–113
Vietnam War and, 73
Lindsay, John V., 80–115
about, 87–89
election (1965), 89–90, 139
Jamaica initiative, 80–85, 94–103, 106, 406
labor problems, 90–91
Maguire and, 80–86, 95–115
old age, 114
progressive platform, 89
reelection (1969), 84, 103–107
unpopularity in Queens, 82–83
Lindsay, Mary Harrison, 87
Lob-Levyt, Julian, 349–350, 352–353
Locklin, Ken, 346
Lon Nol, 127
Long, Russell, 205
Lott, Trent, 330, 331
Ludi, Gerard, 40

M

MacDonald, Gordon, 292
Maddox, Lester, 76, 189–190
Maguire, Andy (Andrew George, grandfather), 7
Maguire, Andy (Gene Andrew): personal life
activism, 2–4, 7, 179, *198–200*
adolescence, 20–24
altruism and activism in youth, 9–11, 18, 117, 380
athleticism, 21–22
children, 4
college years, 23–24
education, 2, 21–24, 27, 37–42, 49–50, 53
father's influence, 10–24, 26, 33, 69
first experiences with racism, 33–34
graduate work at Harvard, 38–42, 49–50, 53
life's vocation, 18
marriages, 3–4, 97
as parent, 4
parents of, 6–14
personality, 2–4, 7, 145, 175–176, 350, 380, 385–386
photos, *195–197, 202*
public speaking, 9, 12
racism, 13–14, 33, 39
undergraduate at Oberlin College, 23, 27, 37–38
Maguire, Andy (Gene Andrew): professional life
about, 2–4, 379–387
activism, 26, 37–38, 117, 179, *198–200*, 379
on Africa, 47–49, 69
African studies at Harvard, 38–42, 49–50, 53
antiwar movement, 26, 73
apartheid, 65, 66, 181–182
at Appropriate Technology International (ATI), 308–313, 318–323, 324–326, 382–383, 391, 401
Bill Steiger Memorial Bill (1979), 221
Bordering on Trouble: Resources & Politics in Latin America (Maguire & Brown), 282–284
building of new Queens Civil Court, 101–103
cancer and environment, 215–218, 220, 368
Capital Availability for Higher Education Act (1975), 221
on Carter, 203, 207, 211–214, 246–248
civil rights activism, 2, 26, 33–37
at Clean Air-Cool Planet, 358, 360–365, 383
Clinch River Breeder Reactor, 224–225
as consultant in later years, 343–377
criticism of, 174–180, 184–186, 380
dissertation, 41–42
energy as signature issue, 242
energy policy, 162–167
at EnterpriseWorks Worldwide, 324–326, 333–342, 391–392, 401–402
environment and, 294–298, 382
at Environmental Defense Fund (EDF), 367–370, 383
Fair Access to Higher Education Act (1979), 221
first job, 49–50
Food for Furniture amendment, 244–246
Ford Foundation, 79, 122, 268
on Ford's oil policy, 164–165
Global Alliance for Vaccines and Immunization (GAVI), 348–353, 383
graduate work, 38–42
at Harvard, 38–42, 49–50, 53, 281–282
House of Representatives: as freshman Congressman, 2, 158, 162–164, 176, 389
House of Representatives: campaign for Congress, 116–117, 120–125, 132–140
House of Representatives: election to, 144–151
House of Representatives: loss of seat, 265–266, 380
House of Representatives: Maguire and House majority leader campaign, 208
House of Representatives: reelection (1978), 229–233
House of Representatives: reelection to second term (1980), 193–194, 255, 261–265
how to get things done, 107–108
at Improshare, 267–268, 288

inspired by Edward R. Murrow, 6–7
interns working for, 400
internship with "Scoop" Jackson, 31
Jamaica initiative, 80–85, 94–103, 106, 108, 109–111, 380
journalists covering, 400–401
on Latin America, 282–284
lobbyists and special interests and, 218–221, 225–227
"Maguire Report," 2, 217, 369
Maguire-Steiger bill, 221
management style, 174–180, 184–186, 380, 385–386
natural gas policy in 1970s, 169–171
New Jersey issues and, 242–244
in New York City under Lindsay, 80–86, 95–115
at North American Securities Administrators Association, 302–303
oil price decontrol, 256–257
Panama Canal, 221–222
photos, *195–197, 202*
post–ATI/EWW activities, 343–377
post–State Dept. opportunities, 78–81
practice of politics, 204–207
retirement, 383
Senate aspirations, 270–273, 381
Senate campaign (1978), 227–228, 270, 276, 381
Senate campaign (1982), 270–275, 381
Sikes and, 182–187
societal change and, 26, 37–38, 117
South Africa, 65–69
at State Department, 49–78
student loans, 220–221
supporting Adlai Stevenson, 14–18
supporting John F. Kennedy, 28–31
in Tanganyika, 40–42
at Union of Concerned Scientists (UCS), 375
at United Nations, 53–68
US Senate seat campaign, 227–229
on Vietnam War, 73–75
work habits and methods, 2, 152–153, 175, 204–207
at World Resources Institute, 282, 283, 294–295, 382
in years 2003–2014, 343–377

Maguire, Bruce (father), 1, 7–8, 10–24, 26, 33, 145–146, 274
Maguire, Jeannie (grandmother), 7
Maguire, Marjorie (sister). *See* Shultz, Marjorie "Marj"
Maguire, Meg (wife), 97, 116, 117, 122, 134, 231
Maguire, Ruth Leitch (mother), 7–9, 19, 23, 26, 33, 145, 146
"Maguire Report," 2, 217, 369
Mahon, George, 155
Mailer, Norman, 104
Malecela, John, 47–48
Mandela, Nelson, 40
Mandela, Winnie, 42
Mao Zedong, 128
March on Washington, 25
Marchi, John, 103–104
Markey, Ed, 218, 258, 359, 364
Martin, Angie, 264, 392
Matalin, Mary, 325
Mathias, Charles, 226
McCain, John, 301, 354, 363, 372
McCarthy, Eugene, 76, 248
McCarthy, Joseph, 5–6, 15, 372
McClellan, John, 156
McConnell, Mitch, 373, 374–375
McCord, James, 140
McDew, Charles, 34, 35, 36
McGovern, George, 77, 125, 129–132, 190, 317
McHenry, Donald F., 54–55, 61, 66, 67, 74, 79, 403–404
McHugh, Matt, 245
McNamara, Robert, 72, 74–75
Meany, George, 173
Medicare, 260, 266, 329
Meir, Golda, 105
Meisner, Bill, 121
metalizing, 344
Meyner, Helen, 177
Mezzacappa, Dale, 401
microloans, 341
Middle East
Arab oil embargo, 119, 162–163
Camp David Accords, 222–223
Operation Desert Storm, 314–316
Saddam Hussein, 314
Six Day War, 58–67
Yom Kippur War, 119
military services, gays in, 327–328
Mills, Wilbur, 155
Minish, Joseph, 177, 179, 180
Mitchell, John, 143, 167
Mitchell, Parren, 228
Mobil Oil Corp., 170, 256
Moffett, Toby, 157, 163, 170, 174, 181, 212, 247
Mohammad Reza Shah, 238
Mondale, Walter, 147, 190, 205, 252, 253, 262, 296, 317
Moore, Curtis, 293
Moose, Dick, 68
Morris, Adele, 362
Moses, Robert, 86
Moss, John, 169
Mossadegh, Mohammad, 238
Mudd, Roger, 185, 250
Murphy, Phil, 273
Murrow, Edward R., 6
Muskie, Edmund, 129–130, 140, *198–200*, 245

N

Nader, Ralph, 332, 355
NAFTA, 332
Nasser, Gamal Abdel, 58–59

National Cancer Institute, 215–217, 369
National Dairy Development Board of India, 338
National Energy Act, 214
National Labor Relations Board, 288
National Taxpayers Union, 232
natural gas, 169–171
Nemtsov, David, 135
Nepal, *202*, 333, 338
New Jersey
  cancer mortality rate, 215, 220
  Carter and, 206
  industrial pollution in, 215–216
  Maguire and, 242–244
  natural gas in 1970s, 169–171
  Senate race (1982), 270–275
  television station of its own, 241–242
  Union of Concerned Scientists (UCS), 375
New York City
  building of new Queens Civil Court, 101–103
  Dinkins as mayor, 114
  Giuliani as mayor, 114
  Jamaica initiative, 80–85, 94–103, 106
  Koch as mayor, 113–114
  labor problems under Lindsay, 90–91
  Lindsay as mayor, 80–115
  Maguire and Lindsay administration, 80–85, 94–103, 106
  Mets World Series win (1969), 105
  Office of Jamaica Planning and Development (OJPD), 83–84, 106, 108, 109–111, 380, 406
  rail transportation to JFK airport, 99
  Regional Plan Association, 80, 84, 95, 406
  rerouted Jamaica subway "el," 99–100
  teacher's strike, 91
  Transport Workers Union strike (1965), 90
  York College created, 100–101
Ngo Dinh Diem, 45
Nguyen Van Thieu, 156
Nicaragua, 222, 286–287
nitrosamines, 215
Nixon, Richard M.
  about, 15, 73, 111–113, 125, 190, 277–278, 289
  Allende affair, 127–128
  China visit, 128
  conservatism of, 111–112
  Department of Justice under, 168–169
  domestic affairs, 112, 126, 289
  Eisenhower and, 15
  election, 77–78, 79
  global affairs, 126–129
  impeachment, 143, 149
  inflation and, 160
  reelection, 129–131
  resignation, 143
  "Saturday Night Massacre," 142
  "smoking gun tape," 143
  USSR, 128, 129, 143
  Vietnam War and, 25, 74, 78, 118–119, 126–127
  Watergate affair, 140–144, 149, 153
  White House Plumbers, 142
nonviolence, civil rights movement, 35, 36
Noonan, Peggy, 298
North American Securities Administrators Association, 302–303
North, Oliver, 287
Nyerere, Julius, 38, 46

O
Obama, Barack
  about, 204, 289, 331
  American Recovery and Reinvestment Act, 373
  climate legislation, 365
  Deepwater Horizon oil spill, 365
  environment and, 358–359
  first campaign, 370–372
  Maguire on, 365
  presidency, 358–360, 365, 372–375
  reelection, 373–374
Obamacare, 359, 373, 374
Oberlin College, 23, 27, 37–38
Occupational Safety and Health Administration (OSHA), 112, 269, 288
Office of Jamaica Planning and Development (New York City), 83–84, 106, 108, 109–111, 380, 406
oil
  Anglo-Iranian Oil Company, 238
  Arab oil embargo (1973), 119, 162–163
  Carter's policy, 210, 247–248
  climate change and, 291
  corporate average fuel efficiency (CAFE) standard, 165, 166
  decontrol of oil prices, 256–257
  Deepwater Horizon oil spill, 365
  Energy Policy and Conservation Act (1975), 165
  Ford's policy, 163–165
  oil crisis (1979), 235–237
  windfall profits tax, 247–248
oilseed press, ATI and, 307, 310–311
O'Neill, Tip, 184, 208, 237, 257, 280, 285
Operation Desert Storm, 314–316
O'Rourke, Bea, 135, 397–398
OSHA. *See* Occupational Safety and Health Administration
Oswald, Lee Harvey, 70
ozone, climate change, 291–295

P
Pahlavi, Mohammad Reza Shah, 238
Palin, Sarah, 372
Panama Canal, 221–222
Papp, Joe, 244
Parsekian, Ned, 133, 138, 139
"pass laws," South Africa, 65

Pataki, George, 328
PATCO. *See* Professional Air Traffic Controllers Organization
Patman, Wright, 155
Patten, Eddie, 208
Peace Corps, 43, 46
Pedersen, Richard Foote, 50, 54–55, 57, 61, 73, *196*
Pelosi, Nancy, 360, 385
Pentagon Papers, 142
People for the American Way, 346
People's Republic of China, Nixon and, 128
Perot, Ross, 317
Pesky, Johnny, 234
PHIA Project. *See* Population-based HIV Impact Assessment (PHIA) Project
Philippines, 222
Pinochet, Augusto, 128, 222
Poage, William, 155
pollution
  Clean Air Act (1970), 219
  Clean Air Act Amendments (1977), 219
  emission standards for cars, 220, 224
  industrial pollution, 215–217, 219
Pomerance, Rafe, 220, 282, 292, 293, 301, 357, 361, 404
Population-based HIV Impact Assessment (PHIA) Project, 395
populism, 372
Porter, Michael, 311, 312
Porter, Sylvia, 160
Potter, Paul, 26
Powell, Lewis, 112
Procaccino, Mario, 104–105, 107, 150
Professional Air Traffic Controllers Organization (PATCO), 280
Putin, Vladimir, 374, 385

Q
Quayle, Dan, 298, 315
Quayle, Marilyn, 315
Quill, Michael J., 90

R
Rabin, Yitzhak, 57
racism
  Maguire's father on, 13–14, 33, 39
  Maguire's first experiences with, 33–34
  See also civil rights movement
Rae, Kathy, 134–135, 398–399
Rall, David, 216
Rappoport, Mike, 136
Ray, James Earl, 76
Rayburn, Sam, 177
Reagan, Nancy, 279
Reagan, Ronald
  about, 88, 184–185, 204, 255–256, 266, 284, 383
  air traffic controllers strike (1981), 280–281
  Alzheimer's disease, 296–297
  assassination attempt, 278–280
  critique, 284–288
  domestic policy, 279, 288
  election of 1976, 184–186, 188–189, 192
  election of 1980, 253–255, 258–261, 264
  environmental appointees, 289–291
  Environmental Protection Agency and, 289–290
  foreign policy, 159, 241–242, 277–281, 285, 286
  greenhouse effect, 292
  Iran-Contra scandal, 159, 241–242, 285, 287
  political career, 188–189
  presidency, 277–281
  Reaganomics, 289
  reelection campaign (1984), 295–297
  tax cuts, 279, 280, 285
  UC Berkeley and, 187
  unions and, 280–281
Reaganomics, 289
Redford, Robert, 231
Regional Oils Project, 310
Regional Plan Association (New York), 80, 84, 95, 406
Regulation Q, 158
Rehnquist, William, 112
Reid, Harry, 364
Reilly, William, 301
Relief International, 342
Rendering on Trouble: Resources and Politics in Latin America (Maguire, ed.), 44
Republic of China, 128
Resolution 242 (UN), 59, 62–63
Reston, James, 211
Reuss, Henry, 155
Reuther, Walter, 219
Reza, Mohammad Shah, 238
Rhodes, James, 127
Rhodesia, 222
Ribicoff, Abe, 77
Richards, Ann, 328
Richardson, Elliot, 142, 168
Rinaldo, Matt, 177
Robertson, Pat, 298
Robinson, Jackie, 12
Rockefeller, David, 240
Rockefeller, Nelson, 108, 109, 188
Rodino, Peter, 143, 158, 177, 247
Roe, Bob, 176, 208
Roe v. Wade, 137–138, 261
Rogers, William P., 54
Romney, Mitt, 373–374
Roosevelt, Franklin D., 12, 43, 209, 289, 343
Roosevelt, Kermit, 238
Rosa Pepe, Jim, 399–400
Rosen, Howard, 271–272
Rostow, Walt, 72, 74
Rotberg, Robert, 38, 40, 181, 352
Roth, William, 230
Roukema, Marge, 229–233, 261–265

Rove, Karl, 354
Ruckelshaus, William, 112, 142
Rumsfeld, Donald, 356
Rusk, Dean, 56, 72
Russia
 interfering in 2020 presidential campaign, 374–375
 Russian wheat deal (1972), 133, 148–149
 See also USSR

S
saccharin, ban on, 217–218
Sadat, Anwar, 222, 240
SALT II arms treaty, 222, 240, 259
Sandinistas, 286–287
Sasser, Jim, 245
"Saturday Night Massacre," 142
Saxby, William, 168
Scheuer, James, 104
Schlesinger, Arthur, 73, 251
Schlesinger, James, 212, 237
Schumacher, Ernst Friedrich, 304, 305–306
Schumer, Chuck, 385
Schweiker, Richard, 188
Schwerner, Michael, 259
Scowcroft, Brent, 315
Seaver, Tom, 105
segregation. *See* civil rights movement; racism
Selikoff, Irving, 216, 243
sexual revolution, 51–52
Shanker, Albert, 91
Shapiro, Peter, 272, 274, 275
Sheehan, James, 193
Sherwood, Kenneth, 121, 125
Shriver, Sargent, 131
Shultz, Marjorie "Marj" Maguire (sister), 8, 13, 14, 16, 18, 19–20, 22, 145, 146, 327
Sigmund, Barbara, 274
Sihanouk, Norodom, 127
Sikes, Bob, 182–187
Simba Rebellion, 47
Sirhan, 77
Sirica, John, 141
sit-ins (civil rights movement), 34
Six Day War, 58–67
Sleeper (movie), 91
Slim, Carlos, 351
Small Is Beautiful: A Study of Economics As If People Mattered (Schumacher), 305, 306
Smith, Margaret Chase, 226
Smith, Steve, 108–109
smoking, Carter policy on, 214
SNCC. *See* Student Nonviolent Coordinating Committee
Social Security, privatizing, 366
Solzhenitsyn, Aleksandr, 173–174
Somalia, *200, 201*
Somoza, Anastasio, 287
Sorensen, Ted, 251
South Africa, 65–69
 apartheid, 65, 66, 181–182, 222
 Bipartisan Monitoring Group, 81, 181
 Maguire trip to, 181–182
South Korea, 222
Southern Christian Leadership Conference, 34
Soviet Union, 12
Spain, 349
Speak Truth to Power: A Quaker Search for an Alternative to Violence (American Friends Service Committee), 10
Speth, Gus, 282, 293
Staggers, Harley, 164, 220
Starr, Kenneth, 331
states rights, 259
Steiger, Bill, 221
Stevenson, Adlai Ewing, I, 14
Stevenson, Adlai Ewing, II, 5, 14–18, 32, 55, 383
Stokes, Louis, 155–156
Stone, Oliver, 325
student loans, 220–221
Student Nonviolent Coordinating Committee (SNCC), 33–35
Students for a Democratic Society (SDS), 26
Suharto, 171–172
Sukumaland, 41, 42
Sununu, John, 300–302
Superstorm Sandy, 376, 377, 383
Suzman, Helen, 40
Swift, Susan, 312, 313, 319, 324, 347–348, 350, 351, 404–406

T
Taiwan, 128
Tanganyika, 40–42, 46–48
Tanzania, 40, 47, 310–311
Tavoulareas, William, 256, 257
taxation
 carbon tax, 302, 362
 Kemp-Roth tax cut, 230
 Reagan and, 279, 280, 285
 windfall profits tax, 247–248
Tea Party, 365
Texaco, 171
Theodore Roosevelt (aircraft carrier), 67
Thompson, Frank, 177, 208
Thurman, Howard, 10, 389
Thurmond, Strom, 111
tobacco, Carter's policy on, 214
Torricelli, Bob, 276
Toussaint, Donald, 57, 73
Toward "Uhuru" in Tanzania: The Politics of Participation (Maguire), 42
Towery, F. Carlisle, 84–85, 93, 94, 102–103, 108, 109–110, 406–407
Toxic Substances Control Act (1976, TSCA), 367
toxic waste, Carter on, 215–217
TransAlta, 345
Transport Workers Union strike (1965), 90

treadle water pump, ATI and, 307
Truman, Harry, 12, 43
Trump, Donald
  about, 64, 256, 284, 289
  campaign of 2020, 374
  compared with Reagan, 284–288
  COVID-19 pandemic and, 288
  crimes of, 64, 159
  denial of facts, 384
  election (2020), 374–375
  influence of, 385
  path to, 112–113, 266, 284, 372
  support of white evangelical Christians, 261
Trump, William, 169
Trumpism, 112, 113, 370
TSCA. *See* Toxic Substances Control Act
Tucker, Richard P., 283
Turkey, 337

U
UCS. *See* Union of Concerned Scientists
Udall, Morris, 190
Ukraine, 385
UN Capital Development Fund, 322, 334, 337
Union of Concerned Scientists (UCS), 375
United Nations
  apartheid, 65
  Maguire at, 53–68
  Resolution 242, 59–60, 62–63
  Six Day War, 59–63
  on South Africa, 65, 67
United States
  1950s, 11–12, 44
  1960s, 25–26, 44–46, 51–53, 111–113, 266
  1970s, 118–119
  Abscam, 268–270
  Acid Rain Program, 360
  Affordable Care Act, 359, 373, 374
  American Clean Energy and Security Act (2009), 359–360
  American Recovery and Reinvestment Act, 373
  antiwar movement, 25–26
  on apartheid, 66
  Arab oil embargo, 119, 162–163
  Bay of Pigs invasion, 44
  Bill Steiger Memorial Bill (1979), 221
  Capital Availability for Higher Education Act (1975), 221
  Civil Rights Act (1957), 71
  Civil Rights Act (1964), 51, 71
  civil rights movement. *See* civil rights movement
  Clean Air Act (1970), 219
  Clean Air Act Amendments (1977), 219
  counterculture of 1960s, 52
  Energy Policy and Conservation Act (1975), 165
  Environmental Protection Agency, 112, 126, 215, 219, 289, 396, 397
  Export-Import Bank Amendment Act (1978), 68–69
  Fair Access to Higher Education Act (1979), 221
  Family and Medical Leave Act, 327
  Food for Furniture amendment, 244–246
  Foreign Corrupt Practices Act, 288
  Frank R. Lautenberg Chemical Safety for the 21st Century Act (2016), 369
  "the Great Society," 71–72
  Guaranteed Student Loan Program, 220–221
  Gulf of Tonkin Resolution, 46
  Gulf War, 314–316
  Helsinki Accords, 172–174, 191–192
  Iran-Contra scandal, 159, 241–242, 285, 287
  Iraq War, 79
  Israel and, 119
  Kennedy election, 28–31, 32
  Kyoto Protocol, 358
  Latin America policy, 43–44
  liberalism. *See* liberalism
  Maguire-Steiger bill, 221
  March on Washington, 25
  Occupational Safety and Health Administration (OSHA), 112, 269, 288
  Operation Desert Storm, 314–316
  Pentagon Papers, 142
  Pinochet in Chile, 127–128
  populism, 112
  Roe v. Wade, 137–138, 261
  Russian interference in 2020 presidential campaign, 374–375
  SALT II arms treaty, 222, 240, 259
  setting the stage for Trumpism, 112–113, 266, 284, 372
  sexual revolution, 51–52
  Simba Rebellion, 47
  social change, 11–12, 25–26
  on South Africa, 65–69
  Toxic Substances Control Act (TSCA), 367
  Trumpism, 112, 113, 370
  Vietnam War, 25, 44–46, 52, 72–76, 78, 118–119, 126–127, 144, 156–157
  Voting Rights Act (1965), 51, 71
  Watergate affair, 140–144, 149, 153
  Waxman-Markey climate bill, 346, 359–365
  Yom Kippur War, 119
United States Agency for International Development (USAID), 306, 308, 310, 320, 323, 325–326, 340, 341, 402
United States Mission to the United Nations (USUN), 53–79
Unity Resources Group (URG), 347
University of California at Berkeley, 187
US Congress
  Carter and, 203–209
  fall of Saigon and, 156–157

lobbyists, 218, 225
special interests, 218–221
US Department of Justice
under Ford, 168–169
under Nixon, 167–168
US House of Representatives
criticism of Maguire, 174–180, 184–186, 380
Democratic Study Group, 389
Ford's oil policy, 164–165
freshman (Watergate) class (1974), 153–156, 389
Maguire and Bob Sikes, 182–187
Maguire as freshman Congressman, 42, 158, 162–164, 176, 389
Maguire election to, 144–151
Maguire leaves House, 265–266, 380
Maguire on Commerce Committee, 158
Maguire reelection to second term, 193–194
Maguire work methods at, 2, 152–153, 175–180
natural gas policy in 1970s, 169–171
US Senate
about, 225–226
Maguire campaign for (1978), 227–228, 270, 276, 381
Maguire campaign for (1982), 270–275, 381
Maguire's aspirations to serve in, 270–277, 381
Toxic Substances Control Act (1976, TSCA), 369
US State Department
antiwar protesters and, 73–74
Maguire at, 49–78
USAID. *See* United States Agency for International Development
USSR
Bay of Pigs invasion, 44
Nixon and, 128, 129, 143
SALT II arms treaty, 222, 240, 259
wheat purchases (1972), 133, 148–149
See also Russia
USUN (United States Mission to the United Nations), 53–79

V
vaccination, Global Alliance for Vaccines and Immunization (GAVI), 348–353, 383
Vallone, Peter, 114
value chain, 311–312, 339, 340
Vance, Cyrus, 222
Viet Minh, 157
Vietnam War
about, 52, 72–76, 127, 144
consequences of, 144, 193
fall of Saigon, 156–157
Ford and, 156
Johnson and, 45–46, 72–74, 76, 78
Nixon and, 25, 74, 78, 118–119, 126–127, 144
Pentagon Papers, 142
Vietnamization, 126
Volcker, Paul, 256, 271
"voodoo economics," 230, 254
Voting Rights Act (1965), 51, 71
Vreeland, Frederick, 55, 57, 62, 79

W
Wagner, Robert F., Jr., 87, 104
Walcott, John, 400
Walker, Jimmy, 87
Wallace, George, 70, 77–78, 190
Waring, Fred, 136, 139
Wasserman, Lee, 362
Watergate affair, 140–144, 149, 153, 193
Watt, James, 290, 291
Waxman, Henry, 220, 359, 361
Waxman-Markey climate bill, 346, 359–365
"We Shall Overcome" (song), 35
Weinberg, Melvin, 268–269
Welch, Joseph, 6
Welker, Bob, 124
Werber, Barbara, 120, 121, 132
Weyand, Frederick, 156
wheat, Russian wheat deal (1972), 133, 148–149
White House Plumbers, 142
Widnall, William, 133, 140, 146–148, 149, 150
Williams, Harrison "Pete," 177, 269–270, 381
Williamson, Rich, 325, 338
WIN campaign, 161–162
windfall profits tax, 247–248
Wolfowitz, Paul, 79
women's movement, 18–20, 26
Woodcock, Leonard, 219–220
Woodward, Bob, 141
World Bank, 79
World Resources Institute (WRI), 282, 283, 294–295, 382
Wright, Jim, 163, 184, 208, 209, 247
Wrubel, Arthur, 123, 124
Wyngaarden, Marge, 133, 138, 140

Y
Yannarelli, Cyril, 272
Young, Andrew, 68, 244
Young Men's Christian Association (YMCA), 10–11
Yunus, Muhammad, 341

Z
Ziegler, Ron, 140
Zimbabwe, 222, 310–311, 339
Zimmer, Dick, 375, 377, 407–408
Zinn, Howard, 73

ADVANCE PRAISE FOR *AHEAD OF THE CURVE*

"Michael Takiff's masterful storytelling illuminates an era when America made costly errors abroad and faltered at home, but victories could still be won. This unusual book chronicles Andy Maguire's direct involvement at seminal moments in American history: as a peace agreement is approved by the UN Security Council in the aftermath of a Middle East war, when the most far-reaching reforms ever undertaken in Congress are adopted, and as a new cohort of environmental warriors labor to clean up America's air and water, safeguard the world's natural resources, and forestall the ravages of intensifying global climate change. Takiff and Maguire offer a compelling account of who, what, where, and how public interest activists can mobilize consensus towards progressive goals."

—**Rafe Pomerance**, Former Deputy Assistant Secretary of State for Environment and Development (1993–99); President, Friends of the Earth; Founder, National Clean Air Coalition and American Rivers; Chair, League of Conservation Voters and Arctic 21

"Author Michael Takiff's documentary-drama of a book brings decades of history to life through the triumphs and near misses of one political reformer determined to make improvements in our world, whether in the halls of Congress or the highlands of Bolivia and Nepal. Takiff captures it all with a 'see it now' style that makes the past feel like yesterday. A great read!"

—**Kathleen Rae**, Trustee, America's Public Television Stations

"In an early phase of his career, Andy Maguire served at the United States Mission to the United Nations. There he impressed all who knew him with his idealism, passion, energy, and dogged determination, all fired by a sharp intellect and all in the name of the public good."

—**Ambassador Donald F. McHenry**, former Permanent Representative of the United States to the United Nations; Distinguished Professor of Diplomacy, Georgetown University

"Andy Maguire's record of service demonstrates the enormous impact a person of intellect, determination and principle can have in confronting archaic and destructive public policies. Honed by his early experiences in the struggles for civil rights and consumer protection, Maguire's career reflects how even relatively junior legislators can change national priorities. Maguire's story—one of successes and failures, electoral victories and losses—is told by Michael Takiff in an informative and unabashed manner, and serves as a valuable addition to the literature of how politics is really practiced at the highest levels. This is the kind of personal and institutional history that can help inspire a new generation of reformers to enter the arena."

—**John A. Lawrence**, Ph.D., author, *The Class of '74: Congress After Watergate and the Roots of Partisanship; Arc of Power: Inside Nancy Pelosi's Speakership*

"Andy Maguire wanted to grow up and 'make a difference.' Despite only six years in Congress, he did just that, laboring passionately for six decades in the vineyards of the public interest—a frayed liberal concept that Maguire's eventful life story can help revive."

—**Jonathan Alter**, author, *His Very Best: Jimmy Carter, A Life; The Center Holds: Obama and His Enemies*

"When Andy arrived in Congress he immediately became a reform leader of an institution that for too long was in decline. Andy and his class challenged the power structure, changed the rules, made the old bulls accountable to the rest of the Congress and American people. What they did was historic and it took courage and strategic leadership. Andy was one of the first to articulate the need to address the looming environmental crisis our planet was facing because of our reliance on fossil fuels. His long-distinguished career of public service was marked by justice: racial justice, enviro justice, and justice and opportunities for women."

—**David Bonior**, Congressman from Michigan 1977–2003; House Democratic Whip, 1991–2002

"This book is about the journey of a pioneer and a changemaker who delivered on the promise of building a better world. Andy's inspiring life is a must read for those who want to understand how both hard-fought

American politics and strategically savvy international development can transform people's lives. I loved the structure of the book with the protagonist imbedded in succeeding historical epochs—a thoroughly engrossing and engaging rendering by author Michael Takiff."

—**Valeria Budinich,** Senior Advisor, Systems Entrepreneurship, The Legatum Center, Massachusetts Institute of Technology; Harvard Business Review/McKinsey M-Prize for Management Innovation; author, *Answering Society's Call: A New Leadership Imperative*

"Andy Maguire's career reflects an axiom that too many politicians fail to grasp: 'Live your life so that even if you lose, you're ahead.' Andy made a difference for racial and environmental justice and helped clean up the Congress after the scandals of Vietnam and Watergate. However, as with some other agents of change, Andy was felled by revanchists who opposed his work—an abrupt personal surprise after three remarkable terms in Congress. But Maguire didn't miss a step in his continuing work for social justice and economic and environmental progress, in the U.S. and abroad."

—**Les AuCoin,** Congressman, Defense Appropriations Subcommittee; Trustee and Professor, Business Ethics, Southern Oregon University; Advisory Board, Maxwell School National Security Studies Program; author, *Catch and Release: An Oregon Life in Politics*

"This is more than a biography and a brilliant insider's insights during important turbulent times. It is more than the journey of someone 'ahead of the curve.' It is the story of a man of principle and courage who shows the power of a single voice. He is a model to be emulated. That voice, when accompanied by a deft understanding of how to assemble coalitions and manage organizations, can 'move mountains,' especially when character and conviction are buttressed with a willingness to confront power or adversaries in the pursuit of fairness and justice.

This is a 'must read' book for those of us who still believe in democratic values, courage and 'winning.'"

—**Charlan J. Nemeth,** Professor of Psychology Emerita, University of California at Berkeley; author, *In Defense of Troublemakers: The Power of Dissent in Life and Business*